S0-AHR-100

Anti-Semitism
and the Holocaust

PERSPECTIVES ON THE HOLOCAUST

A series of books designed to help students further their understanding of key topics within the field of Holocaust studies.

PUBLISHED:

Holocaust Representations in History,
Daniel H. Magilow and Lisa Silverman
Postwar Germany and the Holocaust, Caroline Sharples

FORTHCOMING:

Sites of Holocaust Memory, Janet Ward
The Holocaust in Eastern Europe, Waitman W. Beorn

Anti-Semitism and the Holocaust

Language, Rhetoric and the Traditions of Hatred

Beth A. Griech-Polelle

Bloomsbury Academic
An imprint of Bloomsbury Publishing Plc

B L O O M S B U R Y
LONDON · OXFORD · NEW YORK · NEW DELHI · SYDNEY

Bloomsbury Academic

An imprint of Bloomsbury Publishing Plc

50 Bedford Square	1385 Broadway
London	New York
WC1B 3DP	NY 10018
UK	USA

www.bloomsbury.com

BLOOMSBURY and the Diana logo are trademarks of Bloomsbury Publishing Plc

First published 2017

© Beth A. Griech-Polelle, 2017

Beth A. Griech-Polelle has asserted her right under the Copyright, Designs and
Patents Act, 1988, to be identified as Author of this work.

All rights reserved. No part of this publication may be reproduced or transmitted
in any form or by any means, electronic or mechanical, including photocopying,
recording, or any information storage or retrieval system, without prior
permission in writing from the publishers.

No responsibility for loss caused to any individual or organization acting on or refraining
from action as a result of the material in this publication can be accepted
by Bloomsbury or the author.

British Library Cataloguing-in-Publication Data
A catalogue record for this book is available from the British Library.

ISBN:	HB:	978-1-4725-8692-6
	PB:	978-1-4725-8691-9
	ePDF:	978-1-4725-8693-3
	ePub:	978-1-4725-8694-0

Library of Congress Cataloging-in-Publication Data
Names: Griech-Polelle, Beth A., 1964- author.
Title: Anti-Semitism and the Holocaust : language, rhetoric, and the
traditions of hatred / Beth A. Griech-Polelle.
Description: London ; New York : Bloomsbury Academic, an imprint of
Bloomsbury Publishing Inc, [2017] | Series: Perspectives on the Holocaust|
Includes bibliographical references and index.
Identifiers: LCCN 2016029704| ISBN 9781472586926 (hardback) |
ISBN 9781472586919 (paperback)
Subjects: LCSH: Holocaust, Jewish (1939-1945)–Sources. | Holocaust, Jewish
(1939-1945) | Antisemitism–Europe–History. | Germany–Politics and
government–1933-1945. | BISAC: HISTORY / Holocaust. | HISTORY / Modern /
20th Century. | HISTORY / Europe / General.
Classification: LCC D804.19 .G75 2017 | DDC 940.53/18–dc23
LC record available at https://lccn.loc.gov/2016029704

Series: Perspectives on the Holocaust

Cover design: Jesse Holborn
Cover image: The exhibition "The Eternal Jew" in the Reichstag (Parliament) Building in
Berlin, November 1938. Photograph © ullstein bild/ullstein bild via Getty Images.

Typeset by Integra Software Services Pvt. Ltd.

To the memory of my beloved parents,
Helen and Robert Griech.

CONTENTS

LIST OF FIGURES

1

Introduction: "Us" versus "Them"

The whole truth is much more tragic and terrible.
—ZALMEN LEWENTAL[1]

This book is not an attempt to provide a comprehensive account of all aspects of the Holocaust. Nor is it an exhaustive account of the long history of anti-Semitism. Instead, it focuses on the theme of the power of language and how language and rhetoric can result in deadly actions. In this respect the work is heavily influenced by the writings of the French political scientist Jacques Semelin. Semelin, in his work *Purify and Destroy: The Political Uses of Massacre and Genocide*, wanted to examine how genocide comes about, how is it possible that ordinary people could become murderers sometimes hundreds of times over? And what is the point in making the victims suffer torture, deprivation, and sexual violence before they are murdered? For most historians of the Holocaust, this is a question that we must ask ourselves repeatedly and, certainly, our students ask us quite frequently. Whether we can ever truly arrive at a complete answer is questionable, but it is most definitely our task to attempt to find explanations.

In Semelin's work, he traces the development of the extermination of enemies. He tracks the development of ideologies whose rhetoric revolves around three main themes: identity, purity, and security. For those who find themselves designated as the "enemy outsiders" they are portrayed as severe threats to those designated as the "insiders." In this "Us" versus "Them" world, insiders are told that their very existence is threatened by an enemy who seeks to defile, pollute, and destroy the coherence of "us." The threatening imagery of "the Jew," as I will argue, was built up over the course of centuries. Destructive legends, myths, and stereotypes all contributed to a type of acceptable language about Jews which enabled Hitler to play upon well-established tropes. Images of the "diabolical, cunning" Jew could be used to instill fear and anxiety and could serve as an explanation as to why an average German person felt stymied in their personal and professional development. They were told repeatedly that the enemy, the Jew, was standing in their way of creating a peaceful, harmonious society united by commonly shared principles. Only by destroying the "other" can "we" emerge triumphant and victorious. In order for the German people, the *Volksgemeinschaft* (People's community), to live, Jews had to die.

The Volksgemeinschaft could only achieve purity, security, and a reaffirmation of their identity through the destruction of "the Jew." The "other" is portrayed in language that suggests Jews are dirty, foreign, corrupt, corrupting, and never to be trusted. They are depicted as being in league with the devil, perpetrating every evil known to mankind. Because there was a long-established tradition of depicting Jews as outsiders seeking to destroy whatever society in which they lived, a leader such as Hitler could easily argue that Germans had to attack Jews in a kind of preemptive strike. Destroying the Jews first only "proved" that the German people were the real victims of nefarious Jewish plots. The Germans were only acting in self-defense to protect themselves from an imagined future annihilation. In this equation, the Germans were drawn more closely together. As scholar Thomas Kühne argues in *Belonging and Genocide: Hitler's Community, 1918–1945*, by persecuting and killing Jews, Germans from all walks of life "participated in community building through mass crime."[2]

One can see the development of the "us" versus "them" construct resulting in lethal violence in volumes 1 and 2 of Saul Friedländer's *Nazi Germany and the Jews*. In Friedländer's works, he uses the phrase "redemptive anti-Semitism" to explain how many Germans, in building their Volksgemeinschaft, needed to destroy Jews in order to save the world from complete Jewish domination. The image of "the Jew" as it was constructed throughout history allowed Hitler to connect everything that he deemed as evil in history with the work of the Jews. Jews were associated most clearly with the destruction of the basic core of all nations, corrupting and polluting everything they came into contact with, threatening to overtake the German *Volk* (people) by unleashing another world war.[3] The threatening image of the Jew, as an active agent of disruption and destruction, allowed Hitler to remind the German Volk of the need for them to be constantly mobilized to react to any and all Jewish threats. Friedländer's work argues that Nazi Germany effectively produced an "anti-Jewish culture," and that Hitler's hold over Germans stemmed from three "salvation creeds: The ultimate purity of the racial community, the ultimate crushing of Bolshevism and plutocracy, and the ultimate millennial redemption borrowed from Christian themes known to all. In each of these traditions the Jew represented evil per se."[4] Within this context, we can again see Semelin's concept of identity, purity, and security. The image of "the Jew" was now a figure standing outside of history, an eternal enemy to "us."

Throughout this work, I have endeavored to use the latest compilations of primary source documents to illuminate the theme of how language and rhetoric influenced the construction of "the Jew" as eternal enemy and how that type of language led to the violence and annihilation of European Jewry in the Holocaust. Students will hear the voices of average people, both

German and Jew, trying to make sense of the events going on around them. I rely heavily throughout the book on the speeches of Hitler, the diary entries of Nazi propaganda minister, Joseph Goebbels, and the reports of Nazi spies on the general German and Jewish populations' reactions to Nazi policies. The multivolume works edited by the United States Holocaust Memorial Museum on Jewish responses to persecution provide extremely rich and detailed accounts documenting the perception of Jews as they lived through such threatening times. Using Jews' and Germans' own words, one can see the impact that the language of segregation had on both communities. We will trace the creation of destructive and threatening language about the Jews in the opening chapters and then we will move on to explore in more detail the division of German society into the Volksgemeinschaft versus "the Jews" and the dire consequences that division brought about.

In Chapter 2 we will explore the origin of some of the most destructive and long-lasting images of Jews: that of "Christ-killers" who stubbornly refused to accept Jesus of Nazareth as the Messiah. From this moment in history on, Jews would find themselves associated with the forces of evil, for who but the devil would want to kill God's Son? As Christianity came to dominate the Roman Empire, Jews found themselves labeled as religious outsiders. This gave rise to religiously based anti-Semitism, which posited that if Jews would only convert to Christianity, then there would no longer be a "Jewish problem." From there, the chapter explores the rise of other anti-Semitic stereotypes and legends. Many of these myths and legends about the Jews would become accepted "truths" as time progressed, allowing many Christians to justify debasing, humiliating, and even murdering Jews. With the rise of the Age of the Enlightenment, secular societies began holding out the promises of liberty and equality, but would that be applied to Jews as well?

Chapter 3 begins with one of the most powerful ideologies of the nineteenth century: that of nationalism. What did it mean to belong to a nation-state? Who truly was a member of that society? Could Jews be accepted as members of secular nations? Here we will encounter the rise of Social Darwinism and more modern "scientific" forms of anti-Semitism, all of which were used to justify why Jews could never be fully trustworthy citizens entitled to all of the promises of liberty and equality. Political demagogues will emerge in this period in history who will denounce the idea that Jews could be emancipated and become full-fledged members of the nation-state. The questions of belonging to the community and to sharing a common identity with gentile citizens would again be raised with the outbreak of the First World War in 1914. Here was an opportunity for Jewish men to fight against the stereotypes that they were cowardly or effeminate and that they could be just as nationalistic as their gentile counterparts were. Yet, by the end of the devastating war, Jews would find themselves depicted in various reports that "proved" Jewish men were disloyal shirkers who avoided fighting for their respective countries. Throughout the 1920s in Germany, the specter of defeat, shame, and humiliation would be blamed on the "internal enemy" who had been seeking Germany's destruction: the Jews. Racial anti-Semites put forward their pseudoscientific theories explaining why Jews and Germans were incompatible.

Chapter 4 continues the exploration of Weimar Germany, a site of cultural modernism coexisting with a sense of misery and violence. In the tumultuous atmosphere of Weimar Germany, we will examine Adolf Hitler's early views on Jews and his rise to political power. We will examine the powerful rhetoric that Hitler deployed in this early time period, combining what he called the emotional imagery of anti-Semitism with his preferred "anti-Semitism of reason." In forging the "Volksgemeinschaft" Hitler began the process of consolidating his power. He simultaneously provided the German people with a sense of dynamism, for they were all working together to create a new Germany, but he also gave them the bond that would unite them: aiming to destroy the "outsiders" of German society, most notably the Jews. In this chapter we will track the ways in which Hitler sought to isolate and humiliate Jews, following his "anti-Semitism of reason" while random acts of violence against Jews provided those who ascribed to "emotional anti-Semitism" a release valve. Law after law will be promulgated against the Jews in this time period, taking away any emancipation German Jews had once experienced. We will explore Jewish writings at the time as they try to assess how dangerous Nazi Germany had become for the Jewish community.

In Chapter 5 we continue the story of the radicalization of Nazi anti-Semitic policies, examining the division of German society into "healthy Aryans" who were eligible for full membership in the Volksgemeinschaft versus anyone deemed unhealthy, including the Jews. We will see how Hitler's focus on saving and fostering the further growth of the healthy Aryan people was intertwined with his foreign policy objectives to acquire *Lebensraum* (living space). Throughout this time period, Hitler's regime encouraged Jews to emigrate away from Germany, yet their public declarations of endorsing Jewish emigration would be contradicted by their numerous restrictions placed upon Jews who were attempting to escape the Third Reich. As Hitler's rhetoric became more nakedly aggressive toward foreign powers, so too did his government take a more openly aggressive stance against the remaining Jews of Germany. With the invasion of Poland on September 1, 1939, the Second World War had begun. Hitler, however, continued to emphasize that he was a man of peace who did not want war. He was only engaging in violence because an international conspiracy of Jews and people controlled by Jews was seeking to destroy the Aryan people. At the same time, Hitler initiated a program to destroy the mentally and physically handicapped living within Germany's own borders as part of his "domestic purification" policy.

Chapter 6 explores the destruction of Poland and what implications that had for the large population of Jews now trapped by the Nazi war machine. Mobile SS squads, called Einsatzgruppen, were sent in to combine "emotional anti-Semitism" with the colder "anti-Semitism of reason."

Various Nazi plans were made as to what to do with such a large Jewish population ranging from marching Jews from small villages and towns to large cities forming a "Jewish reservation" to shipping Jews to far off islands such as Madagascar. While men such as Heinrich Himmler sought to address the issues of what to do with so many Jews, he was also focused on moving hundreds of thousands of ethnic Germans closer to the region of Germany. In this massive transfer of populations, thousands of people would lose their lives. This project of "resettling" ethnic Germans closer to the "Old Reich" while simultaneously removing the "enemy Jew" further away from Aryans further reinforced the notion that Germany's existence was dependent upon the removal of the Jews. One cannot separate these policies from one another. To purify the German homeland, one needed to push Jews as far away as possible so they could no longer pose a threat to German security. Quarantining the Jews became necessary, so ghettos were established of varying sizes throughout occupied Poland. On the home front, German Jews faced increased restrictions as to where they could and could not go while Nazi propaganda churned out stereotypes of "the dangerous Jew." The Volksgemeinschaft, by 1940, was demanding further segregation and isolation of the Jews.

Chapter 7 explores the radicalization of Nazi policy regarding the "Final Solution of the Jewish Question." With the invasion of the Soviet Union, and the subsequent acquisition of still more Jews, the Nazis had to address what they planned to do with the conquered territory and with all of the Slavic and Jewish people living in it. As formal plans for the colonization of Soviet territory were being drawn up, SS Einsatzgruppen men were sent in to execute Jews and Bolsheviks. Of course, part of the assumption the Nazis had made was that all Jews were Bolsheviks. As the mass shootings at pits occurred, the search was on to find a less psychologically taxing way for the killers to murder large numbers of Jews. For this, Nazis could rely on early technological developments made in the Euthanasia project. Gas chambers had already been used since 1939–1940 in Germany, and the question was how to apply the technology to events on the eastern front. Various experiments were conducted, using gas vans as opposed to permanent gassing facilities like the ones that had been used to destroy mentally and physically disabled adults back in Germany. In the Old Reich, German Jews faced yet more segregation as well as the new stipulation that they must wear the yellow Star of David on their outer clothing. Reminiscent of the medieval "Jew's badge" now all Germans could be a part of a surveillance society, making sure that anti-Semitic laws were enforced properly. Moreover, 1941 would also be the year that Jews living in the Old Reich experienced their first taste of deportations to the mysterious East. Rumors abounded, but what did being "evacuated" to the East really mean?

Chapter 8 takes us through the rest of the war years tracking the Wannsee Conference and its plans for the Jewish population of Europe. The quest to find the "Final Solution of the Jewish Question" was now

in high gear. We will examine some of the major death camps designed
to kill large numbers of people in an efficient manner. What was it like
to be a Jew deported to a killing center? What was it like to be kept
barely alive and used as slave labor in a camp? What happened to the
German home front as the war turned against them? How did they react
to the rumors about what was being carried out against the Jews? By the
war's end, the German Volksgemeinschaft had bound themselves to the
mission to eradicate "the Jew," but now, as defeat loomed, many of those
same Germans saw Allied bombing raids and invasion of the Fatherland
as "Jewish retribution." The fear of what Jews might do in revenge only
intensified most people's acceptance that they had been correct; "the
Jews" were the eternal enemy of the Aryan people who now sought their
complete destruction. Hitler had won in the sense that he had been able to
use centuries of anti-Semitic language to convince the Volksgemeinschaft
that it was either "them" or "us."

The Holocaust raised powerful and disturbing questions for all of human
society. It is not simply a "Jewish-thing." It is a universal "thing." Language
fails to fully convey the suffering, the violence, and the visceral sights and
smells that people experienced during the Holocaust. But we must explore
the suffering as best as we can if we are to fully explore the question that
philosophers such as Emil Fackenheim have asked, "Can humanity be trusted
after the Holocaust?" In his work *God's Presence in History*, Fackenheim
attempted to inspire all of us, but especially the Jews, with the notion that
"we, as Jews, are not permitted to hand Hitler any posthumous victories."[5]
How can Hitler be defeated? By remembering, by surviving, by testifying
to the truth of what was done to millions of innocent men, women, and
children who lost their lives in the Holocaust. It is our universal duty to
record and remember for the sake of those whose voices were never allowed
to speak. If not, "Damned be those of us with enough to eat and drink and
[who] forget about these children."[6]

2

The Rise of Religious Anti-Semitism: The Foundation of Myths and Legends about the Jews

In the beginning was the Word:
The Word was with God
And the Word was God.
—JOHN 1:1

Introduction

In this chapter we will cover a sweeping span of history, from the ancient Roman world to the Tsars of nineteenth-century Russia. Throughout this time period, we will be tracking the rise of popular myths, legends, and stereotypes about the Jews, all of which will serve as the foundation for later periods of the language of anti-Semitism. As Jews become a minority population in Europe, deprived of the rights they once enjoyed in the ancient Roman Empire, their lives will become increasingly difficult. However, the rise of the Enlightenment and its new language about freedom, equality, and emancipation seemed to hold out the promise that life in Europe would improve for Jews. As we shall see, for some Jews there was improvement, but when we turn to life inside the Russian Empire, we will find that not much of the Enlightenment ideals had penetrated into Russian everyday life.

The ancient world: From Roman citizen to "Christ-killer"

In the ancient Roman Empire, Jews living in the region called Judea (later Palestine, later still Israel) had to comply with their political overlords, the Romans. Fortunately, for many Jews, the Roman authorities generally allowed other religions to coexist in the pagan environment of the empire. For Jewish men, there was still a possibility that they could obtain Roman citizenship and thus earn for themselves all of the rights and privileges that other non-Jewish Roman men enjoyed. In practical terms that meant that as a citizen of Rome, Jewish males could own property including slaves. They could fight in the Roman army, and even if they did not join the military, they were allowed to carry weapons in order to protect themselves as well as their property. They could also own slaves and could participate fully in the life of the citizenry. This does not mean that Jews, under the control of the Roman Empire, were living in an ideal world. They could, in fact, find themselves facing persecutions. However, most of these persecutions revolved around political problems, rather than religious differences.[1] Nevertheless, the region of Judea by time of the year 1 BCE was a hotbed of highly charged political and religious sentiment. What were the people of Judea so stirred up about?

Judea, as a provincial outpost of Rome, often faced rebellions and insurrections against the emperor's authority. By the time of the year 1 BCE, there were many segments of the Jewish community who were theorizing about the possibility of a new leader for the Jewish people. This leader, or Messiah, was imbued with many qualities and characteristics depending on the individual thinking about freedom from Roman domination. For groups of Jewish leaders, such as the Pharisees, many of them might have imagined a Messiah with authority to impose greater compliance to Jewish law and ritual. The Zealots, a group of Jewish fanatics, knew what they wanted: a Messiah to lead them politically against Roman control, while at the opposite end of the spectrum were the Essenes, who withdrew from daily life in Judea up into the mountains, longing for a spiritual Messiah who would revolutionize men's hearts. While many of these groups had overlapping ideas concerning a savior, the birth and ministry of Jesus of Nazareth would challenge many of the assumptions people had concerning what a savior was actually going to do for the Jewish people.[2]

As Jesus of Nazareth practiced his ministry, travelling among the various Jewish communities of Judea, he put forward a certain core message to anyone who would listen. He spoke about the need to not only forgive one's enemies but also love them. He asked people to treat one another as they themselves would like to be treated. He promised his listeners that there would be a time in history when the dead would be resurrected and the kingdom of Heaven would reign supreme.[3] For centuries numerous Christian writers have presented Jesus's teachings as the opposite of Judaic teachings rather than portraying Jesus's message as extending Jewish rituals and beliefs. In many Christian traditions, whatever Jesus stood for, Judaism supposedly was against. So, for example, many Christians have been taught that many Jewish leaders believed Jesus's attitude toward observing many Jewish laws and rituals was lax, and that he was therefore often regarded by the community leaders as a rebel who was not truly following the rules of Judaism.[4] The dominant narrative continues on by arguing that as Jesus's following seemed to be growing, some of the Pharisees met and decided that Jesus would have to be tried for the crime of blasphemy. In their minds, Jesus had proclaimed himself the Son of God, and, since they did not believe that he was the Son of God, he was considered a false Messiah.[5] This element in the story of Christianity is vital to the historic roots of religiously based anti-Semitism, for the story of Jesus's trial, torture, and crucifixion remains a central part of the long history of justification for anti-Semitic behavior.

Let us turn then to the way in which the Gospel writers (Matthew, Mark, Luke, and John) tend to tell the story of Jesus's arrest and death, recognizing that each Gospel writer(s) had their own agenda which influenced the ways in which they constructed the narrative. The group of Pharisees, angered that Jesus had entered Jerusalem at the time of the Passover, met and decided that Jesus was to be arrested, tried before the Sanhedrin, and found guilty of the charge of blasphemy. Jesus was arrested and brought before the leaders of the Sanhedrin. They found him guilty and with that came the death sentence. However, Jewish leaders, living in Judea, had no political authority to carry out a death sentence. So, the leaders handed Jesus over to the one person who did have the right to pronounce a death sentence: the Roman governor, Pontius Pilate. After interrogating Jesus and having him scourged, Pontius Pilate had to make a decision: should he proclaim Jesus guilty of portraying himself as "King of the Jews" or should he not get involved in what he believed to be an internal fight among various Jewish community leaders. Biblical accounts vary, but Matthew's Gospel shows that the Roman governor decided to remove himself from the decision-making process by publicly washing his hands in front of the crowd. Observing a tradition during Passover, Pontius Pilate announced that he would have two convicted men stand before a crowd and the crowd could decide which man would go free while the other would have his sentence enforced. Pilate hedged his bets a bit and put a known, convicted murderer, named Barabbas, up against Jesus of Nazareth. In the various Gospel accounts, we are told that the crowd, when given the opportunity to free Jesus, instead began to yell out for his crucifixion.

What is also worth exploring in the story of Jesus's crucifixion is how language changes throughout the different Gospel accounts. In what is thought to be the earliest of the four Gospel accounts of Jesus's ministry and preaching, Matthew writes that it was the chief priests and the members of the Sanhedrin who do not recognize Jesus as the Messiah and therefore hand him over to Pontius Pilate. It is also the chief priests and the elders who persuade the faceless mob to call out for Jesus's death.[6] Likewise in the Gospel accounts of both Mark and Luke, it is still the chief priests and the scribes who inspire the crowd to demand Jesus's crucifixion. However, by the time we arrive at the Gospel according to John, there is a more generalized account of Jesus's death: "From that moment Pilate was anxious to set him free," but the JEWS shouted, "If you set him free you are no friend of Caesar's; anyone who makes himself king is defying Caesar" (John 19: 12–13).[7] John's Gospel, more than likely written by John's followers, shows an evolution in the story of the crucifixion. Although the chief priests and scribes are still the main drivers, now *all* Jews are involved in calling out for Jesus's death. The portrayal of a collective, "the Jews," as all sharing in the guilt of the crucifixion has served as the fuel of religiously based anti-Semitism for hundreds of years. As Yehuda Bauer has argued, the charge of deicide, the killing of a god, has been leveled at Jews since the time of Jesus of Nazareth. This legend, that all Jews throughout all of time have the blood of Jesus upon their hands, has inspired the language that portrays all Jews everywhere as "Christ-killers."[8]

In the Roman Empire, the early followers of Jesus were often regarded as merely another breakaway sect of Jews, only those particular Jews followed the anointed one, or, the Christ. They were therefore known as Christians. In the pagan environment of the empire, various religions competed for followers and the early Christians were no different. As they sought to spread the news about Jesus of Nazareth and to bring about conversions, many early church leaders also searched for ways to show that they were not just another Jewish sect.[9] In their quest to differentiate themselves, the church leaders had to convince other people that Christianity was a whole religion; it was connected to an older religion (Judaism) but the new religion of Christianity brought with it the fulfillment of the prophets. In this respect early Christianity had to walk a fine line: many people believed that for a religion to be considered legitimate it had to have ancient roots. However, early church leaders also wanted to make it clear that Christianity, while connected to the past through scripture, was now a stand-alone religion. This desire to break free of connections with Judaism, while simultaneously portraying Christians as the new chosen people of God, is called supersessionism. We can see the roots of supersessionism being planted in the writings of St. Paul.

The early Christian Church

St. Paul, before his conversion to Christianity, was known as Saul of Tarsus. Saul was a Pharisee, one who wanted to see Jewish law and custom preserved, and in his earlier days, Saul persecuted Jews who had gone astray, meaning that they had converted to Christianity. Saul had an epiphany and became the very kind of person whom he had been persecuting: a Christian. He took the name Paul to symbolize his transformation into a new person and he emerged as a true leader in the early church. In the Acts of the Apostles, Jesus appears to a disciple called Ananias, telling Ananias to go to restore Saul's eyesight and baptize him. At first Ananias refuses due to Saul's reputation as a persecutor of early Christians. Jesus rebukes Ananias, stating, "You must go all the same, because this man is my chosen instrument to bring my name before pagans and pagan kings and before the people of Israel ..." (Acts 9: 15–16). Note that Saul/Paul's primary mission will be to convert pagans, not Jews, to Christianity. That will necessarily mean that Paul must work to convince potential converts that they do not need to be Jews in order to be Christians. Christianity is a stand-alone religion.

From Paul's surviving letters to the early Christian community, we can see the effort that is being made to impress upon converts that there is no need to practice Judaism first.[10] In Paul's letter to the Romans, he states:

> Let me put another question then: have the Jews fallen for ever, or have they just stumbled? Obviously they have not fallen for ever: their fall, though, has saved the pagans in a way the Jews may now well emulate. Think of the extent to which the world, the pagan world, has benefitted from their fall and defection—then think how much more it will benefit from the conversion of them all. Let me tell you pagans this: I have been sent to the pagans as their apostle, and I am proud of being sent, but the purpose of it is to make my own people envious of you, and in this way save some of them. (Romans 11: 11–15)

Here Paul argues that pagans who convert to Christianity will ultimately help to bring about the conversion of at least some unbelieving Jews. Clearly, Christianity is for the gentile world as much as it is for Jews. On a slightly more humorous note, Paul writes "in large letters" to the Galatians that there is no need for men to be circumcised, that is, practice a religious ritual of Judaism, in order to become Christians. Paul writes, "It does not matter if a person is circumcised or not; what matters is for him to become an altogether new creature" (Galatians 6: 15–16). One might guess that grown pagan men, wishing to convert to Christianity, heaved a huge sigh of relief when they were told they did not have to first become Jews in order to become Christians. In much newer scholarship, the emphasis is now on Paul, not leaving Jews out of salvation history, but rather as being intensely concerned with showing his followers that God still has a place for Jews in salvation (Romans 11: 17–26).[11]

As theologians and historians debate when the seeds of separation between Judaism and early Christianity were planted, we can see the beginning of language separating Judaism from Christianity in the New Testament.[12] With subsequent church fathers, further separation is stressed arguing that the members of the Christian Church have now become the specially chosen people of God; that the Jews in their refusal to accept Jesus as the Messiah, Son of God, have forfeited their special relationship with God. In their rejection of Jesus as Messiah, Jews have broken the covenantal relationship they once enjoyed with God. The Christians are now portrayed as the "New Israel." In the writings of church fathers such as Ignatius of Antioch, St. John Chrysostom, and many others, the church has now superseded that of the synagogue. Jews are no longer the brothers of Christians, sharing the common root of Jesus's Jewish heritage, but instead, they are now accused of a hardness of heart, a willful blindness, and of being in league with the devil seeking to bring death and destruction to God's chosen Son. To Ignatius of Antioch, he puts forward the argument that Jews are all Christ-killers, condemning an entire people for the acts of a mob. St. John Chrysostom saw the synagogue not as a sacred place of worship, but rather as a pigsty, where Jews went to worship the devil. St. Cyprian argued that only gentiles would inherit God's kingdom as the Jews, through their actions of killing the Christ, had forfeited their special covenantal relationship with God.[13]

Perhaps no other early church father had as much of an impact on the language and doctrine of the Roman Catholic Church regarding the Jews than did St. Augustine, bishop of Hippo in the fourth century (345–430). St. Augustine came to be regarded in the early history of the church as one of the leading intellectuals whose opinions were constantly being sought out. As bishop of Hippo, Augustine watched from afar the sacking of Rome at the hands of the Visigoths. In this environment of a world turned upside down, Augustine set the tone that would profoundly influence the course of Christianity in the West regarding the church's position on treatment of Jews. So what did Augustine have to say about Jewish people?

Augustine argued that Jews had to be kept alive as they served as living testimony to the truths of the Old Testament. However, he also argued that good Christians could humiliate, debase, and persecute the Jews in order to reaffirm the triumph of Christianity over Judaism. In the writings of scholar Paula Frederickson, she argues that Augustine's position was actually helpful to the Jews of Europe in that he strongly condemned the idea of annihilating the Jews. In effect, his position helped to save Jewish lives, although it did not improve their lives amid a Christian majority population. In addition, St. Augustine also wrote that it was not the job of the Christians to convert the Jews. He believed that God had a plan for the Jews and that God would bring about their conversion when He wanted it to happen. This bifurcated policy, of mistreating and harming Jews, but stopping short of actually killing them, became the official position of the Roman Catholic Church for hundreds of years. One can see how this policy reinforced the idea of the supersession of the church over the synagogue, as anyone living near Jews would have seen them as an oppressed and downtrodden minority population.[14]

Tertullian, writing from a Roman pagan perspective, offered his opinion about the Jews. In *Adversos Iudaica* (Against the Jews), he spoke of the ways in which the Jewish population stood apart from the pagan Roman world.[15] However, the pagan Roman world was changing rapidly with the spread of Christianity over the empire. As Christianity gathered more and more converts, Jews were still able to maintain most of the rights and privileges they had been granted; however, things were soon to change. In 313, the Roman emperor Constantine converted to Christianity. Although he converted he did not issue a decree that all of his subjects must also convert. His conversion did, however, bring about many other conversions, some of which were no doubt heartfelt while others were perhaps more in the line of opportunism. Whether people were converting out of true conviction or not, Christianity was in the ascendant. By 380 Theodosius the Great issued an edict whereby he decreed that all worship of pagan gods was now illegal. All of his subjects were expected to adhere to the principles of Christianity. With this decree, Christianity became the dominant religion of the Roman Empire, but what implications did that have for the Jewish minority?

The loss of Jewish rights under Rome

For Theodosius, Jews worshipped the same God as did the Christians: the God of Abraham and Isaac. It was one thing to ban the worship of a Jupiter or of a Juno, but could one stop Jews from worshipping, particularly if they worshipped the same God to whom Christians were praying? The emperor's decision was that Jews had to be allowed to continue to worship. His decision was enshrined in the *Codex Theodosianus* compiled between 429 and 438. In the Codex, Jews were granted the freedom to practice their religion openly. Their property rights and synagogues were also protected by law. However, since Jews had steadfastly refused to convert to Christianity, the Codex also began placing limitations and restrictions upon the Jews of the empire. These were primarily limited to removing Jews from service in the Roman army and prohibiting Jews from serving in public office. In all, the Codex marks the very first small steps in the language of segregating Jews from other subjects in the land. Jews were now losing some of the rights of citizenship that had once been the hallmark of the diverse world of Ancient Rome.[16]

As the Roman Empire declined, many Jews found themselves living now under either Muslim empires or the Orthodox Byzantium Empire. It would only be a small percentage of Jews who would be living within Roman Catholic–dominated European societies. The spread of small Jewish communities in Western Europe first appeared along ancient Roman trade routes. Jewish merchants generally led the way in establishing these small outposts, and by the ninth century, many of these Jewish communities had been granted charters by French and Germanic kings. These charters allowed Jews as individuals to live under the king's protection, establishing the image of Jews as dependent upon alliances with royalty, and leading some local Catholic Church leaders to complain about unfair advantages given to non-believing Jews over that of believing Christians. For the most part, however, rulers such as Louis IX and Charlemagne allowed these Jewish merchant families into their territory primarily because they saw economic benefits from such alliances.[17]

Over the course of decades, these small Jewish merchant families expanded into Jewish communities, with the first ones forming gradually along the Rhine River. In these small Jewish settlements, Jews were able to live relatively unharmed, further developing Jewish culture and scholarship as they grew. For some local church authorities, the Jewish communities presented a problem; however, until approximately 1096 with the preaching of the First Crusade, Jews were able to enjoy certain rights and privileges, including that of owning land and slaves. Jews worked as craftsmen, as silk weavers, glass blowers, and dyers of fabrics. Jews were also producing wine and breeding livestock and horses. For a time, Jews were able to receive rights as individuals to practice their trades, but over the course of the next several centuries, Jews' legal position would deteriorate.

The First Crusade as a turning point for European Jewish communities

One such turning point in the deterioration of Jewish lives in Europe was the preaching of the First Crusade. Pope Urban II, staying in Clermont, France, issued a call for Christian warriors (knights) to go on an armed pilgrimage. Although he did not call it a "crusade," later authors would do so. What was the objective of the pilgrimage? Ostensibly it was a twofold project. One portion of the agenda included helping the Byzantium emperor fend off Muslim invaders from the walls of Constantinople. In this regard Pope Urban hoped to heal the schism between the Roman Catholic and Orthodox Christian Churches. In addition to this aim, the warriors were to continue on to free the Holy Land from Muslim control. Urban, in an effort to convince the knights that they should participate in this expensive and dangerous undertaking, promised that any knight who took up the cross for this endeavor would be freed from performing earthly penance for his sins. Since knights often sinned, this seemed to be a good deal. However, the response was relatively lukewarm to Urban's appeal. Other preachers, wishing to stir up a good crowd, decided to offer plenary indulgences. This meant that if one participated in an armed pilgrimage against the "infidel"/"non-believer," then that individual's soul went straight to heaven—no penance, no purgatory, just reward. Not surprisingly, hundreds of people—men, women, and children—showed up for this type of promise. In the medieval world where life was short, eternity guaranteed in heaven seemed quite a bit more intriguing to many people. But how did this largely Christian versus Muslim affair impact Jews?

Beginning in 1096, as the crowds of would-be crusaders were whipped into a frenzy, many of them decided that, if killing the infidel was part of the plan for their eternal salvation, why go all the way to the Holy Land to kill them when Jews were living right there in their midst? Jews were nonbelievers, too, since they had rejected Jesus of Nazareth as the true Messiah. Although the idea of killing entire communities of Jews was officially against the church's teachings, many lower level clergy ignored those teachings and encouraged the crowds to perpetrate acts of violence against Jews. To be fair, many higher level clergy, who had the benefit of being drawn from the aristocracy with some modicum of education, did in fact try to protect Jews from violence, but they were often at the mercy of mob action if they attempted to interfere.

To the crusader hordes, it was outrageous that Jews should be allowed to live—especially since they were the actual "Christ-killers!" As the undisciplined crowds surged across Europe, Jewish communities, particularly those along the Rhine River, would be attacked mercilessly. It is difficult to know exact numbers; however, historians estimate that approximately 5,000 Jews were murdered or committed suicide rather than be forced to convert to Christianity. As the crusaders passed through German territory, the Jews of Mainz, Speyer, Worms, and Cologne were particularly hard hit. Hebrew Chronicles, written a generation after the events, provide insight into the actions of the persecuted Jews. One can read that some Jews tried to bribe officials to protect them and their families; others fled, sometimes to the local bishop's residence (hoping that he would offer them protection due to official church teaching); still others fasted, prayed, and hid. In many instances, Jews opted for martyrdom. In the Chronicle of Solomon bar Simson, we read about the Jews of Worms, hiding in the bishop's courtyard, attacked by the crusaders: "The Jews, inspired by the valor of their brethren, similarly chose to be slain in order to sanctify the Name before the eyes of all, and exposed their throats for their heads to be severed for the glory of their Creator. There were also those who took their own lives.... Fathers fell upon their sons, being slaughtered upon one another, and they slew one another—each man his kin, his wife and children; bridegrooms slew their betrothed, and merciful women their only children. They all accepted the divine decree wholeheartedly and, as they yielded up their souls to the Creator, cried out, 'Hear O'Israel, the Lord is our God, the Lord is One.'"[18]

The chronicler, although not an eyewitness to the events, tells the reader that the crusaders then stripped the dead Jews naked, dragged their bodies along, and then forcibly baptized some of the surviving Jews. In all, there were two days of this type of violence, with the end result that at least 800 Jews who had once lived in Worms now were dead. Although many historians debate the accuracy of the chroniclers, what cannot be debated is the effect that the Crusade had upon the Jewish communities of Western Europe. Particularly in the hardest-hit areas along the Rhine, Jewish communities ceased to function for a considerable length of time. In addition, the Crusades had significantly shifted Jewish-Christian relations for now it was unquestionable that Christians could assault Jewish communities in direct contradiction to the early teachings of St. Augustine. No Jew could place their trust in the words of Augustine any longer, but the Crusades and their violence do not represent the lowest point of medieval Jewish-Christian interactions.

FIGURE 2.1 *Image of the "Eternal Jew" from Elvira Bauer's* Trust No Fox on His Green Heath and No Jew on His Oath *published in Nazi Germany in 1936 for children. Courtesy Randall Bytwerk Collection, German Propaganda Archive, Calvin College. The accompanying text reads (in translation):*

From the start the Jew has been
A murderer, said Jesus Christ.
And as Our Lord died on the cross
God the Father knew no other race
To torment His Son to death,
He chose the Jews for this.
That is why the Jews now claim
To be the chosen people.
When Christ the burden of the cross
Too heavy found, He sought to rest
One moment 'gainst a door.
But from the house a Jew came out
Cursed Him and upbraided Him,
Telling Him to move on further.
For 'twas a Jew that owned that house.
It was the Jew Ahasuerus....
Since then that Jew has borne a curse.
Two thousand years he has sought rest,
That wretched Jew Ahasuerus,

The curse has passed to all his race,
Restless he wanders far and wide,
One land to another.
He has no home to call his own,
The alien Jew, that scurvy knave.
His nomad soul finds nowhere rest,
Everywhere he's just a pest.
Four centuries have come and gone,
Ahasuerus crops up everywhere
Now in Hamburg, next Berlin,
In Denmark and in Danzig too.
Dresden, Paris have seen that Jew.
Believe me, children, it is quite clear,
Ahasuerus haunts us still
Under the skin of every Jew.
Now, children, keep a good look out
Whenever you see a Jew about.
The Jew creeps round, a regular fox,
Keep your eyes open, or you'll be on the rocks.

The development of popular anti-Semitic myths and legends

For many of the crusaders, Jews were an offense to God. Allowing them to live in the midst of Christendom seemed an outrage. In the medieval world, Jews found themselves also portrayed as poisoners, polluters, and defilers. Images of Jews as wanderers exploded in medieval Europe, in particular because of the popularity of a fairly simple story. The original version of the story concerned a man, Ahaseurus, a shoemaker by trade, who heard a knock at his humble door one night. Ahaseurus heard a stranger on the other side of the door, asking to stay the night inside of the shoemaker's home. Fatefully, Ahaseurus refused to provide hospitality to the stranger. For his refusal, Ahaseurus was condemned to walk the face of the earth, constantly in search of a safe haven, for the stranger he had sent off into the dangerous night was Jesus. This simple story morphed into a destructive legend that stipulated that Ahaseurus was a representative of the Jews. Since Jews rejected Jesus as the Messiah, it would make sense in the story to name the shoemaker as a Jew. The image of the wandering Jew also corresponded to the teachings of church leaders such as Augustine, who believed that Jews had condemned themselves through their refusal to convert. It was also in keeping with church teaching that Jews were to wander the earth, destitute and hopeless, to serve as reminders of what happened when one did not believe in the saving mission of the church. This type of imagery was so prevalent that down to this day there is even a plant known for growing very quickly and spreading out all over. Its name is the Wandering Jew.

Along the same lines of stories about wandering Jews, other legends about Jews gained in popularity during the medieval time period. Jews were often the victims of accusations that they had poisoned a community's well water and that they were the cause of many disasters such as earthquakes, floods, and outbreaks of disease. When the Black Death erupted in 1348 in Europe, widespread fear and panic swept across countries—and with good reason, as historians estimate that approximately half to one-third of Europe's total population was wiped out. In the face of such devastation, many people began to search for a cause: Why were so many people dying so rapidly and in such astonishingly high numbers? Were all people equally at risk of succumbing to this terrible plague? Many religious fanatics, called Flagellants, often went around the infected areas of Europe, and in their religious fervor, they often blamed the presence of the Jews as the source of the plague. Believing that God was punishing Christians for allowing nonbelievers to live among them, some Jews were attacked in a desperate attempt to stave off the plague. The plague continued despite the Jewish deaths.

In addition to medieval people blaming Jews for what we, in the modern world, would attribute to natural disasters, Jews were also targeted, beginning in the year 1144 for another crime: that of blood libel or ritual murder. This legend states that Jews seek to kill Christians, especially Christian children, in order to use their blood for ritualistic purposes. In Norwich, England, a young boy went missing. Later, when his corpse was discovered out in the woods, a local priest and some other villagers examined the child's body. They saw tiny marks on parts of the child's body and declared this was proof that Jews had drained the child's body of its blood to use for their own nefarious practices. This made the young child into a martyr for the faith although it could have been that the tiny marks on the child's body were from birds or other wild animals. These blood libel accusations were leveled against Jews repeatedly over the centuries. In England, charges of ritual murder would appear in 1255, in Austria in 1472, and the list could go on. Tsar Nicholas II of Russia used the charge of blood libel in 1911 in Kiev. The last known official charge of blood libel levied against the Jews occurred in Kielce, Poland, in 1946. Some historians believe that Jews were connected with the death of children after the events of the First Crusade: the argument goes that Christian crusaders witnessed Jews killing their own children rather than convert, and therefore they posited that Jews could of course kill Christian children if they could kill their own. This theory may be correct; however, we simply do not know the exact origins or the reasoning of the local villagers in Norwich in 1144. What we do know is that the charge of blood libel/ritual murder was used throughout history to enact violence, intimidation, and the death of Jews living throughout European society.

Decline of Jewish rights in medieval and early modern Europe

As the twelfth to fourteenth centuries progressed, Jewish-Christian relations would further worsen. Beginning in the twelfth century, European laws began to change which resulted in the decline of Jewish rights and privileges. One of the first laws to be changed regarded property ownership. Jews, since the Roman Empire, had had the opportunity to own land if they were citizens of Rome. By the twelfth century, a new law was introduced which now stated that in order to mortgage a piece of land, a Christian oath was required. No Jew could legitimately swear out a Christian oath, so therefore, Jews could no longer hope to purchase property. This was especially harmful because in the medieval world, a person's power, prestige, and importance in society were directly tied to how much land he controlled. By depriving Jews of the right to purchase land, Jews were effectively being denied access to power in the feudal hierarchy of Europe. What followed fairly quickly was another law that required a Christian oath in order to be a member of a craft guild. Again, Jews could not swear a Christian oath, so they were locked out of the medieval Christian economic structure. Jews could, in some areas, form their own all-Jewish craft guilds, but that would be the extent of the exception to the law.[19]

Other laws followed such as those limiting the number of Jews allowed to receive honorific status and awards. In still other places Jewish men were placed into the same legal category as women, clerics, and merchants. This meant that Jewish men were no longer allowed to carry weapons and that, theoretically, knights were supposed to behave in a chivalric way toward unarmed Jews. In 1236 the Holy Roman emperor Friedrich II defined the Jews living in his territories as *servi camerae* (chamber serfs).[20] What did this legal definition of Jew as chamber serf mean? Originally serfs were peasant farmers legally bound to the soil with very limited rights and many obligations to the man who controlled the land on which they lived. Since Jews were not allowed to own land, designating them as still a "serf" meant that Jews were defined as subservient to masters, even if they were not bound to the land. The idea that Jews now served the Christian leaders became clear in the law. Due to these new limitations, many Jews found themselves reduced to limited occupations, and, most notoriously, they were finding themselves forced into the job of money lending. Since the Catholic Church had decreed lending money with interest from one Christian to another Christian the sin of usury, church leaders had no problem with Jews committing that sin. Of course, Jews who did lend money were often on the receiving end of hatred and violence, thus increasing Jewish unpopularity in Europe and helping to create the illusion that all Jews had access to money through their connections. In their role as moneylenders, Jews were relegated to an economic outsider status.

As the secular world attacked Jews through the legal system, the Catholic Church continued to chafe amid the Jewish presence. The Fourth Lateran Council met in 1215 and one of the issues for the church authorities was what to do about Jews and Christians still interacting with one another. To address their concerns, new legislation was adopted which would further ostracize Jews from a Christian world. Under this new legislation, Jews and Christians were forbidden to eat meals together, they were not allowed to marry nor engage in extramarital intercourse, and Jews were now required to wear special clothing and markers which would designate them as social outsiders. These requirements ranged from having Jews wear yellow belts to what were called "Jew badges" affixed to outer clothing; for Jewish women it meant wearing veils out in public, and for Jewish men it could also mean wearing silly or ridiculous pointed hats. All of these new requirements suggest to the historian that if laws have to be passed against Jews and Christians eating together or having sex, then we can guess that Jews and Christians were in fact engaging in these very activities prior to the creation of the new legislation. In addition, these new restrictions worked to enforce a kind of public surveillance system in society. If one saw a person marked as a Jew, then one would know what activities a Jew could engage in within the community. Forcing Jews to be marked in a public fashion resulted in what historians call their "social death." Jews were ostracized, forced to live apart from the rest of their communities, and so disappeared from many Catholics' world.[21]

The impact of St. Thomas Aquinas

Into this charged atmosphere, one could find echoes of Augustine's original teachings in the writings of St. Thomas Aquinas (1225–1274). Aquinas, one of the most influential medieval theologians of his day, considered the interactions between Christians and Jews. Much of what he argued had already been said by Augustine; however, Aquinas added some new elements. Like Augustine, Aquinas argued for the contradictory position that the church had always held: Jews could be kept in abject humiliation but Christians should stop short of annihilating them. What Aquinas added was the notion that Jews had souls and therefore could be at least theoretically "saved." Somehow, Jews were to be converted voluntarily— despite the persecutions and horrendous depictions of Jews as being in league with the devil, desecrating the Host, and reenacting the crucifixion of Jesus.[22] Most Jews did not feel as though they would be welcomed as converts; however, some Jews did in fact convert to Christianity. The converts often became weapons in the church's arsenal to show the moral bankruptcy of Judaism.

Nicholas Donin, a recent convert to Christianity, became one of the thirteenth century's weapons to be used against his former coreligionists, the Jews. In 1239 he served as the Christian representative in a public disputation in Paris in which the primary goal was to bring about public ridicule. The aim was to use Donin's "insider knowledge of Judaism" since he had been a practicing Jew, to put further pressure on Jewish communities and to reveal to the generally Christian audience the bankruptcy of Judaism as a faith. Of course, any Jew forced into the open debate had no chance of winning the argument; the odds were already aligned against him. In the 1239 Paris debate, Donin attacked the writings of the Talmud in particular, arguing that the rabbinic texts had pulled Jews away from the real teachings of the Old Testament, and this had resulted, according to the convert, in Jewish blindness with regard to the "true" faith of Christianity. Once the disputation had concluded, the king of France Louis IX followed up on Donin's argument: if the Talmud was what poisoned Jews' minds against Christianity, then all of the Talmudic literature should be collected and burned. In 1242, twenty-four wagonloads full of Talmuds from all over France were transported to Paris, where they were publicly burned. The destruction of precious Jewish literature was so extensive that only one complete copy of the Talmud from this time period from France exists to this day, and it is kept in an archive in Munich, Germany.[23]

These types of public disputations, rigged as they were against the Jews, served only to further strain Jewish-Christian relations. It also helped formulate goals for many church leaders: if the Talmud produced heresy on the part of the Jews, then all Talmudic literature should be removed. Further disputations occurred throughout Europe, including a famous one in Barcelona in 1263. These displays of shaming and humiliation of Jewish belief and teachings helped the general public to develop their language regarding the treatment of Jews. It reinforced the Christian majority's contempt for Judaism and raised Christianity's awareness that, if the Jews had shifted in their religious beliefs to a reliance on the oral law (that of the Talmud) instead of the written law (that of the Old Testament), then the Jews were no longer the same people whom St. Augustine and Thomas Aquinas had defended. That belief had serious implications for Jews in Europe because if they were following rabbinic teachings, they were practicing willful heresy, and there should no longer be any injunctions against persecuting, forcibly converting, and murdering Jews.

The result of public attacks—both intellectual stylized debates and forced markings of Jews—led to an overall decline in the standard of living for most European Jews. Historians debate what had changed in the overall atmosphere from European Jewish life pre-1096 with that of post-1096 Crusades, and generally we can conclude that as Europe experienced a series of upheavals and threats, the position of Jews became more precarious. For some scholars, they point to the harsher segregation policies of the Catholic Church, the creation of the Dominican and Franciscan orders in the thirteenth century, and their extreme positions against non-Christians; however, this does not seem quite enough of an adequate explanation. European-wide threats and fears seem to have contributed to the deterioration of the Jews' position in Christian society, fears such as the growing threat in the rise in Muslim empires, the fears of internal heresy, as well as changing, more centralized governments. There was also a rise in prejudice against any type of nonconformist behavior, and Jews certainly stood out as refusing to adopt the dominant culture's religious beliefs.[24]

As time progressed and further challenges rose up in European people's lives, the public ostracizing of Jews increased, with popular literature churning out stories of Jewish perfidy and their adoption of willful unbelief. Attacks against Jews in imagery increased as well, often depicting Jews at "work" desecrating the sacred Host, reenacting the crucifixion, performing ritual murder against unsuspecting Christian child-martyrs, and as Jews were increasingly limited in what types of occupations they could pursue in the Christian world, the imagery of the shyster Jew, lending money at exorbitant interest rates abounded in the popular imagination. With tensions increasing, Jews often faced expulsions from whatever country they happened to be living in at the time. In 1290 King Edward III ordered all of the Jews out of England; the king of France followed up on this in 1306. The Austrian duke Albrecht V decided that keeping Jews in his territory was no longer profitable for him so he not only ordered the majority of the Jews out but also had 200 of the once wealthiest Jews arrested, bound together and burned alive on a pyre in public in 1420. While all of this proved time and again to the general public that Jews were religious outsiders, it also demonstrated that Jews were economic outsiders as well, fully dependent upon the whims of rulers.

Expulsion for outsiders

No case better demonstrates Jews' precarious position than expulsion at the whims of rulers than that of Spain in 1492. Back in 1469 Ferdinand, heir of the kingdom of Aragon, married Isabella, heir to Castile. Their union was supposed to end the warfare that had existed between the two kingdoms and it was to forge the foundation of modern-day Spain. The problem faced by the new royal couple was how to define who was truly a Spaniard, and as it turned out, it was easier to define people according to what they were not: if one were not a Muslim or a Jew, then one could be a Spaniard. In medieval Europe, the largest and oldest Jewish communities were located in Spain. Prior to a violent outbursts of violence against Jews in 1391, most thought of Spain as a place where Jews could exist alongside that of Christians, even when the rest of Western Europe was witnessing a decline in Jewish-Christian relations. So what had changed by 1391 in Spain? Historians cite class hatred, economic difficulties, and rising religious intolerance as the causes of the pogrom. In the violence meted out to the Jews of Castile and Aragon, a strange reaction occurred: unlike in the time of the First Crusade where so many Jews preferred martyrdom to apostasy, masses of Jews converted to Catholicism. So many converted that a new name was created to describe the new Christians, the "conversos." It seems that Jews had decided to convert for a variety of reasons, including some out of a sense to preserve their lives, still others converted because they were tired of the persecutions and humiliations, and others simply converted out of a true call to Christianity. In the popular imagination of the day, however, the new Christians were still Jews, not to be trusted. The slang used to describe the converts was the derogatory word "Marrano," or "swine." The general suspicion was that the converts were secretly still practicing Jews and that they sought to somehow disrupt Catholic Spain by infiltrating "true" Catholic families.[25]

The Catholic Church responded to these suspicions by sending in inquisitors to investigate the forced (and sometimes voluntary) conversions. Jews who had converted, whether it was forced or not, were frequently the victims of persecution. Contrary to modern-day misperceptions about the Catholic Inquisition, Jews as Jews were not rooted out. Instead, the inquisitors were looking for those people who had professed to be Catholics but were accused of being heretics (in this case secretly being Jewish). The inquisitors burned heretics at the stake, again reinforcing to the general public that being a nonconformist was life threatening. By 1492, Ferdinand and Isabella took another bold step: they signed an expulsion order for all remaining Jews to leave Spain. They feared that if they allowed unconverted Jews to remain in Spain, then the "conversos" would be drawn back into the Jewish communities they had supposedly left behind. For the Jews who were forced to leave, and approximately 150,000 of them left, where would they go? The vast majority of them went to neighboring Portugal; however, those who did so were forcibly converted in 1497. Others fled to parts of Italy and to the Ottoman Empire. To all of those forced to leave Spain behind, no matter where they ended up, the mass expulsion represented a truly low point in European Jewish history.[26]

With the forced migration of Jews from Spain, new Jewish communities began to grow in parts of Italy, the Ottoman Empire and even in Eastern Europe. For the Jews who came to live in Italian territories, they were about to experience the new trends of Renaissance thought and culture, the Reformation and the revolutionary invention of the printing press. As the medieval period came to a close, Jews still living in Western European communities would have seen that fundamentally Jewish men were now people without rights. Forbidden to own land, join a craft guild, and pursue certain professions, segregated from Christian communities, abandoned by many church leaders, expelled by kings, princes, and dukes, the everyday life of Jews was fairly grim. Most Jews recognized how precarious their coexistence alongside Christians actually was, for they had experienced firsthand how quickly the local population could turn their fear and loathing into violent actions for supposed crimes. The bishop of Speyer noted in 1519 that Jews were "not humans, but dogs." How would the new humanism of the Renaissance and the challenges of the Reformation impact the Jews?

The Renaissance and Reformation's impact on Jewish lives

For some Jews, particularly those who now found themselves living in Italian lands, they would be exposed to Renaissance humanistic thought. This was especially true for those who lived in Florence, the main center of Renaissance thinking. Although Renaissance thought did have an impact on some Jewish scholars, mainly because some Renaissance thinkers wanted to learn how to read Hebrew to help them with source materials, most average Jews still experienced a life of restrictions. Indeed, it was in the Italian territories that Jews were first confined to ghettos with the earliest known ghetto being established in Venice in 1516. Pope Paul IV decreed that Jews were now required to move from outlying regions into urban areas where certain neighborhoods or streets would be designated as appropriate living space for the Jews. At first these ghettos were billed as ways to contain Jews, so that they would have fewer opportunities to "contaminate" Christians. It was also argued that ghettos would help to convert the Jews, although forcing them to live in relatively overpopulated, squalid neighborhoods does not seem to have brought about the desired conversions. One of the unintended consequences of the ghettoization of the Jews in Italy, however, was the now forced interaction between Christians and Jews. It turned out that by forcing Jews into limited urban spaces, more Jews and Christians actually came into contact with one another. Another consequence would be the long-held association that Jews were an urban people.[27]

Christian Humanists did consider the position Jews found themselves in, but most were loath to change the status of the Jews. Noted northern humanist, Erasmus of Rotterdam, famous for his satirical works demanding toleration and peace, continued to hold a deep-seated hatred for the Jews. The Dutch Calvinist philosopher Hugo Grotius offered his expert opinion on the Jews. He argued that Jews should in fact have freedom to worship, but he tempered that with ideas regarding the establishment of quotas for how many Jews could live in an area, restrictions that forbade Jews from holding any public offices, and he added that Jews should also be required to listen to Christian sermons. Clearly, some doors were opening for Jews, while others remained shut in this time of great change. Adding to the insecurity of the times would be the challenge to the seemingly unlimited power of the Catholic Church, that of the Reformation, led by Martin Luther.

Luther, a former Catholic monk, had agonized over what was required for a good Christian to achieve salvation. His studies had led him to develop his own theories of salvation through justification by faith alone, and, when combined with the many rampant abuses present in the Catholic Church of his day, Luther began to search for ways to reform the church. As he pursued his reformist agenda, Luther also thought about the position of the Jews. Early in his career as a reformer, Luther wrote a pamphlet titled "Jesus Christ was born a Jew" (1523). In his quest to bring salvation to as many souls as possible, Luther believed that taking a gentler approach to the Jews would bring about their conversion—to his brand of religion, not to the Catholic Church. In reminding his readers that Jesus of Nazareth had been born a Jew, Luther was attempting to bridge some of the divide that had arisen due to supersessionism. However, as the years turned into decades, with few to no Jews converting to Lutheranism, Luther's ire became provoked. By 1543 he penned a much different work "Concerning the Jews and Their Lies." In this violent attack, Luther spewed forth his hatred of the Jews. In this work he suggested that Jewish houses of worship should be set on fire, as should their schools, private homes, and prayer books. He recommended that Jews be confined to urban environments where they could be watched more closely than if they lived out in the countryside. He wrote that Jews should be deprived of their money and that they should be forced to perform physically demanding work. Finally, he warned Christians to stay away from

Jews lest they be corrupted by them. Luther's vitriolic language against the Jews also included the now familiar accusations that Jews committed blood libel, poisoned wells, and served Satan. If Jews had pinned their hopes on the Reformation bringing about a radical change in attitudes toward them, this was clearly not the result for which they might have wished.[28]

Poland as a possible refuge for Jews

In the midst of all of the restrictions, discriminations, and persecutions, Jews did have one hopeful spot in Christian Europe: the kingdom of Poland. As more expulsions occurred across Western Europe, some Jews made their way into the land of King Kasimir the Great. Legend has it that King Kasimir had acquired numerous mistresses; however, his favorite mistress happened to be a Jewish woman and that inclined him toward inviting Jews into his lands. In reality, as early as 1264, King Boleslas Pius of Poland made special offers to Jews to enter his kingdom as men working for his treasury. King Kasimir in 1364 did issue another invitation to Jews, offering them the protection of the king, if they settled in his territory. For the persecuted Jews of Europe, Poland became at least a temporary safe haven for them as they worked for royalty primarily in economic roles such as leasing land, taxation farming, trade, and manufacture. Although royalty and other aristocrats tended to welcome the participation of Jews in the economy, Jews did still face criticisms at the hands of local church leaders as well as rising middle-class burghers. Despite these criticisms, Jews were able to form a council that allowed them to rule according to their own religious laws. This council was made up of the wealthiest of Jewish men in Poland. In addition, as life stabilized further, Jewish centers of learning flourished, establishing Poland as a leading center of Jewish studies.[29]

As Jewish academies flourished, there was great interaction with Jews all over Europe and the Ottoman Empire due to the printing press. Printed copies of the Talmud circulated, allowing rabbinic studies to be more widely discussed and debated in the academies. Jewish culture continued to thrive in Poland, and, under the improved living standards by the seventeenth century, there was a dramatic increase in the Jewish population of Poland. Not all was well, however, and in 1648 a Ukrainian Cossack leader, Bogdan Chmielnicki, led a vicious assault on the Jews of Poland. It is estimated that anywhere from 50,000 to 100,000 Jews were massacred or enslaved in these pogroms. To Chmielnicki and his followers, the Jews had acquired too much economic power in Poland—as moneylenders, as leaseholders, and so on, and the assaults were intended to drive the Jews out of the country. Despite the enormous loss to the Jewish community of Poland, the survivors rebuilt their communities and they continued to grow so much so that by the end of the eighteenth century, Poland had the largest single center of Jewish life in all of Christian Europe.[30]

The Enlightenment and optimism

Let us now turn to another promising development in the improvement of life for the Jews of Europe: the age of the Enlightenment. With the Enlightenment came the idea that perfect societies could, in fact, be established if the philosophes (intellectuals) of the era could study human nature and discern what types of laws could be written that would be in keeping with human behavior. Once those laws could be written, presumably a utopian society would emerge. This intellectual movement, beginning in Paris in the eighteenth century and sweeping into the other urban areas of European cities, was filled with optimism: could man, through the acquisition of knowledge, truly create an ideal world? Would the use of man's ability to reason, to inquire logically, to arrive at objective truths, restructure the imperfect world that most people were currently living in? This emphasis on man's ability to use reason inspired great confidence in ideas of progress, but the philosophes of the day also looked around and saw that the world they were currently a part of was riddled with imperfections of all kinds. Philosophes such as John Locke, Jean Jacques Rousseau, and Baron de Montesquieu all contributed to critiques of their societies.

These intellectuals saw absolutist systems of government, based on inherited rights and privileges as defying rationality. Why should a man have certain rights guaranteed to him based solely on having the right last name? The philosophes were searching for ways to bring about the ideas of meritocracy, natural rights, and the creation of a secular society ruled over by men of property and education. Their ideas would prove to be so radical that they would help to fuel major revolutions: in the Americas as well as in France, Belgian, and the Netherlands to name but a few. The philosophes emphasized the ideas of natural rights: the right to life, liberty, and property (happiness in the case of Thomas Jefferson). In particular, their powerful attachment to the concept of individual liberty, that is, that a man should have the ability to maximize his freedom and that all men were equal in the eyes of the law, would have a dramatic impact on the position of Jews throughout all of Europe. As a visibly oppressed minority group, living in ghettos, under countless restrictions regarding occupational choices, Jews certainly had much to gain from such powerful ideas about ending society's enforced inequality. One voice rose to the forefront in this age of classical liberalism: that of a German Jew, Moses Mendelssohn (1729–1786).

Mendelssohn had been born in Dessau in a Jewish ghetto, to a fairly impoverished family. However, his obvious intellectual abilities had catapulted him into the higher echelons of education where he studied general philosophy and science. As a young man, Mendelssohn moved to Berlin, where he became acquainted with German intellectuals and artists such as the famous playwright Gotthold Lessing and the philosopher Immanuel Kant. What should strike the reader at this moment is the recognition that Lessing and Kant were not Jewish. Mendelssohn's great mind, his ability to speak eloquently, and the ability to debate issues brought him into contact with the non-Jewish intellectuals of the Berlin salons. Mendelssohn rose in their esteem, many of their circle wondered why Mendelssohn would not convert to Christianity, but Mendelssohn had developed his own philosophy about Judaism and he would not leave it behind. Still, many Enlightenment thinkers continued to pressure Mendelssohn—if he truly endorsed the universal values of Enlightenment thought, how could he still maintain his Jewishness? To answer these challenges, Mendelssohn wrote his influential work *Jerusalem*.[31]

In this philosophical work, Mendelssohn argued that church and state should indeed be separated and that Locke's ideas of natural rights should be extended to encompass Jews' abilities to practice their religion freely. In addition, Mendelssohn attempted to lay out his own definition of Judaism and he tried to show how Judaism was consistent with Enlightenment ideals. Unfortunately, much of Mendelssohn's definitions of Judaism lacked an emotional appeal that remained unconvincing for many Jews, including that of Mendelssohn's own children (most of whom converted to Christianity). Despite the fact that *Jerusalem* was not resonating with people of his time, it was Mendelssohn's attempt to show that Judaism and Enlightenment thought were not wholly incompatible. His life also proved that a believing Jew could move in the non-Jewish world and be successful. Toward the end of the eighteenth century, Mendelssohn was asked to write a plea for the emancipation of German and French Jews. He declined, but his gentile friend, Christian von Döhm (1751–1820), a political theorist, diplomat, and historian, took up the challenge instead.

Döhm, in 1781, wrote that Jewish men should be given political equality both in German territories and in French ones. Believing in the ideals of the Enlightenment, the scholar argued that Jews deserved political equality because "the Jew is a human being even before he is a Jew."[32] While that might not sound particularly enlightened, to recognize that Jews were indeed human beings, Döhm had put forth what seemed like a radical idea, especially in many German-speaking lands. For many Germans, the idea of emancipating the Jews and bestowing full civic equality upon them smacked of too much, too soon. Many German intellectuals paternalistically argued that Jews were unfit for emancipation, that they would not know what to do with such equality. While many Germans might have thought this was too much, with the eruption of the French Revolution and the Napoleonic Wars, Enlightenment ideals were coming to Germany no matter what they wished.

The revolution in France

Back in France, many of the revolutionaries of 1789 had decided that, in the name of equality, they would have to grant Jewish men civic rights. This was not at all an obvious choice because many philosophes, including the most famous of all, Voltaire, despised the Jews and saw no need to extend the ideals of the Enlightenment their way. Despite this, many liberals, in the name of equality, fought for Jewish emancipation. This did not necessarily mean that the liberals embraced social equality for Jews; instead most of them focused on the ideas of civic, legal equality which would make Jewish men as individuals equal in the eyes of the law. In December of 1789 in France, the revolutionaries declared Jewish emancipation. But declaring emancipation and living emancipation are two different things, and for many Jews, life was still filled with restrictions and countless discriminations.

As the French Revolution convulsed through various stages, a relatively young military genius, Napoleon Bonaparte, rose to great power and fame. As he acquired more and more influence, Napoleon led the Grand Army of France across the continent of Europe. Wherever Napoleon and the Grand Army conquered land, they enforced French law—and with it, French ideas of the Enlightenment. Wherever the French came to occupy and control German-speaking lands, Jews seemed to derive the greatest benefits from the French document "The Declaration of the Rights of Man and Citizen." This document had been decreed in the early phases of the French Revolution and it boldly stated that all men are born free and equal, that all men are entitled to life, liberty, and property (called natural rights), and that all men are given the freedoms of speech, assembly, security, the press, and religion. For Jews living in conquered German territories, these ideas were quite radical.

For many German Jews, life revolved around restrictions, not emancipation. In the mid-1700s Jews living in German lands would have found that in some towns, no Jews were allowed to live there at all. In still other towns, such as Ulm, only one Jew was permitted to reside within the town's walls. Other larger cities, such as Nurnberg, did not allow Jews to reside within the city; however, a Jew could enter during the day to conduct business. This entailed going through the cattle gate of the city—the one cattle were driven through, not the gates reserved for Christians. In addition, each Jew would have to pay a tax to get inside. Usually this was the same amount a livestock breeder would have to pay for a head of cattle, further stressing the dehumanized Jew's status. Upon paying the cattle tax and entering through the gate, the Jew would find a group of elderly Christian women. He would have to select one of the women to accompany him throughout his travels in the city. She would monitor his behavior, and at the end of his business journey, he would have to pay the woman for her "work."

For Jews going to Frankfurt, they would find that it was a "liberal" city. That meant that Jews could actually live inside the city walls, but they had to be confined to the Jewish quarter, a ghetto, called the Judengasse. The Judengasse could only be entered or exited through gates and the gates were locked each night at sunset. Quotas were set which meant that no more than 500 Jewish householders could reside inside the Jewish ghetto at any given time. That meant that the 500 men could bring their families, which comes close to approximately 3,000 individuals living in the Judengasse. In order to live there, a Jewish man had to have a permit which he had to renew every three years; he paid regular taxes as well as special fees if he was a newcomer to the city. There were other strict regulations applied to residents as well. For average Jews living inside the ghetto, this meant that only the oldest son could marry and only after the father of the house had died—that way the number of householders remained stable. In addition, if there were younger brothers, they had to either remain unmarried for the rest of their lives and stay in Frankfurt with their family or move away and establish a new family for themselves. As the eighteenth century progressed, Frankfurt's city fathers decided to become more "liberal" and allowed Jews to own shops outside of the Judengasse's walls.

Not all German-speaking lands dragged their feet in regard to Jewish emancipation. The Enlightened ruler Friedrich Wilhelm III adopted a sweeping program of reforms in 1812, including granting Jews in his territory of Prussia the rights of citizenship and corresponding political rights as well. To the south and west, however, German speakers found themselves conquered by Napoleonic forces and, whether they wanted Jews to be emancipated or not, was immaterial. French law was imposed and Jews were given equal rights according to the "Declaration of the Rights of Man and Citizen." Chafing under defeat at the hands of the French, many German intellectuals began to dream of a united German nation-state, one which would be able to throw off French tyranny and all things associated with France. This dream led to a reaction against the ideals of the French revolution, with many thinkers denouncing the ideas of "Liberty, Equality, and Fraternity" as being un-German.

The dream of a United Germany— where do Jews belong?

In the new, modern, secular Europe, many German thinkers were beginning to imagine what a united German land might be like. In their imaginings, we can see a language being developed that moves away from religiously based anti-Semitism to that of a more modern type of discrimination. Who were some of these individuals who were contributing to this new type of language? Perhaps the first and most notable of these men was the young German philosopher Johann Gottlieb Fichte (1762–1814). Fichte has often been granted the title of "Father of German Nationalism" as well as "Father of Modern German Antisemitism." Why? How is German nationalism related to German anti-Semitism? At first, Fichte watched the unfolding events of the French Revolution from afar and he at least mildly approved of some of the changes occurring. However, once he found himself living under French laws, he began to argue that German speakers needed to unify into one powerful German nation-state. He, as a philosopher, could envision how a united Germany might alter the balance of power in Europe. Under French domination, he decided to deliver a public address. He obtained the French-occupying authorities' permission to give the public lecture and he fired his opening salvo for German nationalism. In his address he opened dramatically by stating that he was "speaking to Germans and of Germans only." Since there was no united German nation-state yet, Fichte was already revealing his idea that a unified Germany could in fact become a possibility. He continued on in his address by telling his audience that if they could just hold on, in their hour of defeat at the hands of the French, that German greatness was waiting for them. He was promising them a messianic future, if they could unify and act together to defeat the French. Considering that he died in 1814, one year before the great Napoleon Bonaparte would be decisively defeated at the Battle of Waterloo, Fichte was quite optimistic about the future.

In other writings, Fichte considered the question of Jewish emancipation. Earning his title of "Father of Modern German Antisemitism," Fichte denounced this idea of emancipation as a French idea, effectively conflating the terms "French" and "Jew." To Fichte, to say the word "French" was to say the word "Jew," and he claimed that all French and Jewish ideas were the same. He added in for good measure that these French-Jewish ideas were not only all the same but also obnoxious. In this way, Fichte began to develop the language that allowed Jews to become associated with the ideas and values of the French Revolution and, by extension, the ideals of the age of the Enlightenment. Fichte also warned that Jews living in German lands were a divisive presence, calling them a "state within a state," which would work to weaken and undermine the German nation. (Remember that there was no German nation yet!)[33]

Fichte was certainly not alone in his denunciations of the French Revolution, of liberalism, or of progress. One could point to the Austrian leader Metternich, to the pope, and to the Russian Tsars and find many of them rejecting what others had called "modernity" or "progress." But with Fichte we can definitely see how questions of identity (e.g., who are the Germans?) were combined with questions of belonging. If you do not belong in a society as a citizen, then what position do you actually occupy? How are you, as an outsider, defined by the dominant population?

Contributing to this type of insider-outsider language was Friedrich Ludwig Jahn (1778–1852). Jahn, a founder of the nationalist gymnast movement, also weighed in on the idea of a German nation and who would potentially belong in it. Jahn helped create the concept of German nationalism with his refinement of the term "Volk." Technically one could define "Volk" as meaning a people, a nation, but Jahn invested this term with another level of meaning. He argued that there was an "essence" to the word "Volk" and that this so-called essence transcended commonalities such as speaking the same language, sharing similar cultural and social practices. To Jahn, the term "Volk" implied something mystical that transcended all of those shared commonalities. He could not quite show people who the Volk was, but he could tell people who could never be included in the Volk: the Jews and the Sinti and Roma (gypsies). He argued that if a German nation was to be created, it would not include Jews or Gypsies, partly because they were people who wandered—or were "rootless" in his words and the state would have to be Christian. In Jahn's world, Jews would always be considered outsiders who simply could never belong to the German Volk.[34]

Overlapping in time with Jahn was another intellectual who was helping to create this language of exclusion. His name was Christian Friedrich Ruhs (1781–1820). Ruhs was a historian at the University of Berlin. Like Fichte, Ruhs believed that Jews were a divisive presence, again picking up on the language of Jews as a "state within a state." He argued that Jews could never become German citizens because they were not Christians. Ruhs elaborated on this idea by stating that only Christians could be expected to be loyal and therefore Jews were ruled out as potential members of a German state. Ruhs went further than Fichte or Jahn, however, in that he suggested the revival of the medieval Jew badge. He wanted Jews to be forced to wear yellow patches of fabric on their outer clothing so everyone else would know that they were aliens who did not truly belong.[35] Once again, the idea of a unified German state brought with it questions about identity: who would be counted as a full member of the state and what rights would they be entitled to—despite the fact that no German nation-state existed yet.

Despite this divisive language of historians and philosophers, the position of most European Jews was improving over the course of the nineteenth century. England had granted emancipation to its Jewish population in 1826, and by 1858 the first Jewish man was elected to Parliament. Even German territories would be swept up in the "Year of Revolutions" of 1848 when a new cycle of Liberalism arose. Beginning in Paris in February 1848, a loose coalition of middle-class men, liberal students, and working-class people rose up to try to bring about the promises of the French Revolution that they felt had never come to fruition. Once revolutionary behavior emerged in France, every single capital city throughout Europe, with the exception of Great Britain, Russia, and Turkey, erupted in attempted liberal uprisings. The heady ideas of liberty, equality, and fraternity were once again on the march, except in all of these uprisings, the romantic notions of ill-organized liberals were doomed to be put down by the forces of reactionary conservatives. The Liberals had been too weak and too disorganized to withstand the reactions that were to follow, and by 1852, all of the attempted liberal revolutions had been squelched. The ending of revolutionary dreams was followed by yet another set of social commentators who reacted strongly against the ill-fated revolutions they had witnessed.

Post-1848 reactionaries

The German scholar Paul de Lagarde (1827–1891) argued that his studies of the "Orient" had led him to conclude that Jews were vermin, destroying

German life and culture. Another professor, Christian Lassen (1802–1871), combined his expertise of ancient civilizations with linguistics. In his work he divided the peoples of the world into two large categories: the Aryans and the Semites. Using the tools of linguists, he argued that Semitic-speaking peoples were selfish, exclusive to their own people, and intolerant, and they generally destroyed civilizations and culture. In contrast, he found Aryans to be the polar opposite: they were tolerant, altruistic, creative peoples who built up civilizations and culture. Still another, Arthur de Gobineau (1816–1882), a French social commentator, added his opinion that racial questions overshadowed all of history. To Gobineau, European society was degenerating and it was due to racial mixing. He did not single out the Jews specifically, but they would have been included as those marrying into gentile families and bringing about such families' "decline." Finally, we could add the voice of composer Richard Wagner (1816–1883). Wagner, known for his operatic compositions such as Parsifal, Rienzi, and the Niebelungenlied, not only revived Teutonic mythology for his musical works. Wagner had lived through the 1848 revolutions, had seen it fail, and became a reactionary conservative. He firmly believed that German music was being corrupted by compositions by German Jews, but his beliefs about Jewish pollution went further than just the realm of music. Before Wagner died, he collected many of his writings into fourteen volumes. Out of the fourteen volumes, only four of them deal with music. The remaining ten volumes represent his rantings and ravings about the dangers of Jews to German life. As a famous and outspoken composer, Wagner had far-reaching influence. He fought vociferously to exclude Jews from all segments of German life. It is no wonder that Wagner became Adolf Hitler's favorite composer.[36]

All of these men, from Paul de Lagarde to Richard Wagner, represent the voice of reactionary conservatism following on the heels of the attempted liberal revolutions of 1848. All of these men represent a time in history when differences among peoples were being stressed, where ideas about racial superiority were rampant, and where anti-Semitism was beginning to move into the realm of racial ideology. To these thinkers, it would be impossible to fully assimilate Jews into European culture, and all of them fought emphatically to deny Jews emancipation in their territories. As bad as all of this was, for many Jews in the nineteenth century, living in a German-speaking land was considered to be a viable option—especially if they were living in Russian-controlled land.

Tsarist Russia: A land untouched by Enlightenment ideals

Over the course of the European Enlightenment, the Tsars of Russia had been able to largely ignore the revolutionary ideas espousing liberty and equality for all men. By the late 1880s Russia had become the home of approximately 40 percent of world Jewry. Why? Poland had been the home to the largest concentration of Jews for centuries, but with the partitioning of Poland, Russia now found itself with much of the Jewish population of Poland living in its territory. Under the Enlightened Despotism of Catherine the Great, the partition of Poland in the 1790s resulted in a large number of Jews falling under the control of the Russian Empire. Catherine, although a person who had read much of the Enlightenment philosophy, worried about the Jewish population—as well as the Polish aristocrats who might object to Russian control. Partly in an effort to keep Jews from "contaminating" the Russian Orthodox Christian population and partly in response to Russian businessmen's fears of Jewish economic competition, Catherine created a special area in which Jews were required to live. This area, representing approximately 20 percent of European Russian land, was called the Pale of Settlement. It included Polish-Lithuania, Latvia, Belarus, Moldova, Ukraine, and parts of western Russia. Historians estimate that anywhere from 4 to 5 million Jews lived within the Pale.[37]

What followed for Jews after Catherine the Great died would be a litany of further tightening restrictions upon their communities. Under Tsar Alexander I, Jews were no longer allowed to live along any borderlands, they could not live in villages alongside Russian Orthodox Christians, and they could no longer sell alcohol to Christians by 1804. His successor, Nicholas I (1825–55), decided that Jews needed to be assimilated, which really meant that they should stop being Jews and become Russian Orthodox Christians, so he developed an assimilationist plan. Jews living in the Pale, mostly in all Jewish settlements called *shtetls*, would now be required to fill quotas in the Tsar's army. All Jewish males aged 12–25 years were eligible for a term of service of twenty-five years. Some Jewish families reportedly held wakes when their sons were about to report for duty because they understood that they might never see them again. In addition, if a twelve-year-old boy was taken, his twenty-five-year term of service would not begin until the boy became eighteen years of age. For six years, from the ages of twelve to eighteen, these young boys were kept in special units where every effort was made to convert them to Orthodox Christianity, and, at the very least, these children were certainly not allowed to receive instruction in Judaism. To Nicholas I, this plan, of removing marriageable age young men in particular from Jewish communities, would necessarily decrease the Jewish population. It also worked to pull young men away from their faith and religious rituals and customs as no special allowance would be made for them as Jews. The plan also had the further bonus in that it often resulted in one Jewish community raiding another Jewish village in order to kidnap young boys and hand them over to Russian authorities in fulfillment of their quotas. Even within the same villages, wealthier Jews often paid poorer Jews to send their sons to fill the requirements. This pitted Jews against other Jews, breaking down communities and setting one group against another.

By the time we arrive at Tsar Alexander III (1881–1894), Jews living within Russian lands found themselves facing a new threat—that of government-sponsored pogroms. Alexander III and his advisors had a new plan to solve Russia's "Jewish problem." The plan was a straightforward mathematical equation that stipulated that under the harsh living conditions, combined with outbursts of extreme violence, one-third of Russian Jewry would emigrate, one-third of the Jewish population would die, and the remaining one-third would be converted to Orthodox Christianity. Violent pogroms, instigated by Alexander III's government, made life increasingly difficult for Jews. Now they not only had to worry about violating laws; they also had to worry about being brutally murdered. Large numbers of Jews did in fact flee westward, beginning in 1881. Some Jews went to Germany, but the goal for many was to come to the United States of America, where they hoped they would be free to live as Jews. By the time of Nicholas II (1894–1917), the last Tsar in Russian history, Jews who were left behind in Russia were increasingly poverty-stricken, persecuted politically, and desperately seeking to escape from Russia's oppressive grip.[38]

For the Jews of Europe, the promise of the Enlightenment ideals of progress, liberalism, and emancipation had not been fulfilled whether one lived in Russia or in France. To the gentile world, Jews were not living up to their end of the bargain. As we saw with Moses Mendelssohn, many enlightened individuals believed that in order for Jews to become accepted members of society, they had to shed their "Jewish" ways. But for many Jews, their religious practices were a private matter, and emancipation a political matter. The question for many Jews was how far they should go in their assimilation efforts. As the nineteenth century wore on, another problem regarding assimilation was about to hit Jews: the question of nationalism. Where would Jews fit in, when so many gentiles saw the Jews as rootless wanderers, unable to be loyal to whatever nation they resided in?

For your consideration

Below you will find primary source documents that address some of the themes of this chapter. Our first source is taken from the New Testament. Each excerpt is the Gospel writer's version of the crucifixion of Jesus of Nazareth. As you read each passage, think about the ways in which the Jews are described. What role do they play in the sentencing of Jesus? Is it a specific group of Jews who are named in the process as being responsible for the Roman governor Pontius Pilate's decision? How might the role of the Jews as they are depicted in these passages lead to the myth of deicide?

Matthew 27: 20–26:

The chief priests and the elders, however, had persuaded the crowd to demand the release of Barabbas and the execution of Jesus. So when the governor spoke and asked them, "Which of the two do you want me to release for you?" they said "Barabbas." "But in that case," Pilate said to them, "what am I to do with Jesus who is called Christ?" They all said, "Let him be crucified!" "Why?" he asked. "What harm has he done?" But they shouted all the louder, "Let him be crucified!" Then Pilate saw that he was making no impression, that in fact a riot was imminent. So he took some water, washed his hands in front of the crowd and said, "I am innocent of this man's blood. It is your concern." And the people to a man shouted back, "His blood be on us and on our children!" Then he released Barabbas for them. He ordered Jesus to be first scourged and then handed over to be crucified.

Excerpt from The Jerusalem Bible Reader's Edition

John 8: 42–47:

Jesus answered: "If God were your father, you would love me, since I have come here from God; yes, I have come from him; not that I came because I chose, no, I was sent, and by him. Do you know why you cannot take in what I say? It is because you are unable to understand my language. The devil is your father, and you prefer to do what your father wants. He was a murderer from the start; he was never grounded in the truth; there is no truth in him at all; when he lies he is drawing on his own store, because he is a liar, and the father of lies. But as for me, I speak the truth and for that very reason, you do not believe me. Can one of you convict me of sin? If I speak the truth, why do you not believe me? A child of God listens to the words of God; if you refuse to listen, it is because you are not God's children."

Below is an excerpt from Martin Luther's pamphlet, "Concerning the Jews and Their Lies" (1543). Luther wrote this pamphlet after trying to convert Jews to Lutheranism for twenty years. He had had very little success and now his anger spilled out in this work. How does Luther paint a picture of Jews? What qualities does he believe Jews have? What recommendations does he make for Christians regarding their relationships with Jews? How does Luther's portrayal of Jews rely on medieval prejudices? How might this writing have influenced early Protestants in their opinions about Jews?

dear Christian, be advised and do not doubt that next to the devil, you have no more bitter, venomous, and vehement foe than a real Jew, who earnestly seeks to be a Jew.... Therefore the history books often accuse them of contaminating wells, of kidnapping and piercing children, as for example at Trent, Weissensee, etc....

... they hold us Christians captive in our own country. They let us work in the sweat of our brow to earn money and property while they sit behind the stove, idle away the time, fart, and roast pears. They stuff themselves, guzzle, and live in luxury and ease from our hard-earned goods. With their accursed usury they hold us and our property captive. Moreover, they mock and deride us because we work and let them play the role of lazy squires at our expense and in our land. Thus they are our masters and we are their servants, with our property, our sweat, and our labor. And by way of reward and thanks they curse our Lord and us! Should the devil not laugh and dance if he can enjoy such a fine paradise at the expense of us Christians?...

So we are even at fault in not avenging all this innocent blood of our Lord and of the Christians which they shed for three hundred years after the destruction of Jerusalem, and the blood of the children they have shed since then.... We are at fault in not slaying them. Rather we allow them to live freely in our midst despite all their murdering, cursing, blaspheming, lying, and defaming; we protect and shield their synagogues, houses, life, and property. In this way we make them lazy and secure and encourage them to fleece us boldly of our money and goods, as well as to mock and deride us, with a view to finally overcoming us, killing us all for such a great sin, and robbing us of all our property....

What shall we Christians do with this rejected and condemned people, the Jews? ... I shall give you my sincere advice:

First, to set fire to their synagogues or schools....

Second, I advise that their houses be razed and destroyed....

Third, I advise that all their prayer books and Talmudic writings, in which such idolatry, lies, cursing, and blasphemy are taught, be taken from them.

Fourth, I advise that their rabbis be forbidden to teach henceforth on pain of loss of life and limb....

Fifth, I advise that safe conduct on the highways be abolished completely for the Jews. For they have no business in the countryside, since they are not lords, officials, tradesmen, or the like. Let them stay at home....

Sixth, I advise that usury be prohibited to them, and that all cash and treasure of silver and gold be taken from them and put aside for safekeeping....

Seventh, I recommend putting a flail, an ax, a hoe, a spade, a distaff, or a spindle into the hands of young, strong Jews and Jewesses and letting them earn their bread in the sweat of their brow, as was imposed on the children of Adam....

Excerpt taken from Steve Hochstadt, Sources of the Holocaust, *13–14.*

Suggestions for further reading

Alexander Altmann, *Moses Mendelssohn: A Biographical Study* (University, AL, 1973).

Yehuda Bauer, *A History of the Holocaust* (New York, 1982).

David Biale, ed., *Cultures of the Jews* (vols. 1–3; New York, 2002).

Robert Bonfil, *Jewish Life in Renaissance Italy* (Los Angeles, CA, 1994).

Robert Chazan, *Church, State, and Jew in the Middle Ages* (West Orange, NJ, 1980).

Robert Chazan, *In the Year 1096: The First Crusade and the Jews* (Philadelphia, PA, 1996).

Robert Chazan, *Medieval Jewry in Northern France* (Baltimore, 1973).

Robert Chazan, *Reassessing Jewish Life in Medieval Europe* (New York, 2010).

Jeremy Cohen, *Living Letters of the Law: Ideas of the Jew in Medieval Christianity* (Los Angeles, 1999).

Mark R. Cohen, *Under Crescent and Cross: The Jews in the Middle Ages* (Princeton, NJ, 1995).

Philip A. Cunningham, Joseph Sievers, Mary C. Boys, Hans Hermann Henrix, and Jesper Svartvik, eds., *Christ Jesus and the Jewish People Today: New Explorations of Theological Interrelationships* (Grand Rapids, MI, 2011).

Paula Fredericksen, *St. Augustine and the Jews: A Christian Defense of Jews & Judaism* (New Haven, CT, 2010).

John Friedman, Jean Connell Hoff, and Robert Chazan, eds., *The Trial of the Talmud, Paris, 1240* (Toronto, 2012).

John Gager, *The Origins of Anti-semitism* (New York, 1983).

Gavin Langmuir, *Toward a Definition of Antisemitism* (Los Angeles, CA, 1990).

Amy-Jill Levine, *The Misunderstood Jew: The Church and the Scandal of the Jewish Jesus* (New York, NY, 2006).

Moses Mendelssohn, *Jerusalem*, translated by Allan Arkush (London, 1983).

Yohanan Petrovsky-Shtern, *The Golden Age Shtetl: A New History of Jewish Life in Eastern Europe* (Princeton, NJ, 2014).

Leon Poliakov, *The History of Anti-Semitism*, translated by Richard Howard (vols. 1–3; New York, 1965–1975).

Peter Pulzer, *Jews and the German State: The Political History of a Minority, 1848–1933* (Detroit, MI, 2003).

Peter Pulzer, *The Rise of Political Antisemitism in Germany and Austria* (New York, 1964).

David B. Ruderman, "Between Cross and Crescent: Jewish Civilization from Mohammed to Spinoza," in *Great Courses* (Chantilly, VA, 2005).

David B. Ruderman, *Early Modern Jewry: A New Cultural History* (Princeton, NJ, 2011).

David B. Ruderman, "Jewish Intellectual History: 16th to 20th Century," in *Great Courses* (Chantilly, VA, 2002).

Robert Seltzer, *Jewish People, Jewish Thought* (New York, 1980).

Joseph Shatzmiller, *Cultural Exchange: Jews, Christians, and Art in the Medieval Marketplace* (Princeton, NJ, 2013).

Joshua Trachtenberg, *The Devil and the Jews* (New Haven, 1943).

3

The Rise of "Modern" Anti-Semitism and War

The Jews Are Our Misfortune!
—HEINRICH VON TREITSCHKE

Introduction

Over the course of the nineteenth century, many European Jews believed that they could integrate into gentile European society while simultaneously retaining their Jewish faith and heritage. In the age of flourishing nationalism, a minority of the Jewish community became even more nationalistic than their gentile neighbors. However, the majority of European Jews looked to furthering the ideals first started with the Enlightenment, embracing internationalism, socialism, and universal liberalism. They would also be confronted with a new type of anti-Semitism: that of the political anti-Semite. Although political anti-Semites could be found in all European nations, we will focus on those primarily in Germany and the Austro-Hungarian Empire because of the legacy of language and rhetoric these disreputable individuals left for later political leaders such as Adolf Hitler.

The new modern German nation-state: Who belongs?

Germany, a united nation-state, had finally been formed in January 1871. Thanks primarily to three short, victorious wars, the German nationalism that men such as Fichte had dreamt of, now made a new reality in the balance of power in Europe. Now, sitting in the middle of Europe was a new country, Imperial Germany (or, the Second Reich), complete with an emperor/kaiser, an imperial chancellor, and a military that had taken on first Denmark, then Austria, and finally France and had beaten them all in quick, devastating succession. For many historians, the lateness of German unification led to an identity crisis. What did it mean to be "a German," who belonged in the Second Reich? As we noted in Chapter 2, the question of German unification almost always was accompanied by these types of questions of belonging. Was it enough that a person living in German territory spoke German, or practiced German customs, or was there an "essence" that was required to qualify as truly German?

The new empire quickly began to modernize and industrialize. Between 1871 and 1914, the new Germany came to rival that other industrial powerhouse, Great Britain. It seemed that every day new inventions, new products, new ways of living were emerging. This was terribly exciting for many people, but it could also be terrifying. Who knew where all of this change was leading? Was change itself a positive for the German nation? Many Germans identified with the romanticized version of their history whereby Germans lived in idyllic pastoral communities, producing the image of German as a nation of *dichter und denker* (poets and thinkers). Beginning in 1873, just two short years after Germany's creation, the country found itself in the grip of a financial panic, followed by six long years of economic depression. For some, they began to question where Germany was headed and they asked who might want to see the infant nation fail so early on?

Some politicians began to blame Germany's tough economic times on policies endorsed by the Liberal parties. But by this time, to say the word "liberal" in some German circles was to also say the word "Jew." Indeed, for many of these political leaders, the assumption they made was that all Jews were Liberals since Jews seemed to benefit the most from Liberal ideas and policies. In addition, the belief was there that Jews, with their access to wealth and international connections, had caused the financial panic in an effort to weaken the new country which would then enable them to take further advantage of the economic woes of average gentiles. The attack on Jews and Liberals gained momentum as the Depression worsened. Now, a new breed of political speakers appeared on the scene. These were popular agitators who, unlike the Conservative Party members, claimed to speak for the "little guy," the one who had been severely impacted by the economic downturn.

The first political anti-Semite to emerge in this crisis atmosphere was a failed journalist, Wilhelm Marr. In 1873, Marr had been fired from his position at a German newspaper, but he knew the "real" reason why he had been let go: a Jewish conspiracy at the paper had plotted to remove him since he was not a Jew! Ignoring the facts of an economic downturn, Marr decided to use his journalistic skills to quickly produce a pamphlet, "The Victory of Jewry over Germandom." The pamphlet, appearing in 1873, was extremely popular. It eventually went through twelve editions in just six years. Marr told his readers that Jews had come to wield too much influence in German society. He adopted Christian Ruhs's concept of the essence of the Volk as part of his German nationalism and he suggested that Jewish superiority was ruining the Germany he loved (even though Germany was only two years old). He subtitled his pamphlet "Regarded from the Nondenominational Point of View," as he sought to disassociate himself from religious anti-Semites. He was convinced that the problem lay in racial differences. Marr also began thinking about how to speak about the Jews. He realized that when he would go to speak to groups of respectable middle-class men, some of them might feel uncomfortable when he discussed his hatred of the Jews. The word he would have used was "Judenhass," or Jew hatred. Marr thought he needed a new word, one that smacked of modernity, of science, of progress: a word that suggested there was a scientific reason to hate the Jews, not some old-fashioned religiously based antagonism to them. The word he adopted is the word most of us in the modern world immediately recognize: "anti-Semitism."[1]

To Marr, this word, "anti-Semitism," would make his audiences feel more enlightened, less uncomfortable. One could easily imagine attending a dinner party and announcing that one was an "anti-Semite" without any degree of embarrassment, unlike saying "I'm a Jew-hater," which sounded as if one was from the gutter. In reality, they meant the same thing, but respectable, educated people would feel that "anti-Semitism" was a much more sophisticated word that could be used in polite company. Marr did not invent the term, but his writings were so popular that the phrase took hold in society. What he had done was take the term "semite" from the realm of linguistic study, while realizing that linguists would have said that ancient peoples from the Middle East, parts of North Africa, and elsewhere were all classified as "semitic speaking" peoples. This classification would have included the ancient Hebrews. Marr's real triumph in popularizing the word "anti-Semite" was that everyone knew that when someone said "I'm an anti-Semite," they did not mean they were against people from North Africa. Everyone knew that this term targeted Jews specifically and only Jews. Marr was able to place his terminology within the confines of science and this gave the term a wide range appeal. The word is so appealing to its alternative of "Jew hatred" that we still use it to this day.

Marr was not some creative genius. He was smart enough, though, to realize the tenor of the times. In the 1850s the writings of Charles Darwin's *Origin of the Species* had led to new theories about evolution and biological adaptation. Darwin's theories were so compelling that a group of people began to argue not only that evolution was a universal law but that it could be applied to human civilizations. These thinkers, applying Darwin's ideas to society, called themselves "Social Darwinists." In their depiction of civilizations' evolution they believed that Western civilization was the most successfully evolved of all civilizations. They therefore spent a great deal of time classifying large groups of people, arguing over where they fit in. Whites were superior to people of color, men were superior to women, Christians were superior to non-Christians, rich people were superior to poor ones, and so on. Questions arose whether a white, Christian European woman would therefore be inferior to a black African man, but Social Darwinists expressed an ethos that was quite appealing to many European Christian men. Social Darwinists also became associated with the catchphrase "survival of the fittest," as their ideology seemed to embody a struggle of civilizations where only the strongest and most adaptable emerged triumphant.

Other voices added to this Zeitgeist, men such as Houston Stewart Chamberlain (1855–1927). Chamberlain had been trained as a botanist but his real fame came as he emerged as a leading racial theorist. Using the scientific language of botany, Chamberlain pronounced Germans as the truly superior Aryan race and he promptly decided that he no longer wanted to be British. He moved to Germany, married the daughter of famous composer and anti-Semite Richard Wagner, and announced that he was now German! His frequent correspondence with Kaiser Wilhelm II no doubt reinforced his image as a German. His book *Foundations of the Nineteenth Century* contained his arguments about German racial superiority, but despite the overlay of a scientific veneer, his work relied on "spiritual differences." He invested German/Aryans with all the positive qualities one could imagine. Aryans were pure; standing in stark contrast he argued that the Jews were, like the Devil, associated with all things evil.[2] His book would influence a leading Nazi Party theorist, Alfred Rosenberg, who wrote his own treatise on the superiority of Aryans called *Myths of the Twentieth Century*.

Although Chamberlain couched his work in the language of science, we are really back to much earlier works which stressed the connection between Jews and the Devil.[3] This idea of Jews, like the Devil, being out to control the entire world resonated so much in European society that a special document was produced to "prove" the Jewish plot. This document, called *The Protocols of the Elders of Zion*, has appeared in book form all over the world, in various languages. Even today in some Arab nations, the *Protocols* is still published as proof of a Jewish conspiracy. So what does the story say? The claim is that the work represents the minutes of a secret meeting, where twelve Jewish men met in a cemetery in Prague. In the story the twelve Jews (representing the twelve tribes of ancient Israel) conspired to spread out over the rest of the world, sow chaos wherever they went, throw the world into complete disarray, then rise up and take it over. This seems like a very large task for twelve men. Nevertheless, the *Protocols* was published over and over again. Excerpts from the *Protocols* were used by anti-Semites to "prove" Jews were in fact conspiring to take over the world. Henry Ford in the United States believed in the veracity of the *Protocols*. He had parts of it published in the *Dearborn Independent* newspaper in the 1920s. Eventually Ford was forced into printing a retraction as, time and again, others had proven that the *Protocols* were actually a forged document and had no basis in fact.

FIGURE 3.1 *Image of the "Jewish Congress." The caption reads: "Let the Goyim believe that we can be Americans, Englishmen, Germans, or French. When our interests are at stake, we are always Jews, and nothing but." Taken from* Der Stürmer, *July 1934, Issue #34. Courtesy Randall Bytwerk Collection, German Propaganda Archive, Calvin College.*

Throughout all of these books, articles, and speeches is the idea that the Jew is always the outsider, the eternal "other." Jews are portrayed, even in supposedly "modern and scientific" works, as forces of disorder and evil. They are associated with darkness, with plotting, and with polluting whatever place they inhabit. The idea that Jews really were a "problem" for Europeans to deal with had gained a foothold in many people's minds. Maybe one could posit that one Jew was alright, but as a group, the Jews posed a serious threat to stability, peacefulness, and purity. No case encapsulates these themes better than the Dreyfus Affair in 1894.

The Jew as outsider

Captain Alfred Dreyfus stood out from the other French military officers on many different levels. Dreyfus had been raised in Alsace and he spoke French with a slight German accent. Dreyfus was also a family man who did not gamble, keep a mistress, or spend time in officers' clubs. He also stood apart from his peers because he was the only Jew in the officer corps. In 1894, the government of France discovered that some of its military secrets had been sold to the hated enemy, Germany. With national security endangered, the search was on to discover the traitor. All fingers pointed to the outsider, the Jew. Dreyfus was arrested, charged with betraying his country, and was publicly humiliated with his officer's sword broken and his epaulets torn from his jacket. He was also marched in front of the French people where they had the opportunity to yell and curse at him. The final moment came when sentence was pronounced: Dreyfus would be remanded to France's worst prison, located off the coast of French Guiana, called Devil's Island. There, he would be kept in solitary confinement for the rest of his life.[4]

French society was riven in two by this trial. There is no underestimating the impact this event had on the public. There was the Dreyfussard camp, who defended Dreyfus as a man falsely accused and wrongly sentenced. There was the anti-Dreyfussard camp, who believed Dreyfus was a traitor. The press covering the trial shouted from its headlines that this trial was about more than just one man. It was about *all Jews*—could Jews be trusted to hold positions of power and authority in society? Could Jews, the eternal aliens, truly be loyal to a nation? The most extreme of the French papers, *La Libre Parole*, argued vehemently that Dreyfus was proof that a Jewish conspiracy did exist. As people all over Europe considered the questions raised by the Dreyfus Affair, Captain Alfred Dreyfus lay in his cell in Devil's Island.

By 1898, France had a new president, Emile Loubet. Loubet wanted to know if Dreyfus was still alive, and, if he was, could he be brought back to France for another court martial? It seems that Loubet thought this would be a good idea to mobilize the public once again for the spectacle of a traitorous Jew's trial. As it turned out, Captain Dreyfus was still alive. He was brought back to France for yet another display. Meanwhile, another French officer, Major Walsin-Esterhazy, had fled secretly to England. Walsin-Esterhazy had been the traitor who had sold France's military secrets to Germany. He wrote a letter to President Loubet explaining how he had needed money to settle his debts, and he alone was the traitor. The president then had to make a decision: What to do about the public retrial of Dreyfus? Loubet's answer was to approach Dreyfus with a deal: in return for Dreyfus lying and claiming that he had played a role in selling French secrets, the president would offer Dreyfus a presidential pardon. Dreyfus did not want to go back to Devil's Island and so he accepted the deal. Although it was a complete lie, Dreyfus sadly noted that, had he been the president of France, he would have offered the same deal. Dreyfus then retired, his name and reputation still ruined in many people's minds.

In the trial of Dreyfus one can see all of the ways in which Jews were being put on trial. They were never truly considered members of whatever society they lived in; they were the outsiders trying to fit in unsuccessfully. Centuries of language about the Jews, portraying them as incapable of loyalty, untrustworthy, and power-hungry, came to be embodied in this trial. It was clear to most observers that the Dreyfus Affair was an attempt to put all Jews on trial: Could they ever be "real citizens"? The trial reveals that for many there was, in fact, a "Jewish problem." But what should be done about it?

The spread of political anti-Semites

Part of the answer to the question of what could be done about a Jewish presence in society was already being addressed in Germany and Austria-Hungary. Beginning in the 1870s, both countries witnessed the proliferation of political anti-Semites. The political anti-Semites used the rhetoric of attacking the Jewish presence in German life in order to gain votes. This trend, beginning in the 1870s, continued unabated until the outbreak of the First World War in 1914. These men began a type of language that could be used in public to make attacking Jews appear respectable and acceptable. These agitators were able to play upon people's fears that there was a "Jewish problem," and that if nothing was done soon to stop the Jews, then Germany and/or Austria-Hungary would lose its identity and culture.

One of the very first men to adopt political anti-Semitic rhetoric was Adolf Stöcker. Stöcker came from a modest background: his father had worked alternately as a blacksmith, then a soldier, then as a warden of a prison. The younger Stöcker decided to go a different path: he wanted to study theology and become a minister. Stöcker realized his dream. He became a Lutheran pastor attached to the Berlin Cathedral during the height of the Franco-Prussian War in 1870. From his influential position, Stöcker became known for his nationalism. He also was appalled by the increasingly secularized society of the new Germany. Not content with giving sermons, Stöcker decided to establish his own political party. He had come to despise social progressives and he especially detested the Marxists. In 1878, the minister put posters up all over Berlin announcing the first meeting of his new political party, the Christian Social Workers' Party. The first meeting proved to be somewhat of a disaster as Social Democratic supporters showed up and fighting broke out among the audience members. Nevertheless, Stöcker persevered, and by fall of 1878 his party was campaigning for pensions for the elderly and infirm and for factory legislation which would improve the working conditions at the plants, and a progressive taxation policy was also put forward as well as a call to restore usury laws. In Stöcker's mind he was preaching the social Gospel. His party lost in the elections.

Minister Stöcker then decided to shift tactics. He began to incorporate blatant anti-Semitic rhetoric into his campaigning. What he found was that his followers had changed: now the workers who had once come to his party's meetings no longer appeared, but instead he had gained a new following of anti-Semites. To Stöcker, the "Jewish Problem" could be fixed, if Jews would only convert. In many respects, Stöcker more closely resembles a religious anti-Semite, because in his mind, if a Jew converted (preferably to Lutheranism, but at least to some form of Christianity), then the "Jewish Problem" was solved. Stöcker was successful enough to get elected, but once he was in parliament he did not accomplish very much. By 1879 his party had to compete with other anti-Semitic parties that had emerged on the scene.[5]

One of Stöcker's early competitors was a young, brash 27-year-old man named Ernst Henrici. Henrici, a former school teacher, founded the Reich Social Party and he appealed to the most radical and nationalistic tendencies in Berlin. He was also the first politician to popularize the writings of Wilhelm Marr, helping to turn the term "anti-Semitism" into a household word. Unlike Minister Stöcker, Henrici believed that the solution to the "Jewish Problem" was not a matter of converting the Jews to Christianity. Henrici believed that the core of the problem was a racial one, which implied that even if a Jew did convert, he would still consider that person a Jew. His position was so inflammatory that he was able to spark pogroms against the Jews of Pomerania, with attacks on Jewish individuals and the burning of their synagogue following one of Henrici's speeches. By 1880, Henrici presented a document to the kaiser, simply titled "Anti-Semites' Petition."[6]

In the "Anti-Semites' Petition," Henrici's position is clearly illuminated. In order to solve the "Jewish Problem" he argued that all Jews must leave Germany. In the petition, he asserted that Jewish dominance in German life has led to a loss of the sense of the "Volk" and that this loss will continue to occur so long as Jewish power remains unchecked. To solve the problem, he makes four suggestions to the kaiser: end all immigration of Jews into Germany; exclude all Jews from governmental positions; have only Christian schools; conduct a census of Jews and their belongings in Germany. The kaiser did not act upon any of the suggestions; however, Henrici pointed out that, while he might be a relatively uneducated man, he was saying the exact same thing as Germany's most famous historian Heinrich von Treitschke (1834–1896). The only difference Henrici saw was that Professor Treitschke was more sophisticated.

Treitschke was an historian at the University of Berlin. In 1879 he had authored a series of articles for a German journal in which he examined who truly belonged in the Second Reich. Treitschke was quite selective in who he thought could be truly German. He disapproved of Catholics, arguing that "real" Germans were Lutherans, but his real ire was reserved for the Jews of Germany. The last line in the last article ended with the ominous phrase "The Jews are our misfortune!"[7] To men like Henrici, the professor's voice had added an air of learning and authority to what political anti-Semites had already been saying. Treitschke's work also provoked a reaction from one of the leading Jewish scholars of the day, Heinrich Graetz (1817–1891). Graetz, like Treitschke, was also an historian of great importance. His eleven-volume work, *The History of the Jews*, attempted to show how Christian rulers had harmed Jews, using the position of Jews in different societies as a way of testing how morally healthy a society was. If Jews were harmed and mistreated by non-Jewish rulers, then that society was corrupt. He also argued that if Jews were deemed unfit for emancipation, like Treitschke had argued, it was because non-Jewish governments had held Jews down, leaving them in an inferior state.[8]

Both Graetz and Treitschke used their interpretations of history to justify Jewish-Christian relations. Treitschke found Graetz's work to be infuriating because Graetz refused to idolize Treitschke's Germanic heroes such as Martin Luther and Immanuel Kant. In addition, Graetz found Christian ethics lacking in comparison to Judaism's ethical teachings, which further enraged Treitschke. In challenging the Christian scholarly world, Graetz hoped to defend the integrity of Judaism against forceful detractors. Likewise, another noted Jewish scholar, Abraham Geiger (1810–1874), also took on the Christian scholarly world and formed what was called "Reform Judaism." In particular, Geiger was one of the first Jewish scholars to study the New Testament. He believed that he could understand Jesus and his ancient world better than most Christians could, because of their shared heritage of Judaism. He also argued that Christianity owed a debt to Judaism—completely upending the supersessionist myth. He wrote that Jesus was a liberal Pharisee, interested in bringing about reform. He therefore saw that Reform Judaism was something pure that Christians needed to understand.[9] Yet another Jewish scholar, responding to the pressures faced by many German Jews, was Samson Raphael Hirsch.

Hirsch (1810–1888) was a contemporary of both Graetz and Geiger. Unlike the other scholars, Hirsch developed "Neo Orthodoxy," which meant that he believed German Jews should continue to practice Judaism as it always had been. However, he also argued that German Jews needed to join German secular culture. He encouraged Jews to emerge out of their isolation, to learn German, to think, look, and act like everyone else. Even though Hirsch rejected the Enlightenment's emphasis upon the individual subjective experience, he embraced the idea that a faithfully observant Jew could still be a good citizen of whatever country a Jew happened to live in.[10]

Austria-Hungary's political anti-Semites

Questions about belonging, of being a good citizen, also arose within the Austro-Hungarian Empire. The political trendsetter there was a man of middle-class standing, Georg Ritter von Schönerer. Although his name had an aristocratic title, "Ritter von," meaning "knight," Schönerer's father had received the honorific title for his years of loyal and efficient service as a railway engineer. Nevertheless, Schönerer in 1873 had decided to run for election in Bohemia. He wanted to improve the welfare of the peasantry and, with his knowledge about agriculture and his charisma, he was successful. Schönerer, when thinking about the position of Jews in Austrian life, remained fairly obscure early on in his political career, mentioning only vague references to Jewish "money and words." However, by 1882, he had developed what was called his "Linz Program," and by 1882 he had a much stronger anti-Jewish position. He was also beginning to stress the Germanity of the Austrian people, making him an extreme German nationalist despite living in Austria. By 1885, he had adopted the position that Jews living in the Empire should be excluded "from all sections of public life."[11] Although Schönerer never led a mass movement, he was successful enough in getting his voice heard among Austrian citizens. One such Austrian, Adolf Hitler, was very familiar with the Linz Program of Schönerer and agreed with both the nationalism and the anti-Semitism of the platform.

Schönerer's star faded, particularly in 1890, when he assaulted a journalist and was sent to prison for four months. In addition to jail time, the former politician was stripped of his political rights for the next five years, and, to add insult to injury, the court took away Schönerer's honorific title of "Ritter von." Like so many of the political anti-Semites, Schönerer was destined to disappear from the public mind, but another more suave, sophisticated man was emerging on the Viennese political anti-Semitic scene. His name was Karl Lüger (1840–1910).What makes Lüger so intriguing for biographers and historians is that no one can say for sure if he was truly anti-Semitic or not. Most authors argue that Lüger was using the rhetoric of attacking "Jewish influence" out of political expediency. Even if he did not mean the words he was saying, Lüger contributed to an increasingly accepting atmosphere that one could be well educated, charming, and anti-Semitic. Lüger's great claim to fame is that he made the language of anti-Semitism politically respectable and viable. So what did he actually say?

Lüger believed that the best place in all of the world was Vienna. He had no desire to go anywhere else. He lived, ate, and slept thinking of Vienna. His widowed mother had encouraged him to go to law school, and as a young man, he became a lawyer working right alongside another lawyer who happened to be Jewish. There was reportedly no friction between the two men, thus adding to the mystique surrounding Lüger's adoption of anti-Semitic rhetoric. While still working as a lawyer, Lüger decided to enter the world of local Viennese politics and he was successfully elected to city council. He certainly had made contact with Catholic reformers as a city councilman, but he was also familiar with local anti-Semites. He had voted to support Schönerer's platform several times and he was delving deeper into the world of Christian Socialism, which was dominated by young anti-Semitic priests in Vienna. Legend has it that he was attending a political rally, listening to an anti-Semitic tirade being delivered by a priest, when he leaned over to the man seated next to him and asked, "How can I follow this man?" The man next to Lüger reportedly said, "that is easy, just be more anti-Semitic than the priest." Lüger then stood up and delivered his own anti-Semitic screed and the crowd ate it up. Whether this story is accurate or not really does not matter; what matters is Lüger's policies as an elected official in Vienna. What appears is that he never enacted any anti-Semitic legislation, lending credence to the idea that he was using the rhetoric of anti-Semitism out of political expediency. When Viennese voters occasionally confronted Lüger on his lack of persecutory legislation against the Jewish population, the charming political leader would answer, "I decide who is a Jew."[12]

Lüger's tactics regarding the position of Jews in Vienna allowed him to become the shining star in the political anti-Semitic firmament. Elected mayor of Vienna several times over, Lüger proved that one could be educated, middle-class, sophisticated, and anti-Semitic. His way of speaking made the rhetoric of anti-Semitism politically viable and even respectable. Many other political aspirants would watch Lüger and learn from his posturing, including a young Adolf Hitler. Although Hitler never met Lüger, he certainly adopted some of the Viennese mayor's propaganda moves and strategies, seeing in them an acceptable way of winning over masses of people to the anti-Semitic cause.

In the late 1800s through the outbreak of the First World War, political agitators espousing the language of anti-Semitism continued to carve out a following, particularly among the middle classes in both the Austrian and German empires. These small craftsmen, teachers, civil servants, white-collar workers, and small business owners found a wide range of anti-Semitic opinions to select from when voting for representatives. For many of these middle-class men, they voted for political anti-Semites out of a deep sense of frustration, in many cases believing that there was some outside "force" standing in their way of social mobility and achieving a higher social status. There were, however, political alternatives to anti-Semitic parties, particularly in the 1890s, with August Bebel leading the German Social Democratic Party (SDP). Bebel was famous for labeling anti-Semitism as "the socialism of fools," and he steadfastly refused to allow the SDP to become infected with the anti-Semitic trend of the times.[13] How did Jews react to the rise of political anti-Semitism?

Jewish reactions to political anti-Semitic attacks

For many European Jews, watching and living with the rise of racial theories with their ties to various political parties meant thinking deeply about social inequality. For the vast majority of European Jews, they were left wondering whether the promises of equality, even in enlightened Europe, would ever truly be achieved. Witnessing events such as the Dreyfus Affair in France led other Jews to fear that true equality was unobtainable, and they began to think about the possibility of a Jewish nation. Given that Jewish assimilation into the larger European society had not been fully achieved, some Jews argued that only a self-governing Jewish nation-state would provide Jews with true equality and freedom from discrimination. In their minds, Jews living in a Jewish state with their own separate society would be the solution to the "Jewish problem" in Europe. This idea, of an all-Jewish autonomous nation-state, is called Zionism, and it was only one of many proposed solutions to improving Jewish lives in the modern world.

Modern Zionists were only speaking for a minority of European Jews. Other solutions to the traditional Jewish problems of economic, political, and social oppression in Europe were put forward. Perhaps the least favorable suggestion was the idea of Jewish emigration from the oppressive Russian Empire westward. But for the majority of the Jewish community, there was the idea that Jews should be at the forefront of restructuring governments and thereby societies so that Jews could actually be fully assimilated into whatever nation they happened to reside in in Europe. That resulted in many Jews becoming affiliated with more radical ideologies which promised complete social and political change. The notion was that by radicalizing society, anti-Semitism would be wiped out as a more egalitarian society emerged. Socialism was therefore seen as a way of ending the problem of anti-Semitism as prejudices of all kinds were supposed to fall away. These more radically liberal ideas promised to forge a "classless" society where the proletariat ruled and was treated justly. Particularly for Jews living in the Pale of Settlement areas of the Russian Empire, this was a dream. One small group of East European Jews formed a socialist organization simply called the "Bund."

Members of the Bund worked toward restructuring Russian society along Marxist lines, and although their radical ideas were embraced by only a minority of Russian Jews, the Bund was at first a vital component within revolutionary Russian intellectual circles. As the Bund became increasingly marginalized from other socialist thinkers, its members worked to improve the lives of the Jewish workers within the Pale of Settlement. It also promoted the use of the Yiddish language. Yiddish was a hybrid of German and Hebrew, and in the Pale of Settlement it was the language of the common people. Ultimately the members of the Bund came to reject Lenin's vision of a proletariat dictatorship. Instead, they endorsed a more gradual program of change which would lead at some point in time to public ownership of the means of production.[14]

Modern Zionism

As was mentioned earlier yet another response, by a minority of Jews, to the oppression and anti-Semitic attacks of the late nineteenth century was that of modern Zionism. Once again, we can see Jewish intellectuals searching for ways to solve the "Jewish Problem" of integration into Christian-dominated European society. In the case of Zionism, however, there was a real sense of defeat. For Zionists, Jews had cooperated and had tried to assimilate into Christian society. They had integrated themselves into the culture of their respective nations and they had educated themselves according to Christian European standards, but, for all of the changes that Jews had made, they still were not seeing the principles of the French Revolution and the Enlightenment put into real practice. With the dramatic rise of racialist theories attacking Jews, not simply on the grounds of religious differences but also upon the idea of "blood purity," many Zionists simply concluded that Jews would only be safe and free if they had their own nation-state.

Some of these earlier Zionist thinkers, men such as Moses Hess (1812–1875) and Leo Pinsker (1821–1891), authored books arguing that in order to maintain a Jewish identity, Jews would have to form their own nation-state like other peoples had. Hess, a friend of Karl Marx and Friedrich Engels, had written *Rome and Jerusalem* in 1862 and *Plan for the Colonization of the Holy Land* in 1867. His works, however, tended to be ignored in the 1860s, primarily because German Jews reading his books believed that their lives were actually improving in Germany so there was no need to consider uprooting one's family to move to the Holy Land. For Pinsker, his work *Auto-Emancipation* (1882) came out following Tsar Alexander III's government-sponsored pogroms and found East European Jews open to the idea of establishing a Jewish nation-state in order to escape persecution. The man most credited with developing and popularizing the idea of modern Zionism, however, was an unlikely man, Theodor Herzl (1860–1904).

Herzl, raised in the Austro-Hungarian Empire, in a tight-knit Jewish family, dutifully studied law as a young man. In his youth he encountered no discernible acts of anti-Semitism that he could recall with the one exception of an event in his college days. At his university, he wanted to join a men's dueling society but was rejected because the society did not allow Jewish members. Herzl's life went on; he became a lawyer, but then decided that he would prefer to work as a journalist. It was in his role as a journalist that Herzl became a convinced Zionist. While working for an Austrian newspaper, Herzl was dispatched to Paris, France, to cover the infamous Dreyfus Affair. Witnessing the denigration of Captain Dreyfus and the public outrage, Herzl came to the conclusion that if a Jewish man could not receive a fair trial in the birthplace of the Enlightenment, then where on earth would a Jew be treated fairly and equitably? His response was to author a brief work, *Der Judenstaat (The Jews' State)*, in 1896. In this work, Herzl argued that anti-Semitism existed everywhere, that it was incurable, and that the only possible solution was for Jews to establish their own self-governing state.[15] He mentioned in his pamphlet how Jews had attempted to integrate into the "Volksgemeinschaft" while still preserving their own faith. He concluded, "One does not allow it."[16] To achieve the end goal of a Jewish nation-state,

Herzl worked tirelessly to organize a gathering of Jewish delegates from all over the world at the First Zionist Congress in Basle, Switzerland, in 1897.

The Zionist Congress met with 204 Jewish delegates present. Their mission was to debate the idea of Zionism before the public (here Herzl drew on his journalistic connections). The result was the creation of the World Zionist Organization, which would work to endorse the goals of each year's congress. Debates within Jewish communities were rife on the controversial topic of Zionism. Some individuals, such as Herzl, endorsed the idea of political Zionism—meaning that he was not concerned with the religious devotion of Jews to Judaism. Likewise, Jacob Klatzkin (1882–1948) argued that Jews simply needed a nation-state of their own in the land of Israel. He was not concerned with concepts such as Jews as a "chosen people" with a "spiritual uniqueness." Others, though, such as Asher Hirsch Ginsberg (1856–1927), argued for an elite group of Jewish intellectuals to go to Palestine, and establish a model society and a model Jewish culture for all Jews worldwide to emulate. He was not interested in mass emigration of Jews to Palestine. As we can see from just these few examples, there were many debates and arguments about the issue of Zionism, but while the debates continued, small groups of primarily East European Jews began to board ships to return to the biblical homeland of their people. By the eve of the First World War, approximately 100,000 Jews had immigrated to the land of Palestine.

The outbreak of the First World War

The shattering event of the First World War (1914–1918) would have serious consequences for Jews in Palestine as well as in Europe. Conversations about Zionism, political anti-Semitism, and the "Jewish Problem" would be buried under the drive to attain unity within warring European nations. Like so many other divisive issues, such as women's rights, European political leaders attempted to set aside internal conflicts within their countries in the effort to forge a common bond needed to fight the enemy. For many political anti-Semites, that meant the end of their careers. For Zionists, the war could mean being attacked as disloyal to one's birth nation, or at least being accused of having "dual loyalty." In the face of fervent nationalism, many controversies were driven underground. Most leaders believed in the myth of the short war, in the idea that war would be a purifying agent which wiped away all domestic problems. To each man who marched off to battle in the summer of 1914, they mistakenly believed that the war would be over quickly, that they would be home by Christmas, and that the war would be providing them with an opportunity to become extraordinary men. These ideas—of a short, victorious war; of ordinary men being transformed into something extraordinary; of war as purifier—would all come into question as the war dragged on and on for four excruciatingly long years.

Jewish men, across the board in each European nation, rushed like their gentile neighbors to support the war effort. Statistically, Jewish men served out of proportion to their percentage in the population, meaning that more Jewish men served than was expected. This is important to note as reports about Jewish military service would be published after the war in Germany that attempted to deny this fact. In fact, 96,000 German Jews served in the military during the war years, 35,000 were decorated with medals, and 12,000 died.[17] Not only did average Jewish men enlist to fight in support of their country but Jewish scientists worked alongside gentiles to develop weaponry and chemicals which would give their particular country the winning edge over their enemies. Men such as Fritz Haber, who was born into a Jewish family, but who had converted to Christianity as a young man, would develop ways of harnessing artificial nitrates, which allowed an increase in food production but which also helped to kill soldiers in the trenches through chemical weaponry. Walter Rathenau, a very successful and wealthy industrialist, used his own personal money to help finance the German war effort. On August 5, 1914, the Berlin-Charlottenburg Synagogue held a worship service led by Rabbi Leo Baeck, in which 2,000 seats were filled and the crowd overflowed out into the street. Even Martin Buber exclaimed, "never has the concept of 'Volk' become such a reality for me in these weeks."[18] All of these men demonstrate the pull of nationalism and the desire to show their support for Germany. These were men who strongly identified as Germans who happened to be of Jewish origins, and they wanted to defend their country just as much as German Christian men did. With the rise of Nazi Germany, this fact would largely be forgotten or misrepresented to the German public.

Jewish men, much like their gentile counterparts, enlisted, fought, and died for their respective warring nations. For most Europeans alive in 1914, there was no memory of what war actually looked like when all of Europe joined in combat to murder one another. The last time such an event had occurred was in the early 1800s, when armies of Europe aligned themselves for or against the great military genius Napoleon Bonaparte and the Grand Army of France. So, for many Europeans, the first rush to war in August 1914 meant that there had been almost a "century of peace," and most individuals thought that war would not only be glorious; it would be quick. For European leaders, such as Kaiser Wilhelm II of Imperial Germany, war was not something to be feared as it would promote social cohesion and unity on the home front, papering over all of the seemingly limitless internal challenges facing his regime. As Germany entered the conflict, Kaiser Wilhelm II spoke publicly of a *Burgfrieden*, or "peace in the castle" implying that Germans must set aside their internal divisions, form a true community, or "Volksgemeinschaft," and win the war. In his speech, in front of the Berlin Palace, Wilhelm II said, "In the battles that are now to come, I no longer recognize any parties in my people. Among us there are now only Germans."[19]

As millions of men rushed to join in the war effort, a myth of "comradeship" came to dominate the imagery of Germany's western front. As thousands of men sat in trenches, wondering whether they would live to see another day, the German home front was reading about the ability of the German soldiers to pull themselves together into a cohesive fighting unit that transcended all possible divisions. This type of imagery, of soldiers from all social strata joining together into a "band of brothers," reached its zenith in the postwar literature of Erich Maria Remarque's *All Quiet on the Western Front*. Remarque, himself a frontline trench soldier who had fought for Germany in the war, wrote his book believing that it would deliver a devastatingly pacifist message—and it did, to a certain extent. However, historians such as Thomas Kühne argue quite convincingly that Remarque's book also went a long way toward convincing the average reader that only men who had fought in the hell of the trenches could have truly experienced the bonding of a real community.[20] In Remarque's novel, the main character Paul Baümer goes home on leave, only to find that he no longer feels that he belongs alongside the civilians of Germany. Only his fellow soldiers understand what he has experienced: they don't even need to talk about the specifics, but they simply intuitively understand what each man has endured.[21] This portrayal went quite a long way in postwar Germany, allowing political leaders to argue that the comradeship of the trenches was the only true community and all others who had not shared in that experience were outsiders.

Although many soldiers did share in the building of community at the frontlines, they also experienced the shock of industrialized killing on a level and scale which had hitherto been unknown in human history. The development of the machine gun, ever lighter and faster; the use of airplanes as weapons of war; the invention of biological and chemical weaponry and flamethrowers; and so on meant that soldiers now saw that "old fashioned" notions of *cran* and *elan* (guts and spirit) would not be enough to carry them out of the inferno alive. In this new style of trench warfare with its miles and miles of barbed wire and churned-up earth of No Man's Land meant that an order for men to go "over the top" was essentially a death order. Now, sitting in cement pillboxes and waiting for the enemy—the defensive posture—was proving to be the superior strategy. As wave after wave of soldiers emerged from their trenches, they marched and then ran directly into the withering machine-gun fire and artillery of their enemy. Yet, countless military leaders, still believing that a dashing charge was the preferred way to attack, continued to exercise a lack of imagination and sent hundreds of thousands of men to their deaths.[22] Until the German military leadership devised a way to break the superiority of the defensive position, in the spring of 1918, soldiers on Germany's western front would face this surreal world of dirt, filth, and the ever-present stench of death. One man who experienced the nightmare world of the trenches was Adolf Hitler, an Austrian who had enlisted in August 1914 to serve in a Bavarian army regiment. As a dispatch runner, Hitler spent his time running from rear trench lines to the front lines in order to deliver messages. This was an extremely dangerous position and one in which Hitler reportedly performed quite bravely, earning the Iron Cross for his actions. Like countless other men, Hitler was also a victim of the new advances in military weaponry and he was temporarily blinded in a poison gas attack. This resulted in Hitler going to hospital to recuperate, and this is where, at least according to *Mein Kampf*, Hitler received the news that the war had come to an end on November 11, 1918. In *Mein Kampf*, Hitler described being in the hospital recovery ward and hearing a man enter the room declaring the armistice. At that moment Hitler remembered hearing that his beloved Germany had lost the war and he wrote, "it [the news] cut him to the core."[23]

Like most Germans, Hitler's reaction to the end of the war was one of utter shock. Due to strict wartime censorship of the press, many Germans simply could not acknowledge the military defeat of their country. It is worth remembering that on November 11, 1918, the day German civilian representatives went into a railway car in the forests of Compiegne, France, to sign the unconditional surrender of Germany, no enemy forces were occupying any German territory. For many Germans, they could not understand how their country could declare itself defeated yet they saw no British, American, or French forces in their German towns. This feeling of disbelief gave way to anger for some Germans and they suspected that their country had been betrayed by "internal enemies." Their suspicions were confirmed when the second-highest-ranking military leader of the war General Erich Ludendorff began to loudly exclaim that the German military would never have surrendered and that Germany had been betrayed by elements on the home front who wanted to see Germany fail.[24] This myth, called the *Dolchstosslegende*, or the "stab-in-the-back legend," began to acquire more and more believers, including the devastated recovering Hitler. But who might those weak, corrupt civilians be who were willing to see Germany defeated?

German defeat in war

General Ludendorff had an answer to that question. Ludendorff had fled the field of battle toward the end of the war—going to live in exile in Sweden temporarily. In this way, he was not around in the final weeks of the war and hence disassociated himself from the decision to sign the unconditional surrender in November 1918. Over the years, Ludendorff had morphed from a German Protestant into a racist who came to believe that Germans should truly practice pagan rites as their ancestors had once done. After his return to Germany in 1919, Ludendorff devoted himself to endorsing nationalistic causes, frequently leveling charges against Marxists, Jesuits, and Jews.[25] After the war's end, Ludendorff sponsored several "studies" about one group he had deemed especially unworthy of belonging to the German nation: the Jews. In these diverse studies, statistics were gathered and skewed in ways that reinforced long standing imagery of Jewish men as natural traitors and as unmanly cowards.

In some postwar studies, arguments were made that attempted to "prove" Jewish disloyalty by demonstrating voting records of Reichstag delegates during the war. Those delegates who had voted against supporting war credits for the German government were shown to be disloyal traitors, and over half of them were supposedly Jewish. Another study argued that Jewish men in Germany had not enlisted to fight for the country, thus underscoring that Jews were unpatriotic and unsupportive of a German victory. This study in particular was statistically inaccurate as German Jewish men served out of proportion to their percentage in the population, thus demonstrating that Jews were just as nationalistic as gentiles. Finally, yet another study gathered data on injuries sustained by frontline soldiers and interpreted their data to "prove" that Jewish men were not injured as often or as severely as their counterparts had been, implying that Jewish men were what Hitler called "shirkers" who exhibited cowardice and unmanly attributes. One could turn those explanations on their head, however, by arguing that if the rates of injury were lower for Jews, then perhaps Jews were better fighters. Yet another work, conducted by a Jewish scientist in England, named Redcliffe Salaman, measured the feet of Jewish and gentile British men. In his study he found that one out of six Jewish men were flat-footed as compared to non-Jews, where it was one out of forty. This study was later used by a racial scientist in Germany to "prove" that Jews could be recognized by their distinctive, shuffling, "soft" gait.[26] No matter how these studies were interpreted, they were shared with the general public as proof positive that stereotypes about Jewish men were true, and with heroes such as General Ludendorff storming around, declaring Jews, like the Marxists, as traitors to Germany, many average people moved closer to accepting this mythology.

Contributing to this imagery of Jewish men as disloyal and effeminate was the supposed connection between Marxism/Leninism/Bolshevism and Jewish-ness. Ever since Karl Marx and Friedrich Engels had published *The Communist Manifesto* in 1848, Marxist thought had come to be associated with Jewishness. Perhaps partly due to the reality that Marx himself had been raised in a converted Jewish household although he had become an atheist, men such as Ludendorff were quick to point out that the ideas of Marxism had sprung from the head of Jew. It is especially ironic that much of the accusations leveled against Jews in the late nineteenth and twentieth centuries were that they were both the engineers of capitalistic society and avid socialists seeking the destruction of class systems. Marx himself was against the Judeo-Christian heritage, and in Marxist thinking Jews were associated with—as we have seen from the Middle Ages onward—capitalism, exploitation, and greed. Marx believed that the "Jewish problem" would disappear as soon as class warfare had ended the capitalist systems. In a further irony, many Jews were attracted to Marxism because it seemed to promise them an end to the intolerance and prejudice of class-based systems. Their hope was that a radicalized approach to revamping society would end in the creation of a harmonious, peaceful society of equals, thus ending anti-Semitism entirely. Unfortunately, Marxist ideology provided fodder for anti-Semites who denounced Jews as both capitalist exploiters and radical communists seeking to destroy all private ownership. This dual image of the Jew—as both capitalist and communist—emerged in postwar German society.

A new government for Germany

At the close of the war, Kaiser Wilhelm II had abdicated his throne and he left Germany (while it was still at war on November 9, 1918) to reside in Holland. Upon his abdication, the powers of the German government had been given to a civilian politician, Friedrich Ebert of the Social Democratic Party (SDP). It had fallen upon Ebert's shoulders to dispatch representatives to sign the November 11, 1918, armistice, and it was now his responsibility to create for the German people a new form of government. He had announced that on January 19, 1919, elections based on universal suffrage would be held to elect delegates to the National Assembly. The National Assembly's job would be to write a constitution for the German nation, thus providing Germany with a new government. Ebert faced many challenges, particularly from the cofounders of the German Communist Party (KPD), Karl Liebknecht and Rosa Luxemburg.

Liebknecht and Luxemburg despised Ebert as they believed that, although he was a member of a socialist political party, he was not truly open to social revolution. The cofounders of the KPD decided to organize an uprising that would supposedly stop the January 19 elections from ever taking place, thus plunging Germany into either revolution or civil war.

Liebknecht and Luxemburg were able to hastily draw together approximately 200,000 people to march through the streets of Berlin, threatening to take over government facilities and generating general chaos in the streets. The march began on January 5, 1919, and both Liebknecht and Luxemburg hoped that revolution would follow, thus ending Ebert's temporary government and short-circuiting the January 19 elections. Their plan proved to be unsuccessful, partly due to the haste in which it was planned but also due to the general atmosphere of German society in 1919, where most people were exhausted and wanted no further radical changes in their lives. Nevertheless, the marchers dubbed themselves the "Spartacists," and their singing of Russian revolutionary songs and violence out on the streets struck fear into the hearts of most middle-class Germans. In the end, the "Spartacist Uprising" was violently put down by the combined efforts of the regular German army with Freikorps (paramilitary) units. By January 12 the event was over, leaving approximately 100 Spartacists and 13 Freikorps dead. Liebknecht and Luxemburg were captured, interrogated, and then escorted to two different cars. Liebknecht was shot and his body was thrown from the car. The official announcement was that he had been "shot while trying to escape." This would have been quite difficult to do since both Liebknecht and Luxemburg had been knocked unconscious as they were loaded into the awaiting cars. As for Luxemburg, she too was shot and killed but her assassins thought it best to throw her body in the nearby river. What did this uprising have to do with being Jewish?

Rosa Luxemburg had been raised in a Jewish household, and like Marx in an earlier age, she had become an atheist. The imagery that had long been associated with Jewish acceptance of radically liberal ideologies from the time of the Enlightenment to the new association of Jews being heavily involved in and supportive of Marxist ideology now seemed confirmed in many average people's minds. Luxemburg, due to her Jewishness, was willing to engage in illegal acts against the German state in a desperate attempt to impose communism on the German people. As a result, all Jews became suspect and were frequently accused of attempting to implant communism on German soil. Particularly for the German middle classes, who actually owned property, "Jewishness" and "Bolshevism" (the Russian version of communism) were almost synonyms. Despite this overarching belief that Jews promoted worldwide revolution and class warfare, the same people also believed that Jews had successfully engaged in war profiteering throughout the war years, and they accused Jews of attempting to profit from the postwar inflation that Germany was wracked with as well. So, the double image of Jew as exploitative capitalist could sit comfortably beside the image of the Jew as communist revolutionary sowing discord and upheaval in the same person's mind.

Despite the Spartacist Uprising's intentions, the elections for the National Assembly moved forward on January 19, 1919. All German men and women over the age of twenty could cast a ballot to send a representative to the assembly. Voter turnout was phenomenally high, with a reported 85 percent voter participation record. It would become the National Assembly's main task to design a constitution for the German people, in keeping with the voters' wishes. When the ballots were counted, Ebert's Social Democratic Party had not won a majority of the votes; instead mostly moderate, center-of-the-road political representatives had been elected. Their first job was to decide where the assembly should meet. It became apparent that many of the representatives did not want to meet in Berlin. Berlin as the capital of the kingdom of Prussia and then of Imperial Germany smacked of warmongering, saber rattling, and overall militarism. Most of the delegates wanted to portray Germany once again as a nation of "poets and thinkers," not war-crazed military dictators. They opted to meet in the beautiful city of Weimar, a place where one of Germany's greatest writers, Goethe, had once lived. This was thought to be more in keeping with the new image the National Assembly wanted to promote to the world.

The delegates got down to business in Weimar, writing the new constitution that would form the basis for the new German government. Because of the meeting site, the new government would be called the "Weimar Republic." In a reflection of voters' wishes, the constitution created Germany's first ever Democratic Republic. The man most responsible for drafting the bulk of the constitution was a member of the DVP, a constitutional law scholar, Hugo Preuss. Incidentally, Preuss also happened to be Jewish. The Weimar constitution provided the German people with a president who would be elected by a plebiscite of the people to serve for a seven-year term and he or she would have limited powers. The president would be served by a chancellor, a vice-chancellor, and a cabinet of ministers. All of these officials would be responsible to the Reichstag (parliament). Reichstag members would be elected on the basis of universal suffrage, but Preuss wanted to ensure the greatest amount of representation he could so he designed the election format to include proportional representation. Proportional representation meant that in an election it would not mean "winner take all," but rather, if a political party could win 3 percent of the total number of votes cast, that political party would then get a corresponding proportion of seats in the Reichstag. In Preuss's mind, this would allow even smaller political parties to voice their constituents' opinions, thus giving even more democracy to the German people. In addition to these offices, the constitution guaranteed all of the basic freedoms—of the press, of speech, of assembly, of religion, and so on. The constitution was formally adopted on July 31, 1919.

The Weimar Republic and the Treaty of Versailles

Although many Germans did, at first, support the creation of the Weimar Republic, it was off to a shaky start. Extremists on the right refused to support the constitution as valid and they linked its "foreignness" to the fact that a Jewish man had mainly been responsible for writing it. They argued that Germany had historically never had a democratic republic and now it was being foisted upon the German people by an "alien" outsider—a Jew. Men such as Axel von Freytagh-Loringhoven argued that Jews could not ever be citizens because they did not share the lineage of the German people. They might adopt the German language and even German culture, but they could never truly belong to the Volksgemeinschaft. His core belief was that only those who were of "German blood" could be part of the state; therefore Jews should not have the right to vote, hold office, or obtain citizenship.[27] Such men also connected their disgust with the new government to the earlier announcement of the Treaty of Versailles.

Almost one month earlier, on June 28, 1919, German delegates had been summoned to the Palace of Versailles to sign the treaty which would officially end the war. Toward the very end of the First World War, the soon-to-be victorious powers dropped leaflets all over German territory, raising many German people's hopes that they would be treated as equals at the Paris Peace talks. The leaflets espoused the president of the United States of America Woodrow Wilson's promise of a "Peace without Victory." The leaflets promoted Wilson's idealistic Fourteen Points, and many began to hope that under Wilson's guidance, the peace talks would be structured to provide Germany with a "fair deal." Wilson's rhetoric regarding the peace promise argued that what had caused Europe to slide into the recent catastrophe was Old World diplomacy—the world of secret treaties, secret alliances, and corruption. In his mind, the peace talks should be open, fair, with no secret side deals; a place where victor was indistinguishable from vanquished. Naturally, as German hopes for victory began to slide away, more stock was placed in the leaflets as many Germans thought they could at least expect to be treated with dignity and fairness. This was not to be the case.

Of the "Big Four" leaders present—Woodrow Wilson representing the U.S., David Lloyd George representing Great Britain, Vittorio Orlando from Italy, and Georges Clemenceau representing the French—Clemenceau would emerge as the driving force of the treaty talks. Clemenceau, who had lived through the siege of Paris during the 1870–1871 Franco-Prussian War, had witnessed the triumph of Prussia, the birth of the modern German nation, and the humiliation of France all at the Palace of Versailles in 1871. From that moment on, Clemenceau was a man devoted to the cause of destroying and humiliating the Germans, quenching the French thirst for revenge. Clemenceau also understood how devoted President Wilson was to the idea of creating a League of Nations—a kind of international peacekeeping force which would troubleshoot world conflicts before they devolved into warfare. Because of Wilson's commitment to this league, Clemenceau was able to prevail in many other areas of the peace talks. He held the trump card: if Wilson did not let him prevail, then France would not join this new league and the league would immediately fail. So, Clemenceau now had the opportunity to enact revenge for the humiliation France had suffered at German hands in 1871. The German representatives, waiting to begin negotiations with the victorious powers, were summoned to the Palace of Versailles.

On the grounds of France's most illustrious palace, approximately 10,000 people were anxiously waiting to see history in the making. At the outset of war in 1914, the French government had announced they would turn off all of the outdoor water features at Versailles and that they would not turn them back on until France had achieved victory. The German representatives were escorted into the exact room where German unification had been announced (the Hall of Mirrors), and the German representatives were informed that they had to sign the treaty "as is" or else the war would resume.

To the German representatives, this must have come as quite a shock. More than likely they had imagined that they were there to read the clauses of the treaty and then sit down to begin negotiations—as had been promised in all of those leaflets. Instead, they were compelled to sign. As the first German representative took out his fountain pen and began to sign his name, the water features outside were turned back on, alerting the thousands of people that France's victory was now secure. Amid the cheering and shouting outside of the palace, the second German representative signed his name as well. Back in Germany, when the terms of the treaty were delivered to the government, the first chancellor of the Weimar Republic Phillip Scheidemann asked, "What hand would not wither when it signed such a treaty?" He then resigned his post in protest of the humiliating treaty. What were some of the terms that shocked and upset so many people?

The Treaty of Versailles stipulated that Germany would lose much of her territory. For example, the French reclaimed the lost territories of Alsace and Lorraine; Germany lost all of her overseas colonies, with a special statement inserted that "Germans were unfit to rule there." This was seen, in a world still dominated by the racism and prejudice of Social Darwinists, as a slap in the face to white, Christian German men—they were now called "unfit" to rule over Africans and Asians. In addition to these losses, Germany lost control of Belgium; they also had to cede land to the newly independent nation of Poland, cutting Germany into two pieces, bisected by the "Danzig Corridor." In addition they were required to relinquish a portion of the territories of Schleswig and Holstein, and there was a special clause inserted that forbade the unification of Germany with what was now left of Austria. Finally, an industrialized region of Germany, called the Saarland, was to be occupied by the French for the next fifteen years. At the end of the fifteen-year time span, the people living in the Saar would vote by plebiscite to either go back to German control or to formally join France.

In the realm of military punishments, the Treaty of Versailles also stipulated that the German army could have no more than 100,000 men in its standing army at any given time. The German Navy was reduced to no more than 15,000 men. There were numerous restrictions that Germany could not develop tanks or submarines; nor could Germany have an air force. The river Rhine, a natural boundary between Germany and France, was declared, on the German side, to be a "forever demilitarized zone," which in effect meant that Germany could not defend its western border from possible French attacks. To enforce German compliance, the French also now had the right to station an occupying military force on German soil—and to further humiliate the Germans, the French decided to send in French African soldiers to enforce the treaty's clauses.

All of these clauses were seen as harsh, humiliating, and destructive to Germany's future interests; however, the one clause that was the most hotly debated throughout the 1920s and 1930s was Article 231, also known as the "War Guilt Clause." In this portion of the treaty, Germany and the other Central

Powers were declared to be solely responsible for the war. As a corollary to this idea, the treaty argued that since Germany was responsible for the devastation that the war had brought, Germany now had to make reparations payments. For most German political leaders as well as average German people, the notion that Germany was solely responsible for the beginning of the conflict was outrageous and unacceptable. They therefore quickly moved to reject the demand for reparation payments as they rejected the premise of Article 231. This immediately set the stage for Germans of all political stripes to loudly reject the hated treaty, referring to it as the "Versailles Diktat." The treaty was now portrayed as something that had been foisted upon an unwilling Germany; it was not at all what Germans had been expecting with their raised hopes based upon Wilson's leaflets. When the treaty was signed in June 1919, it was also quickly associated with the newly created Weimar Republic, which now meant that this new form of government was linked in many people's minds with the humiliation of defeat and the hated "Diktat."

Given the lengthy historical tradition in many German circles that argued that liberal, enlightened ideals were French and not in keeping with the German character, many angry German leaders looked around and found that Jews seemed to benefit the most from the postwar chaos and the establishment of the Republic. Once again, Jewishness was associated with foreignness—particularly French foreignness—and the French were the enemy who had inflicted suffering upon Germany. So, the Treaty of Versailles, the adoption of the new Weimar constitution, and the new government of Germany were, in the minds of many, products of liberal, French, Jewish scheming to bring about the weakening and eventual destruction of the German nation. Clearly, the Weimar Republic was off to a shaky start.

To demonstrate the sense of alienation that was already beginning to permeate German people from their new Republic, one could simply look at the controversy that emerged over the new flag. The Weimar political leaders, who desperately wanted to distinguish the "new Germany" from the authoritarian and militaristic Kaiser's regime, adopted a new flag as symbol of the nation. Its colors were red, black, and gold. Many segments of the German population rejected this new flag and all that it stood for, refusing to fly the new colors. Instead, the military, the shipping industry, and many from the old right-wing political parties insisted on flying the old imperial colors of red, white, and black. The issue over what colors the flag sported represents on a small scale the Weimar Republic's deeper sense of alienation. Already in the early 1920s, Weimar's government was associated with the end of Germany's glory, the loss of status, and a rejection of the liberal ideas embodied in the Weimar constitution.

Many segments of the population, including the old officer corps, the educated middle class, high-ranking civil servants, and industrialists. were beginning to move away from the Weimar Republic due to its association with Germany's defeat and humiliation at Versailles. President Friedrich Ebert unfortunately incorrectly believed that, despite these individual's expressions of discontent, they would serve Germany faithfully and honorably no matter what type of government was in charge. Ebert's government therefore did not go through a restructuring process, seeking out new employees and officials who were committed to seeing the Weimar Republic thrive. Enemies of the new Republic denounced the new flag, suggesting that there was a conspiracy of "Red Internationalists," that is, the Communists; the "Black Internationalists," that is, the Catholics; and, standing behind the Red and Black, the "Yellow Internationalists"—the Jews. They could clearly point to Hugo Preuss's involvement in drafting the constitution to "prove" that Jews stood behind the grand plot to destroy German greatness.

Weimar's troubles multiply

The Weimar Republic was plagued with a series of problems that went well beyond the refusal to acknowledge the new flag of the nation. Beginning in 1919 economic and political turmoil marked the landscape of the new government. One chancellor after another came and went; between 1919 and 1928, there were fifteen different cabinets, with the shortest term of office lasting a mere three months. Why were chancellors coming and going so frequently? In most cases, the chancellors were faced with fulfilling clauses of the hated Versailles Diktat, so, rather than comply and meet their obligations, the chancellors would resign in protest, which would then trigger a new chancellor and a new coalition cabinet would be formed. The problem of such short-lived, unstable government leadership came precisely at the same time when workers were taking to the streets, demanding an increase in wages, which further hindered economic stability.

In such chaotic times, the government began to increase the printing of paper money in Germany, which led to catastrophic levels of inflation. For example, one American dollar in 1914 was worth approximately four marks on the exchange market. However, by 1922 that same American dollar was now worth approximately 191 marks; by November 1923, one American dollar was the equivalent of 4.2 trillion marks. This complete erosion of the value of the mark meant that any person who had carefully saved money for retirement or as a nest egg was financially ruined. It meant that civil servants on a fixed income could not keep pace with the rising cost of all products in their country. Anyone with any type of savings was wiped out. As the paper money lost its value, children could be found playing with stacks of the worthless paper, folding the bills into kites. Other people, now rendered homeless, used the worthless currency as wall paper in their shanties to keep the wind from whistling in between the cracks in the corrugated metal. Prices on all goods in stores were changed throughout the day, and the prices were always going up. Workers who still had employment would be paid several times per day at their jobs. Eventually the crisis reached such proportions that the government could not afford to keep printing new bills, so people would have to take their money to local banks where tellers would stamp extra zeroes on the face of the bill to reflect its new value. For those unable to keep their jobs, unemployment was rising. There was a general hardening of attitudes present in society as suffering had become so pervasive and a fact of everyday life.

Under such fears, cries of exploitation and black marketeering exploded in the Berlin neighborhood of Scheunenviertel at the height of the inflation. In particular, anti-Semitic agitators blamed the inflation and the suffering on the presence of Jews, more specifically targeting groups of East European immigrants living in and around the neighborhood. Lootings and robberies erupted, and the police moved in, but not before at least one person had been killed and many more seriously injured. There could not be much doubt in people's minds that Jewish shops were the target—gentile business-owners tried to save their stores from the looting by placing signs in their storefront windows stating "Christian business people."[28] Despite their efforts at deterrence, over 200 mostly non-Jewish-owned stores were still robbed. Incidents such as these were not isolated to big cities like Berlin. In Neidenburg demagogues told the crowds, "Just go to the Jew Lazarus, and take the millions for yourself, and smash [his] skull in for me, if you have the courage! Who are the blood-suckers? The Jews! Who provoked the war? The Jews!"[29] There were individuals who denounced the anti-Jewish violence, such as Michael Faulhaber, cardinal of Munich. Faulhaber, reacting to the upsurge of attacks made against Jews, openly preached that hatred of the Jews was un-Christian. That was helpful; however, he followed that sentence with the more ambiguous statement "every human life is precious, even that of an Israelite."[30] With talk such as that, it is unsurprising that the violence continued.

Ilya Ehrenburg, a Russian intellectual, was living in Berlin in the 1920s and wrote how he found the city to be a place of violence and misery. He encountered a stranger who offered to take him to an "interesting" night spot. They traveled by underground and arrived at a middle-class family's apartment. They were served drinks and then the host's two daughters appeared, naked, and began to ask their Russian visitor about Dostoyevsky's novels.[31] Not only were middle-class families resorting to prostituting their own children for foreign currency, Germany in the 1920s was rocked by many different mass murders. The images of black marketeers, pimps, and murderers became common tropes in this time period. One need only look to Bertold Brecht's work *The Threepenny Opera* to see some of these themes popularized, contributing to the atmosphere of instability.

Another element that began to arise was the emergence of counterrevolutionary movements backed by various Freikorps units. Freikorps, which were paramilitary units originally intended to supplement the now diminished German army, were growing in numbers in the Weimar era. They could range in size from 100 members to 8,000 men in a unit, and they were recruiting among the discontented middle and upper classes in society. These growing militias engaged in street fighting with political opponents on a daily basis. Sebastian Haffner recalled that as a young boy he had experienced the First World War as a series of newspaper notices but now, after the collapse, he saw street fighting and heard gunshots almost every day in the 1920s.[32]

In such a destabilizing and violent atmosphere, attitudes toward those less fortunate than oneself were beginning to become much more calloused. Europeans in general had already lived through a massive bloodletting in the war, never having experienced such enormous losses before. For some, there was a growing numbness to brutality; a work by Ernst Jünger, *The Thunder of Steel*, talked about the transformation of young men who had become political soldiers who only knew how to kill and fight. But these attitudes also extended into the realm of medicine and law. In 1920, Alfred Hoche and Karl Binding, a psychiatrist and a lawyer, co-wrote a book, *Permission for the Destruction of Life Unworthy of Life*. In this work, the two educated men argued that children and adults who were mentally or physically handicapped should be eradicated in order to allow healthier people to prosper. Their arguments, stemming from the eugenics movement of the late 1800s, put forward the concept that some lives were more worthy than others, and therefore, the "unworthy" did not deserve to live. This went well beyond what most eugenicists were arguing, most of whom thought that the physically or mentally ill should be forcibly sterilized to prevent any chance of reproducing. Hoche and Binding's arguments about the destruction of life contributed to an attitude that placed individuals into categories of "more valuable" and "less valuable" to society. Once a person began to accept the so-called logic of this premise, they were on a slippery slope to endorsing the murder of individuals deemed "unworthy of life."[33]

As we have already seen there were numerous thinkers who had already endorsed the ideas of racial superiority and inferiority, but Binding and Hoche went much further than merely categorizing groups of people; they had a definitive plan to end the threat these "useless eaters" posed to healthy, productive members of society. Another work appearing in the 1920s and 1930s, and one which carried enormous influence in Nazi circles, was Hans F.K. Günther's *The Racial Characteristics of the Jewish People*. Günther, who was born in 1891, studied linguistics, earned his doctorate, and went on to publish many books and articles which established him as a leading figure in the field of "racial science." Originally, Günther wrote *The Racial Characteristics of the German People* in 1922, which earned him the nickname "Race-Günther."[34] After the successful publication of the 1922 book, Günther then decided to write the book on Jewish characteristics. The author argued that Jews had descended from non-European races who, he claimed, passed on psychological and cultural qualities such as the "commercial spirit."[35] In a terrible misuse of scholarship, Günther used the works of Jewish scholars such as Samuel Weissenberg to promote his own conclusions about Jews. In one part of Günther's work, he went to great lengths to describe what made Jews stand out as a separate Volk (people). In this segment of his work, Günther described Jews as exhibiting fatty necks, small skulls, "bulging lips, heavy eyes, large fleshy ears, loose skin, hairiness and a prominent nose."[36] His stereotypes of Jews continued into the realm of how Jews walked, talked, and even smelled. He claimed that a specific odor could be attributed to Jews, partly due to the chemicals in their perspiration but also due to their liking for garlic.[37] Perhaps most shockingly, Günther claimed he was actually not an anti-Semite because he said he was not arguing for the racial inferiority of Jews, but was merely pointing out their "otherness."[38]

Günther did warn Germans against mixing racially with Jews. He believed that the two races were incompatible, arguing that when a German married a Jew, they had smaller-sized families and that the children of these "mixed marriages" tended to become "psychopaths and neurotics," "physical deviants," and criminals.[39] Günther suggested that Jews should emigrate and he applauded Zionists for their well-developed belief that Jews were a separate people. His works were published in many editions and went a long way toward popularizing racial anti-Semitic ideas. With just a dash of scientific information, Günther's work went on to serve as a stimulus for future eugenicists, anthropologists, and Nazis. Let us now turn to an examination of Hitler's attitudes toward the Jews.

For your consideration

Below is an excerpt from Heinrich von Treitschke (1834–1896), one of the most famous historians of his day in Germany. Thousands of students attended his lectures at the University of Berlin. He also edited the important academic journal *Prussian Yearbooks*. As a German conservative-nationalist, he attacked Socialism, Catholicism, and Jews. In this selection, how does Treitschke portray Jews? What types of problems in German society does he see and who does he blame for these problems? How might the words of such an influential professor influence the respectability of anti-Semitic views?

We Germans, however, have to deal with that Polish branch of Jews, in whom the scars of many centuries of Christian tyranny have been imprinted; according to experience, they are much more alien compared to European, and especially to the German being.

What we demand from our Israelite fellow citizens is simple: they should become Germans, feel themselves simply and justly as Germans— without prejudice to their faith and their sacred old memories, which all of us find honorable; for we do not want an era of German-Jewish mixed culture to follow thousands of years of German civilization. It would be a sin to forget that many Jews, baptized and unbaptized, Felix

Mendelssohn, Veit, Riesser among others—not to mention ones now living—were German men in the best sense, men in whom we revere the noble and fine traits of the German spirit. It remains just as undeniable that numerous and powerful groups of Jews definitely do not cherish the good will to become simply Germans. It is painful enough to talk about these things; even conciliatory words are easily misunderstood here. I think, however, many of my Jewish friends will agree with me, with deep regret, when I maintain that recently a dangerous spirit of arrogance has arisen in Jewish circles, and that the influence of Jewry upon our national life, which in former times was often beneficial, has recently been harmful in many ways.... There is no German commercial city which does not count many honest, respectable Jewish firms; but it is incontestable that the Semites have a great part of the falsehood and deceit, of the bold greed of business excesses, a heavy guilt for that contemptible materialism of our age, which regards all work only as business and threatens to suffocate the old comfortable joy in work of our people; in thousands of German villages sits the Jew, who buys out his neighbors through usury. Among the leading men of art and science, the number of Jews is not large; much greater is the bustling horde of Semitic talent of the third rank....

Most dangerous, however, is the unjust preponderance of the Jews in the daily press... For ten years public opinion in many German cities was "made" mostly by Jewish pens.... What Jewish journalists achieve in abuse and mockery against Christianity is plainly outrageous, and such blasphemies are offered to our people in our language as the newest achievement of "German" Enlightenment! Hardly was the emancipation obtained, when one insisted boldly on their "certificate"; one demanded literal parity in all and everything, and did not want to see that we Germans are, after all, a Christian people and the Jews are only a minority among us; we have experienced that the removal of Christian pictures and even the introduction of the Sabbath celebration in mixed schools was disbanded. If we consider all this—and how much more could be said!—then the noisy agitation of the moment appears only as a brutal and spiteful, but natural reaction of the Germanic national consciousness against an alien element which has taken too much space in our life. It has at least the one involuntary merit of having freed us from the ban of an unspoken falsehood. It is already a gain that an evil, which each sensed but nobody wanted to touch, is now openly discussed. Let us not deceive ourselves: the movement is very deep and strong.... Up to the best educated circles, among men who would reject with horror any thought of Christian fanaticism or national arrogance, it sounds today, as from one mouth: the Jews are our misfortune!

Excerpt taken from Steve Hochstadt, Sources of the Holocaust, *26–27.*

The following excerpt is from a 1912 pamphlet titled "If I Were the Kaiser," written by Heinrich Class. Class was a leader of a pan-German league in the years leading up to the outbreak of the First World War. He was against liberalism, socialism, and democracy—all ideologies which Class connected to Jewish influence. Twenty-five thousand copies of Class's pamphlet were published in Germany before the war and after Germany's defeat in the First World War, the pamphlet was reprinted in the 1920s praising the young Nazi party and its leader Adolf Hitler. As you read the excerpts, what types of influence does Class believe Jews have in German society? Does he see Jews as being German? How does he portray German gentiles? Does Class believe in racial anti-Semitism?

The carriers and teachers of the materialism that today is dominant are the Jews; its German-born supporters are dupes seduced and alienated from their inborn instincts.

Having achieved economic power these racially foreign guests on German soil spread from all areas of national life—a tragi-comic contradiction in itself—but because it was tolerated, it has become historical fact. Publishing, theater, journalism were taken over; law, academia, medicine became special fields of Jewish activity and influence.

And according to the law of his being—no person can get out of their skin; this is valid too for everything that is racially inherited—the Jew remains a Jew in everything he undertakes. If he engages in politics, he can only do so as a Jew, i.e., without sense or understanding for self-integration, for subordination, without love for what has grown historically and organically. If he becomes a lawyer, he acts subversively, because his inborn notions of justice stand in contradiction to those to be found in written German law. He resorts to those Talmudic tricks that turn justice into injustice. If he pursues art, he lacks the inwardness that is the basis of every creative achievement. We know that the so-called German theater is almost completely in Jewish hands today. Only the few people who reflect on the fact that the performance of new works depends on the judgement of Jewish theater directors and their advisers, who decide whether a piece is worth staging, realize what this means for German artistic creativity. The judgement, coming from the Jews, will correspond to the Jewish conception of what is stageworthy, and we can categorically state that many works for the stage emerging from good, German minds, gather dust in the desks of poets, because they are found not to be stageworthy by critics of alien blood. "Sensationalism", however, is their measure of stageworthiness, and the German-born writer who wants to write for the stage has to change and write like a Jew....

Even worse is the influence of the Jewish press, because it affects the popular masses directly day by day.... Jewry has seized hold of the press.... If a newspaper is not under Jewish ownership; or if the editors are not Jewish, then it is the advertising that determines the attitude of the paper—at least on all questions that concern Jewry.... What do these people know of German freedom, which sets boundaries through voluntary restraint? What do they know of the necessary subordination of everyone? What is the fatherland and the state to these homeless and stateless people? What is military discipline to them? What is monarchy to them?

Excerpt taken from Roderick Stackelberg and Sally A. Winkle,
The Nazi Germany Sourcebook: An Anthology of Texts, *20–22.*

Suggestions for further reading

Alex Bein, *Theodore Herzl: A Biography Hadassa Ben-Itto, The Lie That Wouldn't Die: The Protocols of the Elders of Zion* (New York, 2005).

Jean-Denis Bredin, *The Affair: The Case of Alfred Dreyfus* (New York, 1986).

Michael Burleigh, *Death and Deliverance: "Euthanasia" in Germany 1900–1945* (New York, 1995).

Amos Elon, *The Pity of It All* (New York, 2003).

Edward Flannery, *The Anguish of the Jews* (New York, 2004).

Adolf Hitler, *Mein Kampf*, translated by Ralph Manheim (New York, 1999).

Jacob Katz, *Out of the Ghetto: Social Background of Jewish Emancipation, 1770–1870* (New York, 1998).

Thomas Kühne, *Belonging and Genocide: Hitler's Community, 1918–1945* (New Haven, CT, 2010).

Paul Massing, *Rehearsal for Destruction: A Study of Political Antisemitism in Imperial Germany* (New York, 1949).

Peter Pulzer, *Jews and the German State: The Political History of a Minority, 1848–1933* (Detroit, MI, 2003).

Peter Pulzer, *The Rise of Political Antisemitism in Germany and Austria* (New York, 1964).

Alan E. Steinweis, *Studying the Jew: Scholarly Antisemitism in Nazi Germany* (Cambridge, MA, 2008).

Fritz Stern, *Gold and Iron: Bismarck and Bleichröder and the Building of the German Empire* (New York, 1979).

4

Hitler's Rise to Power and the Radicalization of Anti-Semitic Policies

Why Are We Anti-Semites?
—ADOLF HITLER, AUGUST 1920

Introduction

In the years immediately following the defeat of Germany in "the Great War," the German people adopted a new constitution giving them a level of freedom that they had never experienced before. Those freedoms of expression came to dominate the postwar imagery of the Weimar Republic in the minds of the general public. Weimar Germany was a place of instability, violence, and suffering, yet it was also seen as a cultural mecca, the place to go if one wanted to experience the avant-garde. These extremes, of left-wing cultural dominance, combined with growing right-wing extremism, prepared the soil for the growing Nazi Party. In this chapter we will examine the rise of Hitler and his political party, the NSDAP, to power with a focus on Hitler's anti-Semitic attitudes. We will follow the course of anti-Semitic policies and actions once Hitler becomes the chancellor of Germany.

The Weimar years

One of the most outstanding aspects of Weimar Germany was its cultural modernism. The Expressionist movement, emphasizing the artist's feelings as well as the emotional response from the audience, was the dominant artistic movement of the 1920s. Painters such as Otto Dix and George Grosz, authors such as Kurt Tucholsky, and composers such as Arnold Schoenberg challenged their contemporaries to restructure German society in radical ways. Expressionists tended to be left-wing intellectuals who believed that if Germany remained on its present course, then another war was almost inevitable. These intellectuals and artists attacked the institutions that seemed to be holding onto power, just as they had wielded power before and during the First World War. That meant attacking the conservative industrialists, the established churches, the civil servant bureaucrats, and the officer class of the military in particular. Through their writings, paintings, sculptures, and more, they fought to reveal the dirty underbelly of German life—depicting German veterans with amputated limbs out begging on the streets, showing the "new woman" of the 1920s with her bobbed hair, wearing makeup, sheer clothing, and drinking and smoking in public. They challenged gender roles, even in the realm of architecture, where graduates of the Bauhaus school of architecture designed kitchens that now looked like laboratories, acknowledging that now with more women out in the workforce, men as well as women needed to feel comfortable in the kitchen. They even wanted to force their audiences to see the world in different colors, painting cows that were yellow and horses that were blue. To most of the Expressionists, Germans had to revise their world drastically, otherwise things would continue on as they always had—and that path led to more war.[1]

As jazz music blared in countless small cabarets, inflation and unemployment continued to rise, particularly after the 1929 stock market crash in America. Expressionists continued in their heavy critique of the shortcomings of the new Weimar Republic, using the very freedoms granted to them by the Weimar constitution to declaim its failings. Unfortunately for so many of these left-wing intellectuals, in their quest to save Germany from itself, they neglected to gauge the public's mood. For many Germans, life after the war was filled with challenges, fears, and instability. Most people felt exhausted. They had sacrificed all in the name of a victory which never came and now life as they had once known it was erased. There was no Kaiser, the behaviors of men and women were forever changed, money had no stable value, and most people were longing for a return to something more familiar. But the Expressionists kept on insisting that still more change was required, that the work of creating a new Germany was only at its beginning. They failed to have their fingers on the pulse of the average person. Most people did not necessarily want to work for still more change.

In the tumultuous times of the Weimar era, there were moments of stability. In what historians refer to as "the Era of Stresemann," the falling mark was exchanged for a new currency, the government was able to clamp down on both left- and right-wing attempted coups, but this idyll would only last for a few brief years (1923–1929). Gustav Stresemann is credited with giving the Germans some temporary relief from the economic and political turmoil of earlier years. However, Stresemann could only achieve so much, first as chancellor and then as foreign minister of Weimar Germany. With his death in 1929, his "policy of fulfillment" regarding the hated Treaty of Versailles was at an end. Once Americans began to call in their loans to German companies and towns, economic disaster seemed to be lurking around the corner again. For many, the fear that the inflationary rates of November 1923 would come again coupled with the psychological fear of losing one's job was captured in Hans Fallada's novel *What Now, Little Man?* In this instantaneous best seller, Fallada portrayed the effects of the depression on a lower middle class man who feared losing his job and sliding down the social scale into the working class, or worse still, into the homeless ranks. Feelings of isolation, alienation and insecurity raised the question—where was the sense of community to be found now? Where had the Burgfrieden declared by Kaiser Wilhelm II in 1914 gone?

The early Nazi Party

The triumph of Hitler and the Nazi Party in this troubled Weimar era was deeply connected to the fears of most average people. They were concerned about the future—both their own, personal futures and the future of the German nation. Nazi propaganda aimed to convince Germans that if they felt alienated from Weimar—both in politics and in its culture—it was due to the fact that Weimar was dominated by Jews. Everything that was deemed culturally modern—from art to music to film—was designated as international, cosmopolitan, urban, and Jewish. To the Nazis, true German culture and political life sprang from a sense of the Volk, and the Volk was presented as being nationalistic, simple, rural, and Aryan. In fighting to recreate the sense of comradeship and community that had supposedly existed in the trench lines during the war, the Nazi Party fostered the division of German society into categories of "us" versus "them." The group categorized as "them" were the outsiders, those who could never truly belong to the Volk, and their very existence was seen as an existential threat to the healthy Volksgemeinschaft. How did the Nazis, and more specifically Hitler, define these "outsiders"?

When we last left Hitler, he was in hospital recovering his eyesight when he received the devastating news that Germany had signed the November armistice. In the greatly reduced postwar German army, Hitler was selected to be one of the 100,000 men left. Partly this was due to his abilities as a charismatic speaker, and in part it was due to his extreme German nationalism. His job in the reduced army was information officer, which meant that he was tasked with keeping up the morale of the men. He was also to gather information on political clubs and organizations. He was to visit the political organizations and feel them out to see whether they could assist the military in the event of a crisis. This role provided Hitler with the opportunity to enter into the local political arena around Munich. In September 1919, Hitler as information officer attended a meeting of a local, small right-wing party. The party's name was the German Workers' Party (DAP). It had been founded by an unassuming man, Anton Drexler, who wanted to provide German workers with a conservative alternative to communist or socialist parties. The group's membership was so miniscule in 1919 that Drexler numbered membership cards beginning with the number 500; if a participant became member number 507, they were, in reality, the seventh person to officially join the DAP.

Hitler listened to the men of the German Workers' Party that evening and he discovered that many of those present also held membership in a secret organization called the Thule Society. One could question just how secret the society was since Hitler was a newcomer and was told about it, but nevertheless, the men told Hitler about the group. Both groups, the DAP and the Thule Society, were in keeping with many of the ideas and prejudices that Hitler already held. Between the two groups, Hitler found that they preached Aryan supremacy, racial anti-Semitism, anti-Marxism, and extreme German nationalism. Hitler had found a political home. He joined the party officially in the latter part of September. Hitler became member #555, although in later years he claimed he was member #7.[2] Drexler thought Hitler was a bit absurd when they first met. Little did Drexler know that his underestimation of Hitler would soon result in Drexler being eclipsed by the latest member of the very party he had established.

Hitler was still in the German army working as an information officer; however, he now was also engaging in political discussions with the men of the DAP. In September 1919, Hitler, now a thirty-year-old, wrote a letter to another veteran, Adolf Gemlich. This would be one of Hitler's first written statements addressing the "Jewish Question." In the letter, Hitler attempted to differentiate between an emotionally based type of anti-Semitism with that of a political doctrine.[3] He argued to his fellow veteran that most Germans had a personal antipathy toward Jews after having encountered them; however, he claimed that this emotionally negative response to a Jewish person would not be able to sustain a political movement. "Anti-Semitism as a political movement may not and cannot be determined by flashes of emotion, but rather through the understanding facts." What was needed, he continued, was a "clear understanding of the consciously or unconsciously systematic degenerative effect of the Jews on the totality of our nation."[4]

The argument Hitler was making to Gemlich was structured around the so-called facts about Jews. Hitler vehemently declared that Jews were a racial community, not a religious one, and that centuries of in-breeding had inculcated the abhorrent qualities of materialism and greed into the Jewish racial character. Hitler intermixed religious imagery, however, with his racial claims about the Jews, arguing that they "danced around the golden calf," and that the essence of their character was about money and power. He saw Jews as the ultimate exploiters, arguing that as Jews, they had failed to develop higher spiritual and moral ideals. Gemlich was told that Jews were a "racial tuberculosis" that only an "anti-Semitism of reason" could effectively and permanently combat. Hitler's plan said that only "the systematic legal combatting and removal of Jewish privileges" could lead ultimately to "the removal of the Jews altogether."[5] We do not know Gemlich's response.

FIGURE 4.1 *Image of "Loyalty." The poem reads: "The sword will not be sheathed./ The Stürmer stands as ever/ in the battle for the people and the fatherland. It fights the Jews because it loves the people." Taken from* Der Stürmer, *November 1935, Issue #48. Courtesy Randall Bytwerk Collection, German Propaganda Archive, Calvin College.*

Hitler, following in the long established tradition of racial anti-Semites, continued to promote his idea of the "anti-Semitism of reason" as he became further involved in the German Workers' Party. By February 1920, Hitler had acquired enough influence with the DAP to hold his first authentic mass meeting. That night, over 2,000 people attended the meeting. Hitler was reportedly ecstatic to see so many people in attendance. He announced the new party platform. In his speech, Hitler said that the platform would now have twenty-five points, one of which spoke of "positive Christianity." Hitler denounced the Versailles Diktat, the "November Criminals," and the Jews. He said that this party would glorify war and violence, arguing that violent acts revealed just how committed a man was to the cause. Finally,

Hitler announced that the party would now have a new name: the National Socialist German Workers' Party, or NSDAP. At this point in time, the NSDAP, or Nazi Party, was committed to effecting change by revolutionary means. Hitler had officially entered the rough and tumble world of Munich politics.

Hitler on the "Jewish Question"

On August 13, 1920, Hitler spoke to a group in the ballroom of the Munich Hofbräuhaus. The speech lasted for several hours and came to be known as Hitler's foundational speech on the subject of the "Jewish Question." Its title was, "Why Are We Antisemites?" Now making a subtle pivot away from the Gemlich letter's argument, Hitler told his listeners that they had to understand and accept the scientific principles of the true racial differences between Jews and Germans, but they also had to combine that with emotionalism in order to create a mass following. Apparently Hitler had acquired enough political experience by the summer of 1920 to understand that he needed the colder, "logical" reasoning of racial anti-Semitism to be combined with a more emotional appeal to the masses. This theme of combining the "science" of Jew hatred with the appeal to mass outrage against the Jewish population was again revisited by Hitler in yet another speech in September 1921. Placing himself firmly in the camp of earlier racial anti-Semites such as Wilhelm Marr, Hitler was essentially arguing that Jews were unable to change because their qualities were inherited. They therefore could never truly be assimilated nor could they alter their innate behaviors, "And in this characteristic, which he cannot transcend, which lies in his blood … in this characteristic itself lies the necessity for the Jew that he must present himself as destructive to the state. He cannot do otherwise, whether he wants to or not."[6] Unlike Marr, however, Hitler was proposing action, not mere words. The only solution was to separate the Jews from the larger population, protecting the gentile majority from Jewish corruption.

In the same August speech, Hitler gave voice to his own description of the Volksgemeinschaft for the first time. Organizing his talk around the concept of "work," Hitler presented the idea that only the Nordic races had evolved to a higher level, beyond that of instinctual preservation. He argued that due to harsh external conditions, Nordic peoples learned to work not just to keep themselves alive, but to protect their clan. He threw in Social Darwinism, too, by stating that the Nordic peoples purified their race because the weak and unfit died. What remained was a "race of giants in strength and health."[7] Duty, racial purity, health, and a deep spiritual inner life all helped Aryans develop states and culture. In contrast, Jews were unlike the Nordic races. They could only exist "as parasites on the bodies of other people (Völker)"; the "vermin of the Volksgemeinschaft" did everything to destroy the community.[8] The concept of Volksgemeinschaft and its ideas of inclusion necessarily meant the active practice of excluding those deemed to be a threat to the community's purity and survival. From as early as this speech in 1920, Hitler offered his followers a vision of an exclusionary society, where the positive creation of a vibrant, healthy "Volksgemeinschaft" meant that, by necessity, violent actions had to be taken to remove those standing in the way, most notably the Jews. This does not mean that Hitler, back in 1920, had already planned for the murder of Jews; in fact, he ended his speech with: "the removal of the Jews from our people, not because we begrudge them their existence... but because the existence of our own Volk means a thousand times more to us than that of a foreign race."[9]

The Munich Beer Hall Putsch

As Hitler and the NSDAP continued to grow and expand beyond the Munich environment, Hitler's charisma and speaking skills led to an invitation by the self-proclaimed leaders of the state of Bavaria: General Otto von Lossow and Gustav von Kahr. Lossow and Kahr had essentially seized control of the state government, forcing the legally elected representatives—at gunpoint—to relinquish their authority. The Weimar government had passed the "Law for the Protection of the Republic," which made anti-republican activity illegal; Kahr and Lossow protested this law, arguing that it interfered with states' rights. The two men had a deep hatred for the Weimar Republic, and by their actions had virtually declared a civil war against the federal government of Germany. Both men wanted to return Germany to its more conservative heritage and they were more than willing to foment counter-revolution in the name of ending the hated Weimar "system."

Kahr and Lossow had watched, along with most other Europeans, as Benito Mussolini and his black-shirted fascists had marched through the streets of Rome, demanding that the king of Italy, Victor Emmanuel III appoint Mussolini as the prime minister of the country. The march by thousands of angry, fist-waving blackshirts worked and Mussolini became the first fascist leader in the world to acquire real power. The spectacle of the fascists destabilizing a government inspired Kahr and Lossow to hatch a plot.

By 1923, the Weimar Republic was devolving into near chaos in many places. The French and their allies had decided to occupy another industrialized region of Germany, the Ruhr, in an attempt to force the Germans to make good on their reparations payments. The workers in the Ruhr carried on passive resistance activities such as work slowdowns to thwart the French. Kahr and Lossow, in October 1923, took the bold step of taking over the army in Bavaria. Meanwhile the two men also began to plan for a Mussolini-inspired march through the streets of Munich. They wanted the march to spark off a nationalist counter-revolution but they needed someone to spread the message of the impending march. They enlisted the aid of Hitler. He was known to them already as an extreme German nationalist who despised the Republic, and they knew of his outstanding speaking skills. Hitler agreed to coordinate the political and propagandistic preparations for the putsch.

Everything seemed ready to go by November 1923; however, in a last minute meeting, Kahr, Lossow and the Commander-in-Chief of the Reischswehr (army), General von Seeckt, Seeckt informed the co-conspirators that he could not guarantee that the army would remain neutral during such a march. On November 8, 1923, Kahr and Lossow summoned a meeting of their followers to the Burgerbrau Cellar and Kahr attempted to explain to the audience why the march now had to be delayed. An enraged Hitler entered the hall from the back, with two pistols reportedly drawn, and he tried to force Kahr and Lossow to go along with the original plans. Kahr and Lossow seemingly pretended to agree with Hitler and the order was given that the very next day, November 9, 1923, the march would begin right in front of the beer hall.

In the early morning hours, Hitler arrived at the beer hall, only to find that Kahr and Lossow had abandoned the plan. However, Hitler's spirits were lifted when the infamous First World War hero General Erich Ludendorff appeared and proclaimed himself ready to take part in the march. The march began, the army did not remain neutral, and shots were fired. Reportedly Hitler was one of the first to be slightly wounded; he was put into a waiting car and rushed away from the scene. Ludendorff walked right through the gunfire. The march ended with several killed, many others wounded, and even Ludendorff was arrested. Thus ended the Beer Hall Putsch of November 1923, a miserable failure in the short run as it had failed to achieve the goal of stimulating a nation-wide counter-revolution that would bring about the end of the Weimar Republic.

In the long run, however, the Beer Hall Putsch resulted in helping Hitler's political career. He, like Ludendorff and many other marchers, was arrested. Gustav Stresemann insisted that there should be a trial since the men had participated in an act of treason against the state. Ludendorff was acquitted—no jury in Germany would sentence such a famous war hero. Kahr and Lossow, the originators of the putsch idea, were not charged with anything. Hitler, however, understood that as he was a virtual nobody compared to the likes of a Ludendorff, he would be the one blamed for the putsch. Although it may have appeared that Hitler's days as a political leader were over, Hitler found that the judge trying the case was sympathetic to right-wing causes. In addition, the judge allowed Hitler unlimited speaking time at his trial, a true gift for a man who based his success upon his ability to sway crowds. The court case received a great deal of nationwide coverage, with major German newspapers sending journalists to report on the details of the trial.

Hitler was able to turn the trial to his advantage as he was able to portray himself as a patriot who only wanted what was best for the German nation. In his rousing closing statements he declared himself innocent:

> For, gentlemen, it is not you who pronounce judgment upon us, it is the external Court of History which will make its pronouncement upon the charge which is brought against us. The verdict that you will pass I know. But that Court will not ask of us, "Did you commit high treason or did you not?" That Court will judge us ... as Germans who wanted the best for their people and their fatherland, who wished to fight and to die. You may pronounce us guilty a thousand times, but the Goddess who presides over the Eternal Court of History will with a smile tear in pieces the charges of the Public Prosecutor and the verdict of this court. For she acquits us.[10]

These were powerful words from a "nobody." Hitler became an overnight sensation in the press. Now, instead of being finished as a potential political leader, he was a household name throughout all of Germany. The court did sentence him, but it was with the understanding that Hitler would be out of prison long before the sentence had been served. He was given five years in the Landsberg Fortress Prison, but he would be released in less than one year. While in the prison, Hitler enjoyed a steady stream of well-wishers and curiosity-seekers, all of whom had read the defiant words of the "patriot" who wanted what was best for Germany. While in prison, Hitler was treated like the superstar he had become so he received special meals and was allowed unlimited visitations. In his spare time, Hitler used his incarceration to create his autobiography, *Mein Kampf* (My Struggle). In the long run, the royalties from the sale of *Mein Kampf* would make Hitler a fairly wealthy man. In *Mein Kampf*, Hitler predicted that Jews were in league with Satan in an effort to destroy the world:

> If, with the aid of his Marxist creed, the Jew triumphs over the peoples of this world, then his coronation will be the dance of death for humanity, and this planet will once more drift through the ether devoid of human life, as it did millions of years ago. Eternal nature is relentless in avenging transgressions of her laws. Hence, I believe I am acting in accordance with the wishes of the Almighty Creator: by defending myself against the Jew, I am fighting for the work of the Lord.[11]

Perhaps the greatest lesson Hitler took away from the failed putsch was that the German people were not truly revolutionary. No matter how much they railed against the hated Weimar government, they were not willing to break with law and order and take to the streets. Germans would not arm themselves and overthrow the Republic by force. This resulted in a new strategy for the Nazi Party. From the time of Hitler's release from prison in

December 1924 to his appointment as chancellor of Germany in January 1933, the focus would now be on using democracy to gain votes, obtain real political power, and then destroy democracy itself.

Building the Nazi Party

If Hitler was now going to try to appeal to more voters, how did this impact his earlier focus on anti-Semitism? The Nazi leader still retained his beliefs that "anti-Semitism of reason" coupled with the emotional imagery of anti-Semitism were necessary, but he incorporated a broader set of appeals in order to obtain a wider base of support for the party. That did not mean abandoning the core of his principles regarding the supposed danger Jews posed to society, but it did mean uniting German gentiles into a greater community, the Volksgemeinschaft (the People's community). Excluding the Jews while building up an Aryan community were two sides of the same coin. Perpetrating acts of discrimination and persecution against the Jews would effectively bind Aryan-Germans together. In the words of historian Thomas Kühne, "Nothing makes people stick together better than committing a crime together."[12] Hitler himself pointed this out in a 1932 speech, stating, "There are two things which can unite men: common ideals and common criminality."[13]

As the Nazi Party rose to ever more power, these two sides of the same coin were exploited to their fullest. On the one hand, Hitler could ask Germans to stand up, unite, and work to bring Germany out of the ashes of defeat, despair, and humiliation. He could promise them in countless speeches that he, as leader of his party, wanted to restore the Volksgemeinschaft, and end all of the alienation that so many people had experienced in the postwar years. While delivering this more positive message, it was clear that there would be groups of people who would be excluded from joining in this national reawakening. They were the outsiders, the aliens who simply did not, nor could not, become accepted members of the national community. The two messages were inseparable, and "anti-Semitic violence was thus not merely a means of National Socialist politics; violence against Jews was the core of those politics."[14]

Throughout the 1920s the NSDAP organized countless "actions" against Jews. This achieved the two goals of Hitler: attacking Jews made life difficult for them so hopefully they would leave Germany and attacking Jews bound the attackers together in a community of violence. Regional SA units were often gathered together and would be sent into towns in the countryside. There, they would march, sing songs, honor the war dead, hold a rally, offer a concert, and march away by torchlight in the evening. This pattern could also be punctuated by attacking Jews. In addition, Nazi newspapers such as the rabidly anti-Semitic *Der Stürmer* (The Attacker) continued to foist its views on the public. In article after article, *Der Stürmer* claimed to be able to reveal Jewish plots all over the world, encouraging the readers to unite to fight against the Jewish menace. Quite frequently SA (SturmAbteilung) brownshirts would threaten pedestrians passing by, particularly those identified by the thugs as "looking Jewish." In September 1931, 1,000 SA men shouting "Germany awake, Judah die," and "beat the Jews to death" rampaged down Berlin's elite shopping street—the Kurfürstendamm. It was Jewish New Year and the SA used the occasion to assault pedestrians.[15]

As Michael Wildt's research has shown, Prussian police reports revealed a dramatic escalation in violent attacks at political events. In 1929 the records indicate 579 violent outbursts. By 1930 the number was up to 2,494; 2,904 in 1931; and then in 1932, 5,296 reports were registered in Prussia alone.[16] In most cases, the men of the SA would attack Communists, Socialists, and Jews. The Nazis were fighting two fights at once: against the existence of the Weimar Republic and against the Jewish community. In both of these arenas, we can see once again the use of the positive message of forging a true "Volksgemeinschaft" while simultaneously enacting the negative message that certain people should disappear from the country.

Inclusion and exclusion were forged in these early years of the NSDAP, but the Weimar Republic did show instances of resistance to the powerful double message of the Nazis. For example, police did actually intervene in many of the instances, attempting to restore order in their communities instead of turning a blind eye to the attacks. Jewish leaders in the Centralverein (CV) often wrote articles demanding protection for Jews and tried to counteract the violence with slogans such as "Humans, be humane!"[17] The CV also had opportunities to lodge legal complaints against attackers. Liberals and Social Democrats staged protests. All of this was still possible in the heated atmosphere of the Weimar Republic, but meanwhile the Nazis continued to use slogans such as "Work and Bread" to win elections, and as the economic conditions worsened for the Weimar government, it appeared that only the political extremes were left as viable options for most Germans. One could support either communism or Nazism. There seemed to be no moderate alternative.

Hitler's seizure of power

In the final years of the Weimar Republic's existence, the aging president Paul von Hindenburg began to invoke one of the truly important powers that the Weimar Constitution had granted to the president: Article 48, or, the "Emergency Clause." This clause allowed whomever was serving as president to declare an emergency and thus suspend parliamentary democracy. It allowed the president of Weimar to appoint a chancellor, vice-chancellor and a cabinet of officers, not based on what the voters had sent to the Reichstag, but based on what he thought would be needed to end the crisis. Beginning in 1930, using Article 48, Hindenburg appointed a gaunt First

World War veteran and politician, Heinrich Brüning, as chancellor. Brüning had an overwhelming sense of self-sacrifice based on his experiences during the war with a machine gunners' unit which had lost every single man but him. He was also, at the age of forty-five, well versed in the intricacies of the budget of the government. Hindenburg's advisors thought they had found the correct man to steer the Republic out of financial disaster. They had not. Brüning's austerity measures only incensed the German public, earning him the nickname the "Hunger Chancellor." Despite his attempts to pull Weimar out of its downward economic spiral, he was replaced by Hindenburg in 1932. Again using Article 48, Hindenburg's government announced a new chancellor, a Catholic Center Party conservative, Franz von Papen.

Franz von Papen, an aristocratic conservative, was the darling of Hindenburg. He was charming and conniving. During the First World War Papen had been in America, spying for Germany. He was discovered and was sent back to his homeland. Now, in 1932 he was called to fight against the mounting unemployment, rising prices, and fighting in the streets between Nazis and Communists. Again, like his predecessor Brüning, Papen failed to correct any of these problems. By December 1932, Hindenburg had decided to select General Kurt von Schleicher as Papen's successor as chancellor. Schleicher had approached Hindenburg with a plan to split the Nazi Party into two factions. The retired General had a meeting with a top Nazi leader, Gregor Strasser, asking him if he would join Schleicher's cabinet in order to represent the Nazi Party. Schleicher, a master of intrigue, thought that Strasser would leap at the chance to have real power, thus splitting the Nazi Party into two factions: one faction around Hitler, the other around Strasser. What Schleicher did not factor into his plans was loyalty. Strasser went to Hitler and told him of Schleicher's offer. Hitler, unsurprisingly, told Strasser to reject the deal. Strasser did just that. With the collapse of Schleicher's scheme to divide the Nazis among themselves, Franz von Papen began to whisper in President Hindenburg's ear: perhaps Hitler was able to be tamed? Why not replace Schleicher with Hitler? To reassure Hindenburg that Hitler would be controlled by nationalistic conservatives, Papen volunteered to become Hitler's vice-chancellor.

At first, Hindenburg, who despised Hitler, dragged his feet. He even received a warning note from his former First World War colleague, Erich Ludendorff. By 1932, Ludendorff and Hitler had had a falling out and Ludendorff told Hindenburg not to appoint Hitler chancellor. Ludendorff wrote a note to the aging president, "I solemnly prophesy that this accursed man [Hitler] will cast our Reich into the abyss and bring our nation to inconceivable misery. Future generations will damn you in your grave for what you have done."[18] Eventually, however, Papen's advice won out and on January 30, 1933, Hitler was legally appointed chancellor of the Weimar Republic.

Hitler had done exactly what he had set out to do since the failure of the November 1923 Beer Hall Putsch. Using innovative campaigning techniques, the Nazis had acquired a substantial electorate. They had used the apparatus of democracy to achieve power and now Hitler would turn to destroy it. That night, as the evening newspapers announced that Germany had yet another chancellor, the fourth in less than four years, crowds began to gather under torchlights to sing popular Nazi songs. Hitler stood in the window of the Reich Chancellery window for hours that night as thousands upon thousands of exuberant Nazi supporters turned out to cheer his success. A kind of electricity spread over Germany; there was clearly a feeling that this was no mere change of chancellors. One woman from Hamburg greeted the announcement of Hitler's cabinet with great joy. She later described her city's torchlit procession a few nights after the announcement as "a wonderful uplifting experience for us all." She acknowledged that there were also "cries of Judah, die, and songs sung about Jewish blood squirting under knives, but she added after the war, 'Who at the time took that seriously?'"[19]

Hitler as chancellor

With the news that Hitler was now the legal chancellor of Germany, the SA ran wild on the streets. They were celebrating that their "revolution" had succeeded and they believed that they could now perpetrate any acts of violence and illegality so long as it promoted the NSDAP agenda. For many segments of the German population, that meant that the door had been opened to outright physical intimidation and destruction of property. There was a sense that the SA intended to "settle old scores" with political rivals, with perceived threats to the party, and so on. For some Germans, their belief was that Hitler would not last in power for very long. Sebastian Haffner, as a 25-year-old man, discussed the appointment of Hitler with his father. They decided that the new regime "had a chance to wreak a pretty large amount of harm, but hardly a chance to rule for long."[20] Leaders of the CV urged Jews in Germany to follow a "wait and see" attitude.[21] Jewish speakers at events immediately following the appointment argued that between the constitution and the conservative leaders in the cabinet, Hitler would be unable to put into practice what he had campaigned on in his rise to power. One man, a Jewish butcher exclaimed at one such meeting, "They won't do anything to us—after all, we're Germans."[22]

Meanwhile, Hitler made it clear that his government was going to pursue a policy called *Gleichschaltung*. Gleichschaltung can be translated as "coordination" or "consolidation," and it meant that now the Nazis were aiming to infiltrate every aspect of an average person's life with Nazi ideology. This now meant that every choice a person made carried a political significance. The way one dressed and wore one's hair, the newspapers one subscribed to, the movies and concerts one attended, the furniture placed in one's house—all of this was going to be filtered through the Nazi lens. As a young man, Hitler had fancied himself a great artist/architect, and he promised that once the Nazis had seized power, there would be a cultural rebirth in the German nation. "Aryan" art, music, architecture, etc. would all come pouring forth to combat the "poisoning" of German culture that Hitler claimed had occurred during the Weimar years. He clearly labeled Expressionist, Abstract and Modern Art as "Jewish intellectualism" and depicted anything deemed "modern" as the product of internationalism, cosmopolitanism, and Bolshevism. The Nazi worldview was to be an all-encompassing one, one which touched on every aspect of a person's life.

In the political realm, Hitler moved quickly to dispel notions that Gleichschaltung was only going to be reserved for culture. Almost immediately after his appointment, Hitler declared that the Reichstag representatives would be sent home while new elections would follow. In addition, freedom of assembly was prohibited, making it immediately more difficult for would-be opponents to meet and organize any type of open protests against the Hitler government. Watching the events, an author for the newspaper *Der Israelit* argued that Hitler and his colleagues would not be able to fulfill any of their anti-Semitic promises to their Nazi supporters: "they not only cannot do this because many other crucial factors hold their powers in check, ranging from the Reich president to some of the political parties affiliated with them, but they also clearly do not want to go this route,"[23] because they must act as a European power. This was the tenor of many Jewish leaders' voices, urging watchful waiting, not overly optimistic but also believing that Hitler would be subject to the system of checks and balances of the government, which would constrain him.

Not all Jewish leaders responded in the same way. One writer for a Zionist newspaper, on February 3, 1933, wrote of the ever-present reality of anti-Semitism in Germany: "Quite apart from the fact that Jews are being systematically shut out of economic and cultural life, anti-Semitism has come to dominate the psychological atmosphere. This actually also has the effect that the Jew again knows he is a Jew, for no one lets him forget it."[24] The author continued on, urging German Jews to join together, to hold their heads high, to draw together in solidarity for the Jewish cause. In this writer's mind, Jews had to recognize that assimilation had failed and promises of integration were only dreams. This article was seen as a response to the CV's reaction to the news of Hitler's appointment, which put forward the idea that Jews should remain calm and restated the view that Jewish rights would be protected by the constitution.[25]

Placing their faith in the constitution and the laws of Germany, many Jews as well as gentile Germans were unprepared for what followed. On the night of February 27, 1933, the German Reichstag building was engulfed in flames. The Prussian Minister Without Portfolio and Nazi Party leader, Hermann Göring, appeared at the scene of the fire. Amid the fire trucks, police officers, and crowds of onlookers, Göring announced that this fire was supposed to signal a Communist uprising throughout Germany. He claimed he had proof of this conspiracy to unseat Hitler before the chancellor could really begin to govern. The proof of the conspiracy was a young man, Marinus van der Lubbe. Lubbe was pulled from the burning building, covered in soot and ashes, and when his pockets were searched, the police found that Lubbe was a card-carrying member of the Dutch Communist Party. Lubbe, who seemed to be half-crazed, was whisked away and, following a trial in Leipzig, was executed. Hitler met with Göring and, as the fire was still smoldering at the scene, Hitler announced a new, emergency decree.[26]

The decree of the Reich president, "Law for the Protection of the People and the State," stated that now, in such a time of crisis, many of the freedoms that had been granted to German citizens by the Weimar constitution were going to be "temporarily suspended." What did this mean to average citizens? It now meant that freedom of speech, freedom to assemble publicly, freedom of the press were all curtailed. It also meant that now an individual could be arrested, taken into police custody, and be denied access to family members, a lawyer, or a judge. It also stipulated that the arrested individual was not entitled to a speedy trial—in fact, they were not guaranteed that there would ever be a trial at all. The government reserved the right to tap people's phones and listen to their conversations and they could open people's mail—all without obtaining a warrant first. The government could also confiscate a person's private property.

This decree was sold to the German public as only a temporary measure during a crisis; however, it is worth noting that this decree was never rescinded. With the passage of such a decree, historians such as Detlev Peukert have argued that this marks the very beginning of the "atomization" of society. Using the positive language of "protection" the Nazi regime enforced their power through the use of intimidation and the threats of violence. Many Germans—both Jews and gentiles—now opted to keep their opinions about the Nazi regime to themselves out of fear of arrest and indefinite imprisonment. For those who had placed their hopes in the checks and limitations placed upon Hitler's power, this was truly a troubling sign.

The Nazis used the Reichstag fire to silence some of their most organized opponents—not the Jews, but another group of "outsiders," the Communists. In the early morning hours of February 28, the new government ordered the arrests of approximately 4,000 German Communists. This should not have been a shock to German's military leaders as Hitler had told them in an earlier meeting in February, "Complete reversal of the present internal political situation in Germany. No tolerance for activities of any kind of ethos that opposes the objective. Those who will not let themselves be converted must be made to bend. Extermination of Marxism, root and branch."[27] Göring had also made his position clear regarding those who opposed Hitler's new government, telling German police on February 17 to "oppose the operations of subversive organizations with the sharpest methods" and "when necessary, ruthlessly make use of firearms."[28] Göring also deputized 50,000 members of the SA, SS, and Stahlhelm to function as auxiliary police officers.[29] For those who were arrested following the fire, they could expect to be beaten with truncheons, rubber hoses, leather belts, and whips. They could expect to be tortured and some were murdered. For Jews arrested during this time, their arrest was linked to their being classified as Communists, not as Jews specifically. However, a Jew accused of being a Communist could expect to be charged with committing "high treason." Marion Kaplan's work *Between Dignity and Despair* tells the story of a Jewish father and daughter who were arrested. They were suspected of being "leftists" because they had been taking pictures at a socialist demonstration.

> Officials confiscated her camera and jailed her. She recounted: "The women were put in the same room as female criminals. They were not beaten, they could read books and write letters, but they heard the screams of men being tortured." After three weeks both she and her father were freed. The father had been tortured to such an extent that the cleaners asked if the man whose suit they were cleaning had been hit by a car.[30]

Despite such terror, the new elections to the Reichstag on March 5, 1933, did not produce a total victory for the Nazi Party, proving that even Hitler at this point in time still needed conservative nationalists in his cabinet. Meanwhile the violence and acts of intimidation continued on the streets of Germany. In Königsberg on March 7, 1933, the old synagogue was lit on fire. In the following days a number of Jewish stores were also lit on fire. Some of the SA men in the town then grabbed Max Neumann, a local film theater manager. They beat him so badly that he later died of his injuries.[31] On March 11, 1933, the Prussian political police received a telephone call from Breslau's Police Superintendent. The superintendent reported:

> Early this morning the peace and quiet of Breslau was disrupted by the SA, which forcibly entered Jewish department stores and shops. The police were brought in and quietly restored order, dispersing the SA. There were no incidents. The department stores have now "voluntarily" closed until Monday. The SA also forced its way into the District Court and Local Court, and dragged Jewish lawyers and judges from their offices. Once again, the police was deployed.[32]

The telephone report continued, describing further acts of intimidation, stating that "the SA put up roadblocks on all the larger highways today around Breslau. Automobiles departing Breslau were halted and searched by the SA, apparently to prevent Jews from leaving the city...." The local leader of the SA told the Superintendent that the SA would not stop its actions as "he is obliged to further the forward advance of the national upsurge."[33]

By early March 1933 various SA and other Nazi leaders had established what were called "wild camps." These would be the forerunners of the concentration camp system. Although Jews as Jews were not being targeted for arrest, that did not mean that the daily terror felt by so many was any less frightening. Report after report came in to local police stations all across the nation, telling authorities that the SA, SS, and other Nazi Party men were going to push their agenda further. The phrase used by the thugs in the street was that Jews were being taken into "protective custody," implying that they were doing the Jew in question a favor by taking them into their control. From Dortmund: "on the afternoon of 28 March 1933, 100 Jews in Dortmund were taken into protective custody by the SA."[34] From Oberhausen: "On 28 March 1933 Jewish shops were closed by deployment of sentries outside. Five Jews, including the rabbi, were led through the streets, preceded by placards. Another four Jews, including the Local District Court councilor Dr. Asch, were taken into protective custody by SA men...."[35] These types of reports, that prominent Jews, rabbis, lawyers, and business owners were being targeted by the SA abound. In addition, in many police reports, destruction of Jewish shops, particularly by smashing windows of storefronts, was an almost daily occurrence throughout the country. The dominant feeling in this growing atmosphere of lawlessness for most Jews was fear. A Jewish woman living in Nuremberg said, "The most frightening fact at this moment was being deprived of the protection of the law. Anybody could accuse you of anything—and you were lost."[36]

By March 23, 1933, Hitler felt confident enough with his position to put forward a new decree, "the Enabling Act." In this decree, Hitler, as chancellor, would be able to pass laws in the Reichstag without receiving the Reichstag's approval. In fact, this would make him the legal dictator of Germany—but only if the politicians in the Reichstag consented to the measure. Sadly, only one man, the leader of the Social Democratic Party, Otto Wels, was courageous enough to stand up and denounce the proposal. He and Hitler locked eyes and Wels urged all parliamentary members to vote "no." He made allusions to the terror being inflicted on political opponents and he encouraged the representatives to maintain their honor and dignity. When the vote was taken, all of the SPD delegates had voted "no" but the rest of the Reichstag members had voted "yes." Hitler was now the legal dictator of Germany. Consolidation of power would continue on. For many Jews, the Enabling Act did not alter very much for them in the sense that they were still being subjected to random acts of violence, intimidation out in public even though Hitler had called for "the strictest and blindest discipline" and prohibited "isolated actions" as an affront "against the national government."[37] That might have given some Jews hope that Hitler was against such acts of violence; however, they could not know that behind the scenes, Hitler was planning a much more coordinated act in the pursuit of his own anti-Semitic agenda.

The first phase of Nazi anti-Semitic policy

Between March 26 and 28, 1933, Hitler held meetings in Munich with various Nazi regional leaders. The meetings were designed to outline a plan for a nationwide boycott of Jewish owned shops. The ultimate aim was to strangle Jews economically in the hopes that life would become so untenable for Jews that they would be forced to leave the country. On March 28, Hitler issued an appeal to all organizations within the Nazi Party to boycott the Jews; part of his appeal stated, "After fourteen years of inner conflict, the German Volk—politically overcoming its ranks, classes, professions, and religious divisions—has effected an uprising that put a lightning end to the Marxist-Jewish nightmare.... National Socialists! Saturday, at the stroke of ten, Judentum will know upon whom it has declared war."[38]

In this appeal Hitler argued that Jews were involved in a conspiracy to smear Germany's name abroad, that Jews in Germany were traitors to the Volk, and that they were working to destroy Germany's economy. Again we can see how both sides of Hitler's agenda came together: on one hand, he was calling on all German Volk to unite, but they are asked to unite in a negative way, fighting against the Jews. The Volksgemeinschaft would be built only through this bonding experience.

Originally the appeal was to call for a boycott that would last for a week; however, in the end, the official boycott itself lasted only Saturday,

FIGURE 4.2 *SA men on April 1, 1933, in Berlin, Germany, distributing boycott pamphlets to passers-by. The sign held by one of them reads: "Attention Germans! These Jewish owners [five and dime] stores are the parasites and gravediggers of German craftsmen. They pay starvation wages to German workers. The chief owner is the Jew Nathan Schmidt." United States Holocaust Memorial Museum, #77490. Courtesy of National Archives and Records Administration, College Park.*

April 1, 1933. Throughout Germany, bands of SA thugs and members of the Hitler Youth (HJ) placed themselves in front of Jewish businesses, attempting to stop would-be customers from going inside to shop. Countless store windows had the Star of David painted on them so that passersby could see that the store was operated by Jews. Still other stores' windows were smashed and some stores were looted. Stories also surfaced of Jewish men wearing their German First World War uniforms, standing silently at the entrances to their stores to remind people that they, too, were German and had risked their lives for their nation. One woman, Olga Eisenstädt, stood outside her small shop on April 1, saying to anyone who would listen, "I was a soldier's widow, that I had received the Emperor's Service Cross in the First World War and the Cross of Honor for soldiers' widows from Hindenburg ... I had taught hundreds of soldiers' wives and widows [how] to make supplies for the army."[39]

Mally Dienemann wrote in her diary of her reactions to the April 1 boycott: "I thought, how unvarying is our fate; now we are [supposedly] harming Germany with fairy tales about atrocities, while in the Middle Ages it was we who were supposed to have poisoned wells, etc.... Could people really do this to each other? And why, why?"[40] In the aftermath of the official boycott, Jews were left wondering how people could actually believe the propaganda that the Nazis had unleashed against them. They might have taken some heart, however, in the sense that the average German did not necessarily support the boycott. In fact, some Jewish businesses and doctors' offices reported an upsurge in business on April 1. Sarah Gordon argues that the boycott had to be rescinded after its first day mainly due to the apathetic response of Germans. They were simply not interested in participating in large numbers in this shameful act, although many were against it simply because it threatened the overall economy of the country. While this response is gratifying on some levels, in some ways it gave German Jews a false sense of hope. Perhaps "good" Germans were still out there, and that Hitler wouldn't be tolerated in power much longer. For Jews, holding onto these hopes could have life threatening consequences. Underestimating Hitler, as so many others did, many Jews thought he would soon be gone from power; instead, government-sponsored anti-Semitic actions were only just beginning, as Hitler now began to pursue his "anti-Semitism of reason" through the passage of legislation.

On April 7, 1933, the "Law for the Restoration of the Professional Civil Service" was announced. This was to be the very first anti-Semitic law of Hitler's regime. Section 3 (1) stated, "Civil servants who are not of Aryan descent are to be retired."[41] That same day the "Law Regarding Admission to the Bar" also announced that lawyers of non-Aryan descent "may be denied admission to the bar," while it also provided for the revocation of lawyers already practicing.[42] Civil servants in Germany at this time included government bureaucrats, postal workers, teachers, and many other professional people.[43] Immediately the Nazi regime had to follow these laws up with a legal definition of "non-Aryan descent." On April 11, 1933, the decree said, "A person is to be regarded as non-Aryan if he is descended from non-Aryan, especially Jewish, parents or grandparents. It is enough for one parent or grandparent to be non-Aryan." The decree continued, "If Aryan descent is doubtful, an opinion must be obtained from the expert on racial research attached to the Reich Ministry of the Interior."[44]

Once these decrees were promulgated, a flood of anti-Semitic legislation followed, further attempting to separate German gentiles from Jews. For some Jews the new decrees, which made them social outsiders, were simply too much to bear. Suicides among Jews following the boycott and subsequent laws climbed to 300–400 in the months of April and May 1933 alone.[45] Fritz Rosenfelder, a Jew living outside of Stuttgart, found that his sports league had decided to exclude "non-Aryans." For Rosenfelder this was too much to bear and he resolved to kill himself. He wrote a letter to his friends:

A German Jew could not bear to live, knowing that the movement in which the people of Germany place their hope for the future views him as a traitor to the Fatherland!…and thus I am attempting through my suicide to jolt my Christian friends into awareness. The step I am taking will show you how things look for us German Jews. How I would have preferred to sacrifice my life for my Fatherland!…let the truth be known, help the truth to triumph.[46]

Rosenfelder's suicide note was reprinted in the Jewish press but, a few days later, the local Nazi newspaper picked up the story, "where an author gleefully recommended that other Jews follow Rosenfelder's example."[47]

As these anti-Semitic pieces of legislation were decreed, Jewish life was dominated by knowing what the latest, newest restrictions were. Teachers lost their jobs, as did many lawyers and judges. Universities were told to adopt restrictive quotas. School children came home with cuts and bruises as they faced not only anti-Semitic teachers but also school bullies. Outside of Frankfurt, in Fulda, a young Jewish boy was attacked by an "Aryan" child. The "Aryan" spat in the Jewish child's face and shouted, "Damned Jew, aren't you out to Palestine yet?"[48] That same Jewish boy's father saw two German women reading *Der Stürmer* which contained Nazi allegations of Jewish ritual murder. He heard one remark to the other, "Isn't that horrible…. And it must be true otherwise the Jews wouldn't stand for it!"[49] Images and stereotypes of Jews from medieval times forward now abounded in Nazi newspapers. The German Jew who had converted to Protestantism, Victor Klemperer, witnessing the boycott and its after effects remarked, "I have also truly felt myself to be German. And I have always imagined the twentieth century in central Europe is something different from the fourteenth century in Rumania. Mistake."[50]

Klemperer, who was married to an Aryan woman, astutely recognized how thin the layer of civilization went. For many German Jews, in such desperate times, a warm greeting from a neighbor, or a seemingly sympathetic smile from a person on the street, could buoy one's sagging spirits at least temporarily. But Jews in Germany were beginning to experience what many historians call "social death." Suddenly colleagues no longer worked side by side with Jews, neighbors who used to chat over garden plots or fences stopped speaking to one another, invitations to celebrations no longer appeared. Marta Appel, from Dortmund, used to meet with her non-Jewish friends in a café on a regular basis but in this growing atmosphere of fear, she had stopped attending their weekly get-togethers. She ran into one of these friends who begged her to come and join them at their next meeting. Marta agonized whether she should go or not. She overcame her fears and went to the café:

> It was not necessary for me to read their eyes or listen to the change in their voices. The empty table in the little alcove which always had been reserved for us spoke the clearest language … I could not blame them. Why should they have risked losing a position only to prove to me that we still had friends in Germany?[51]

The Nazi regime was already working in April 1933 to ostracize Jews. The basic premise was simple and straightforward: if a German did not know any Jews well or intimately, then presumably that same German would not care what was happening to Jews. The Volksgemeinschaft was growing stronger in its identity as discrimination and persecution of Jews was largely accepted and continued.

Throughout the rest of 1933, German Jews were exposed to further restrictions, most of which were designed to harm Jews economically and then, by extension, socially. If Jews could not maintain their standard of living, they would have to move to cheaper places where there would be no longstanding neighborly connection. German Jews found that even if they could stay in their neighborhood, their gentile neighbors had already begun to separate from them:

> But after some months of a regime of terror, fidelity and friendship had lost their meaning, and fear and treachery had replaced them … With each day of the Nazi regime, the abyss between us and our fellow citizens grew larger. Friends whom we had loved for years did not know us anymore. They suddenly saw that we were different from themselves. Of course we were different, since we were bearing the stigma of Nazi hatred, since we were hunted like deer.[52]

Alongside the Nazi decrees seeking to place limitations upon Jews, random acts of violence continued with the aim of publicly humiliating Jews at every turn. In Kassel, in the summer of 1933, the local government reported that a number of Jewish men had been gathered up and accused of having sexual relations with Aryan women. "Before being handed over to the police, the Jews in question were paraded publicly through the streets. This was accompanied by repeated spontaneous anti-Semitic demonstrations by the agitated crowd. The Jews were taken into protective custody and released a few days later."[53] These types of public spectacles, which almost always drew a crowd of curious onlookers, were done deliberately. The public shaming of men and women who had refused to discontinue their friendships flew in the face of Nazi logic. Displays of public humiliation such as these were designed to warn anyone who might still be considering maintaining their friendship with a Jew that today it was that group of men shamed, but tomorrow it could be you. But if one left one's Jewish friends behind then an Aryan could settle into the welcoming embrace of the Volksgemeinschaft.

Further exclusions against Jews and policy setbacks

Although the year 1934 saw no further anti-Semitic decrees, Jews were still going through the process of exclusion and impoverishment. Great emphasis was placed upon removing Jewish involvement in the German economy. The "Aryanization" of Jewish businesses was already taking place as many Jews were pressured into selling off their companies at a fraction of their true value. Schools also continued their drive to further isolate Jews from non-Jews, forcing many children to attend all-Jewish educational facilities. Many German Jewish women, mostly from middle class families, now took on new roles within their families. Since Nazi propaganda tended to focus more on stereotyping Jewish men, it seemed somewhat more possible for Jewish women to "pass" as Aryans out on the streets. Due to worsening economic restrictions, many Jewish women had to earn money for their families now that the men's employment was curtailed. This changed the dynamics within Jewish families, most of which had been patriarchal in structure, but women still had the challenge of convincing their husbands to go along with a woman's request. For some women, they sensed the growing danger more quickly than did their husbands. The men didn't see the younger children coming home in tears, they did not experience the awkwardness or outright rudeness at the local shops. Some women tried to convince their husbands it was time to leave Germany but Marion Kaplan's research has shown that in most German Jewish households the decision to emigrate still tended to rest with the husband.[54]

In some ways, 1934 was a difficult year for Hitler to achieve his policies. In foreign policy he had experienced his first major setback. The Nazis had a branch of the party in Austria; many of the Austrian Nazis were pushing for the annexation of their country to Germany. The Austrian chancellor,

Dollfuss, was a supporter of fascism, but of the Italian kind, not the German variety. Behind the scenes, Hitler was encouraging the Austrian Nazis to put pressure on Dollfuss to violate the Treaty of Versailles which had expressly forbidden the unification of Austria with Germany. Dollfuss vehemently refused. In 1934, Austrian Nazis burst into Dollfuss's office and shot him in the neck. As he lay bleeding to death on the couch in his office, it appeared that Hitler might get his wish of annexation. However, Benito Mussolini, wanting to impress the Western world with Italian greatness, intervened in the crisis. He mustered Italian troops to the Brenner Pass and told Hitler that annexation of Austria was forbidden by the Treaty of Versailles. Hitler backed down.

This issue of Austrian unification with Germany was a loss for Hitler in the short run; however, he derived other benefits in the long term. After Mussolini had challenged Hitler and forced him to back down, the Italian leader had anticipated more respect from the Western powers of Europe. Mussolini was grossly disappointed in the Western powers' responses, so after this event, Mussolini began to draw closer into a "friendship" with Nazi Germany. Ultimately this shift in alliances would result in the 1936 Rome-Berlin Axis treaty whereby the pact of friendship between the two fascist states was solidified. Although relations between Germany and Italy were improving in 1934, there were other internal problems Hitler thought he needed to address. The most pressing issue by the summer of 1934 for Hitler was what to do about the rising power of the SA and its calls for further revolution within Germany.

The Night of the Long Knives

The leader of the SA was a man named Ernst Röhm. Röhm had been with Hitler and the NSDAP since the 1920s and had successfully built up the SturmAbteilung (SA), known for their brownshirt uniforms. Röhm was a populist who would take any and all men who were willing to engage in the brutal street fighting of the day. It was the SA who provided the bulk of the muscle power for Hitler as he rose to prominence. It was also the SA who were incessantly engaging in Jew-baiting and outright murder of Jews. By the summer of 1934 rumors were spreading that perhaps Röhm and the SA would push further in their quest for more power, and it was said that they might be interested in supplanting the regular German army with the SA leader in charge. German officers came to Hitler and demanded that he restrain Röhm. They wanted Hitler to make a clear choice: either it was the regular German army or the SA. Hitler made his choice.

On the night of June 30, 1934, Hitler authorized a competing Nazi paramilitary force, the Schutzstäffel (SS), to round up Röhm and other top SA leaders for execution. This murderous event, sanctioned by the chancellor of the country, was called "Night of the Long Knives." Not only were SA leaders killed, but former chancellor Kurt von Schleicher and his wife were murdered in their home, as was Nazi member Gregor Strasser. Franz von Papen's private secretary was killed, as were many leaders of Catholic organizations.

What is perhaps the most shocking element in this story is how the German public responded; according to Ian Kershaw in *The Hitler Myth*, Hitler's popularity increased dramatically despite his open acknowledgment of ordering the murders. In a speech Hitler delivered on July 13 to the Reichstag he claimed that seventy-four had been shot (it was much higher than this):

> If anyone reproaches me and asks why I did not resort to the regular courts of justice, then all I can say is this: In this hour I was responsible for the fate of the German people, and thereby I became the supreme judge of the German people. It is no secret that this time the revolution would have to be bloody; when we spoke of it we called it "The Night of the Long Knives." Everyone must know for all future time that if he raises his hand to strike the State, then certain death is his lot.[55]

Here Hitler was making it very clear that he would be the one to determine how violence was to be used in the state; he later threw in the comment that Röhm had to die since he was a homosexual. Röhm was indeed a homosexual—Hitler had known that for years—but now, when it was politically useful, Hitler argued that Röhm insulted German womanhood by preferring men. This was just an added bonus to Hitler's rationalization for these violent acts. The final reward for Hitler came from the regular German army: they swore an oath of loyalty to protect the person of the Führer. This would have long-lasting consequences as many soldiers in later years would refuse to join in any plot to assassinate Hitler because they had sworn to protect him.

For the Jews in Germany, 1934 was a year to regroup and consider how their lives had already drastically changed. With the lack of further anti-Semitic restrictions, many Jews became more hopeful that perhaps Hitler was in fact more moderate and once the Night of the Long Knives had occurred, hadn't Hitler shown them that he was against the thuggish behavior of the SA? Again, this contributed to a fatal underestimation of what Hitler was all about. Jews were no different than most other people who believed that Hitler was simply an extreme conservative nationalist and now that men such as Röhm had been destroyed, things might in fact settle down. Jewish life was adjusting to the restrictions of 1933 and the separation between Germans from Jews was still proceeding apace.

Nazi secret reports on Jewish activities in 1934 are replete with statements such as the one from Aachen: "During the course of this month in the local region, the Jews have not been conspicuous, except in the district of

Scheiden. They live completely among themselves and are active principally in their own associations...."[56] While Jews continued to experience social isolation, reports also gleefully mentioned:

> In the rural communities, propaganda against the Jews has strengthened. In some localities, signs proclaiming "Jews not wanted here" and "Jews— entry prohibited" have been placed at the entrance to the locality and mounted on houses. In some localities, hatred against the Jews has increased significantly because their consequent bearing and behavior also lacked the requisite reserve. As a result, there have also been attacks on Jews.[57]

Some of these secret reports also contain proof of the growing divide between police and the Jewish community: "The openly demonstrated self-assurance, aplomb, and purposeful activity of the Jews can act to spark ill-feeling in the population. In all parts of the Reich, this ill-feeling is manifested in violent attacks, placing the police in the unpleasant position of having to protect the Jews and their property against the incensed population...."[58] Despite these signs of growing animosity toward Jews, some still remained optimistic. In an article written by Jacob R. Marcus entitled "Will German Jewry Survive?," Marcus responded to the question of German Jewry's future. He answered:

> German Jewry has the will to survive. It is exerting every effort possible to human beings to maintain its vitality in the face of overwhelming odds.... The lesson of Jewish history lends us further assurance that, barring wholesale expulsion or massacre, which seem rather remote even under the implacable hatred of the National Socialists, what has been called the "Jewish genius for survival" will manifest itself in Germany.[59]

Although some Jews had reason to hope that they had lived through the worst the Nazis had to give, they could not know that changes were being made at higher levels that would dramatically impact the relationship between Jews and the Nazi State. In April 1934 Heinrich Himmler took over the secret police (Gestapo) and he delegated the day-to-day running of the office to the brutal Reinhard Heydrich. Heydrich also headed the powerful SS intelligence gathering agency, the Sicherheitsdienst (SD, or Security Services). Heydrich, nicknamed the "Blonde Beast" by his colleagues, immediately contacted Jewish representatives of the CV, ordering them to desist from collecting information regarding anti-Semitic activities across Germany. This was followed by another order instructing CV members to stop submitting reports to authorities about attacks on Jews or their property.[60]

1935: Calls for increased anti-Semitic legislation

In an ominous sign of things to come, a January 1935 secret report was submitted to the Chief of Police in Berlin. This report, reviewing Jewish activity from November and December 1934, claimed that Jews were becoming more aggressive in denouncing the state; they were supposedly overheard sharply criticizing National Socialist structures and leaders. The author of the report concluded the following: "very large segments of the population do not comprehend why the authorities are exercising such restraint in dealing with this aggressive behavior."[61] The increasing demands for more anti-Semitic restrictions were coming from many segments of the population, arguing that Jews were becoming "haughty" once again and had the temerity to request that they receive compensation for economic damages committed against their property. "Generally the reports on the Jews note that they are now much more self-assured than before. Jews who believe somehow that they have suffered economic damage report this now directly to the Reich economic ministry in Berlin. In any event, unfortunately once again, the Jew is rather optimistic about his future in Germany."[62] In addition to reports on prevailing moods throughout Germany, Nazi newspapers such as *Der Stürmer* and *Der Angriff* began demanding further separation between Germans and Jews. One authority declared, "But it is in any event intolerable that we still have any Jewish judges at all in the German courts."[63]

As more calls went out to Hitler that further measures were desired by the German population against the Jews, Hitler prepared for a foreign policy success. In January 1935, the people of the Saar were scheduled to vote in a plebiscite whether they should revert to German control or officially join France. This was part of the hated Treaty of Versailles's stipulation that France had the right to occupy this industrialized region of Germany for fifteen years. Ninety-one percent of the vote went for German reincorporation. The vote on the Saar would also have an impact on Jews. Many of those Jews who had been living under French law in the Saar endorsed the status quo—meaning that they preferred to remain in French hands. This view was expressed by the Reich League of Jewish Combat Veterans and the CV's branch in the Saar.[64]

For Jews living within Nazi Germany, reports began to surface that Jews were celebrating the Saar results for Germany by displaying Swastika flags over their homes as well as at their businesses. Again, there was a public outcry that Jews were behaving in inappropriate ways: "On the occasion of celebrations for the Saar victory, many Jewish stores and private homes displayed the swastika flag, hoisted by Jews, and this has resulted in a certain sense of unrest in the population. Since according to National Socialist principles, Jews do not belong to the Volksgemeinschaft."[65]

Throughout the early months of 1935 increasing voices were added to the claim that Jews were, once again, trying to reassert their "dominance" in German life and culture, "…in their behavior, which is becoming even more haughty by the day. They cannot and do not wish to comprehend that they are only aliens in the Third Reich. Their intent basically is to slowly steal their way back once again into the Volksgemeinschaft."[66] For adult Jews, negotiating the public spaces of life was becoming increasingly questionable in the face of these complaints. There was great uncertainty about where one could still go and whether it was possible to have a "normal" life at this time. Jews noticed that now just stepping outside meant having to decide how to say "hello." By 1935 most Aryan Germans insisted on using the "Heil, Hitler" greeting, official letters were signed "With German greeting," and Hitler Youth regularly paraded through the streets singing songs that included lyrics such as "Jewish blood spurting from the knife." In addition to these daily stresses, parents were increasingly taking note that German schoolteachers were joining the NSDAP, ostracizing and humiliating their children. One teacher, named Lukas, told his seven- and eight-year-old pupils the following:

> The Jews are cheats. It is because of the Jews that we now find ourselves in a battle for the Saar. The Christian children should tell their parents not to buy anything from the Jews. The Jews pulled out the Christians' legs and arms. The Jews should pack up their bundles and go to Africa or Spain with their Jewish teachers. He would much rather teach without any Jews.[67]

By March 16, 1935, Hitler was ready to violate yet another portion of the Treaty of Versailles. He announced the reintroduction of conscription to the military, a clear violation of the treaty's clause limiting the German army to no more than 100,000 men. The Western powers did nothing in response to the violation and by June 1935 Germany had concluded a naval treaty with Great Britain. These successes only augmented support for Hitler. Some German Jews thought conscription might be a welcome opportunity to demonstrate their love for their country. One Jewish group wrote:

> In this important moment in world history, in which the German Reich has reclaimed its military sovereignty, we young German Jews also feel the urge to express our support for this development. Just as our fathers fulfilled their clear duty to the Fatherland between 1914 and 1918, we also declare our willingness to serve, in line with our motto: Ready for Germany![68]

Any hopes that some Jews may have harbored regarding military service for Germany, however, were dashed when the May 21, 1935, law announced conscription excluded all "non-Aryans."

As the spring and summer turned to fall, increasing numbers of anti-Semitic incidents were reported, local agitators appeared to stir up populations, and papers such as *Der Stürmer* continued on with their calls for further restrictions against Jews, peppering their articles with stories denouncing "white Jews," i.e., those individuals who continued to sympathize with the plight of the Jews. Police were now intervening at much slower pace whenever violence and abuse against Jews was occurring. The police would show up late, after much of the destruction had already been accomplished. Numerous reports began to appear asking the Nazi state to clarify what police officers were supposed to do when Nazi Party activists were targeting Jews—not because the police felt great concern for the Jews, but because they worried that they might fall into the category of "white Jews" when they enforced the law. One report from Kassel asked for just such clarification as the police officers found it "embarrassing," "because when they must act under orders to protect Jews, they acquire the name, against their will, of being Jew friends."[69]

By September 1935, Hitler was ready to address some of the issues being raised about the proper way to deal with the "Jewish Question." At the annual NSDAP rally in Nuremberg, the regime announced two very important laws which would set the tone for further social isolation and ostracism of the Jewish population. The first law, "Reich Citizenship Law," stipulated that after September 15, 1935, "A Reich citizen is only that subject of German or kindred blood who proves by his conduct that he is willing and suited loyally to serve the German people and the Reich."[70] This law now meant that German-born Jews could be banned from citizenship within their own nation. The next law, "Law for the Protection of German Blood and German Honor," announced on the same day as the citizenship law, made marriage between Jews and non-Jews illegal. It also made extramarital intercourse between Jews and non-Jews against the law. This would be called "Rassenschande," or race defilement, if an Aryan were to engage in sexual acts with a Jew. Jews were also forbidden to fly the flag of the Reich or display the colors of the Reich (black, red, and white). In addition, Jewish households could no longer employ German women as servants unless they were over the age of 45.[71] These laws are typically grouped together and simply referred to as "the Nuremberg Laws." Taken together, these laws were designed to further drive home the point that there was a line dividing Germans from Jews. Again, Hitler believed that if no German Aryan knew a Jew well or intimately, then that German would be indifferent to whatever fate befell the Jews.

Luise Solmitz, married to a converted Jew, heard the announcement of the Nuremberg Laws and recorded in her diary how the new rules would impact her small family. She and her husband had one child, a daughter named Gisela, and Luise immediately recognized that their daughter, categorized as being "half-Jewish" would now be "an outcast, excluded, despised, deemed worthless. A mother has to suffer this. No career, no future, no marriage. Whatever the children of relations and acquaintances or [even] our domestic help are entitled to do, the things they aspire to and can achieve—these are things that G.[Gisela] has no chance of attaining."[72]

For some Jews, there was the recognition that they would not be permitted to fully participate in the life of their own country. For still other Jews, there was a tendency to interpret the Nuremberg Laws as clarifications that now German Aryans and German Jews could coexist, and the hope was that violence against Jews would finally come to an end. Willy Cohn, after listening to Hitler's broadcast on September 15, 1935, wrote in his diary about Hitler's remarks: "although he said that the Jewish people had caused all the problems plaguing the German people, he believed that the Reich government had taken measures that would lead to a tolerable relationship between the German and Jewish people."[73] A few days later Cohn wrote, after reading the news reports, "On an uplifting note, Jews were recognized as a people. And with this any future for assimilationists in Germany has definitively disappeared."[74] As Cohn and Solmitz's remarks indicate, Jews were struggling to interpret what these new restrictions would mean in their everyday lives in Germany.

Immediately following the announcement and posting of these new restrictive laws, reports were sent from various regions throughout Germany trying to capture the public reaction to the news. One report wrote that the new laws "have sparked a mood of depression among Jews, since they see themselves excluded in actual fact from the Volksgemeinschaft by these measures."[75] Still another noted the satisfaction of the general population with the Nuremberg Laws, noting that Jews were becoming more reserved in their behavior once again,[76] and the hope was repeatedly expressed that these laws might result in an upsurge of Jewish emigration. Alongside these types of reports were demands that still more restrictions be placed upon businesses run by Jews and that "Jewish cattle dealers" be subject to more control out in the countryside.[77] In addition to these claims, there was a massive uptick in accusations of race defilement in 1935.

In the racist thought of 1935, Jewish men were all potential sexual predators, looking to seduce or rape Aryan women in order to pollute their blood. This was despite the fact that most images of Jewish men in Nazi propaganda had portrayed them as weak, cowardly, and effeminate. These images of sexual predator remained.[78]

Particularly in cases of "race defilement," crowds would gather while the victims of the accusations were publicly humiliated. In many cases the accused victims were made to wear signs around their necks with statements such as "I gave myself to a Jew-pig," or "I defiled a German maiden." In these situations, the power of the perpetrators was further stoked by the excitement of the crowds for such a spectacle. Historians such as Ian Kershaw, David Bankier, Sarah Gordon, and Otto dov Kulka have debated the level of involvement of these crowds, but even if one was a passerby, that individual was now complicit in the action.[79] The more these types of events occurred and then were photographed and printed in the Nazi press, the more the Volksgemeinschaft was involved in the emotionalism of anti-Semitism. Once a person had witnessed one of these public shamings even silently choosing not to intervene meant that that person was guilty of complicity. What many Nazi leaders realized was that a person did not have to be the active fanatic causing the actual suffering, but they could simply be onlookers who, by doing nothing, were now bound to the community of common guilt. This made many people less likely to offer vocal opposition to Nazi policies since they were already guilty to a lesser extent of standing by while others suffered. Here one can see the combination that Hitler had recommended in 1921: emotional anti-Semitism from the masses combined with the "anti-Semitism of reason" in the form of the "Blood and Honor laws."

As accusations of alleged affairs between Aryans and non-Aryans intensified, the Nazi Party began to publicize the names of Aryan women who were thought to be having affairs with Jewish men. In Breslau, this developed into a public ritual whereby on each Sunday in the mid-afternoon, Nazi SA men would shout out the names of the accused women and then march to the old pillory where the list of names were then posted. The pillory was then guarded by SA men so that no one could tear down the list.[80] One woman actually brought charges against the SA for putting her name on the list but the Breslau district court rejected her claims, stating, "the concept of race defilement referred not only to the 'sexual union of an Aryan female with a non-Jewish male and the other way around'" but "also [to] every other friendly interaction insofar as it extends beyond the framework of pure business."[81] Here again, the public played an essential role. The research of Robert Gellately into the actions of the Gestapo in Würzburg has revealed that 54 percent of cases of alleged "race defilement" came from the general public, which then forced the police to investigate the claims.[82] Like a vicious cycle, the media reported the upsurge of predatory Jewish males, the public saw race defilement in the mere hint of a friendship between a Jew and an Aryan, and denunciations flew.

The practice of public shaming at the pillory was a longstanding tradition from medieval Europe forward in time. The association of shame with the loss of honor was deeply embedded in these traditions. By targeting Aryan women, the Nazis were using the age-old notions that a woman's honor rested on her sexual chastity. She was to be virginal until marriage, then remain steadfast in her sexual relationship with only her husband. If a woman was accused of sexual impropriety, she brought dishonor upon not only herself, but also upon her father or husband as well. Ute Frevert calls this a "double violation of honor."[83] The male relative's reputation was damaged as well by his connection to the shamed woman. To Michael Wildt, "'honor' was in fact a suitable medium through which to impose the 'Volksgemeinschaft.' There is virtually no other concept that reveals more clearly the nexus between language and the practice of social power."[84]

FIGURE 4.3 *Decorative sign in a public park in Berlin, Germany, from 1937. The sign reads: "Citizens protect your public spaces. Keep your dogs on a leash. The yellow benches are for Jews (in accordance with the Reich's laws) for their free use." United States Holocaust Memorial Museum, #64462. Courtesy United States Holocaust Memorial Museum, Provenance, Julien Bryan Archive.*

By November 1935, the Nazi regime decided that they needed still further clarifications of the Nuremberg Laws. Supplementary laws were then added to determine who was and was not legally a Jew. According to Nazi definitions, a Jew was a person who had three or four Jewish grandparents. A "Mischling" (mixed race) person was someone who had only one or two Jewish grandparents. However, further classifications were needed to decide just how "Jewish" a Mischling actually was. So, for example, with a mixed race person had "two Jewish grandparents who had in some form demonstrated allegiance to the Jewish religion (e.g., paying their state-collected church taxes to the Jewish community), or if, on September 15, 1935, they were married to a Jew, then they would be deemed Jews themselves."[85] These supposed "clarifications" revealed the complexity of categorizing people and the Nazis fused ancestry, religious practice, and social criteria[86] in order to carry out their discriminatory practices.

Likewise, amendments were added to the "Blood and Honor" law which, if possible, made the question of marriage even more complex. Mischlinge who had only one Jewish grandparent could not legally marry either full Jews or other mixed race people. That implied that the people placed into this category could legally marry Aryans. Yet, if the Mischling had two

Jewish grandparents, then they needed special permission to marry either Aryans or Mischlinge with only one Jewish grandparent. The bottom line of these supplementary laws was that it was increasingly clear that Jews were not a part of the Volksgemeinschaft and relationships between Aryans and Jews were now to be ended. To Hitler, this was a perfect way not only to segregate the Jewish community from the larger Aryan community, but also as a way to further divide Jews against themselves. Now, a hierarchy of "Jewishness" was enshrined in the law—were you a "full Jew," a "half-Jew," or a "quarter-Jew?" Depending on what category a person was placed in, different restrictions applied, so Jewish unity was shattered as there was no sense of a "shared fate."[87]

Further decline in Jewish-German relations

From this point in time on, the Nazi regime did not enact nationwide anti-Semitic legislation until 1938. However, it would be a mistake to portray these intervening years as ones of peaceful coexistence where Jews enjoyed a modicum of legal security. This theory, once advanced by Uwe Adam, that Jews had a respite from Nazi terror tactics is now seen as outdated.[88] So what was happening to Jews between 1936 and 1938? In 1936 Heinrich Himmler was made Chief of the German Police as yet another part of his duties. Now Himmler could use the regular German police when he wanted to enact Nazi policies within the guise of the law, and when he needed to work outside of the law, he could use his SS troops. For Jews this would mean they could not rely on police assistance in any immediate sense. Once again, public actions such as taking Jewish men forcibly out of their places of business and marching them through the streets, often resulted now with the police only intervening once most of the violence had been enacted. The Jews were generally then taken by police into "protective custody" to save them from the crowds' hostility.

Hitler's popularity among the Aryan population was a high point in 1936, particularly since he violated the terms of the Treaty of Versailles in March 1936 by marching German troops back into the Rhineland towns. People living in these areas had not seen German troops stationed in their towns since 1919 and now, on one Saturday morning, military marching bands accompanied the troops while crowds turned out to enjoy the festive spirit. The French were incensed at this direct violation of the treaty; however, they did not want to challenge Hitler's government singlehandedly. When they looked to the British government for support, there was no desire to take action. Victor Klemperer wrote in his diary: "A new act of 'liberation' by Hitler, the nation celebrates—what is internal freedom, what do we care about the Jews?"[89]

Nothing breeds success like more success. In the immediate aftermath of Hitler's wildly popular move to "protect" Germany's western border, Reichstag "elections" were held on March 29. In some towns, potential voters who attempted to avoid casting a ballot were "escorted" by SA men to the voting booths. In other towns, voters did not even bother to use booths. Some districts reported 100 percent voter turnout with 100 percent of the votes cast for the Führer.[90] Public intimidation was an ever-present reality. In one small town of 800, thirteen residents had actually voted "no." A few days after this, a straw effigy was strung up on a tree with a sign around its neck, "13 traitors to the Volk."[91] For Jews, the constant calling for boycotts, public insults, and attacks continued unabated in this atmosphere. By the summer of 1936, Hitler would find a new way to warn the Volksgemeinschaft about the dangers posed by "world Jewry" and that would be the outbreak of the Spanish Civil War.

The Spanish Civil War had erupted in July 1936 and Hitler had quickly agreed to send aid to General Francisco Franco's rebellious forces. Nazi propaganda portrayed the civil war in Spain as a struggle for either Christianity (Franco's side) or "Judeo-Bolshevism" (the Spanish Republic's side). *Der Stürmer* was replete with images of supposed Jewish Communists fighting to destroy Spain's Catholic churches, murdering countless Catholic clergy, and raping Spanish nuns. Joseph Goebbels, the Nazi Minister of Propaganda and Enlightenment, ordered the Nazi press to refer to the Spanish Republican side as "the Bolshevists." At the annual September Nuremberg party rally Goebbels warned that Europe might never recover from a Bolshevik victory in Spain. The *Völkischer Beobachter* reported on September 11, 1936, that Goebbels had described Bolshevism as "pathological criminal nonsense, demonstrably thought up by the Jews."[92]

Hitler picked up this same theme at the rally, stating:

> What others profess to not see because they simply do not want to see it is something we must unfortunately state as a bitter truth: the world is presently in the midst of an increasing upheaval, whose spiritual and material preparation and whose leadership undoubtedly proceed from the rulers of Jewish Bolshevism in Moscow. When I quite intentionally present this problem as Jewish, then you, my party comrades, know that this is not an unverified assumption, but a fact proven by irrefutable evidence.[93]

Like a page ripped out of the forged *Protocols of the Elders of Zion*, Hitler's goal was to convince the Volksgemeinschaft that there was now an existential threat to Germans in the form of the Spanish Civil War. Jews were at the heart of the destabilization and bloody fighting that threatened to turn the world to chaos. The mayor of Freiburg, assessing the mood of his citizens, wrote in his report: "One exception here though are the events in Spain. The course of the struggle by the Spanish people against the Jewish-Marxist-Soviet bands of murderers is the focus of the greatest attention in all segments of the population."[94] In Bavaria, the political police attended a Catholic Workers Association meeting in September 1936. They were there to test the political reliability of Catholics and were impressed by the local monsignor's address. Monsignor Peter Balleis took his listeners on a "Church Historical Stroll through Spain." In his lecture the priest denounced Jews as pests "feeding on the body of the people and the authors of all revolutions." He spoke against baptized Jews, arguing that the holy baptismal waters would not alter "Jewish characteristics" and "Once a Jew, always a Jew, even if he adopts another religion." In conclusion, Father Balleis stated "that Germany was finished and done with the Jews, Bolshevism, Communism, and godlessness, and the events today in Spain proved just how correct the actions of the government had been."[95] The report ended with the comment that the end of the sermon was greeted with loud applause.

The impact of the Spanish Civil War has generally been considered by political and military historians in light of the benefits Hitler derived from the conflict. The historians note how Hitler drew into a closer alliance with Mussolini in their common fight against "Bolshevism" in Spain. They also note the new alliance between Germany and Japan, the Anti-Comintern Pact, which united Japan with Germany in their quest to end the spread of communism. Military historians point to Hitler using the Spanish Civil War as a testing ground for German soldiers and for new weaponry. At any given time throughout the three years of civil warfare, Germany had approximately 5,000 soldiers rotating in and out of the conflict in Spain. All of this is true, but what tends to be overlooked is how Hitler was offering the events in Spain as "proof" to the Volksgemeinschaft at home that he was, in fact, correct. Jews were trying to sow discord throughout the world. They were involved in a worldwide conspiracy to upset the balance of power in Europe, and this threat might spill over into Germany if General Franco's forces, with the help of Nazi Germany, did not win the conflict.[96]

This emphasis on pending world disaster, perpetrated by the Jews, was presented everywhere throughout Nazi Germany. *Der Stürmer's* display cases were filled with photographs of destruction in Spain, and Goebbel's Ministry of Propaganda published *Das Rotbuch über Spanien* which was filled with photos of Jewish artists, authors, and political figures alongside pictures of anti-religious, pornographic, and communist magazines published in Spain. Chapter titles continued to inflame the public's fear of a potential Jewish-Bolshevik victory. Titles such as "Documents of Terror and Degeneracy," "Mass Terror," and "The Path to Power: Soviet intervention in Spain" reinforced the Nazi argument that Jews in Spain, whether they were liberals or outright communists, had been destroying Spanish society for decades.[97]

Goebbels followed up on this success with a thirty-six-page booklet, *The Truth about Spain*. It became one of his bestselling works in the Third Reich. In the short work, Goebbels argued that Bolshevism was linked to Judaism, stating that "the internationality of Bolshevism" was mainly "determined by the Jews. As a Bolshevist the Jew is indeed the incarnation of all evil."[98] His proposed solution to end the spread of "Judeo-Bolshevism" was Hitler. Only Hitler could take on this crusade and win, thus saving Western, Christian civilization from absolute destruction.

By placing the civil war in such apocalyptic terms, Jews in Germany would be seen as even more threatening to the continued existence of the German people. This led to an increase among German community leaders to demand that Jews be removed from their villages, towns, or cities. By 1937 the SD was proposing, in its January 1937 report on the Jewish Problem, "a dejudification of Germany. That can only come to pass if the Jews in Germany are stripped of any basis for an effective livelihood, their possibility for economic activity."[99] Jews understood that the depiction of the war in Spain now meant further burdens for them at home in Germany. Mally Dienemann noted in her diary entry in September 1936: "This week was the [Nazi] party convention, which gave us something to read. Why actually this identification of Bolshevism and Jewry? ...Today during the speech of H [Hitler], I thought, if there is a war, it will start with the extinction of the Jews."[100]

Many histories portray 1936–1938 as relatively "good years" for the Jews in Germany, primarily because they have focused on Germany hosting the 1936 Berlin Olympics, but it would be false to portray these years as anything other than an increasing radicalization of mistreatment toward the Jewish community. As bad as things were, however, the year 1938 would bring even worse conditions for Jews.

For your consideration

Below is the twenty-five-point program of the National Socialist German Workers' Party (NSDAP) which Hitler announced at the February 24, 1920, mass meeting of approximately 2,000 early followers. As you read the points, realize that this party platform would never be altered. What kind of constituents do you think Hitler was trying to appeal to? Do you see any evidence of Hitler's promise to build a Volksgemeinschaft? Do you see evidence of anti-Semitism?

The Program of the German Workers' Party is limited as to period. The leaders have no intention, once the aims announced in it have been achieved, of setting up fresh ones, merely in order artificially to increase the discontent of the masses, and so ensure the continued existence of the party.

1 We demand the union of all Germans to form a Greater Germany on the basis of the right of self-determination enjoyed by nations.

2 We demand equality of rights for the German people in its dealings with other nations and abrogation of the peace treaties of Versailles and Saint-Germain.

3 We demand land and territory (colonies) for the sustenance of our people and for settling our excess population.

4 None but members of the nation may be citizens of the state. None but those of German blood, whatever their creed, may be members of the nation. No Jew therefore may be a member of the nation.

5 Anyone who is not a citizen of the state may live in Germany only as a guest and must be regarded as being subject to legislation governing aliens.

6 The right to determine the leadership and laws of the state is to be enjoyed by citizens alone. We demand therefore that all public offices, of whatever kind, whether national, regional, or local, shall be filled only by citizens. We oppose the corrupting parliamentary practice of filling posts merely with a view to party considerations and without reference to character or ability.

7 We demand that the state shall make it its first duty to provide the opportunity for a livelihood and way of life for citizens. If it is not possible to sustain the entire population of the state, foreign nationals (non-citizens) are to be expelled from the Reich.

8 Any further immigration of non-citizens is to be prevented. We demand that all non-Germans, who have immigrated to Germany since August 2, 1914, be forced immediately to leave the Reich.

9 All citizens must have equal rights and obligations.

10 The first obligation of every citizen must be to work with his mind or with his body. The activities of the individual may not clash with the interests of the whole, but must proceed within the framework of the community and be for the general good.

We therefore demand:

11 Abolition of incomes unearned by work

Abolition of the Slavery of Interest

12 In view of the enormous sacrifice of life and property demanded of a people by every war, personal enrichment through a war must be regarded as a crime against the nation. Therefore we demand the total confiscation of all war profits.

13 We demand nationalization of all businesses that have previously been formed into trusts.

14 We demand a division of profits of large businesses.

15 We demand a generous extension of old-age benefits.

16 We demand creation and maintenance of a healthy middle class (Mittelstand), immediate communalization of large department stores and their lease at low cost to small firms, and that utmost consideration be given to all small firms in contracts with the state, district, or municipality.

17 We demand a land reform suitable to our national needs, provision of a law for expropriating without compensation land for public purposes; abolition of interest on land loans, and prevention of all speculation in land.

18 We demand struggle without consideration against those whose activities are injurious to the common interest. Common criminals against the nation, usurers, profiteers, etc., are to be punished with death, whatever their creed or race.

19 We demand that the Roman law, which serves a materialistic world order, be replaced by a German common law.

20 The state is to be responsible for a fundamental reconstruction of our whole national education program, to enable every capable

and industrious German to obtain higher education and subsequently advancement into leading positions. The curriculum of all educational establishments must be brought into line with the requirements of practical life. Comprehension of the concept of the state must be the school objective…, as early as the beginning of understanding in the pupil. We demand education of the gifted children of poor parents, whatever their class or occupation, at the expense of the state.

21 The state must see to raising the standard of health in the nation by protecting mothers and infants, prohibiting child labor, increasing physical fitness by obligatory gymnastics and sports, and by extensive support of clubs engaged in the physical development of the young.

22 We demand abolition of a mercenary army and formation of a national army.

23 We demand legal opposition to conscious political lies and their dissemination through the press. In order to facilitate creation of a German national press we demand:

(a) That all editors and employees of newspapers appearing in the German language must be members of the race;

(b) That non-German newspapers may be published only with special permission from the state. These may not be printed in the German language.

(c) That non-Germans shall be prohibited by law from any financial interest in or influence on German newspapers, and that the penalty for violation of the law shall be closing of any such newspaper and immediate deportation of the non-German concerned. Publications which infringe on the national welfare are to be prohibited. We demand legal prosecution of all artistic and literary forms that have a destructive effect on our life as a nation, and the closing of organizations which contravene the requirements mentioned above.

24 We demand freedom of religion for all religious denominations in the state so long as they do not endanger it and do not oppose the moral feelings of the German race. The Party as such stands for positive Christianity, without binding itself confessionally to any one denomination. It combats the Jewish-materialistic spirit within us and around us, and is convinced that a lasting recovery of our nation can only succeed from within on the principle: The general interest before self-interest.

25 That the foregoing may be realized, we demand the formation of a strong central power in the Reich; unlimited authority of the central parliament over the entire Reich and its organizations, and the formation of corporate and occupational chambers for the execution of the Reich laws in the various states of the confederation.

The leaders of the party promise, if necessary by sacrificing their own lives, to secure fulfillment of the foregoing points.

Excerpt from Roderick Stackelberg and Sally A. Winkle, eds.,
The Nazi German Sourcebook: An Anthology of Texts, *64–66.*

Below is an excerpt from the April 7, 1933, "Law for the Restoration of the Professional Civil Service." This was the first piece of anti-Semitic legislation passed under Hitler's regime. The first part of the law, not shown here, stipulates who is legally considered to be a part of the civil service and the law also states that the Reichsbank and the German Reich Railroad Company are also supposed to enforce the new law. In paragraph 2, civil servants hired after November 9, 1918, are to be dismissed if they lack proper training. Who is impacted by this new law? Who is exempted from dismissal? Why? What do you think the title of the law shows?

Law for the Restoration of the Professional Civil Service:
3 (1) Civil servants who are not of Aryan descent are to be retired; if they are honorary officials, they are to be dismissed from official status.
3(2) Paragraph 1 does not apply to civil servants who have been officials since August 1, 1914, or who fought at the front during the World War for the German Reich or her allies, or whose fathers or sons were killed in action in the World War. Further exceptions may be permitted by the Reich Minister of the Interior in agreement with the minister concerned or by the highest state agencies for civil servants working abroad.
Paragraph 4 Civil servants whose political activities to date afford no assurance that they will at any time unreservedly support the national state may be dismissed from the service. Their prevailing salaries will be continued for the duration of three months after dismissal. Thereafter they will receive three-fourths of their pension and corresponding survivors' benefits.
Paragraph 8 Civil servants retired or dismissed under Paragraphs 3 and 4 will not be granted pensions unless they have completed at least ten years of service.

Excerpt taken from Lucy Dawidowicz, A Holocaust Reader, *38–39.*

Suggestions for further reading

James Bernauer and Robert A. Maryks, eds., *"The Tragic Couple:" Encounters between Jews and Jesuits* (Boston, MA, 2014).
Lucy S. Dawidowicz, *The War against the Jews, 1933–1945* (New York, 1975).
Lucy S. Dawidowicz, *A Holocaust Reader* (West Orange, NJ, 1976).
Max Domarus, *The Essential Hitler: Speeches and Commentary*, ed. by Partick Romane (Wauconda, IL, 2007).
Richard J. Evans, *The Coming of the Third Reich*, Vol. 1 (New York, 2004).
Richard J. Evans, *The Third Reich in Power*, Vol. 2 (New York, 2005).
Saul Friedländer, *Nazi Germany and the Jews, 1933–39* (New York, 1998).
Derek Hastings, *Catholicism and the Roots of Nazism: Religious Identity and National Socialism* (New York, 2010).
Ian Kershaw, *Hitler: Hubris* (vol. 1) and *Nemesis* (vol. 2) (New York, 2000).

Ian Kershaw, *The Hitler Myth: Image and Reality in the Third Reich* (New York, 2001).

Ian Kershaw, *Popular Opinion and Political Dissent in the Third Reich, Bavaria, 1933–45* (New York, 1985).

Otto dov Kulka and Eberhard Jäckel, eds., *The Jews in the Nazi Secret Reports on Popular Opinion in Germany, 1933–1945*, translated by William Templer (New Haven, CT, 2010).

Jürgen Matthäus and Mark Roseman, eds., *Jewish Responses to Persecution*, Vol. 1, *1933–38* (Lanham, MD, 2010).

Jan Nelis, Anne Morelli, and Danny Praet, eds., *Catholicism and Fascism in Europe, 1918–45* (Hildesheim, Germany, 2015).

Leon Poliakov, *A History of Antisemitism*, Vol. 4, *Suicidal Europe, 1870–1933* (Pennsylvania, PA, 2003).

Alan E. Steinweis, *Studying the Jew: Scholarly Antisemitism in Nazi Germany* (Cambridge, MA, 2006).

Michael Wildt, *Hitler's Volksgemeinschaft and the Dynamics of Racial Exclusion: Violence against Jews in Provincial Germany, 1919–1939* (New York, 2012).

5

Turning Points

*Outcast, outlaw ... that's the only fate left to the two of us,
the realm that will remain for us.*

LUISE SOLMITZ, DIARY ENTRY FOR 27 APRIL 1938[1]

Introduction

As we saw in the previous chapter, Jewish life in Nazi Germany was deteriorating at a steady rate. In individual localities, signs were posted by local officials in the Nazi Party forbidding Jews' entrance to certain stores, restaurants, movie and concert theaters, and public swimming pools. Yet, for some members of the Volksgemeinschaft, these restrictions were not seen as going far enough. In an National Socialist German Workers' Party (NSDAP) local press officer's report from Münster, the officer noted:

> Among the Volksgenossen, if you listen attentively, very often the question is asked: How is it possible that we still can run into Jews in movie theaters ...? In the view of the prevailing popular mood, it would probably be useful and appropriate here for the press to use its influence to spread the idea that the motion picture theater owners can no longer demand of Volksgenossen that they watch films as part of an audience together with Jews.[2]

The years 1936–1938 were marked by actions such as these, again reinforcing the notion that to create the Volksgemeinschaft, anti-Jewish actions were required. As Germany moved closer to starting the Second World War, further anti-Semitic actions would be taken to solidify the Volksgemeinschaft.

Who belongs in the Volksgemeinschaft?

During these years, Aryan families found to be "healthy" were granted rights and privileges that were denied to "unhealthy" Aryans, Jews, and many other outsiders. Once again, these public policies reinforced the point that the Volksgemeinschaft was only for Aryans and even on that point, only for those deemed physically and mentally fit. Nazi-run agencies discriminated against anyone outside of the narrowly defined Volksgemeinschaft by offering aid and assistance programs only to those who were deemed "worthy." For example, the Nazis had begun a heavy propaganda campaign to promote the image of "kinderreich" ("child-rich") families. They differentiated between large families who were "hereditarily valuable" to the Volk, while denigrating "Grossfamilien" ("large families") who were considered not fit to reproduce.[3] On July 14, 1933, Hitler's new regime had passed the "Law for the Protection of Hereditarily Diseased Offspring." This might imply that the government was going to sponsor programs which would prevent things such as birth defects through better prenatal care of expectant mothers, but instead the law listed several categories of diseases including hereditary blindness, hereditary deafness, epilepsy, and "feeblemindedness." The argument was that families whose members had been classified with any of these conditions were a weakening element in the Volksgemeinschaft. The law to deal with these conditions was to go into effect on January 1, 1934. This led to the beginning of the forced sterilization program in Nazi Germany.

The government set up "Hereditary Health Courts" throughout the Reich. They were typically run by two physicians and one Party representative (usually a lawyer). This panel of judges would try cases that had been brought to their attention by various authorities including local doctors, nurses, social workers, and schoolteachers. Any one of these authorities could raise red flags about a person's "fitness" and their denunciation would often result in a person being brought before the Hereditary Health Courts. For most of the victims brought before the courts, the verdict of forced sterilization was a foregone conclusion. Men and women of all ages were called upon to appear in the courts, receive the court's verdict, and then submit to the medical procedure. In some cases, young women who desperately wanted to have a child would go out and engage in intimate relations in order to conceive before their scheduled sterilization date. They were gambling that if they showed up pregnant at the time of the procedure, the doctors and nurses would have to let them carry their child to term. They were wrong. An amendment was attached to the law stating that if a woman claimed she was pregnant at the scheduled date for sterilization, the medical staff was to first abort the child and then sterilize the woman. It is estimated that at least 320,000 German men and women were involuntarily sterilized in this program. None of this was hidden from the general population. Instead Nazi propaganda stressed how "compassionate" it was to sterilize these individuals, for the sake of the greater health of the Volksgemeinschaft. Women, in particular, were targeted through radio programs and magazine articles to accept it as part of their "motherly duty" to denounce suspected inferiors. Women were told they were the protectors of the race, and as such, it was their highest duty to think about the good of the community, not the good of the individual.[4] In such an atmosphere, where German Aryans were being encouraged to denounce other Aryans, it does not seem very far-fetched to imagine how attitudes to Jews, already deemed pollutants and defilers, would be enforced.

Large Jewish families had already lost by 1935 the right to any state assistance in maintaining their family. There would be no family allowances for Jews. By 1938, Jews, whether they had a large family or not, were finding it increasingly difficult to subsist in Germany. Social and leisure activities were already severely curtailed. Educational opportunities that might have helped Jews in their professional lives were also shut down. By July 6, 1938, the Nazi regime decided it was time to squeeze out Jewish businesses as completely as they could. They announced the total exclusion of Jews from entire sectors of the business world. That meant that the approximately 3,000 Jewish physicians still in practice in July were now banned from working as doctors;[5] 709 of them were allowed to list themselves as "medical practitioners" but they were only allowed to provide services to Jewish patients. In September 1938 only 172 Jewish lawyers were allowed to practice law throughout Germany. In addition, the law stipulated that Jewish lawyers could only have Jewish clients.[6] In the realm of Jewish businesses, the "Aryanization" of the German economy proceeded apace with these new restrictions.[7] Many business owners were forced to sell their businesses to Aryans for a fraction of the value of the company's true worth. The forced impoverishment of Jews across Germany led many families to absolute despair. One woman, after the family was forced to sell their business, wrote: "When one's livelihood is gone, what remains? Worry, despair, unhappiness?"[8]

The issue of emigration

With the loss of economic power, many Jewish families again revisited the idea of emigrating from Germany. Although Nazi propaganda made it clear that Hitler simply wanted Jews out of Germany, Nazi emigration policies made leaving even more difficult by 1938. The regime had passed what it called a "flight tax" on Jews leaving Germany. Technically the tax was valued at 25 percent of an individual person's accumulated wealth. That meant a Nazi assessor would be sent to examine how much money a person had in the bank, but that same assessor would also decide the value of the furnishings in the Jewish apartment, and the value of the apartment or home (if the family owned it). Essentially the goal for the assessor was to inflate the overall value of all assets so that the Jewish family would be financially ruined if they did try to leave.[9]

Throughout 1938 the government made additional moves against Jewish wealth and property, including putting all Jewish bank accounts under government control while appropriating other portions of Jewish wealth.

As Jewish families were forced to move to lower rent areas, any remaining ties they might have retained with their former mostly middle-class Aryan neighbors were dying. Social isolation was occurring at a much more rapid pace now as more and more Jews withdrew into their own family circles or into Jewish associational life. There really were not many other options available to them. Hilma Geffen-Ludomer felt that an "abrupt" transition had occurred "from a nice neighborly atmosphere to one in which friends and neighbors no longer talked to her."[10] Still another remarked, "It was not a matter of SA brutality or SS terror, it was the organized strength of the Volksgemeinschaft which step-by-step transformed Jews into impotent pariahs."[11]

Lebensraum and the Volksgemeinschaft

The healthy Aryan Volksgemeinschaft was getting stronger, especially in the realm of foreign policy. 1938 was a landmark year for Hitler's successes in violating the Treaty of Versailles. Back in November 1937 Hitler had assembled his highest-ranking military officers for a top secret meeting. One of the men present, Hossbach, later wrote down what Hitler had told these men. In effect, Hitler had reiterated his desire to acquire more "Lebensraum" ("living space") for the German people. He wanted to speed up Germany's armament productions in case future actions resulted in a war. He laid out his plans for conquering and annexing territories in Europe. Only two men present offered some reservations about Hitler's agenda. They happened to be the two highest ranking men on the General Staff, General Werner von Blomberg and General Werner von Fritsch. The two men were not against war—that was, after all, their job—but they did express grave concerns about the timeline, arguing that Germany would not be ready for war until at least 1945. Hitler was furious that these two men had questioned him, and, by 1938, Hitler had had both Blomberg and Fritsch removed from the General Staff. Now he could move forward with his plans of Lebensraum without any "foot-dragging."

First on the agenda was the annexation of Austria. The Treaty of Versailles had definitively closed the door on the possibility of an Anschluss (annexation), but Hitler believed the time was now ripe. He invited the current leader of Austria, Kurt von Schuschnigg, to a meeting in Munich. Schuschnigg was isolated with only German military leaders and Hitler in a remote mountain retreat. Hitler bullied him into agreeing to lift the ban on the outlawed Austrian Nazi Party (since the 1934 assassination of Dollfuss). Schuschnigg was instructed to then appoint an Austrian Nazi leader, Arthur Seyss-Inquart, to lead the new government of Austria. Feeling intimidated, Schuschnigg left the meeting and hurried back to Vienna.

Once he was back in Vienna, Schuschnigg attempted to outmaneuver Hitler. The Austrian leader announced that on March 12, 1938, Austrians over the age of twenty-five would be eligible to vote in a referendum. They would be asked the question: "Should Austria remain independent or should Austria be annexed to Germany?" Hitler was livid when he was told what Schuschnigg was attempting to do. He telephoned Schuschnigg and delivered an ultimatum: either Schuschnigg would resign and appoint Seyss-Inquart in his place or else military invasion of Austria would follow. Schuschnigg conceded defeat. By March 12, 1938, German tanks rolled peacefully across the border into Austria. The new leader, Seyss-Inquart, had asked for German authorities' assistance in this time of "crisis" in Austria. Hitler rode in his open Mercedes-Benz, waving to the jubilant crowds. Schuschnigg might have thought that Mussolini would once again intervene and save Austria from German aggression, but, by 1938, the two dictators in Rome and Berlin had developed a pact of friendship. Mussolini no longer cared to help Austria.

For Hitler, the Anschluss represented yet another surge in his popularity. Once again, he had promised the German people that he would restore their sense of pride in their nation. Germany would rise again from the ashes of humiliation and defeat. Without having to fire a shot, in one Saturday morning, Hitler had thumbed his nose at the hated Versailles Diktat and he had incorporated more ethnic Germans into the Reich. Of course, the Anschluss also brought with it additional problems in the form of Austria's Jewish population, approximately 200,000 in number,[12] but the Nazi regime had a plan for them as well. In fact, reports surfaced very quickly that even before the German army had rolled in to the country, wild pogroms broke out in Vienna where the bulk of the Jewish population lived. Carl Zuckmayer wrote in his autobiography: "On that day all hell broke loose. The Underworld opened its gates and released its lowest, most despicable and unclean spirits. The city transformed itself into a nightmare painting by Hieronymus Bosch.... The air was filled with a relentlessly piercing, desolate, hysterical screeching, coming from male and female throats ... And all people lost their faces, and looked like distorted grimaces; some of them in fear, the others in falsehood, and others in wild, hate-filled triumph."[13] As public violence was enacted against the Jews of Austria, the SD sent in Adolf Eichmann to coordinate the anti-Semitic actions.

Eichmann's assignment was to run the Central Office for Jewish Emigration. His desire was to use Austria as a model of how to properly get rid of Jews. His office single-mindedly stripped Austrian Jews of their property and other assets before forcing them out of the country. A representative to the World Jewish Congress reported on the situation for Viennese Jews, who were "constantly taken out of their homes and forced to clean and scrape the slogans from the walls and sidewalks painted in connection with the Schuschnigg plebiscite. The number of Jewish funerals had risen from an average of 3 or 4 to 140 a day; among them 'suicides and heart failures' are the majority."[14]

An anonymous person reporting to the Jewish Telegraph Agency sent a long list of anti-Semitic actions taking place throughout parts of Germany and Austria at this time. Some of the description is as follows: "Austria. The suffering of Jews in Austria continues to increase. The persecution has no end. On the contrary; it becomes ever more vicious.... During the first days of June, around 10,000 Jewish prisoners from Vienna were taken to Dachau concentration camp. An estimated 6,000 Jews were arrested in Austria during the Pentecost week.... All Jewish lawyers have been forbidden from practicing their profession. They must wind up their business affairs within the next three weeks.... Countless young Jewish academics have been sent to perform forced labor on the floodplain of Styria.... Well-informed circles are saying that the number of Jews who have been driven to suicide now exceeds 6,800 [in Austria]. A furniture dealer in the 2nd district [in Vienna] killed himself along with his spouse, son, daughter-in-law, and 5-year-old grandchild. The next day the SA affixed a poster to his shuttered business reading, 'We strongly urge others to follow his example.'"[15] The violence in Austria continued with further restrictions imposed upon the Jewish community, and some of the actions inspired other European nations to imitate what was being done to the Jews.

In Belgium, a Rexist leader, Leon Degrelle, led an anti-Semitic demonstration, with protesters carrying signs with slogans such as "Jews out!," "Down with the Jews!," and "Let us do the same as in Germany and Austria!" through the streets.[16] In Poland, the ruling party declared: "The Jews were treated as alien, even hostile elements of the state. The main task of the Polish state in the future is to reduce the number of Jews through emigration. On the basis of special laws, the Jews will be removed from those branches of public life in which they still play a role."[17]

In Germany, authorities now set the official deadline of June 30, 1938, for Jews to register all of their property; registration applied to non-Jewish spouses as well. Once the Jews were stripped of their assets, they became an even greater liability to the German state, "dependent on outside support and not one that German government agencies were willing to shoulder."[18] Jews who had lost all means of support had to report for forced labor in order to earn any benefits from the regime. This was done so that all public welfare could go to healthy Aryans.[19] Jewish relief and self-help agencies were overburdened with requests for assistance. Meanwhile entire German villages and towns sought to force Jews out to nearby cities so the local town administrators could declare their area "Judenfrei" ("free of Jews"). The NSDAP covering the district of Königshofen reported in May 1938: "In the past, Königshofen was totally infested with Jews.... Today the Jews have not only disappeared completely from public life, but Adolf Hitler Square is also 'judenfrei', and the former Jewish houses and stores all over Königshofen are now without exception in Aryan hands.... Most of the Jews have emigrated and moved away."[20] The NSDAP officer did not bother to inquire where these Jews had moved to; that was immaterial to him.

Beginning on June 10, 1938, the Berlin regional (Gau) leadership ordered all Nazi Party organizations to carry out a "Jews' action":

> The operation reached its high point on 20/21 June 1938, when all the Jewish shops in Berlin and the signs of Jewish lawyers and physicians were painted over with the word "Jew" and the Star of David. In the course of this action, there was some destruction and plundering of Jewish shops, as well as physical assaults. The action ended on the afternoon of 21 June 1938. It was carried out with authorization by the local Berlin police authorities.[21]

Notice the added point that the Berlin police allowed the "Jews' action" to be carried out. For Jews in Berlin, if they had once placed their hopes on protection by law enforcement, this was clear proof that Jews were now on their own.

To further remove Jews from public life, synagogues in various cities were ordered to be removed. The law was called "Law on the Redesign of German Cities." A place that might have given Jews a sense of refuge and community was now also being taken away from them. The destruction of houses of worship played the role of public spectacle. In Nuremberg, the SD reported on the destruction of the city's main synagogue. The local Gauleiter, Julius Streicher, a notorious anti-Semite and editor of the hate-filled *Der Stürmer*, started off the destruction: "on 10 August 1938: Julius Streicher gave the sign for the tearing down of the main synagogue at Hans Sachs Square.... Tens of thousands of Volksgenossen were present at the historical hour."[22] An earlier SD report mentioned that, once the synagogue was gone, the plan was to build an anti-Semitic museum in the empty lot.[23] As more synagogues were sold to local authorities and razed, Jewish hopes were temporarily lifted with reports of an international conference to be held in Evian, France.

The Evian Conference

In July 1938, representatives of thirty-two countries from around the world assembled in Evian. They were there to discuss the growing refugee crisis as Jews desperately sought to flee the persecution in Germany and Austria. Unfortunately the conference was doomed before it even began. The countries agreed to send representatives but only upon the condition that none of the nations present would be pressured to alter their present emigration policies. Jewish hopes were dashed. The only country to emerge from the Evian Conference offering a refuge for persecuted Jews was a brutal dictator, Trujillo in the Dominican Republic. Trujillo wanted to improve his image after he had ordered attacks on neighboring black Haitians near the Dominican Republic's border. He offered to take in several thousand Jews because they were white and he wanted to ensure that his country would not be confused with Haiti's "blackness."[24]

Gerhard Kann, living in Berlin, wrote to his friend Heinz who was living safely in America. Kann's letter reflected his pessimism following the failed Evian Conference and increased attacks against German Jews:

> Germany, Italy, Czecho-Slovakia [sic] ... the problems are becoming ever more daunting, and the need for an overall solution has continued to grow. The fate of individuals has become unimportant, trivial. And one can only hope that the growth of the masses of people who are uprooted will make the world recognize the Jewish problem as one that it cannot ignore and not just a question that it can gloss over with a few conferences and speeches.[25]

By August 1938, the Reich government decreed a further segregation between Jews and Aryans. The new law regarding "Changes of Family Names" now stipulated that Jews could only name their children certain names that had been pre-approved by the government as "Jewish names." For those Jews who already had names, the law stated that, beginning January 1, 1939, those individuals would have to assume an additional given name. For males, the name would be "Israel" and for females, "Sarah."[26] In this way, every legal document would alert officials that the person with whom they were dealing was a Jew. It was yet another way for the Volksgemeinschaft to further distinguish the "otherness" of Jews.

In the meantime, Heinrich Himmler had ordered round-ups and arrests of people who were not suitable members of the Volksgemeinschaft. In the summer arrests, well over 10,000 people, labeled by the regime as "work-shy" or "asocial," were taken into "preventive custody." "Preventive custody" meant that the regime suspected those arrested of having the potential to commit crimes. Fifteen hundred Jews were included in this round-up. All of those taken into custody were then sent to either Sachsenhausen, Buchenwald, or Dachau concentration camps. These camps were run by Himmler's SS, so German Jewish organizations worked extremely hard to secure the Jews' release, as they suspected that Jews in SS hands were more likely to be killed.[27]

Hans Reichmann, one of the Jews arrested and sent to Sachsenhausen, wrote in a letter: "Since that day my strength was broken.... It was all over. It required no such devastating documentation of my, of our impotence to make clear to me that the fate of German Jews had come to an end. I had known it for a long time, but only now did I feel that my ability to fight back was gone."[28] The Nazis used this June action to strike fear into Jews but, as the Evian Conference had shown, where were Jews supposed to go? What country would still take them in, especially if they had already been rendered virtually penniless by the German government?

Germany inches closer to war

In the heated atmosphere of the summer of 1938, Hitler had made it known that he desired more Lebensraum. This time his sights were set on a portion of land belonging to Czechoslovakia called the Sudetenland. In 1938 there were approximately 3 million Germans living in this region of Czechoslovakia and by most accounts the ethnic Germans living there had been treated reasonably well until the Depression hit. A pro-Nazi party, the Sudeten German Party (SdP), led by Konrad Henlein, openly pushed for cultural and political autonomy for Germans. Privately, Henlein was working to get the Sudetenland annexed to the Third Reich. The diplomatic situation was quite tense and it appeared that Hitler was willing to risk war in order to incorporate more ethnic Germans into his growing Volksgemeinschaft. Behind the scenes, Hitler had ordered his General Staff to plan "case Green," the code name for the destruction of Czechoslovakia.

Amid all of the bellicose rhetoric, Hitler consistently claimed that he wanted only peace. However, the only way he could accept peace would be the acquisition of the Sudetenland. As the crisis deepened, British prime minister Neville Chamberlain flew to Munich to meet with Hitler. They spoke and Hitler seemingly agreed that the crisis could be averted if a plebiscite was scheduled and the people of the Sudetenland could vote on the question of annexation to Germany. Chamberlain flew back to England thinking that his policy of appeasing Hitler was working. Just a few days after Chamberlain's departure, however, Hitler suddenly announced that a plebiscite would be unacceptable. The Czechoslovakian government had begun to mobilize their forces and it appeared that war was coming.

The district governor of Upper and Central Franconia assessed the atmosphere:

> In the days when the threat of war was increasing, the nasty disposition of the Jews was made very manifest. The Jews displayed a behavior that was haughty and provocative, emerging from their otherwise customary sneaky reserve and conniving shyness. One could notice that they were waiting for war, which in their calculations was to bring about the destruction of the Reich.[29]

The report continued, revealing what types of actions Jews were facing as tensions were mounting over the Sudetenland crisis. "As a result of the murders and atrocities perpetrated against Sudeten Germans in Czechoslovakia, there was great indignation in the market town of Bechhofen ... and in Wilhermsdorf.... It was directed against the local Jews. The Jews then left Bechhofen and Wilhermsdorf. These localities are now completely 'judenfrei,' like the entire district of Feuchtwangen."[30]

Prime Minister Chamberlain flew back to Munich once again. Chamberlain put forward another proposal but while he and the president of Czechoslovakia, Eduard Benes, were awaiting Hitler's decision, the Führer made his desires very clear, delivering one of his most famous speeches on September 26, 1938. In the speech, Hitler claimed that his demand for the Sudetenland would be his last territorial request. He thanked Chamberlain for his efforts, stating that the German people only desired peace:

> But in the same way I desire to state before the German people that with regard to the problem of the Sudeten Germans my patience is now at an end! I have made Mr. Benes an offer which is nothing but the carrying into effect of what he himself has promised. The decision now lies in his hands: Peace or War![31]

As Hitler continued to work himself up into a lather, he also managed to work in some oblique references to Jews. Speaking of how Germany had changed since its defeat in 1918, he stated, "If at that time a wandering scholar was able to inject into our people the poison of democratic catchwords—the people of today is no longer the people that it was then. Such catchwords are for us like wasp-stings; they cannot hurt us: we are now immune."[32] He notably used words such as "wandering," "scholar," and "democracy," all of which could be seen as attributes of men such as Hugo Preuss, the author of the Weimar Constitution—and a Jew.

Three days after this powerful speech, a settlement was achieved at the Munich Conference. There, representatives from Germany, Italy, Great Britain, and France met to decide the fate of Czechoslovakia. Mussolini portrayed himself as the "honest broker" and the agreement was made. The Sudetenland would be annexed to Germany. Some guarantees to protect what was left of Czechoslovakia were granted.

On October 1, 1938, German troops marched triumphantly into the Sudetenland. Chamberlain flew back to Great Britain, and as he disembarked from his plane, he was waving a newspaper with the headline, "Peace in Our Time!" In actuality the banner should have read, peace in our time, but only for a bit longer. With the resolution of this conflict, the SD reported on Jewish attitudes: "But the peaceful resolution of the Czech question sparked a strong sense of resignation."[33] For the Jews living in the Sudetenland, there was a scramble to flee the territory before annexation. Swiss authorities, worried that there was a possibility of a mass influx of Jews flooding across their borders, signed an early October agreement with Nazi Germany. All passports of German Jews had to be stamped with a red letter "J" for *Jude* on them. More doors were closing for the panicked Jews.

Further laws restricting what occupations Jews could engage in followed. For example, Jews by early November 1938 were not allowed to work in real estate, as tour guides, as lawyers or doctors, nor could they work as traveling salesmen or peddlers. Jewish organizations were merged together or dissolved altogether. Even more regulations were to follow. What is also so striking is how, even in the wake of the resolution of the Sudetenland crisis, Jews continued to be the focus for punishment, with many Germans blaming the tense atmosphere not on Hitler and the Nazis, but on the Jews. Town after town submitted reports of attacks on Jewish people, on their homes, and particularly on their synagogues. The NSDAP leaders in Windsbach issued a leaflet:

> In the last critical weeks, the Jews had the firm intention of hounding a part of the peoples of the world into a frightful war. The German nation was to be defeated and obliterated. Millions of people were to be slaughtered and murdered. Towns and villages of the German Gaue (regions) were to be destroyed. More than hundreds of thousands of German families would have to face unspeakable suffering. That was the will of the Jews.... Our unshakeable will is: in a short time, Windsbach must be Jew free.[34]

In the words of historian Michael Wildt, "The fact that this inversion of reality was plausible to so many people reveals that they were more willing to accept anti-Semitic justifications and to see or even make the innocent suffer than to question their own worldview."[35] The willingness to make Jews the scapegoat for tensions that had been building to a fevered pitch in the summer of 1938 continued unabated into the fall. The push, according the SD report, was to achieve "the final exclusion of Jewry from all areas of life, with the ultimate goal of their removal from the territory of the Reich, by all means necessary, and in the shortest amount of time."[36]

Forced expulsion

To achieve the goal of expelling Jews as quickly as possible from the Reich, the Nazi regime began a series of forced expulsions in October 1938. Jews living in the Sudetenland were forced to flee into the un-annexed portion of Czechoslovakia, but in late October, the Nazis decided to target Polish Jews living within the Reich's boundaries. For many of these Jews, they had lived in Germany for decades; some had even become German citizens. However, the feeling of the time was that Jews were an "internal enemy" that needed to be removed so that no further danger would come to the Volksgemeinschaft. The reason why Polish Jews were targeted for expulsion was connected to the Polish government's announcement that any Polish Jews wishing to return to Poland had a limited amount of time to re-register as Polish citizens or else forfeit their right to return.[37] The Nazis sought to expel their Polish Jews back into Poland before the deadline had expired.

On October 18, Hitler ordered approximately 17,000 Polish-born Jews to be rounded up and deported. The expulsion was to be sudden, brutal, and thorough. Those being expelled would be allowed to take only one suitcase with them; they had to leave all other property behind in Germany to be taken by the Nazi authorities as well as by their German neighbors. The actual attack, led by the Gestapo and German police, began on October 28, 1938.

Here is how one man, named Zindel Grynszpan, recalled the events:

On the 27 October 1938—it was Thursday night at 8 o'clock—a policeman came and told us to come to Region II. He said, "You are going to come back immediately, you shouldn't take anything with you. Take with you your passports." When I reached the Region, I saw a large number of people; some people were sitting, some standing. People were crying; they were shouting, "Sign, sign, sign." I had to sign, as all of them did. One of us did not, and his name, I believe, was Gershon Silber, and he had to stand in the corner for twenty-four hours. They took us to the concert halls on the banks of the Leine and there, there were people from all areas, about six hundred people. There we stayed until Friday night; about twenty-four hours; then they took us in police trucks,..., to the railway station. The streets were black with people shouting, "The Jews out to Palestine." After that, when we got to the train, they took us by train to Neubenschen on the German-Polish border. It was Shabbat morning.... When we reached the border, we were searched to see if anybody had any money, and anybody who had more than ten marks, the balance was taken from him. This was the German law. No more than ten marks could be taken out of Germany. The Germans said, "You didn't bring any more into Germany and you can't take any more out." The SS were giving us, as it were, protective custody, and we walked two kilometers on foot to the Polish border. They told us to go—the SS men were whipping us, those who lingered they hit, and blood was flowing on the road. They tore away their little baggage from them, they treated us in a most barbaric fashion.[38]

The Polish authorities examined these unfortunate people's documentation at the border. They allowed some to enter across the border, but many others—Martin Gilbert estimates almost 7,000 people—were not allowed to enter Poland. Instead, those individuals had to stay in between the border of Germany and Poland. They had to wait to see whether the Polish government would relent and let them cross officially into Poland. Many of them ended up waiting in a small border town, Zbaszyn. While the Jews awaited word from Poland, at least five people in Zbaszyn committed suicide. There was great distress, hunger, and worry. The Grynszpan family had been expelled but were stuck in the no man's land of Zbaszyn. As they waited and worried, the daughter, Berta, sent a postcard to her brother—a young man studying in Paris, France, at the time of the expulsion. Berta's postcard described their brutal expulsion, writing, "No one told us what was up, but we realized this was going to be the end.... We haven't a penny. Could you send us something ...?"[39] Berta's brother, seventeen-year-old Herschel Grynszpan's reaction to his family's ordeal would make history.

Herschel, furious and distraught, bought a gun on November 6. He also bought five bullets. He then boarded the Metro and went to the German Embassy. Once inside the embassy he claimed he had a document for the Ambassador. Instead, he was shown into the office of the Third Secretary, Ernst vom Rath. As vom Rath stood up to receive the "document," Grynszpan opened fire. He fired all five shots, but only two hit vom Rath. The shots did not immediately kill vom Rath, and as news reached Nazi Germany, Hitler ordered his private physician, Dr. Brandt, to fly to France to help the severely wounded man. By the morning of November 8, the press in Germany was condemning the action in Paris, claiming that this event was "proof" that an international Jewish conspiracy did exist and that all Jews were out to kill Germans.

Immediately the government set punishments in motion. All Jewish children still attending Aryan schools were expelled. All Jewish publications were also banned. That meant that Jewish community organizations would have a next-to-impossible time trying to advise and communicate with other Jews. Finally, all Jewish cultural activities were suspended.[40] That was all done for the public; however, in addition to these punitive measures, Jews who had been kept in the Buchenwald concentration camp for months were executed.[41] In the meanwhile, Goebbels and Heydrich gathered information about "spontaneous" outbursts against the Jews.

The violence intensified when the press reported on November 9, 1938, that vom Rath had succumbed to his wounds. It was a Wednesday evening. The radios went silent for two minutes.[42] Hitler was in Munich on November 9 because it was the anniversary of the failed Beer Hall Putsch of 1923. Each year, the Nazis held a solemn ceremony commemorating the men who had fallen during the attempted coup. Speaking events were planned all over Germany to share in this occasion, but now, with the word that vom Rath was dead, all plans were changed. Joseph Goebbels wrote in his diary that after speaking with Hitler, "He [Hitler] decides demonstrations should be allowed to continue. The police should be withdrawn. For once, Jews should get the feel of popular anger." He added, "I immediately give the necessary instructions to the police and the Party. Then I speak in that vein to the Party leadership. Stormy applause."[43] Goebbels's instructions to police were also given to local fire departments—they were not to interfere unless a burning Jewish structure threatened to spread to an Aryan property. The violence erupted that night, November 9.

Kristallnacht and its aftermath

For many Jews, the events of November 9–10, 1938, marked a turning point in their lives in Germany. The violence was nationwide, so all-encompassing, that one could see why they remembered these events as monumental. The pogrom was called *Kristallnacht* by the Nazi leadership to call to mind the shimmering broken glass of Jewish shops, homes, and houses of worship that now littered the streets in the moonlight. For many historians, the events of Kristallnacht are not necessarily a dramatic turning point in Jewish persecution.[44] As we have already seen throughout the summer and fall of 1938 the mood was ripe for explosive violence and indeed we have seen many acts of destruction—all of which preceded the Night of Broken Glass. It would be useful, however, to remember that Kristallnacht was organized from the top down—from Hitler, to Goebbels, to Nazi Party leaders. This was a massive, government-organized and -sponsored attack on the Jews; this could be why so many German Jews saw the nights of violence as so overwhelmingly shocking. Now it was not just local Nazi Party thugs who were engaging in "random" acts of violence; instead, they understood that this was something the top leaders in the government had ordered. For many Jews, Kristallnacht evoked true feelings of despair, knowing that they were most definitely excluded from being considered German. Elisabeth Petuchowski described her grandfather's funeral following his suicide after he witnessed his business turned to ashes and the arrest of his two sons: "Unable to accept a future not resembling his past, he put himself to sleep forever. During these November days, no Jew dared to leave his house. So there we were... at 5 a.m., the time set by the police for his funeral ... we were horror stricken. Not at his death—what more could now happen to him?—but at our nightmare?"[45] The suicide rate for Jews climbed higher in the wake of the destruction.

When all of the damage was surveyed after November 10, 1938, approximately 7,000 Jewish businesses were destroyed, most synagogues were burned down if they had not already been destroyed or sold off to Aryans before Kristallnacht, and almost 30,000 Jewish men were arrested and sent to concentration camps. At least ninety-one Jews were reported dead, with many more beaten and wounded in the attacks. Individual Jewish homes were invaded by SA and Hitler Youth groups. Margaret Czellitzer, who had stayed away from her home during the violence, returned home afterwards. She wrote:

> I found my radio broken at the garden door, my lovely china smashed all over the kitchen floor, the beds overturned, the mattresses cut into pieces, the paintings as well as all other valuables stolen....We were all heartbroken, but especially myself, who had discovered for us...that lovely place and built our little house according to my own ideas ... You children loved it...., and we spent the happiest time in our lives.[46]

With the destruction of Jewish homes, no Jews could try to ignore what was happening in Nazi Germany. For many, their hope was now to emigrate.

Although the Nazi regime made it clear that all it wanted was for Jews to get out of Germany, the government made it as difficult as they possibly could. Verena Hellwig, an Aryan woman married to a Jewish man, feared for the future of her family, especially that of her "Mischlinge" children. Her husband, near retirement age, did not wish to leave Germany. Hellwig spoke to a Nazi official and he told her that "mixed blood" people (meaning her children) were the greatest danger to Germany. "They should either return to Judaism,…and suffer the fate of the Jews or they should be prevented from procreating, like retarded people."[47] Hellwig had reached her breaking point; she wrote that "Her homeland was lost; Germany was dead" for her.[48] She and her son were able to immigrate to England, then they were later joined by her daughter.[49] She did this to ensure a future for her children.

In order to emigrate, Jews had to negotiate a vast array of obstacles. Some took classes to learn new languages in preparation for their move, others tried to obtain new skill sets to better their chances of employment in a new land. While they pursued courses of study, they also had to obtain visas, affidavits, etc. The government, using the "flight tax" law, also worked to bankrupt Jews before they could leave:

> Many people had to sell all their belongings simply to pay this one tax. Gerdy Stoppelmann, for example, sent her husband, recently released from Sachsenhausen concentration camp, ahead to England while she stayed behind to pay the tax: "To be able to pay the … tax I sold our furniture, valuable paintings and carpets … dirt cheap. Many a home of true Aryans, SA and SS became exceedingly well furnished."[50]

In addition to the "flight tax," the Nazis held up Jewish money in blocked bank accounts. After paying the flight tax, Jews would have to put any residual money they had into a bank account. They could then purchase foreign currency with that money; however, they were given unfavorable exchange rates. This would only last until war broke out in 1939, after which Jews were no longer allowed to transfer money into foreign currency.[51] As if these conditions were not devastating enough, Jews were also victimized by unscrupulous Nazi officials who understood that Jews were powerless in this situation. Some male officials expected Jewish women to have sexual relations with them; one woman "is still thankful today that her mother saved their lives by having sex with a bureaucrat who then provided their exit papers."[52] Other Nazis stopped by Jewish apartments, helping themselves to whatever they wanted. Lola Blonder recalled: "They … took whatever little objects they liked—from the wall … from the tables…. I was used to this by now. Whenever a group of Nazis visited, they helped themselves to… valuables. Robbing! Robbing! Every day robbing me!"[53]

The Nazi regime, however, was not satisfied with individual Jews being further impoverished. On November 12, 1938, a new decree was announced. Called the "Decree on a Penalty Payment by Jews who are German subjects," the law stated: "The hostile attitude of Jewry toward the German Volk and Reich, an attitude which does not shrink even from committing cowardly murder, necessitates determined resistance and harsh penalty."[54] In a gross inversion of reality, Jews were portrayed as the "aggressors" who had caused the destruction of Kristallnacht by the murder of vom Rath. Therefore, the Nazi logic went, Jews, as a community, were penalized for the destruction of their own property. The Jewish community of Germany, by this decree, were now ordered to pay 1 billion Reichsmarks to the Reich. The decree was signed by Göring, who was in charge of the Four Year Plan. Although the German press reported that the Volk were "spontaneously" seeking revenge for the death of vom Rath, it was clear that the government had sponsored the nights of violence. Henry Stern, a fourteen-year-old boy in 1938, remembered:

I was on my way to school when I saw the flames and the smoke rising from the big synagogue.... The fire engine stood by but did nothing. There was a huge crowd of people standing there and I remember clearly that there was a complete silence. (Not a jubilating crowd, as was generally reported in the German press). I, of course was in shock and ran home crying.

Later on, he heard Germans saying quietly: This won't end well, nothing good can come when you burn "Gotteshäuser" ("the Houses of God").[55] Fire trucks as well as police primarily stood by during the destruction, doing nothing to stop the violence.

Nothing good would come of the destruction. One Austrian Jew recalled, "Germany had drawn a strong line of demarcation between itself and civilization."[56] For Jews, one of their main organizations, the CV, was closed. After being in existence for forty-five years, on November 10, 1938, the CV was gone. That meant that the organization's advice on emigration rules and regulations, explanations of new anti-Semitic legislation through its press, and maintenance of Jewish cultural activities was gone. The isolation of the Jewish community would continue with only one official organization allowed to operate on a greatly reduced level, the Reichsvertretung. This would, of course, make it even more difficult for Jews to understand and receive news of further attacks, and the source of information would be limited, adding further challenges for Jews desperate to assess their ever-worsening situation.

Amid the destruction, some countries did respond by allowing an increase of Jews into their countries. Sir Martin Gilbert's work *Kristallnacht* is filled with examples of countries such as Australia and Great Britain allowing persecuted Jews to come into their countries. But, by the end of November 1938, the Nazi paper *Das Schwarze Korps* ran an article, "Juden, was nun?"

("Jews, what now?"). The article predicted the further impoverishment of the remaining Jews and proclaimed "the iron necessity of exterminating the Jewish underworld ... with fire and sword."[57]

Kristallnacht, according to historian Marion Kaplan, marked the "social death" of Jews. Now they were excluded from almost all social aspects of the larger community. As Jewish numbers declined, due to emigration, death, or suicide, the regime's obsession with the potential "Jewish threat" continued to grow inversely to the actual number of Jews left alive in Germany. In the NSDAP Women's Organization in Baden, they held a series of lectures on the topic "Germans Become a Volk." What is very revealing about this topic is that the lectures included: "The Jewish Question," "International Jewry," "Judaism and Freemasonry," "The Impact of the Jews," "World Jewry," and "Racial Awakening."[58] The author of the report, after listing the topics for presentation, ended the report with "... and people here feel very sorry for 'the poor Jews!'"[59]

In some respects, this reveals the new hurdle the Nazi regime had to face, for many SD reports following Kristallnacht's destructiveness show that the general mood of the German public was a mixture of shame, worry about the disruption of the economy, concerns about foreign countries' responses to the nights of violence, and in some cases "pity for the Jews."[60] The local Gendarmie of Muggendorf summed up the local German opinions:

> However, the other segment of the population, far larger, thinks that this destruction was improper and unwarranted. Although the other measures against the Jews meets with approval, the prevailing view when it comes to destruction is that property destroyed should have been preserved, and ought to have been put to good use elsewhere for the benefit of the German people.[61]

What emerges is that the majority of Germans, whether active participants or bystanders to the events of Kristallnacht, agreed that the "worst" aspect of the pogrom was economic wastefulness.

Capitalizing on the idea of confiscating still more Jewish property, the town of Bremen's NSDAP district officer wrote in December 1938:

> Assuming that the Jewish Question is proceeding very rapidly toward a further radical solution, so that in Bremen in the near future there will be hardly any Jews left, it has been suggested that the Jewish cemetery in Hastedt be kept available so that a sports ground can later be set up there for the SA. Likewise, a large part of the cemetery remains unoccupied. Later on perhaps a playground for children could be constructed there.[62]

Although Nazi propaganda stressed that Aryans should avoid coming into contact with all things Jewish, they seemed to have no problem with taking Jewish property and making it their own.

The growing Jewish "threat"

Likewise, as the Jews became increasingly ostracized and disempowered, the Nazi leadership began to stress even more vehemently that the Jews were an even larger threat to the German Volk than ever before. The Gendarmie in Maxdorf concluded, "The popular mood is good and confident. The measures taken by the government against the Jews are welcomed and one can generally hear the comment, 'that should have been done a long time ago': now people are slowly beginning to realize that the Jews have only been a source of misfortune for Germany."[63] The less real power and influence Jews actually had, the more Nazi propaganda emphasized the severity of the "Jewish threat." Hitler, who had remained quiet in public regarding Kristallnacht, was about to weigh in on the "Jewish Question."

On January 30, 1939, Hitler delivered a speech to the Reichstag. In the lengthy address, the Führer "warned" Jews that if a war erupted, Jews would be to blame for its beginning. He also claimed that Jews were standing in the way of the German Volk, providing a litany of German suffering in the twentieth century (supposedly at the hands of Jews), and then he made his "prophecy": "Once again I will be a prophet: should the international Jewry of finance succeed, both within and beyond Europe, in plunging mankind into yet another world war, then the result will not be a Bolshevization of the earth and the victory of Jewry, but the annihilation of the Jewish race in Europe."[64] Here one can see Hitler using not only emotional language against the Jews, but also his "anti-Semitism of reason," when he appealed to the peoples of the world to now engage in a war "devoid of all sense for them, and serving the interests of the Jews exclusively."[65] It is interesting to note Jewish listeners' responses to the speech. Victor Klemperer noted: "Politically everything the same. Germany all-powerful. Spain will soon be finished. Campaign against the Jews further intensified. In his Reichstag speech of January 30 Hitler once again turned all his enemies into Jews and threatened the annihilation of the Jews in Europe if they were to bring about war against Germany."[66] For many Jews, nothing Hitler said in his speech was especially noteworthy; they recognized his speech for its "vicious anti-Jewish rhetoric, but by then they had come to expect as much from Hitler."[67]

While Hitler openly attacked the presence of Jews in the Third Reich, he aggressively began to acquire still more territory. In March 1939 he ordered the destruction of what was left of Czechoslovakia and he annexed Memel, a territory of Lithuania. He then made it clear that Germany needed Danzig and the Polish Corridor. With each successive acquisition, Hitler increased his "Jewish problem." If Germany could not force the roughly 525,000 Jews who had been living in Germany in 1933 to emigrate, then how would they deal with the increase in the Jewish population? According to the SD Main Office summary report, they counted 87,000 Jews from Bohemia and Moravia (both of these regions were incorporated directly into the Third Reich). On the morning of March 15, 1939, the president of Bohemia and

Moravia, Emil Hacha, was brought to Berlin and was told that he had to accept German occupation of the remaining parts of the country. On March 16, Hitler appeared in Prague and declared that these lands "had belonged to the 'Lebensraum of the German Volk' for a thousand years, and that they would henceforth form part of the Greater German Reich."[68] He granted automatic Reich citizenship to all ethnic Germans, but that simultaneously made all Czechs and Jews second-class citizens. Hitler's vision was to move Germans into the region, but in the short term he granted the Czech portions of the country a limited form of autonomy.[69]

On March 21, 1939, President Hacha, allowed to remain in office, ended democracy in the former Czech Republic. He dissolved the parliament and approved anti-Semitic measures. Wolf Grüner estimates that approximately 118,310 Jews or more were living in the recently annexed territories. Anti-Semitic violence erupted in various locations during the annexation, following the similar patterns of burning down synagogues, attacking Jews on the streets, and arresting at least several thousand people. Most of those arrested were sent to concentration camps back in Germany.[70] Jewish facilities and organizations were shut down or they were placed under the control of the Gestapo. Various agencies competed to persecute their Jews. After the initial bursts of violence and "emotional anti-Semitism," the "anti-Semitism of reason" took over: law after law was passed seeking to destroy Jews both economically and socially.

On March 17, 1939, the first anti-Semitic laws were passed, which included prohibiting Jewish physicians and lawyers from having their practices, the marking of Aryan businesses, and the removal of Jews from social organizations and industry.[71] Czech associations such as the police, army, and merchant organizations followed suit and distanced themselves from their former Jewish colleagues. As their economic situation worsened, many Jews wanted to emigrate; however, they were held in place by an order issued by Reinhard Heydrich. Heydrich ordered the Security Police to keep Jews where they were, so as to not interfere with immigration quotas for Jews in the "Old Reich."[72] Here, it would seem that Jews closer to the center of power in Nazi Germany had to be pushed out before Jews living in the outer areas of the Reich were expelled.

Hitler himself claimed that the "Jewish Question" should be dealt with by the Czechs themselves. Groups such as Arisjky Boj (Aryan Struggle) demanded that President Hacha begin ghettoizing Jews. Reich Protector Neurath intervened and passed "Regulation of the Jewish Question" in June 1939, using the German Nuremberg Laws as his model. On the same day of Neurath's order, Heydrich finally established a central office to work on Jewish emigration. Adolf Eichmann, who had organized such work against Austrian Jews, was then transferred to Prague to work on these policies as well. While the Nazi representatives were working to impoverish Jews, the Czech government, chafing under German domination, began to pass their own anti-Semitic legislation, calling for the segregation of Jews from restaurants, swimming facilities, hospitals, and clinics. They also demanded that Jewish businesses be marked.[73] With the Nazi invasion of Poland on September 1, 1939, preparations were made to deport Jews in the Czech territories to Poland. The first transport—of 901 men—left on October 18, 1939. The transports to Poland would be temporarily halted for a variety of reasons, but would resume in 1941.[74]

Jewish life in the heart of Germany

Back in the Old Reich, German Jews were struggling to find ways to adjust to the new restrictions being placed upon them. On January 31, 1939, licenses to practice as doctors, veterinarians, and pharmacists were revoked. By February 23, 1939, Jews were banned from using sleeper and dining cars on all train routes. All Jewish precious metals and stones were to be handed over to the government by March 31, 1939.[75]

Jews who were unable to emigrate had to tackle new religious questions such as how to properly care for the ashes of relatives murdered and cremated by the Nazi regime. Because Jewish law forbids cremation, families asked rabbinic leaders what they should do with the remains. One rabbi, Menahem Mendel Kirschbaum of Frankfurt-am-Main, formulated a policy, called a "responsum," to the queries he was receiving. His answer was made into a leaflet for distribution. He recommended that, upon receipt of the death notice, there should be a seven-day mourning period. The urn containing the ashes should be placed on a bier to maintain the dignity of the deceased. He also included a variety of ways to honor the dead during the burial ceremony.[76] There was a recognition that for those still in German territory, the everyday aspects of life and death had to go on in some fashion. But soon Jews would be deprived of the solace of living in their own homes. On April 30, 1939, a new law was passed which restricted the rights of Jewish tenants. This allowed the government to begin moving Jews into "Judenhaüser" ("Jew houses") where they could be more easily monitored by both the government and the Aryan community. The segregation and isolation of Germany Jewry continued on unabated.

One Jewish organization that was permitted to continue its work in maintaining a sense of Jewish life was the Jüdischer Kulturbund (Jewish Cultural Organization). It was answerable to Nazi officials; however, it did attempt to provide some form of entertainment associated with German culture. Until the start of the war, the Kulturbund continued to offer Jews left in Germany programs put on by Jewish actors for a Jewish audience.[77] Another organization left intact after Kristallnacht was the Reichsvereinigung der Juden in Deutschland. Originally this organization was established to promote emigration; after July 1939, it was also charged with organizing a "Jewish school system" and "Jewish welfare work."[78] The further isolation of the Jews of the Greater German Reich continued, prohibiting Jews from using public pay phones and automatic ticket machines, such as might be found at train stations, going to "Aryan" hairdressers or barbers, or going to "Aryan" spas. This was to drive home to the German Volk that even coming into contact with something a Jew had touched could lead to pollution and corruption. The segregation continued.

Escalation in foreign policy

In August 1939, the world was shocked to learn that the Nazi regime had signed a non-aggression pact with its archenemy: the Soviet Union. Hitler, back in May 1939, had already told his General Staff to draw up "case white," the plans for a military invasion of Poland, but Hitler did not want a repeat of the First World War whereby Germany found itself fighting a two-front war. He decided he needed to neutralize the Soviet Union in order to move against Poland safely. Feelers were sent out to Moscow in June and July to see whether Stalin would entertain the idea of a non-aggression pact.

Stalin, who had been trying to reach an agreement with Britain and France in the face of German aggression, realized that the British and French were not taking his concerns seriously. Joachim Ribbentrop, leading the German Foreign Office, offered to sign a twenty-five-year non-aggression pact with his Soviet counterpart, Molotov, by mid-August. Stalin stalled, hoping for more time and requesting clarification on matters of spheres of influence. On August 20, Hitler sent Stalin a telegram pleading with the Soviet leader to sign the agreement. On August 23, 1939, the Ribbentrop-Molotov Pact was finally signed. Under the agreement, Stalin would do nothing in the event Germany invaded Poland. In the secret protocols attached to the pact, the Soviets were invited to take portions of Poland not wanted by Germany, and the Baltic States were noted as belonging to the Soviet sphere of interest, as was Bessarabia. There were other elements in the protocol as well; particularly noteworthy was the agreement that the Soviet Union would provide some war material to the Nazis.

All people, Jews and gentiles alike, were stunned by this news. The Nazis had earned part of their reputation by engaging in street violence against communists, and now they had reached an accord. At the outset of the Spanish Civil War in 1936, Hitler had declared himself the protector of Western, Christian civilization against the Judeo-Bolshevik threat. Now, with the signing of the pact, Nazi propaganda was recalibrated to portray Jews as capitalistic plutocrats, war profiteers, and exploiters of honest, hardworking Aryans. Karl Marx's "dual image" of the Jew as both capitalist and communist provided versatility for the Nazis. People watched and tried to evaluate the increasingly tense environment. It appeared that a war was indeed looming on the horizon between Germany and Poland. One fifteen-year-old Jewish boy in Poland wrote, "A terrifying, interesting, and strange piece of news. The Germans are concluding a 25-year nonaggression pact with the Soviets! What a turn of events. What a capitulation of Nazi ideology.... Chamberlain called the British parliament back from vacation and convened an extraordinary session."[79]

The original plan for the invasion of Poland was set by Hitler for August 26; however, there was a last-ditch effort on the part of the British and Italians to bring about some sort of negotiated settlement regarding German control of Danzig. Hitler believed that he was a gambler, that the Western democracies were weak, and that the Nazi-Soviet Pact had rendered Poland helpless. At 4:45 a.m. on September 1, 1939, Germany invaded Poland. War had come to Europe again.

The war begins

In the face of the invasion of Poland, new regulations and restrictions were announced for Jews in the Reich. A curfew on Jews was immediately announced. Jews would not be allowed outside between the hours of 9 p.m. and 5 a.m. in the summer and between 8 p.m. and 6 a.m. in the winter. Jews were required to hand in their radios, thus depriving them of the news of the day. Jews also received special ration cards. Jews were further restricted in that there were only a limited number of shops in which they could purchase items. The rationing system meant that limitations were placed on what Jews could actually buy. They were not allowed to purchase fresh fruit or vegetables, with one woman recalling how her four-year-old daughter asked for some cherries, but the mother explained that Jews were not permitted to buy the fruit. The child responded, "I'm fed up with this. I shall go into a church and become Aryan."[80]

As Jews continued their daily struggle to make sense of the events around them, reports noted that "In Worms, segments of the population found it exceedingly unpleasant to observe that the Jews are shopping once more in all stores, with their food ration cards; their comportment is marked by a striking air of security and confidence."[81] Still another reported, "The Jews throughout the district are behaving in an impudent manner. Apparently they are listening to foreign radio stations. It's about time to put all the Jews in a concentration camp and to confiscate their radios."[82] One can see the rising tension with the war, as more and more reports came in accusing the Jews of spying, listening to foreign radio broadcasts, and behaving in a haughty manner. One report simply stated, "As I see it, the time has now come to gather all Jews together, confined in a concentration camp, so that they really will no longer be able to have contact with the German Volksgenossen."[83] Throughout the official reports is the underlying belief that the war was the fault of the Jews—not, of course, Nazi policy. One gendarme simply stated, "Everywhere people have understood that only the Jew, and he alone, bears responsibility for the war."[84]

Biological racism escalates

As Hitler prepared for the war with Poland, he received a letter from a father, Herr Knauer. In the letter Knauer explained to the Führer that he and his wife had just recently had a son. The child was born with missing limbs, and was thought to be blind and mentally retarded. Knauer asked Hitler to grant permission to have his son killed. Hitler sent his personal physician to investigate the veracity of Knauer's letter and told the physician that if he found the child to be the way the father's letter had described, the doctor had permission to perform a "mercy killing." The doctor examined the baby. The child was killed. This set in motion a new phase of Nazi eugenics, one more in keeping with the writings of Hoche and Binding from the 1920s.

Hitler subscribed to the concept of "negative eugenics," meaning that if healthy, "valuable" German men were going to die fighting for Germany in Poland, then something had to be done to "prune" the so-called less valuable people living in Germany. The policy of eradicating "life unworthy of living" would supposedly help to balance out the loss of "valuable" healthy Aryan citizens in warfare. This project, of ridding the Volksgemeinschaft of mentally handicapped and physically disabled children and adults, had its beginning thanks to the escalation of tensions leading to war.

Dr. Theo Morrell advised Hitler that children who were mentally or physically challenged were burdens on their parents. He hinted to Hitler that parents might not object if their children happened to die while in the care of a medical facility, so long as the parents had a clear conscience. This suggestion unleashed what the Nazis termed the "Euthanasia Project." Using the language of "mercy killing" incorrectly, they reasoned that children who were suffering with mental illness or physical impairments could never be valuable members of the Volksgemeinschaft. Hitler often referred to these unfortunates as "useless eaters." The next step was to assemble doctors and administrators to go through collected data on "deformed" and "questionable" births. Thirty or so clinics were established throughout Germany where children denounced as disabled were sent. In some of these clinics, now removed from parental supervision or visits, the staff could slowly reduce the rations, thus starving the children to death. In still other clinics, the preferred method of murder was via lethal overdose. The doctors, nurses, and technicians involved in the "Child's Euthanasia Project" varied their killing methods, but they all agreed that these defenseless children were a drain on the Volksgemeinschaft. They had bought into the idea that, in order for the Volksgemeinschaft to live, others had to die. By the end of the war, approximately 5,000 children had been murdered.[85]

Once the children's euthanasia project was underway, Hitler authorized the adult euthanasia project to begin. The eventual headquarters for the administration of the adult program was in Berlin at Tiergartenstrasse 4. The code name given to this project was, therefore, "Aktion T-4." Dr. Viktor Brack told a meeting of doctors, professors, and law enforcement officers on October 9, 1939, that he had done a calculation. He reasoned that out of every 1,000 German people, 10 of them needed psychiatric care; of those 10, he believed 5 would be hospitalized. Of the 5 who were hospitalized in various clinics, hospitals, and other facilities, one should be killed. Germany's population was roughly 70 million people in 1939, so by his calculations, the regime should be targeting the removal of 70,000 individuals.

Recruitment for the "T-4 Project" was relatively easy. There were many doctors, nurses, technicians, scientists, police officers, and common workers who were willing to work for the project. In fact, according the research of Michael Burleigh, who has tracked almost all of these workers, none of those in the T-4 program were forced to be there. Hitler had also backdated a document to September 1, 1939, calling for the "domestic purification" of Germany. This document was on Hitler's private stationery and was shown to individuals who questioned the legality of the program. To gather the victims, the T-4 personnel sent out questionnaires to each medical facility in Germany. The directors and staff were to fill out a questionnaire for each of their patients and then mail the packet back to the Berlin address. T-4 personnel then distributed the questionnaires to physicians hired to be outside "consultants." These "consultants" never saw the people whose fates rested in their hands. All they had were the completed questionnaires. The "consultants" placed a "+" or a "−" sign in the corner of each document. If there was a "+" then that patient's name would be added to the list for euthanasia.

Since the targeted number of victims was 70,000 adults, the T-4 personnel believed that they could not model the killing process on the children's euthanasia project. It would be too slow, too costly, and some adults might be able to fight the process. The aim was to be able to kill large numbers of adults in an effective and secretive way. To achieve this end, the T-4 personnel developed killing centers. After many discussions about how to kill, it was determined that gassing people would be the ideal method to use. Eight disabled men were brought to a Brandenburg jail where a gas chamber had been constructed. Dignitaries and technicians were present. The men entered the gas chamber, chemists outside injected carbon monoxide through a pipe, and the observers watched through a viewing window. All eight of the men perished. The experiment was deemed a success. Hitler was informed of the experiment's results. He authorized the use of gas as a killing agent. The project then moved forward.

The T-4 Project built six killing centers located in various parts of Germany. Each killing center was run by a chief physician who was assisted by one or two junior physicians. In addition there were also non-medical supervisors, who were usually men recruited from the police forces. All six killing centers were equipped with a gas chamber and a crematorium. There were also reception rooms and housing for the staff. There were, however, no facilities for the disabled patients. They would be killed soon after their arrival. Victims were selected from various hospitals, clinics, and nursing homes all over Germany. They would be loaded onto grey-painted buses and transported to one of the six killing centers. The victims would be met by the chief physician and his staff. The staff verified that the paperwork was in order, and often the victims were photographed before being gassed. After the gassing, the chief physician would declare the victims dead and then the "stokers" would ventilate the chamber, remove the corpses, and cremate the bodies. Paperwork would then be filled out, lying to families, telling them that their mother or father or sister or brother had died of "heart failure" or "pneumonia" or a "burst appendix." Victims' families would receive a box with some ashes dumped inside. The ashes were usually accompanied by a letter warning families not to open the boxes. Some families ignored the notice and opened the box. What some found astonished them. In one case, a family opened what they thought was going to be their father's ashes but inside the box were ashes with lady's hairpins. Their father did not wear lady's hairpins, so whose ashes did they have? Still other families questioned the letter explaining the cause of death—how could their brother's appendix have burst when he had had his appendix removed years before? Rumors began to abound in relation to this project. Children sang songs warning each other to stay away from the grey buses. Anyone living close to one of the killing centers also experienced the overpowering odor of bodies being cremated.

The Nazis understood that the T-4 Project was becoming a "known secret." Men such as Protestant pastor Fritz Bodelschwingh, who ran an institution for epileptics, refused to fill out the questionnaires as he suspected that his answers could result in the deaths of some of his patients. A Roman Catholic bishop, Clemens August Graf von Galen of Münster, collected information from Bodelschwingh and his parishioners. On August 3, 1941, the bishop delivered a denunciation of the government-sponsored killing project at the noon Mass. He went back to the bishop's palace afterwards and waited to be arrested by the Gestapo. The Gestapo never came. It seems that the bishop was too high profile to take action against, Hitler feared that arresting or killing the bishop would turn him into a Catholic martyr. Word continued to spread all across Germany about what the government was doing, yet there was never a mass protest by German people out in the streets. Hitler learned a very valuable lesson from the T-4 Project. If German families did not protest openly when people they professed to love were being murdered by their own government, would they really protest when ostracized, isolated Jews, Poles, Russians, and others were being killed? Following the bishop's outcry, Hitler had the T-4 personnel moved off of German soil. They were sent to Poland to oversee the production of killing centers there.[86]

For your consideration

The following is from the Nazi newspaper the *Völkischer Beobachter*, written by "the Blonde Beast," Reinhard Heydrich. Heydrich was the head of the Security Service (SD) and was the second highest ranking official in the SS (Heinrich Himmler was his direct superior). This article appeared on April 29, 1936. Who does Heydrich portray as the opponents of the Volk? Why does he believe they are opposed to National Socialism? How are all of these enemies connected to one another? How does the legacy of religious anti-Semitism and racial anti-Semitism infect Heydrich's article?

Fighting the Enemies of the State

National Socialism, which led the movement's struggle for power on the basis of ideology, also breaks with the liberalist fight against enemies of the state. According to liberalist thinking, the government only fought against the subversive act and the subversive organization as the group responsible for this act.

For the National Socialist it is these opponents' intellectual forces that are crucial; these we want to identify and strike. We know today that they are always the same ones: the Jew, the freemason, and the politicized cleric. Their goals are the same but their organizational forms adapt to what is legally possible at any given time.

So how does the enemy of the people function today? He tries to fight us by legal means, that is, disguised within the framework of the present realities. Always under the heading, "Everything for the National Socialist Reich," he attempts to use all his powers against us, yet without forming an organization that could be apprehended.

Jewry as such, of course, is not isolated as the Jewish race and Jewish people as a result of the Nuremberg Laws. A direct infusion of Jewish blood into the body of the Volk has thereby been averted. But the indirect Jewish intellectual influence has not been completely stopped by any means. In the first place many in academic and intellectual life unknowingly still carry the residues of Jewish, liberal, and Masonic infection. On the other hand, our own German history has shown us that the Jewish goal always remains the same: world dominance through a more or less visible Jewish elite. And if National Socialist policies make political conditions in Germany unsuitable for the attainment of this goal, the Jew will switch to economic and foreign policies. In economic affairs he has always been about to count on egotistical and traitorous elements as collaborators even in Germany. In foreign affairs the Jew works with those organizations that are already completely under his control, Bolshevism and the Masonic Lodges that are still operating freely abroad.

The Communist, whose core is drawn mainly from the ranks of international criminals and who fights with all the methods of modern technology, is especially dangerous, as he must also be regarded as a spy for Soviet Russia. This makes the anarchist criminal at the same time the most dangerous assailant against the elements of national defense.

Even in Germany the Masonic lodges were never more than auxiliary organizations of the Jews. Their purpose was very gradually and imperceptibly to transform the character and mind of the German according to Jewish ideas. With the exception of a few incorrigibles, all Germans now recognize the hostility of the Jews, Communists, and Freemasons toward the state and the Volk, and they approve of their treatment with no holds barred as enemies of the state and the people. One still encounters a considerable lack of understanding, however, with respect to another enemy of the people and the state, the politicized church official..

Excerpt taken from Roderick Stackelberg and Sally A. Winkle, eds.,
The Nazi Germany Sourcebook: An Anthology of Texts, *194–195.*

Below is a portion of Bertel Kugelmann's work *My Story.* Bertel was a nine-year-old Jewish girl living in rural Hessen when Hitler came to power in 1933. Her family had provided her with a safe existence until that time, but now with Hitler in power, her village life began to change. Even as a child, Bertel could sense that Jewish integration into the German community was fragile. How does Bertel describe what began to happen to Jewish-Catholic relations in her village of Fritzlar? How do old stereotypes about Jews appear in her account? How do her parents assess the danger?

We were Jews and our neighbors Catholics, and during my early childhood that was unexceptional. But soon after Hitler came to power in 1933, things slowly began to change. The non-Jewish children form the neighborhood harassed us. Many of them said, "You are a Jew, and you killed Jesus. I can't play with you anymore." I went home crying and asked my parents what was meant by this accusation. My parents tried to comfort me and told me that we weren't to blame for the death of Jesus.... As the persecution of the Jews began to intensify, and one heard from Jews in nearby towns and villages that they had been beaten, that gravestones were overturned, and that windowpanes had been shattered, Jewish families and some of the [single] adult Jews left their homes and the place of their birth, and emigrated.

My father, Joseph Kugelmann, was a grain dealer, highly respected in the community and also among the farmers in the nearby villages with whom he did business. Everyone knew him and came to him when they needed help. Once, when he gave a surety for one of the farmers, he had to put out a good deal of money in order to free him from his debt. He had served in the German army and fought at the front in France throughout all four years of World War I. His father, my grandfather, had served during the Franco-Prussian War. Both felt themselves Germans, like all other veterans. With their wartime comrades, they were members of veterans' associations and organizations. When my mother pressed my father to leave Germany, he would not listen to her. "Don't get yourself worked up," he said. "Nothing will happen to us. After a little while, Hitler will go away again."

Excerpt taken from Patricia Heberer, Children during
the Holocaust: Documenting Life and Destruction
Holocaust Sources in Context, *4–5.*

Suggestions for further reading

Götz Aly, *Final Solution: Nazi Population Policy and the Murder of the European Jews*, translated by Belinda Cooper and Allison Brown (Baltimore, MD, 1994).

Götz Aly, Christian Pross, and Peter Chroust, eds., *Cleansing the Fatherland: Nazi Medicine and Racial Hygiene* (Baltimore, MD, 1994).

Omer Bartov, "Defining Enemies, Making Victims: Germans, Jews, and the Holocaust," *American Historical Review* 103 (June 3, 1998): 771–816.

Doris Bergen, "Catholics, Protestants, and Christian Antisemitism in Nazi Germany," *Central European History* 3 (1994): 329–348.

Michael Burleigh, *Death and Deliverance: "Euthanasia" in Germany* (Cambridge, 1992).

Henry Friedlander, *The Origins of Nazi Genocide: From Euthanasia to the Final Solution* (Chapel Hill, NC, 1995).

Alexandra Garbarini with Emil Kerenji, Jan Lambertz, and Avinoam Patt, eds., *Jewish Responses to Persecution*, Vol. 2, *1938–40* (Lanham, MD, 2011).

Robert Gellately, *The Gestapo and German Society: Enforcing Racial Policy* (Oxford, 1990).

Michael Geyer and John W. Boyer, eds., *Resistance against the Third Reich, 1933–1990* (Chicago, 1994).

Martin Gilbert, *Kristallnacht: Prelude to Destruction* (New York, 2006).

Beth A. Griech-Polelle, *Bishop von Galen: German Catholicism and National Socialism* (New Haven, CT, 2002).

Richard Grunberger, *The 12-Year Reich* (New York, 1971).

Wolf Gruner and Jörg Osterloh, eds., *The Greater German Reich and the Jews: Nazi Persecution Politics in the Annexed Territories*, translated by Bernard Heise (New York, 2015).

Marion Kaplan, *Between Dignity and Despair: Jewish Life in Nazi Germany* (New York, 1998).

Michelle Mouton, *From Nurturing the Nation to Purifying the Volk* (Cambridge, 2007).

Michael Phayer, *Protestant and Catholic Women in Nazi Germany* (Detroit, MI, 1990).

6

Resettlements, Deportations, and Ghettos

There are no Jews here, but there is an active struggle against Jewry both spoken and written...

—NSDAP LOCAL BRANCH REPORT EBERSDORF, 1939[1]

Introduction

In this chapter we will examine how the outbreak of war with Poland impacted Nazi anti-Semitic policies. The war itself would provide convenient cover for the Nazis to commit their racial crimes against the Jews of Europe. Propaganda would continue to stress that Hitler's January 1939 prediction of a war "begun by the Jews" was now a reality. That meant that all Germans were in danger, and that the Volksgemeinschaft was going to be eradicated—unless, of course, Germans bound themselves together to defeat the supposed existential threat. Inverting victim and aggressor, the Nazi regime was able to portray Jews as the "true" danger; they had to be removed from contact with any and all Aryans.

Language that had been used to ostracize Jews from their social surroundings was now escalating into justification for large-scale murder. For some Germans, that meant making the leap from mere anti-Semitic words, to actual anti-Semitic action—with devastating consequences for the Jews who fell into the German grip.

The invasion of Poland and the beginning of war

Prior to Germany's invasion of Poland on September 1, 1939, Hitler told his supreme commanders in the Wehrmacht the following: "I have placed my death-head formations at the ready with the order to mercilessly and pitilessly send men, women, and children of Polish descent and language to their deaths ... Poland shall be depopulated and settled with Germans."[2] This private message was vastly different from the public speech Hitler delivered to the rest of the world on October 6, 1939, declaring that this would not be a war waged on women and children. He did promise, however, that he would attempt to solve the Jewish problem.[3] To anyone living in Poland, they would have clearly understood that Hitler's war was being waged on all Poles alike: bombs did not discriminate between Catholic Poles and Jews.

Germany struck at Poland using its speed and power. Hitler wanted Poland destroyed before its allies, the British and the French, could send in their support. Using the technique of Blitzkrieg (lightning war), the Germans coordinated their Luftwaffe (air force) and Panzers (tanks) with swiftly moving infantry to shock and overwhelm their Polish enemy. Although Poland had the fourth largest army in Europe in 1939, Poland's military was at a disadvantage from the very outset. The Polish government waited too long to mobilize their men, listening to the British and French Allies who advised that Poland should do nothing to provoke a German attack. The Polish military, for its part, lacked adequate planes and mechanized armor and the leadership stubbornly refused to mass their troops along the Vistula River, instead spreading the troops out and attempting to hold the Polish Corridor. The Luftwaffe made quick work of the Polish air force, destroying most of Poland's planes within the opening days of the war. This meant that the Luftwaffe ruled the skies over Poland, striking terror into the population as it bombed strategic areas such as railway lines and bridges, but also as it struck civilian populations as well. One anonymous woman in Kutno, Poland, described the Luftwaffe bombing of her town:

Kutno was bombed already on the morning of September 1. These were likely the first bombs of the war.... The results were terrible: out of a group of recruits waiting for a train near the station, 120 were killed and 200 were wounded. The train never left- there was no one to be transported. On September 2, it was the same thing, the only difference was that 80 were killed and a couple hundred wounded. From then on, German planes visited us every day ... at first the center of town was bombed sporadically, but soon the bombings took on a mass character and claimed so many victims that people started to leave town.[4]

As this woman tried to flee Kutno, she found herself with countless other refugees who were all trying to do the same thing—flee from the German advance. She tried in various ways to reach Warsaw but, in the end, turned back around and went back to her hometown. Upon reaching Kutno, she experienced the worst bombing yet. Entire neighborhoods were in flames; people whose homes were still intact were opening them up to take in wounded soldiers and civilians although there was no medical aid. When the bombing raids finally ended on September 11, the civilians thanked

God. "We all even prayed for the Germans to come so this hell would end. Madness! We didn't realize what we were wishing for! The future would show us soon enough."[5]

Before the bombing of Kutno had ended, the German army had already reached the outskirts of Warsaw by September 8. Because the Poles began using guerilla warfare tactics such as sniper fire and placing burning rags under tanks, the German military retaliated by bombing the city into submission. These were twenty-four-hour, round-the-clock bombing raids with no relief. The civilians trapped in the city lost their lives by the thousands. Things turned from bad to worse on September 17 when the Soviet Red Army attacked Poland on its eastern border. This was part of the secret protocol of the Ribbentrop-Molotov Pact, inviting Stalin to take the parts of Poland unwanted by Hitler. Now, Polish refugees were not sure which way to run: away from the Germans or away from the Soviets. Chaos prevailed as Poland was ripped apart. By September 27, the Polish government was forced to surrender.[6] On that day, independent Poland ceased to exist.

Hitler's plans for Poland

What did Hitler intend to do with the conquered territories of Poland? On September 29, he outlined his tentative plans with Alfred Rosenberg, a leading Nazi ideologue. He told Rosenberg that "the Poles" were frightful material and that the Jews were "the most appalling people one can imagine."[7] He announced that he wanted to divide Poland into three territories. One area would be along the border with Germany. This territory would be colonized by Germans brought in from all over the world. A second territory would be bounded by the Vistula and Bug rivers. This second area was the place that Hitler envisioned for all Jews from all parts of the Reich to be dumped. And he said a wall would have to be built to keep the undesirables away from Germans. The final area would be in between the first two, and it would consist of some form of Polish state.[8]

Once Britain and France rejected Hitler's "offer of peace" on October 6, all notions of an independent Polish state were scrapped. Instead, large portions of former Poland were now directly annexed into the Greater German Reich, adding approximately 7.5 million ethnic Germans. But that also meant that another 8.5 million people were added who were not German. The remaining territory was now called the "General Government region" which included Warsaw, Lublin, and Krakow. This portion of Poland had approximately 12 million people in it, and they were to be governed by German officials and occupied by the German military.[9]

Once it was clear that no peace was going to be negotiated, Hitler made it known privately that the regular rules of war would not apply in Poland. He remarked to military leaders, "The hard struggle of nationalities

(Volkstumskampf) does not allow for any legal constraints. The methods will be incompatible with our principles ... Prevent Polish intelligentsia from becoming a leadership group ... the old and the new territory should be cleansed of Jews, Polacks, and rabble."[10] As Saul Friedlander points out, the type of language used by Hitler made it very clear that he was condoning the mass murder of entire segments of the Polish population in order to guarantee German racial superiority. The code name for the murder of Polish elites and "others" was the "A-B Aktion." Back in Berlin on September 21, Reinhard Heydrich, "the Blonde Beast," had gathered together leaders of special task forces, called Einsatzgruppen. He had already deployed Einsatzgruppen during the Anschluss with Austria and in the invasion of Czechoslovakia; now he wanted to make it clear to these units what their tasks would be in conquered Poland.

At the outset, Heydrich emphasized that there was a "final aim" involving the Jewish question; however, that was only to be accomplished at a later date and was to be kept strictly secret. In the immediate future, the Einsatzgruppen would be tasked with removing Jews from the countryside, forcing them into larger Polish cities. This was to be done quickly and suddenly. Only a few cities were to be used as the gathering sites, preferably cities along major railway junctures. He ordered that, once the Jews had been moved into cities, a Judenrat, or Jewish Council, was to be established, "as far as possible, of the remaining influential personalities and rabbis."[11] The Jewish elders—up to 24 of them per community—were charged with executing any and all German orders. The rest of Heydrich's directive provides details concerning the Aryanization of Jewish businesses; it delineates other responsibilities of Judenrat officials, and attempts to forestall areas of potential conflict among competing German military and civilian administrators.[12]

The Einsatzgruppen move in

Terror was unleashed as the Einsatzgruppen moved into the conquered territory. Three Death's Heads regiments followed closely on the invading German Wehrmacht's heels. Their job was to enact the "A-B Aktion" targeting Polish intellectuals, aristocrats, and priests. These were people who were suspected of being the most capable of launching resistance operations against the invading Nazis. The other portion of the action called for the racial war against the Jews. Thousands of Catholic and Jewish Poles lost their lives in organized massacres, where the victims were machine-gunned at open pits or, in some cases, Jewish victims were herded together into a local synagogue, locked inside and burned alive. Anyone who attempted to escape the fire was shot as they exited the burning building.[13] There were, however, variations on this type of terror. In some cases, the invading Einsatzgruppen toyed with the Jews. In many instances, they specifically targeted Jewish men whose clothing and beards were in keeping with traditional Jewish religious observances. Stopping a Jewish man on the street and forcibly shaving off his beard in front of a crowd was only one part of the public humiliation and torture Jews could now expect.

The men of the SD units re-enacted the events of Kristallnacht in many Jewish communities, burning or boarding up the synagogues, destroying Jewish property, and beating and murdering Jews. In the Polish town of Sosnowiec lived approximately 28,000 Jews, making up roughly 21 percent of the population of the town. On September 4, 1939, German forces entered the town, arrested 300 Jews, and locked them in a local insurance building. That night all 300 Jews were executed. On September 5, 1939, the Germans issued orders that all male Jews were to report to "Schein's factory." There was a camp on the grounds of the factory and all Jews' beards were forcibly removed. The men were subject to brutal torture. Some Jews were also executed on charges of attempted sabotage.[14] By September 9, Jews in Sosnowiec heard a frightening explosion. The synagogue was on fire. "A number of Jews... raced into the burning synagogue to rescue the Torah scrolls. The arsonists shot at them and killed them all. The martyrs were burned together with the synagogue and its Torah scrolls."[15] The surrounding houses caught fire and as Jews attempted to flee their burning homes, "the whole area... had been cordoned off by soldiers, and as soon as a Jew was spotted, he was shot. In a short time the streets near the shul (synagogue) were filled with the bodies of dead Jews."[16]

FIGURE 6.1 *Religious Jews under the supervision of Polish soldiers, digging anti-tank trenches to impede the German invasion. From September 1939, Warsaw, Poland. United States Holocaust Memorial Museum, #33266. Courtesy United States Holocaust Memorial Museum, Provenance, Julien Bryan Archive.*

In Lipno, Jews were uncertain if they were allowed to leave their homes to gather together to pray on the holiest day of the Jewish calendar, Yom Kippur. The local synagogue had already been boarded up by the Germans but many Jews wished to pray together in their homes. Believing assurances that Jews could in fact meet to pray, some attempted to do so. Suddenly, one woman from Lipno later testified:

> I see all the Jews running away in their socks, with prayer shawls and without, in skullcaps or with bare heads, rushing through the streets and chased by the SD. Two acquaintances, Mr. P. and Mr. L., came to our home in a hurry to hide … These two men told us that X [Germans] and SD burst in everywhere where people were praying, beating them with whips and dispersing those who were gathered, who jumped out windows and saved themselves however they could by fleeing.[17]

The Nazis were trying to strike at the heart of Jewish religiosity with these types of attacks; whether it was shaving off a man's beard to violate his religious beliefs or violently interrupting religious services, the fear and uncertainty of what the Nazis would do next was dominant. In addition to these acts of violence, the Nazis also wished to harm Jews economically and socially just as they had already been doing in the Greater German Reich. That meant, in some cases, abducting Jews and demanding that the community pay a large ransom fee to buy the men's freedom. In other cases, Jews were simply forced to work for free, performing difficult and dirty jobs that the Germans thought were fitting for Jews. One eyewitness, who had escaped from Wloclawek, Poland, gave testimony, recorded in Jerusalem on June 7, 1940:

> A few days after they entered Wloclawek, the Germans burst into a private house where Jews were standing in prayer on the eve of the Day of Atonement (Yom Kippur), and ordered those present to get out and run. Then they gave the order "Stop," but some of the Jews did not hear this order being given and went on running; then they [the Germans] opened fire and killed 5 or 6 of them. On the Day of Atonement itself the Germans burned down the two large synagogues. The fire also spread to several private homes. The Jews threw their possessions out [to save them] and there they were robbed by the Polish mob. These fires were mostly set by the men of the SS. The Jews tried to save the burning houses. Then the Germans took all the Jewish men from one of the buildings, 26 persons whom they found there, and forced them to sign a declaration that they themselves had set fire to the building. After they had obtained this declaration the Germans informed the men who had been arrested that they would receive the death penalty for committing arson and could save themselves only if they paid a ransom of 250,000 [zloty]. The Jewish population of Wloclawek collected the necessary sum

amongst themselves and the incarcerated men were released. Then they [the Germans] began to launch hunting expeditions into the houses. They caught about 350 Jews and put some of them in barracks and some of them in the Muehsam factory. From there they were taken out to work every day, but given no food—only their families were permitted to bring them food.[18]

The eyewitness's account continues, explaining the physically demanding types of labor the men were forced to perform. It also states that individual Jews found out on the streets were frequently abducted and forced into the factory as well. It also noted that by October the authorities ordered Jews to wear yellow badges on the back of their clothing, and more ransoms were extracted as "fines" for walking on sidewalks and not in the road, for example. All Jewish stores and factories were confiscated. Jews were required to register all of their property. There were beatings and tortures as well.[19] The town of Wloclawek's experience was not at all unique; the Nazis would re-enact similar events wherever they occupied Polish land.

Further chaos ensued as the Einsatzgruppen also sought to empty hundreds of Jewish villages (*shtetls*) all across the countryside. This was part of Heydrich's order to move Jews into concentrated areas of cities along railway lines. Hundreds of ancient Jewish communities, some having been there since the time of kings Bolesals and Kasimir the Great, disappeared from the map of Poland. Much like the sudden expulsion of Polish Jews in October 1938, these expulsions in Poland followed a similar pattern. The authorities lied to the Jews telling them to take only a few items since they would be back in their homes soon. As Jews were marched toward cities, they were often stripped of what little possessions they had with them, leaving them to suffer from exposure and hunger. Many Jews on these marches would never make it to the cities. One young woman's body was found by some Poles in a ditch. They thought she had something valuable hidden under her coat so they unbuttoned it. They found that the young woman had placed a young toddler inside of her clothing in a last, desperate attempt to save the child from freezing to death. They were both dead. The Poles moved on; there was no "Jewish hidden wealth" here.[20]

The German civilian administration in Poland

As the Einsatzgruppen controlled the flow of human traffic in occupied Poland, back in Berlin, Heydrich's office continued to transmit orders to the German civilian administrators which would further emphasize that the Jews in Poland were social outcasts. On November 23, 1939, the civilian Governor-General for the Occupied Polish Territories, Hans Frank, decreed: "All Jewish men and women in the Generalgouvernement who are over ten years of age are obliged, beginning December 1, 1939, to wear a white band, at least 10 centimeters wide, with the Star of David on the right sleeve of their inner and outer clothing."[21] Jews were responsible for purchasing these arm bands and those who tried to violate the decree were threatened with at least imprisonment.[22] This reinforced Heydrich's concept of the surveillance society. Just as we have seen in the Middle Ages when Jews were forced to wear special badges, veils, belts or hats, so that everyone would know that they were Jews, now the Nazis revived this idea of marking Jews visibly. All of society would now be implicated in enforcing Nazi racial segregation policies.

State Secretary Hans Pfundtner of the Interior Ministry in Berlin emphasized that all future plans for the conquered lands had to consider "whether members of the German Volk are afforded their due preferential position, and, if necessary, that the provisions from the Reich legislation to be introduced are altered such that fremd-völkisch (alien ethnic) Volk members do not become the beneficiaries of German law."[23] To further ensure that German Volk benefitted from the new acquisition of Lebensraum, Hitler appointed Heinrich Himmler the Reich Commissioner for the Strengthening of Germandom on October 7, 1939.

Himmler's task would involve moving hundreds of thousands of people all around Europe. Part of his job was to bring ethnic Germans from all over the world to areas around the newly acquired territory in the East. The Nazi plan was to settle 4 to 5 million Germans into this new land over the course of the next ten years.[24] This was in keeping with Hitler's October 6 speech where he suggested the resettlement of nationalities. Nazi Gauleiter Arthur Greiser saw no problem with Germanizing his new region, called the Warthegau. Greiser made it clear that the indigenous populations—Poles and Jews—were a problem. "Those who want to live must fight, and if a fight is about an entire Volk needing to live and wanting to live, then the soil on which the Volk needs to live and wants to live must also belong to this Volk, and it is impossible for another Volk to also have room on it."[25]

To the Nazi mind, the Volksgemeinschaft had to have this living space and any others living in the same land presented an existential threat to the continued life of the German people. Again, persecuting Jews was the opposite side of the same coin as that of protecting the German Volk. Himmler's resettlement plans for Volksdeutsch necessitated the removal of "volksfremd" (ethnic aliens). Resettlement of ethnic Germans and deportation of Jews and other "undesirables" went hand in hand. The Warthegau was going to be the area for the resettlement of ethnic Germans while the Slavic and Jewish populations living there already were to be deported into the General Government region.

Back on the home front

To "sell" the German home front on the necessity of both resettlement and deportation, Minister of Propaganda Goebbels asked the Wehrmacht to provide footage of Jews in the conquered territories. Wehrmacht propaganda units received the urgent order on October 2, 1939, to provide images of all sorts of "Jewish types" to be used in the weekly newsreels. Goebbels' order explained why he needed so much footage of Jews: "This material is to be used to reinforce our anti-Semitic propaganda at home and abroad."[26]

Newsreels, Nazi newspapers, films, and radio programs all were to stress that the threat of "the Jews" was omnipresent. In the opening two years of the war, Jews were mainly portrayed as the historically exploitative class of capitalists who profited from war and from other people's suffering. Nazi propaganda, not nuanced in the slightest, portrayed the choice in black and white terms: either one was totally "for" the Volksgemeinschaft and "against the Jews" or one was a traitor to the Aryan people. In the words of Robert Ley, "there is no compromise and no settlement. Whoever wants one, must hate the other. Who gives himself to one, must destroy the other."[27] The propaganda was working, as a contact of the SD in Münster reported: "In recent days, a feeling of great bitterness against the Jews has spread in the population, even in [...], so that individual actions are very likely. People are already talking about locking the Jews up, or putting them up against the wall to be shot, 10 Jews for every German killed in combat."[28]

For Jews in the Old Reich home front, further threats and increased demands for still further separation continued. One can find reports of locals demanding that new laws be written prohibiting Jews from all forms of public transportation.[29] Still other reports suggest that Jews living in Germany be "relocated" to Poland.[30] In addition, there are reports where ethnic Germans had been taken into police custody because they have been too "friendly" to Polish-Jewish forced laborers. In one case, the man taken into custody was accused of eating lunch with a Jewish POW and for that, the German had "offended popular sentiment."[31] In the same town of Bielefeld, a group of SA men had stripped a Jewish woman naked and then forced her to dance. Although proceedings were brought against the SA men, they were all granted a "'Führer amnesty'. To date, no consequences of this decision has been noted in the population and its reaction."[32] The "demands from below" in the Volksgemeinschaft to further isolate, humiliate, and deport Jews continued.

The General Government region

Back in Poland, Hans Frank, in charge of the General Government region, issued directives for the establishment of Judenräte (Jewish Councils) on November 28, 1939. For Jewish communities numbering under 10,000 the Jewish Council would consist of twelve men. For communities over 10,000, the Jewish Council would have twenty-four leaders. As Heydrich had laid out back in September, the men serving on the councils would be required to carry out any and all German orders. They would be held accountable for the actions of the Jewish men and women in their communities. All orders from Germans were to be obeyed without question.[33]

As the German civilian administrators took possession of various cities and regions, they began to appoint local "influential" personalities to the Jewish Councils. Many of the men selected did not necessarily want to serve; however, if they refused they would be punished or killed, and then another man would be found to take his place. In the case of Adam Czerniakow, he was in the wrong place at the wrong time. As Warsaw was falling into Nazi hands, the mayor of the city pointed out Czerniakow to Nazi officials and thus Czerniakow was selected to be the chairman of the Jewish Council.[34] Czerniakow was not one of the most prominent men in Warsaw, but since many leaders of the Jewish community had either gone into hiding or had fled to places such as Vilna, Lithuania or to Romania, he would have to do. He was known for his work among young Jewish craftsmen and for his excellent education in engineering.

In the town of Zamosc, Mieczyslaw Garfinkiel's appointment to the council mirrors that of Czerniakow. Garfinkiel was one of the few remaining prominent Jews in Zamosc. He was an attorney and an industrialist, so he was made the chairman. In his case, 7,000–8,000 Jews had fled Zamosc as the Soviet Red Army withdrew from the area. This was done in accord with the secret protocols of the Nazi-Soviet Non-Aggression Pact. The Russians invited Jews to flee with them and many did, fearing the Germans more than the Russians. As the Germans moved in, violent actions took place against the Jews who had remained behind and attacks against Jewish property also erupted. In November 1939 the situation in Zamosc had settled down and the German civilian authorities, assisted by the Gestapo, summoned Garfinkiel and seven other men to a meeting. In Garfinkiel's account, he remembers "the mayor of the city summoned eight Jews, including myself as one of the few members of the intelligentsia who had remained in the city. He informed us that, in accord with an order of the German civil authorities and the Gestapo, we were to form a so-called Council of Jewish Elders of the city of Zamosc."[35]

By the time Garfinkiel was appointed chairman, the first ghettos were being established by the Nazis. On October 8, 1939, the German mayor of Piotrkow Trybunalski (Petrikau in German) ordered the roughly 15,000 Jews of the area into the most dilapidated section of the town by October 31.[36] This ghetto would be located in the region called the General Government, and on October 10 Hans Frank was sworn in as the leader of the region. Frank established himself in the historic palace of Krakow where he would live like a modern-day king. Frank excitedly proclaimed in November 1939:

It is a pleasure to finally have a chance to get physically at the Jewish race. The more of them die, the better; to hit him [sic] is a victory for our Reich. The Jews should feel that we are here. We want to have about one-half to three-quarters of all the Jews east of the Vistula ... the Jews from the Reich, from Vienna, from everywhere; we have no use for the Jews in the Reich.[37]

Ghetto formation proceeded apace.

Adolf Eichmann, working alongside Heydrich in Berlin, developed a plan for the creation of a "Jewish reservation" in the Lublin district of the General Government region. This was called the "Nisko Plan" and reveals the various ways in which the Nazi regime was attempting to address the mounting numbers of their "Jewish problem." With the surrender of Poland, approximately 2.2 million Jews were living under German domination, so something had to be done with all of these potential "threats" to German purity. By December 1939, 90,000 Jews who were living in the Warthegau region under Gauleiter Greiser's control were rounded up and deported into the General Government region as part of Himmler's larger plan to resettle ethnic Germans in places closer to the Old Reich, while simultaneously deporting hundreds of thousands of Poles and Jews away from Germany. During these chaotic times, another grim event occurred. On December 7, 1939, SS units working in the Warthegau region began murdering inmates in asylums through the use of gas vans. SS-Untersturmführer Herbert Lange, leading a special unit, began the project of eliminating the mentally and physically handicapped, forming what Michael Alberti has called "the connecting line between the 'euthanasia' murders and the genocide of the European Jews."[38]

Ghetto formation

The ghettoization process spread slowly to the General Government region. The Warsaw ghetto was formed in October 1940, in Krakow and Lublin by 1941, and in Lwow in Galicia by December 1941. The size of ghettos and their final number are still being researched by the US Holocaust Memorial Museum, but their current estimates are in the thousands. The procedure for the formation of the larger ghettos remained virtually the same. Nazi staff would tour the city armed with street maps, looking for the worst part of the city; the place where windows were broken, running water was a "luxury," and toilet facilities may or may not be working. This would be where the most destitute of the urban landscape already lived and these streets would be marked off as the future site for a Jewish quarter. Orders would then go up on posters throughout the designated area, announcing that all ethnic Germans and "Aryan" Poles had to move out by a particular date. This generally gave the non-Jewish inhabitants some time to look for other housing and to take as many of their belongings with them as possible. Then notices would be put up announcing the sudden movement of Jews from all surrounding regions into the designated streets. The Jews were normally not given as much time to plan for this move. The regime did this purposefully so that more Jewish property would be left behind for plunder. Some of the goods left would be distributed to the local population. In this way, a person was implicated in the guilt of Jewish persecution. They had derived benefits from Jewish misfortune and that would make them less likely to voice opposition to Nazi policies for they were now guilty of complicity too.

Let us examine what this mass movement of people into a small region looked like to observers in Warsaw. In September 1940 close to 80,000 Aryan Poles who were living in the dilapidated section of Warsaw were ordered to move out. On October 3, which was Rosh Hashanah, the Nazi administrators declared the creation of a ghetto in Warsaw. Some 240,000 Jews were already living in this section but on October 16, the Nazis ordered another batch of 140,000 Jews inside. Tosha Bialer, a woman who escaped from the ghetto with her husband and son, described the scene:

> Try to picture one-third of a large city's population moving through the streets in an endless stream, pushing, wheeling, dragging all their belongings from every part of the city to one small section, crowding one another more and more as they converged. No cars, no horses, no help of any sort was available to us by order of the occupying authorities. Pushcarts were about the only method of conveyance we had, and these were piled high with household goods, furnishing much amusement to the German onlookers who delighted in overturning the carts and seeing us scrambling for our effects. Many of the goods were confiscated arbitrarily without any explanation … In the ghetto, as some of us had begun to call it half ironically and in jest, there was appalling chaos. Thousands of people were rushing around at the last minute trying to find a place to stay. Everything was already filled up but still they kept coming and somehow more room was found. The narrow, crooked streets of the most dilapidated section of Warsaw were crowded with pushcarts, their owners going from house to house asking the inevitable question: Have you room? The sidewalks were covered with their belongings. Children wandered, lost and crying, parents ran hither and yon seeking them, their cries drowned in the tremendous hubbub of half a million uprooted people.[39]

At least 400,000 Jews were packed into the Warsaw ghetto. It became the largest Jewish ghetto ever created in history. At first, Jews could travel in and out of the ghetto through twenty-two official entry and exit points so long as they had certificates which proved that they were employed outside of the ghetto's confines. Children were even allowed to leave at first to attend schools outside of the "Jewish quarter." The ghetto itself was part of the Nazi regime's efforts to isolate and segregate Jews from gentiles. By placing Jews in a quarantined area, the Nazis were able to further attack Jews economically and socially. Jews who had once held civil service jobs were fired and businesses designated as "Aryan" were forbidden to employ any Jews. Jews were banned from going into public spaces such as libraries, movie theaters, or concert halls. Nor could they use public transportation. Jewish assets were registered with the occupying authorities as well. Jews could, however, still leave the ghetto and "Aryans" could enter it to sell items inside. All of this changed suddenly on November 15, 1940.

Tosha Bialer describes November 15:

> In the morning, as on every other, men and women go out on their way to work....As they came to the various points where thoroughfares and streets crossed from the Jewish section into the non-Jewish districts, they ran against barbed wire strung across and guarded by German police who were stopping all traffic out of the Jewish section. Hastily they tried other streets, avenues, alleys, only to find in every case barbed wire or a solid brick wall well guarded. There was no way out anymore.[40]

As the panic spread, more and more Jews came out of their overcrowded apartments to see what was happening, and it slowly dawned on people that

> what had been up till now, seemingly unrelated parts—a piece of wall here, a blocked-up house there, another piece of wall somewhere else— had overnight been joined to form an enclosure from which there was no escape. The barbed wire was the missing piece in the puzzle. Like cattle we had been herded into the corral, and the gate had been barred behind us.[41]

Now a mad scramble began in the ghetto. People who had once held jobs outside of the section searched desperately for some kind of employment inside. If a person did not have a job, then that individual would not receive a ration card. If a person lacked a ration card, then starvation and death would quickly take its toll.

Once the ghetto of Warsaw was sealed, German administrators were free to make food allocations in bulk and it would be the problem of the Judenrat leaders to distribute the food to the starving population. The German policy regarding food was to keep the Jews barely alive, and in some cases, no food was delivered into the ghetto at all. Some German ghetto administrators thought that food should be delivered—at least enough to enable some of the Jews to continue to work for the German war effort. Christopher Browning calls these administrators "productionists" who pursued a policy of "destruction through work," as the end result would still be dead Jews, only the Germans would have at least temporarily derived some benefits from free Jewish labor. Other administrators, called "attritionists," saw no reason to keep Jews alive at all, even temporarily; when they moved into power food shipments into ghettos could be stopped for weeks on end. The shuffling of administrators from one post to another kept the Jews in the ghetto guessing about what future supplies might await them.[42]

As historians we know an enormous amount of detail about the life and death of the Warsaw ghetto due to a project undertaken by Emmanuel Ringelblum. Ringelblum was an extraordinary individual. He was thirty-nine years old when the war broke out and he was safe in Geneva, Switzerland attending a meeting of the World Zionist Congress. He decided to go back to his country of Poland to be reunited with his family. He was a trained historian (his dissertation was on the history of the Jews of Warsaw up to their expulsion in 1527), loved to be with people and always had a good joke to tell. He also had a strongly developed social conscience. Understanding the importance of language, he conceived of a massive project for those now trapped with him in the ghetto. Titled *Notes from the Warsaw Ghetto*, Ringelblum sent out questionnaires to inmates of the ghetto, asking them to record their lives and the lives of their Jewish communities. He also had assistants who interviewed the men, women, and even some children who were now trapped in Warsaw. He gathered this information together, seeking to provide documentation on the process of destruction. The group working on gathering all of this information called itself "Onyeg Shabes" ("Joy of the Sabbath"). The collection of documents was buried in milk containers and buckets, so that someday, historians would be able to write what had truly happened to the Jews of Warsaw.

In *Notes from the Warsaw Ghetto*, Ringelblum saw the fierce struggle for Jews to find employment within the ghetto. He noted that as the struggles intensified, a pattern developed. Jews with no jobs sold their jewelry first, then they sold off utensils, and finally, they sold their clothing in order

FIGURE 6.2 *Young forced laborers at the leather and saddlemaking workshop in the Lodz ghetto, Poland, in 1942. United States Holocaust Memorial Museum, #06644. Courtesy of Anatol Chari.*

to purchase food on the black market. He remarked that once a person appeared naked, one knew that that person was soon going to die for they had literally nothing left to sell in order to eat. The German administrators, having no interest in making life any bit easier for the Jews, charged rent for the overcrowded spaces, collected taxes and donations in kind, and they demanded labor quotas. The Judenrat leaders were responsible for getting men to appear for forced labor. Some laborers were marched out of the ghetto and were forced to do physically challenging work nearby while others in Warsaw (about 1,400 men) were taken to forced labor camps near Lublin. Working conditions were abysmal and were life-threatening.

One surviving report on conditions at the Josefow work camp stated that there was no water for washing on the site, there was no dining hall, no infirmary, and no wages were paid. For food, the workers received coffee for breakfast and 400–500 grams of bread. Lunch consisted of one liter of soup, mostly made from porridge or potatoes. Dinner was coffee. The report mentioned that the men were covered in lice, many had fevers, they were emaciated and malnourished, and over 100 of them lacked boots. Several deaths were recorded as well.[43] Within the ghetto, some wealthier Jews were able to pay the Jewish Council a fee in order to be exempted from these types of labor details. While that gave richer Jews certain privileges, the money the council received allowed for the purchase of boots, blankets, and other materials that could then be given out to the less fortunate men drafted into the labor battalions. The disparity between those with some degree of wealth and those without only added to the tensions within the Jewish community of the ghetto and the Jewish Council was caught in the middle.

As chairman of the Jewish Council, Adam Czerniakow was trying to balance the demands placed upon him by the Nazi ghetto administrators, the needs of the Jewish community of Warsaw, and his desire to ensure that the children of the ghetto would outlast the Nazi horrors. We as historians know a great deal about Czerniakow's dealings with the various German administrators and local "Aryan Poles" because he kept a thin, narrow notebook in his trouser pocket and kept notes on all of the deals he attempted to broker with the Nazis. His notebooks, which were purchased by a Warsaw ghetto survivor from an unknown source in 1959, consist of nine different books—with only the fifth notebook missing. Czerniakow's accounts are vastly different from those collected and edited by Emmanuel Ringelblum. Czerniakow did not dwell on the endless suffering. He noted at the beginning that he would never forget the sights, the smells, and the horrors he witnessed. Instead he focused on maintaining records of decrees, forced labor conditions, work camps, apartment evictions, and sanitation challenges. He kept figures for Jewish refugees being herded into the ghetto. His notebooks often began with an entry about the temperature and weather conditions for that day—something that one would be bound to forget if it was not documented. His writings also convey the conflicts, interactions, and social issues that the men serving on the Judenrat had to deal with on a regular basis. All aspects of the German methods of exploitation of the Jews were recorded, revealing the daily struggle for survival in Warsaw.

Perhaps the only times that Czerniakow reveals deep emotion in his diary are when he wonders about the fate of his only child, a son, who had escaped and was supposed to be fighting with the Soviet Red Army. The other time that he allows himself to be emotional is when he describes the children in the ghetto. Most of Czerniakow's efforts to keep education, culture, and religious observance alive in the ghetto were done with an eye to giving the children a sense of normality and a sense of hope that they would one day be able to resume a "normal" life once the Nazis were defeated. Czerniakow praised the bravery of the children; he had smuggling operations raided within the ghetto several times in order to confiscate items such as sardines and chocolates—which he then had distributed to the orphanages in the ghetto. He helped set up underground kindergartens, a lending library, and other educational opportunities for young people. He was arrested and tortured several times by the Nazi authorities; however, he never surrendered his dignity and even earned the respect of one Nazi administrator, named Dr. Auerswald. Czerniakow frequently fought for, and won, certain rights for the Jews, but it was a battle against time.

Let us examine a few entries from Czerniakow's notebooks:

> May 21, 1941—In the morning at the Community. A call from Rozen. They visited Lekno and one other camp. The conditions are horrendous. Nobody can stand it for a month. The firms which supply the food are stealing it from the workers. The beatings of the workers is to cease. The efficiency of the work, admittedly hard, is low. At 9:30 Wielikowski and I reported to Auerswald. We were [then] received by Governor Fischer. At the very beginning he contended that starving Jews was not his objective. There is a possibility that the food rations would be increased... He pointed out that the corpses lying in the streets create a very bad impression....The corpses, he said, must be cleared away quickly....The Governor turned out to be a relatively young man, dressed in civilian clothes, but hearing high boots with spurs. His manner was polite. He completed his remarks by saying that he expects compliance, or else.[44]

This was a typical type of entry for Czerniakow. He names names so he won't forget who he was negotiating with on matters from forced labor to removal of corpses in the streets. The following excerpt, from June 14, 1942, shows Czerniakow in a more emotional state:

> 14 June 1942—Cloudy. Today is Sunday. I am not sure whether the orchestra could perform in the playground. It turned out that it did play in spite of a light rain. I issued instructions for the children from a precinct detention room, organized by the Order Service, to be brought

to the playground. They are living skeletons from the ranks of the street beggars. Some of them came to my office. They talked with me like grown-ups—those eight-year-old citizens. I am ashamed to admit it, but I wept as I have not wept for a long time. I gave a chocolate bar to each of them. They all received soup as well. Damned be those of us who have enough to eat and drink and forget about these children.[45]

Many people were forgetting about the children of the ghetto dying of starvation. In fact, 300–400 people died every single day in the Warsaw ghetto due to starvation and diseases related to malnourishment. Within the ghetto's first year of existence, approximately 43,000 Jews starved to death and another 15,000 died of typhus. Living conditions grew still worse in the winter of 1941–1942 when the sewage pipes froze solid. Since toilets no longer worked, human waste had to be dumped into the streets, bringing still more diseases to the ghetto. The Judenrat, led by Czerniakow, has expected to maintain sanitary conditions but they were not given any supplies. Disinfection brigades were established but sickness continued to spread. In December 1941 the Nazi administrators decided to cut daily rations for adults down to 800 calories a day, shipping in mostly bread, rotten or frozen potatoes, and some ersatz fat. Smuggling became a necessity. Smuggling rings often used young children to run used clothing, utensils, etc. out of holes in the ghetto walls to the "Aryan Polish" side. The smugglers understood that the children were smaller, more nimble, and could maneuver through tight spaces. They also knew that it would be more difficult for Aryan Poles to reject starving, begging children than begging adults. Many of the children in the smuggling rings would not be alive for long as they did not always make it back into the ghetto.

To help stave off the hunger, the Judenrat set up soup kitchens. At times there was not much more than rotten potato peels and sawdust in the soup, but it at least gave people a feeling that their stomachs were filled. As more refugees were dumped into the Warsaw ghetto (mainly from the Warthegau), the Judenrat found it difficult to find housing and employment for the newcomers. Refugees often ended up living on the streets or in abandoned factories and they were more likely to die first from starvation and disease. Men such as Emmanuel Ringelblum began to organize House Committees within the ghetto. This was a grassroots endeavor, seeking to alleviate the suffering in the community by providing shelter, food, and child care. By April 1940, 778 House Committees were functioning and they would climb to 1,518.[46] There was also an intense intellectual life flourishing in the ghetto. There were concerts, plays, lectures, and reading circles; there was even an underground press which published articles which sought to remind Jews to practice moral behavior even in such extreme circumstances. Against these hopeful articles, Emmanuel Ringelblum noted in February 1941 that the sight of people falling over dead in the middle of the street no longer provoked reactions from most people. Children in the ghetto, he said, played a game of rushing to the corpse to tickle it to see who could get the corpse to move one last time. Starvation, typhus, and other illnesses were spreading. Statistically, if conditions in the Warsaw ghetto had remained unchanged, all of the people in the ghetto would have been dead in eight years' time.[47] However, the Nazi administrators had no intention of waiting eight years for the Jews to be gone.

On July 22, 1942, Czerniakow was summoned to the Nazi administrator's office. The Germans had decided to move into a new phase of "liquidating" the ghetto. Czerniakow went back to the Jewish Council's office and wrote his last diary entry on July 23, 1942. In that entry he recorded the Nazi demands to have 4,000 people gathered and ready for transport out of the ghetto by 3 p.m., then by 4 p.m. another 4,000 were to be ready to go. The "Aktion" would be continued throughout the week. At the meeting, Czerniakow had asked the Nazis whether that order applied to the children as well. They said yes, and Czerniakow made the decision that he would not sign the order. Everything he had done in the Warsaw ghetto had been to ensure that someday some of those children would walk out of the ghetto gates alive. If he signed the order, it would be as if he was murdering them himself.

He wrote two letters. In one letter he apologized to his wife for leaving her alone to face an uncertain future without him. In his second letter, to the men serving on the Judenrat, he told them how he had been keeping a bottle of cyanide pills in the back of his desk drawer since September 1939 with just enough pills—one for each man on the council. He advised the men to each take one. Then Czerniakow committed suicide. The deportations from the Warsaw ghetto began.

The Jews forced into ghettos all over Poland experienced similar situations as those in the Warsaw ghetto. There were variations as much depended upon who the Nazi ghetto administrators happened to be, what their attitudes and policies toward the Jews were, and likewise, much also depended upon the leadership of the Judenräte. There was a wide-ranging variety of Jewish leaders—from the modesty and selflessness of Czerniakow to the more power-hungry Mordechai Chaim Rumkowski of the Lodz/ Litzmannstadt ghetto. Rumkowski, who became the "Eldest of the Jews" on October 13, 1939, in Lodz (renamed Litzmannstadt by the Germans), acquired more power in Lodz once the ghetto was sealed off on April 30, 1940. Rumkowski was allowed by the German administrators to move about freely in the ghetto. In a letter written by the German city commissioner, it stated, "Every member of the Jewish race is required to obey unconditionally all instructions given by Elder Rumkowski. Any opposition to him will be punished by me."[48] Rumkowski remains a controversial figure to this day as he exercised his power over all aspects of life in the ghetto. His motto was "Our only path is work," because he believed that at least some Jews could be saved if the ghetto inhabitants made themselves indispensable to the German war effort. This idea was certainly not unique as almost all

Judenräte leaders thought of ways to make their people indispensable. What was unique in Lodz, however, was how Rumkowski came to embody the "Führerprinzip," attacking those who complained about his failures while bribing the population with entertainments and distractions. No matter how controversial Rumkowski was to the Jews trapped in Lodz, his harsh policies did make the ghetto the longest surviving, with forced deportations only beginning in 1944.[49]

The attack on the West

While Jews were starving and freezing to death in ghettos and work camps across Poland, the rest of the world watched from afar, calling the months following the conquest of Poland the "phony war" or "Sitzkrieg." To anyone in Poland, however, this was no "phony war"; it was raging all around them filled with violence and misery under their new overlords. But, to the outside world, the major powers were not battling each other and only skirmishes were reported. This lull would last only until spring 1940—just when most ghettos in Poland were being sealed off from outside society. Hitler launched attacks against Norway and Denmark in April. Denmark surrendered within a few hours of the attack, while Norway was undone by one of its own former war ministers, Vidkun Quisling. Quisling betrayed his country, transmitting valuable military information to the German forces. The British and the French attempted to help Norway but the country also succumbed to the Nazi war machine. Both Denmark and Norway, now conquered territories, lost their independence but, as they were considered countries populated by Nordic Aryans, Nazi rule allowed for some laxness when dealing with the local population.

With the loss of Denmark and Norway, Prime Minister Chamberlain's support in Parliament eroded. He would be replaced on May 10, 1940, by Winston Churchill, the same day that Hitler launched his assault against the West. Churchill's position as a staunch anti-Nazi inspired the British with his lofty rhetoric. On the day of his appointment as prime minister, he gave one of his most famous speeches: "I have nothing to offer but blood, toil, tears, and sweat ... You ask: What is our aim? I can answer in one word: Victory! Victory at all costs, victory in spite of all terror, victory however long and hard the road may be: for without victory there is no survival."[50]

Nazi propaganda and the home front

In the Old Reich, Nazi propaganda continued to churn out its endless stream of supposed Jewish threats to the Volksgemeinschaft. One report from the Reich Security Main Office in April 1940 argued that Jewish authors' works should not be cited in German dissertations, and then suggested that official lists of Jewish scientists, scholars, lawyers, and judges be drawn up so academics would know if the person they were citing came from a Jewish background.[51] Others remarked on the disappearance of Jews from their smaller communities. The mayor of Schwandorf noted in May 1940, "As already reported, there are only three Jewish hags left here. They too will soon disappear."[52] The mayor of Heldenbergen noted that he had ordered Jews in town to relocate to "Jews' apartments," stating that the former residences of the Jews would be used to "accommodate several Aryan families with numerous children...."[53] In the city of Münster, a crowd had gathered at the Gau Air Raid Defense Headquarters where a bomb had landed. One man in the crowd stated: "I know that the two Jews Dr. Rose and Dr. L. Gumprich got a permit to emigrate to England. Who else should have reported on the location of the 'Gau Air Raid Defense Headquarters' but such Jews. This war is certainly a Jewish war, with the help of English soldiers, against Germany."[54] The same person reportedly told the crowd that they should not doubt the spitefulness of the Jews. These types of concerns expressed publicly regarding Jews—as traitors and as taking up valuable living space—must have been gratifying to Nazi propagandists.

For the home front, Goebbels's Propaganda Ministry wanted to produce films that would help German Aryans to understand the "Jewish Problem" they were facing. Although the vast majority of the films produced in the Third Reich were not overtly anti-Semitic, there were some. One was the film *The Rothschilds* which sought to portray Jews as greedy, exploitative, sneaky, and involved in a worldwide conspiracy to destroy the world of non-Jews. Yet another film, *Jud Süss*, was a box-office hit on the home front. The costume-drama set in the 1700s told the story of a Jewish man, Joseph Süss Oppenheimer, who became an advisor to the Duke of Wurttemberg. The movie showed how allowing one Jewish man into "good" German society led to the corruption and destabilization of the entire kingdom. Crowds flocked to see *Jud Süss*, with estimates in the millions for viewership.

The SD office would listen to people's conversations as they exited movie theaters. One report, gathered in Bielefeld, quoted a worker saying, "Why weren't we shown such movies earlier? Here you see the Jew in reality as he actually is. I felt like wringing his neck."[55] One week later the SD office in Bielefeld continued to remark on the film's success with the Volksgemeinschaft, stating, "Probably no film has ever had such an effect on broad circles of the public like this one. Even Volksgenossen who before today have rarely if ever set foot in a movie theater are keen not to miss this film."[56] The success of *Jud Süss* was then followed by the pseudo-documentary *Der ewige Jude* ("The Eternal Jew"). This film, reportedly one of Hitler's favorites, was not a box-office hit, but the SD reports did mention that audiences believed the information presented about the Jews was "well and good, correct, but in the form chosen seemed a bit boring."[57] Other more positive responses to the film applauded the film's ability to drive home the point: "once a Jew, always a Jew, despite all external adaptation to states, languages, and areas of life."[58] All of these films helped to reinforce the message that Jews were eternally the outsiders, disruptive, untrustworthy, and diabolical. They were also being used to justify why German Jews would have to be deported away from the Old Reich.

While millions of German people might attend movie showings, not as many were quite as familiar with the work of the Institute for the Study and Eradication of Jewish Influence on German Religious Life. The Institute, founded in 1939 by Walter Grundmann, brought together academics, theologians, and independent scholars to remove "Jewish influence" in theological writings and in the Bible itself. The group held conferences, presented papers, and worked to prove that Jesus could not possibly have been Jewish. They argued, in fact, that Jesus was an Aryan and the world's first anti-Semite. Perhaps not many Germans would have come into contact with this group until the Institute began to edit the Bible, removing all words that sounded "Jewish" such as "amen" and "hallelujah"; the newly revised Bibles, now "dejudaized," were printed and distributed especially to German soldiers at the front. The Institute also produced new hymnals and as a later project they wished to remove all of St. Paul's writings since Paul was originally a Jew before his conversion. Susannah Heschel, in *The Aryan Jesus*, has shown how the Institute worked to eliminate all that was Jewish in the Bible and in hymns at precisely the same time that deportations of German Jews were beginning in the Old Reich. As Jews were about to be physically removed from German society through deportations to the East, the theologians and scholars at the Institute worked to eradicate Jews spiritually from Protestantism.

As Alan E. Steinweis's research in *Studying the Jew* has shown, numerous other organizations and academic circles participated in the new field of "scientific" studies of Jews. These academics were part of the larger effort to justify the persecution and deportation of the Jews. Likewise, Robert Ericksen's work on theologians under Hitler revealed men such as Gerhard Kittel to be complicit in the project of forwarding the Nazi regime's anti-Semitic agenda. Kevin Spicer's work *Hitler's Priests* reveals the members of the Catholic Church who actively supported the Nazi cause. Claudia Koonz in *The Nazi Conscience* tracked how various intellectuals supported the justification for deporting and murdering Jews.

There are now countless studies which examine the role of scholars in promoting the Nazi worldview, gaining for Hitler's regime an air of respectability and acceptance among the general public. For some Germans, inspiration from the realm of academics was not enough; they wanted to experience the Nazi project in the East for themselves. Elizabeth Harvey's *Women in the Nazi East* explores the role of German women in building the new "Nazi Eden" in Eastern Europe. Harvey's work reveals young Aryan women going to Poland and other occupied territories, as part of their support for the Nazi regime. For many of these young women, their work entailed cleaning up Polish homes—following their brutal evictions by the SS—and then preparing the homes for *Volksdeutsche* (ethnic Germans) to move in and take over. Some of the young women also ran kindergartens, taught German folk music, and even instructed the Volksdeutsche in German language. These women saw in many cases what the two sides of the coin were: on one hand, there was the resettlement of ethnic Germans closer to the Old Reich's borders, but on the other hand, there were the deportations of Catholic and Jewish Poles. Both of these policies were needed to safeguard and strengthen the Volksgemeinschaft.[59]

As the war broadened out with Hitler's assault on the Low Countries on May 10, 1940, more lives would be drawn into the dual policies of resettlement and deportation. Although the Low Countries had declared themselves as neutrals, Hitler had revised the First World War Schlieffen Plan for a daring invasion through the one weak spot on the French Maginot Line. He sent General Erich von Manstein across neutral Belgium and through the heavily forested region of Ardennes. In the meantime, German tanks attacked the frontier between Germany and the Netherlands. After five days of fighting and the aerial bombardment of Rotterdam, the Dutch were forced to surrender. The German forces continued to move through Luxembourg's mountain passes, into the Ardennes forests, and soon enough they were crossing into French territory.

By May 28, 1940, just eighteen days after the invasion had begun, the King of Belgium surrendered. Although many thousands of British troops were able to evacuate at Dunkirk back across the English Channel, German military successes were demoralizing for the Allied Powers. The Wehrmacht continued to move toward Paris. The French military was in disarray, refugees were fleeing south, and even the French government was fleeing. On June 10, 1940, Benito Mussolini, thinking that the war would be over soon, brought Italy into the conflict by declaring war on France. By June 14, the Germans had entered Paris. Most leaders outside of France believed that the French would dig in as they had during the First World War; however, to their surprise, the French surrendered. In six short weeks, France had been crippled by defeat. Almost 2 million French soldiers were now prisoners of war. Most German people on the home front were ecstatic. The "wrongs of the First World War" had been corrected, now Germany was the one bringing the humiliation, not the French. On June 22, 1940, France formally surrendered in the same spot in Compiegne, France that was the site of German shame on November 11, 1918. Hitler was filmed walking along the Champs Elysee, looking the part of military genius and conqueror.

In just over three short months, Hitler had now added Denmark, Norway, Belgium, Luxembourg, the Netherlands, and France to Germany's growing empire. Many Germans were convinced that now the war would end; after all, the shame of defeat in the First World War and the misery of the Treaty of Versailles were now lifted from German shoulders. But there was still one nagging problem: that of Great Britain, now led by the anti-Nazi Winston Churchill. As Churchill noted in a speech following the fall of France, Britain now stood alone. The plan for a naval invasion of Britain, codenamed "Operation Sea Lion," was put on hold while the German Luftwaffe began bombing raids over England. From July through September 1940, Great Britain endured "the Blitz" but by the fall, Hitler had changed his focus from bombing Great Britain to planning for an invasion of yet another country: the Soviet Union. The codename for attacking the Soviet Union was "Operation Barbarossa," and this invasion would mark a major turning point in the war, ushering Germany away from its period of victories into its period of ultimate defeat.

Jewish life in conquered territories

Uncertainty ruled for Jews living in these conquered territories. Some of them were German, Austrian, or East European Jews who had fled the rising Nazi tide much earlier than May 10, 1940. Once their countries had capitulated to Hitler, each country received a variation of Nazi rules and regulations regarding the Jewish population. For Denmark, Norway, Belgium, and Luxembourg, there were relatively low indigenous Jewish numbers to address. For example, in Luxembourg, the vast majority of Jews were fairly well assimilated into the general population prior to 1933. After 1933, however, Luxembourg became a transit point for many Jews fleeing persecution. On May 10, 1940, estimates show that perhaps 4,000 Jews were living in Luxembourg, with approximately 25 percent of them holding Luxembourg citizenship out of a total population of 300,000 people.[60] Most Jews who were citizens of Luxembourg were salesmen, merchants, and small businessmen. The country, as of 1940, had only one Jewish teacher, and Jewish physicians and lawyers were rare.[61] Once the Nazis invaded (and the country was overrun within hours), the German military set up its temporary administration. The military leader, General Alexander von Falkenhausen, took over.

Falkenhausen met with the Grand Rabbi, Dr. Robert Serebrenik, and the General agreed not to attack Jews. Local anti-Semites put up signs and smashed the synagogue's windows, but General Falkenhausen stationed police to protect the house of worship from further destruction.[62] The coexistence of Jews with German occupiers lasted temporarily until the military administration of the region ended and was replaced with German civilian administrators. For Luxembourg that meant Gustav Simon was now in charge as of August 1940. Pro-German groups emerged as did one group called the "Ethnic German Movement" (Volksdeutsche Bewegung) which stressed the German-ness of Luxembourgers. Simon's policy was "The Luxembourger is a German, a German in his entire nature, according to history, according to lineage, language, and the region in which he is born."[63]

According to historian Marc Schoentgen, the Ethnic German Movement had a green applicant card which read, "The German Reich is the homeland of all Germans. The general good is the supreme law. Gaining the soul of the Volk can succeed only if, along with conducting the positive struggle for one's own goals, one destroys the goals of the opponent."[64] The main opponent was the Jews, as the card made clear.[65] Once again, we can see how the positive goal of unifying the German people into a Volksgemeinschaft necessitated the negative goal of fighting against the Jews. For Luxembourg's Jewish community that meant excluding them from any social welfare measures, firing any Jews working in Aryan companies, and creating a card index system listing the names of all Jews in the country.

Anti-Semitic race laws, modeled on what had occurred already in Germany, were enacted and laws allowing for the "Aryanization" of Jewish property were also promulgated. On September 12, 1940, the Gestapo ordered that all Jews in Luxembourg had to leave the country.[66] The actual expulsion was scheduled to take place on Yom Kippur in the following month; however, the order was actually never enforced. Nevertheless, Jews in Luxembourg frantically began to search for ways to emigrate. Some went to France, others to Portugal and Spain.[67] Until October 1941, Jews still were allowed to emigrate from Luxembourg; about 1,450 Jews were able to get out. However, on October 16, 1941, the first major deportation to the "East" (Poland) occurred and the German civil administrators then prohibited any further emigration of Jews.[68] Although Luxembourg can be used as an example of Nazi occupation policies, Schoentgen argues convincingly that the majority of Catholic Luxembourgers were not interested in becoming "German" but, he concedes, of the roughly 3,900 Jews in the region in 1940, at least 1,400 were killed in deportations to camps in Poland, 1,600 individuals survived, and 900 Jewish people's fates are unknown.[69]

Deportations

With each Nazi military success, the "Jewish Problem" was further compounded. The original plan, hatched by Adolf Eichmann at the Reich Security Main Office in Berlin, had been to create a giant Jewish "reservation" in the Lublin area of the General Government region. Eichmann had settled on Nisko, an area near the San River. Hitler approved of Eichmann's plan, and from the end of October 1939 Jews were deported from areas of the Old Reich, including Vienna, to Nisko. No preparations had been made for the arrival of the Jews and fairly quickly the transports were stopped by order of the Reich Security Main Office. The deportation of Jews from the Old Reich was temporarily halted, primarily because Himmler had decided to focus all of his resources on the resettlement of Baltic Germans. The deportations of Jews that did occur were not hidden from the public. A London-based newspaper, *The Jewish Chronicle*, ran an article titled "Vienna Jews Leave for Lublin," on October 27, 1939. The article wondered if the Nazis were planning to reestablish a "pale of settlement" for Jews as in the times of the Tsars of Russia.[70] The Lublin reservation project was eventually shut down in April 1940 and the camp in Nisko was dissolved.[71] Further deportations to the East, however, were soon to follow.

For Jews living in Nazi-controlled territory, news of deportations sparked new waves of anxiety. Jews desperately searched for ways to escape from areas of German control in the hopes of avoiding the deportations. One woman, Mignon Langnas, whose husband and two children had successfully immigrated to America, wrote frantically to her husband when she received her deportation summons. She then wrote to the leader of the Viennese Jewish Community, begging him to ask for a deferral so that she might still rejoin her husband and children rather than be deported. She did receive a temporary reprieve and was granted a postponement; however, she did not have another opportunity to escape from Europe.[72]

In Vichy France, as shown by Robert Paxton and Michael Maurras, the collaborationist regime of Marshal Philippe Petain was willing to enact anti-Semitic restrictions and French leaders were also willing to exchange foreign-born Jews for French POWs, delivering the non-native French Jews into the hands of the Nazis for deportation. In the Netherlands, Jews found themselves suffering under restrictions transmitted to the Jews via the establishment of a Judenrat in Amsterdam. For many European Jews, the Nazi occupation meant further limitations and restrictions on how they could conduct their lives. There was always the fear of being picked up and placed into an internment center such as the camp at Gurs in France. Jews faced increasing impoverishment and hunger with little to no chance of getting their pleas for aid heard by outside organizations. Despite the increasingly poor chances of aid reaching war-ravaged victims, organizations such as the World Jewish Congress continued to attempt to alleviate some of the suffering wherever possible.

The desire to make areas "Judenfrei" led to surprise deportations of Jews from Baden, Mannheim in October 1940. One woman, Clara S., recalled how the police arrived, giving she and her husband one hour to pack their belongings—110 pounds of luggage was all that was allowed. They were taken from their home and made to wait with other deportees, all of whom were racked with anxiety as to what was going to happen to them. Some thought they were going to Poland, but it turned out this group was being sent to the Gurs internment camp. No preparations were made for the sudden influx of 12,000 people about to be dumped into the camp. By November 1940, Gurs was averaging fifteen deaths per day due to the horrendous conditions.[73]

One man, Hans Steinitz, recalled what it was like for these stunned German Jews now finding themselves interned in France. Steinitz's account depicts his ability to recognize how confusing the situation was for the new arrivals at the camp. They had become accustomed to the social isolation of their southwestern German towns, and any act of kindness, such as handing an older woman a glass of water, was gratefully accepted. Steinitz astutely wrote:

> At other locations, the "old Gursers" gave their new comrades some of their coffee, their thin soup, or even a slice of bread—gifts that were accepted with unbelievable astonishment and respectful whispers—"See, here is someone who has helped us." After eight years of living in the Third Reich, the transport in cattle cars to France, and the reception in Gurs, these unhappy people had forgotten what it is like to be regarded as human beings.[74]

For so many of the newly deported, whether they ended up in Lublin, Poland or Gurs, France, they had to try to make some sense of the events happening to them. Perhaps amazingly, many of the deportees continued to hold a sense of "nostalgia for the Germany that had once been their home and to which, despite Nazi anti-Semitism, they continued to feel connected."[75]

Jews in the Old Reich

How did the Jews still residing in Germany feel? Were they still connected to the larger Volksgemeinschaft? Jews in Germany were being further isolated and segregated from the community. Shopping hours for Jews were now restricted in many areas. In Berlin in July 1940, Jews were only permitted to go shopping between 4 p.m. and 5 p.m. That meant that by the time Jewish customers got to the stores, most items that their ration cards allowed them to buy were already gone. Further items were banned for sale to Jews including tomatoes, cauliflower, spinach, chocolate, eggs, and sugar. In addition to these types of restrictions, Jews were, from November 1940 onwards, forced to complete compulsory labor if they were between the ages of eighteen and forty-five. By August 1941, a new decree stated that Jews could only occupy 10–14 square meters per person, so people were now compelled to live in apartments that were grossly overcrowded and most were lacking in sanitary facilities. On September 19, 1941, a new decree went into effect that Jews must all wear the yellow Star of David on their outer clothing. Further measures followed, including ones that forbid the use of public telephones, and the confiscation of furs and woollen clothing.[76] By February 1942 yet another law was passed which made it illegal for a Jew to keep a household pet. The law required that the Jew take the pet to the local veterinarian to have the animal put down. All of these laws were meant to further debase and persecute Jews, making their lives as miserable as possible.

There were individual Germans who felt some sense of pity for the Jewish situation. Lisa Pine notes that occasionally Jewish families would find pastry or fruit on their doorsteps—left anonymously so there would be no risk of denunciation.[77] However, anti-Semitic attitudes were still the prevailing tone. In a report from Münster in March 1941, a dentist reported his anger that Jews were still living in his rental property. He told his listeners that every war was started by Jews and "he thinks it's high time to haul together all the Jews still around Münster and to put them in a ghetto. Better still, it's time to remove them all from Münster. He told me his father said that in an earlier era, Münster did not permit any Jews at all inside the city."[78] A soldier, home on leave, wrote a letter of complaint, stating: "I visited Coffee House Mainz on Sunday afternoon, where the Minari band was playing Jewish music and hot stuff like crazy.... As a German musician and Wehrmacht soldier, I protested that when we soldiers come in looking for some relaxation and decent, pleasant music, what's offered to us in German restaurants with live music is some decadent Jewish-English pseudo-art."[79] One can see the fear of "contamination" by coming into contact with Jews or things owned by Jews also in an NSDAP report from Lörrach. Books had been collected to be sent to the frontline soldiers, but the NSDAP official noted, "The really good books left over after the Jews were removed were soon auctioned off and were gone. What still remains has to be handled with gloves and a protective mask. In the main, these are prayer books and legal texts."[80] In a report written on the general population's reaction to newsreels showing Jews doing physically demanding labor in Belgrade, the report noted, "over and beyond a bit of hilarious laughter following various reports, it was these pictures in particular that again sparked sharp criticism of the Jews remaining in Europe, with whom the German authorities in the occupied territories now have to deal."[81] The Volksgemeinschaft was letting its opinions be known to the Nazi authorities; they did not wish to hear "Jewish music," they did not want to have to physically touch Jewish religious materials, nor did they wish to live alongside Jews in Europe. Further radicalization of Nazi plans were about to occur.

For your consideration

Below is an unofficial army observer's report regarding the use of Jewish men in a labor battalion. One of the first projects for forced Jewish laborers in Poland was to build a defense line near the Bug and San rivers facing the Soviet zone of occupation. This army observer includes a reference in his report to underscore that the labor battalion is not under the German Wehrmacht command. The army observer interviews Jewish men and reports on what they have told him. Why is the army observer there? How much freedom do you think the Jewish laborers have to respond honestly to the German army observer? What type of conditions do the men describe? What are hygienic conditions like in the work camp? Where do the men get their food supplies? Do they get paid for their work?

Report by operations officer of Chief Field Headquarters 179 (Lublin)
  September 23, 1940
Reference: Telephonic order to ascertain the truth of complaints about
conditions of Jewish employment in the anti-tank ditch between Bug and
San.

On the occasion of a tour of the newly assigned local command posts, a
stop was made on September 22 at the Jewish labor camp at Belzec on
the way from Tomoszow.

The impressions gained on one Sunday are not sufficient to generalize
about the whole 80-mile stretch....Since the organization of labor projects
between the Bug and San is evidently completely outside the jurisdiction
of the Armed Forces, clarification would seem to be necessary as to how
far the Chief Field Headquarters may proceed in this matter.

The impressions gained from short, entirely unostentatious
conversations with individual Jews without interpreters. Despite the
Jewish jargon, communication was perfect. The people selected for
conversation made their points in a precise, quiet manner, as answers to
questions put to them. The result is as follows:

I. Work Routine

5:30 Waking

6:00 March to work

7–12 Work on the ditch

12–13 Lunch

13–17 Work on the ditch

18 Arrival in the camp

Thereafter stacking of tools and supper. There is no relief during work.
The men work also Sundays—that is called voluntary.

II. Food Supply. Still in the hands of the Jewish Council of Lublin

Breakfast: Bread and coffee

Lunch: Potatoes, mixed daily with meat. The meat is brought to the work
site in kettles peasant carts.

Supper: Bread and coffee.

Quality of Food Supply:

No vegetables, no fat. Meat in the potatoes is a matter of accident.
Potatoes often underdone.

Bread: One loaf per day per man. [weight unclear]

Impression made by the men varies according to age. Some of the younger men look vigorous, older men mostly undernourished. There appear to be fewer complaints about the food than about quarters.

III. Quarters

Allegedly very crowded, no straw. People lie on the hard floor. In order to sleep at all they lie down head and shoulder on the neighbor and so forth. When the weather becomes colder, there will be a shortage of blankets. The greatest deprivation is felt to be the lack of any opportunity to wash, since the work schedule allows no time for that. This was emphasized several times. They stay for weeks and months without any change of clothes. One would have to check in the camp itself to find out if these allegations are true.

IV. Clothing

The men work in their own clothes. Since they have been here for three months already, there are human figures in literal rags. Those who are clothed better are people who can afford to pay for their own things. They are exceptions.

V. Pay

The men receive only food. Payment in money does not take place, so that supplementary purchases of food or clothes are out of the question.

VI. Hygienic Conditions

So far as can be determined, dysentery prevails, though apparently not to an extraordinary extent. Also fever (perhaps typhus) occurs. Allegedly there is no medical care, though Jewish doctors in sufficient numbers must surely be available.

There are sanitation men (Jews), but their armband with the Red Cross seems to be their only qualification. These conditions are commented on with strong indignation. Lately, men over 60 and the sick have been released.

In answer to a question about deaths, it was said that they occurred, and cautiously added: "also shootings," for example in the morning of yesterday, Sunday. In answer to a question about the reason, there was only a shrug of shoulders.

For the Chief Field Headquarters 379

> *Document taken from R. Hilberg, ed.,* Documents of Destruction:
> Germany and Jewry, 1933–45, 44–45.

This next selection is a poem, composed by a young man, Henryka Lazawert. The poem would have been recited as entertainment in the Warsaw ghetto. It depicts the reality of children as smugglers. Lazawert was killed in the early deportations out of the ghetto to Treblinka concentration camp in July 1942. How does he describe the actions of the child in his poem?

"The Little Smuggler"

Over the wall, through holes, and past the guard,
Through the wires, ruins, and fences,
Plucky, hungry, and determined
I sneak through, dart like a cat.
At noon, at night, at dawn,
In snowstorm, cold or heat,
A hundred times I risk my life
And put my head on the line.
Under my arm a gunny sack,
Tatters on my back,
On nimble young feet,
With endless fear in my heart.
But once must endure it all,
One must bear it all,
So that tomorrow morning
The fine folk can eat their fill.
Over the wall, through holes and bricks,
At night, at dawn, at noon,
Plucky, hungry, artful,
I move silently like a shadow.
And if the hand of destiny
Should seize me in the game,
That's a common trick of life.
You, mother, do not wait up for me.
I will return no more to you,
My voice will not be heard from afar.
The dust of the street will bury
The lost fate of a child.
And only one request
Will stiffen on my lips:
Who, mother mine, who
Will bring your bread tomorrow?

Poem taken from Lucy Dawidowicz,
A Holocaust Reader, *207–208.*

Suggestions for further reading

David Bankier, *The Germans and the Final Solution: Public Opinion under Nazism* (New York, 1996).

Richard Breitman, *Architect of Genocide: Himmler and the Final Solution* (New York, 1991).

Marek Chodakiewicz, *Between Nazis and Soviets: Occupation Politics in Poland* (New York, 2004).

Peter Dembowski, *Christians in the Warsaw Ghetto* (Indiana, 2005).

Robert Gellately, *Backing Hitler: Consent and Coercion in Nazi Germany* (New York, 2002).

Wolf Gruner, *Jewish Forced Labor under the Nazis: Economic Needs and Racial Aims* (Cambridge, 2008).

Raul Hilberg, ed., *The Warsaw Ghetto Diary of Adam Czerniakow* (Warsaw, 1999).

Marion Kaplan, *Dominican Haven: The Jewish Refugee Settlement in Sousa* (New York, 2008).

Ricard Lukacs, *The Forgotten Holocaust: The Poles under German Occupation* (New York, 2012).

Calel Perechodnik, *Am I a Criminal? Testament of a Jewish Ghetto Policemen* (New York, 1996).

Emmanuel Ringelblum, *Notes from the Warsaw Ghetto* (New York, 2006).

Phillip Rutherford, *Prelude to the Final Solution: The Nazi Program for Deporting Ethnic Poles* (Kansas, 2007).

Karl Schleunes, *The Twisted Road to Auschwitz: Nazi Policy towards German Jews* (Illinois, 1990).

Nechama Tec, *Defiance: The Bielski Partisans* (Oxford, 2008).

James Tent, *In the Shadow of the Holocaust: Nazi Persecution of Jewish-Christian Germans* (Kansas, 2003).

Nicholas Wachsmann, *Hitler's Prisons: Legal Terror in Nazi Germany* (New Haven, 2004).

Gerhard Weinberg, *Hitler's Foreign Policy: The Road to World War II* (New York, 2010).

7

Einsatzgruppen, Executions, and "Evacuations" to the East

The entire population feels confident about the new military complications with the Soviet Union. The National Socialists welcome with a sense of joyous anticipation the defeat of Bolshevism and thus of international Jewry, and consider it of great world-historical importance.[1]

(JUNE 1941)

Introduction

The Nazi regime was finding it increasingly difficult in 1940–1941 to find space for the Jews. On December 4, 1940, Adolf Eichmann claimed that Jews were going to be moved to an unnamed location as a preliminary to the "final solution of the Jewish problem."[2] Jews who had already been deported or forcibly marched into the ghettos throughout Poland were dying in large numbers due to the extremely horrendous conditions there. Now Nazi planners began laying out schemes to move Jews further away from the German Volksgemeinschaft. However, these plans were going to be further frustrated as Hitler had decided to expand the war by invading the territory held by the Soviet Union in 1941. As Nazi forces prepared to invade Soviet lands, men such as Reinhard Heydrich and Heinrich Himmler recognized that new plans would have to be drawn up to address the growing "Jewish problem." As more land was conquered by the Nazi war machine, more Jews were added to the growing Reich. This was a situation deemed unacceptable to Hitler. Anti-Semitic language used in Nazi propaganda would escalate, stressing the idea of a "Judeo-Bolshevik conspiracy" out to destroy the Volksgemeinschaft.

The war against the Jews expands

As more and more Jews fell into the Nazi realm of control, various officials attempted to address the growing problem of what to do with so many Jewish threats. One Nazi leader in the foreign office, Franz Rademacher, latched onto a scheme that had been circulating in anti-Semitic circles for some time: moving Jews to the island of Madagascar. Since Rademacher was in charge of the "Jewish question" in the foreign office, he drew up plans for the deportation to the harsh island. The plans for Madagascar were finalized on August 15, 1940. Hitler was notified of the plan and was kept abreast of its developments. The plan originally aimed to deport 4 million Jews from all parts of Europe to the island. This was later revised by Rademacher, who set the goal of sending 6 million West European Jews there, but he suggested keeping young Eastern European Jews as hostages to hold American Jews in check.[3] Despite all of the planning and resources that went into the Madagascar Project, the Nazis could not defeat the British Royal Navy for supremacy of the seas and so the whole project was doomed from the start.

In the meantime, Hitler had decided to expand the war by violating the Nazi-Soviet Non-Aggression Pact. In part, he saw that the Soviet Red Army had been seriously challenged by Finnish forces in 1939; he also knew that Stalin had purged some of his best officers, thus weakening the Red Army even further. However, Hitler also understood that Stalin controlled most of Germany's supply lines for items such as nickel and iron ore, and he worried that Stalin might at any time cut off the supply trains to Germany which were helping to support the German war effort. All of these considerations played a role in influencing Hitler to turn against the Soviet Union; however, the most important reason was that Hitler saw the Soviets as representing the gravest threat to the Volksgemeinschaft's existence. He believed that the "Judeo-Bolshevik conspiracy" was posing the most serious threat to the expansion of the Germanic people into the vast expanses of the East. One of the most troubling aspects, though, when considering the invasion of the Soviet Union, was that anywhere from 4 to 5 million Jews lived there. Again, conquering the territory would increase the "Jewish problem" for the Volksgemeinschaft.

As preparations for a military invasion of the Soviet Union progressed, Nazi propaganda had to now pivot away from selling the war as a "Jewish-capitalist-plutocratic" conspiracy to that of a "Judeo-Bolshevik" threat. Goebbels sent the German military propaganda film crews into areas such as the Lodz ghetto to gather footage for newsreels. These would be used to incite further anti-Semitic outrage once the invasion of the Soviet Union had begun.[4] Research institutes on Jews continued to pour out a constant stream of anti-Semitic theories, carrying with their denunciations of "Jewish influence" the air of respectability—after all, learned academics were the ones making such arguments. One new organization, the Institute for the Study of the Jewish Question, opened in March 1941. Its director, Dr. Wilhelm Grau, stated at its inauguration: "The twentieth century, which at its beginning saw the Jew at the summit of his power, will at its end not see Israel anymore because the Jews will have disappeared from Europe."[5] Yet, how would Jews disappear from Europe?

Thus far we have seen how the Nazi occupation of Poland and various other parts of Europe resulted in brutal acts of violence, particularly at the hands of Einsatzgruppen, then regional leaders established work camps and ghettos, while other Nazi leaders busily prepared fantastical schemes to deport Jews to far-flung places such as Madagascar or to an imaginary "reservation" in Lublin district. In the western areas of occupation, Nazi anti-Semitic policies tended to replicate the pattern of Jewish isolation and segregation that had already been enacted back in the Old Reich. Likewise, in places such as the Warthegau and Upper Silesia, there seems to have been the same policy of forcing Jews to emigrate or be expelled from the regions so that ethnic Germans could be moved in to the area. The Nazis were proceeding in many of these areas following patterns that had already been established within Germany with the understanding that, as long as there were no significant public outcries against the anti-Semitic measures, the restrictions would continue. The general public's acceptance that there was indeed a "Jewish problem" assisted Nazi planners. "If the isolation of the Jews did not provoke any significant protests—and was even welcomed by many—their territorial segregation outside Europe or in some distant part of the Continent would appear as a mere technicality."[6]

The planning stages for war against the Soviet Union

Although the "Final Solution" is not apparent in these planning stages, one can see that when Hitler envisioned how the war against the Soviet Union was going to be waged, he saw it as a war of extermination. This was not going to be an ordinary war for ordinary gains. Rather, it was a war which represented the confrontation of two world views—that of Nazism versus Bolshevism—and it was envisioned as a war where only one of those two views could triumph. The defeated Bolsheviks would be annihilated so as to end the existential threat they posed to Germans. Many of these ideas were explicitly stated in the "Commissar Directive" of March 1941. In this document, modeled closely on the "A-B Aktion" carried out in Poland in 1939, the coming confrontation between Germany and the Soviet Union was noted, calling for the "elimination" of a "Judeo-Bolshevik intelligentsia." Coinciding with this directive, Heinrich Himmler was given special responsibilities from Hitler himself on March 13, 1941. His SS was to be fully independent of the Wehrmacht with the "right to decide who was a member of the 'Jewish-Bolshevik intelligentsia' and who should be liquidated."[7]

It quickly became clear, however, that the SS would need to have the military's cooperation in carrying out the murderous project. By June 11, 1941, General Halder ordered the Wehrmacht to give full support to the actions of the SS.[8] By September 12, 1941, military policy regarding the Jews had escalated. General Keitel issued the following order:

> The struggle against Bolshevism demands ruthless and energetic action, and first of all against the Jews, as the main bearers of Bolshevism. Therefore, there will be no cooperation whatever between the Wehrmacht and the Jewish population, whose attitude is openly or secretly anti-German, and no use is to be made of individual Jews, for any preferential auxiliary services for the Wehrmacht.... The only exception to be made is the use of Jews in special labor columns, which are only to be employed under German supervision.[9]

As the Wehrmacht prepared its plans for attacking the Soviet Union, Heydrich worked in Berlin to assemble the team of Einsatzgruppen leaders who would follow closely on the heels of the invading German army. Beginning in May 1941, SS men were brought in for intensive ideological training at Pretzsch on the Elbe, where they were indoctrinated further.[10] There is no strong evidence that any of the Einsatzgruppen leaders volunteered for this task; however, they did not turn down the opportunity to participate when it was offered to them. Many biographies of various Einsatzgruppen leaders have been written and overall the generalization can be made that these men were well-educated individuals, coming from mostly privileged backgrounds; some had law degrees, some were doctors, and most of them were in their thirties. They were professional men who had joined the SS as part of their career trajectory. Now they were called upon to prove their loyalty to the SS and to Nazi racial ideology. After the war, some historians assumed incorrectly that the men of these mobile killing squads must have been criminals released from German prisons and unleashed on unsuspecting Jews, and that they must have been deviants; however, Raul Hilberg's work *The Destruction of the European Jews* highlighted that these men were highly educated individuals who worked to become efficient killers. Much like Christopher Browning's research on German reserve police officers from Hamburg, one can see the frightening evolution of "ordinary" men into killers.[11]

In June 1941, a meeting took place in Berlin. Himmler had gathered the leaders of the Einsatzgruppen for one last coordinating meeting before the invasion. He made it clear that Jewish males between the ages of 17 and 45 were to be executed as "partisans." The age and gender restrictions would quickly be lifted; by July 1941, all Jews—men, women, and children—were potential targets of "elimination" for the Einsatzgruppen. Himmler later acknowledged this escalation of violence in a 1943 speech to *Gauleiters* (regional leaders):

> Then the question arose, What about the women and the children? I decided to find a perfectly clear-cut solution to this too. For I did not feel justified in exterminating the men—that is, to kill them or have them killed—while allowing the avengers, in the form of their children, to grow up in the midst of our sons and grandsons.[12]

Otto Ohlendorf, one of the leaders of the Einsatzgruppen, stated in his 1947 trial that murdering children was necessary in order to bring about "permanent security."[13] The prosecutor at Ohlendorf's trial understood that the Germans had created the equation whereby Jews had to die in order for the Volksgemeinschaft to live, so he asked Ohlendorf, "That is the master race exactly, is it not, the decimation of whole races in order to remove a real or fancied threat to the German people?"[14] Ohlendorf's lame response to the question was, "Mr. Prosecutor, I did not see the execution of children myself although I attended three mass executions."[15]

The invasion of the Soviet Union and its implications for Jews

On June 22, 1941, as 3 million German and satellite troops began their strike at Soviet outposts, the men of the Einsatzgruppen A, B, C, and D were following, ready to strike. It was understood in June that Soviet Jews were to be placed under curfews, they were to be marked with the Star of David, all Jewish businesses were to be taken over by Aryans, and no Jews could remain in public positions. Jews were also slated for the lowest, minimal rations of all the occupied peoples in the Soviet territory. Some pragmatists, much like the productionists in charge of Polish ghettos, argued that Jews should be kept alive to be used as forced labor, but only when it was shown that Jews were performing an indispensable job that no one else could do. Of course, this only meant a temporary reprieve for the "work Jews" as most of them would starve to death or die as a result of maltreatment in their place of employment. Himmler was not in favor of the productionist argument; he believed that, ideologically speaking, the Jews were too grave a racial threat and that the SS methods of speedy executions were the preferred solution to the "Jewish problem."[16]

Himmler told officers in the Commissariat for Eastern Affairs on July 28, 1941 that Hitler had "placed the responsibility for carrying out this difficult order [to murder the Jews] on my shoulders."[17] There is little reason to doubt that Himmler was not telling the truth. On June 24, Himmler had a forty-five-minute meeting with SS-Standartenführer Professor Dr. Konrad

Meyer. Himmler asked Meyer, who had worked in agricultural offices, to sketch out a plan for resettlement in the soon-to-be conquered East. In just three weeks, Meyer and his co-workers presented Himmler with their draft, called *Generalplan Ost* (General Plan East). The copy of this draft plan as well as a second draft plan have never been found, making it impossible for historians to assess the goals of the regime in July 1941. A third draft of the plan, with notes from Dr. Erhard Wetzel, head of the section on race in the Reich Ministry for the Occupied Eastern Territories does, however, exist.[18] The evolving plan was largely designed in the office for "Strengthening of the German Race" and the Reich Security Main Office. Immediately one can see by the title of the office assigned to the task that increasing the strength of the Volk necessitated the murder of the Jews.

The General Plan East involved "de-Jewing" the entire area under German control and resettling 10 million Germans in Poland and in the Soviet Union. It estimated that 31 million people would have to be "eliminated" in order for this plan to work.[19] Generalplan Ost, according to Wetzel's notes, involved moving many of the people of Eastern Europe into western Siberia in order to make room for 4.5 million German settlers.[20] This raises an important question— if the Generalplan Ost included the idea of moving millions of Soviet Jews further east, then that suggests that the regime had not yet determined the fate of Soviet Jews even at the end of 1941. This is contradicted by the knowledge that thousands of Soviet Jews were already being executed throughout the summer of 1941, months before the General Plan was written.[21] The final version of Meyer's plan was resubmitted and approved by Himmler in May 1942, but by spring 1942 circumstances inside Soviet territory had changed rendering the plan less and less likely to be put into practice.[22] However, that was in 1942, but in July 1941, the Nazi Wehrmacht was experiencing success upon success against the Soviet Red Army.

The idea of the "Final Solution"

In this period of victories, Hermann Göring sent an order to Heydrich, using the phrase "Final Solution of the Jewish Question." The order read:

> Complementing the task already assigned to you in the decree of January 24, 1939 to undertake by emigration and evacuation a solution of the Jewish question as advantageous as possible under the conditions of the time, I hereby charge you with making all necessary organizational, functional, and material preparations for a complete solution of the Jewish question in the German sphere of influence in Europe....I charge you furthermore with submitting to me in the near future an overall plan of the organizational, functional and material measures to be taken in preparing for the implementation of the goal of a final solution of the Jewish Question.[23]

Göring told Heydrich in this July 31, 1941 order to prepare for the mass murders of Jews which in reality were already taking place in the Soviet Union. Heydrich, in order to involve the German civilian bureaucracy in the murderous process, needed a legal order if he was going to be able to coordinate rail transportation with financial administrators. He was also apparently concerned over details such as what to do with Jews in mixed marriages, what to do with "half-Jews" or "quarter-Jews," or Jews who were working in the armaments industries. Heydrich decided to gather various Nazi administrators together. He sent invitations to a "Final Solution" conference to be held on December 9, 1941. The "Final Solution" conference ultimately was delayed due to Japan's surprise attack on Pearl Harbor on December 7, 1941, which threw the Nazi regime's plans into disarray. The conference was re-scheduled for January 20, 1942.[24]

The Einsatzgruppen move in

While men such as Heydrich and Himmler delved into details, the men of the mobile killing squads were busy at work. Their strategy was simple: trap large portions of the Jewish population while they were unaware of their fate. The original strike force had 3,000 men but their killing actions would be quickly followed up with the creation of more Einsatzgruppen.[25] Raul Hilberg noted that part of the ultimate success of the killers was that they created standard operating procedures which streamlined the killing process.[26] Wherever the Einsatzgruppen went, they carried out the systematic murder of Jews. Depending on the size of the Jewish community and the location—urban, countryside, and so on—the method of killing varied, albeit only slightly.

In certain towns, thousands of Jews were murdered in one action that lasted between one and three days. In this way, the Jewish communities of Kiev, Kharkov, Vitebsk, and many other localities were annihilated. In other towns, such as Minsk, Vilnius, Pinsk, and Lvov, the murder of Jews was carried out over several actions, with interruptions between each one. In townships and rural areas, the extermination was carried out by small, mobile Einsatzgruppen units who came to the area, and, helped by the local police, murdered all the Jews in one blow before moving elsewhere to carry out another action.[27]

In order for each killing action to be "successful," the Einsatzgruppen men needed the cooperation of local authorities as well as the local population's complicity. In many cases, the German occupying military authorities exceeded their original agreement with Heydrich's office. The work of Omer Bartov in *Hitler's Army* shows the Wehrmacht soldiers participating in the round-ups of local Jews, requesting that the SS send in Einsatzgruppen to carry out an "action" against the Jews, and participating in the actual killing of Jews as well.[28] In areas of German civil administration, local mayors and village elders were needed to reveal how many Jews lived in the area, where they lived, and where they might be hiding. Locals were also needed to provide information as to where Jews could be rounded up at a "collection point" and they could also be useful in suggesting possible venues for the shootings and burials. Jews were rounded up in various ways. In some regions, notices were posted on local billboards, ordering the Jews to assemble at a certain location by a specific time. The notices frequently made use of the terms "resettlement," "resettlement elsewhere in a ghetto," "resettlement in a sparsely populated location."[29] For Jews already living in confinement in ghettos, there was no need to use such notices. Jews were told to report to a collection point within the ghetto and then they would be marched out to the actual killing site in batches.[30]

The killing units were small in comparison to the number of intended victims, so by definition, the killers needed to be able to enlist the cooperation of local people in the killings. They needed men who could stand guard over the assembled Jews to prevent their possible escape. They needed men who could guard the killing area and they needed others to participate in the actual shooting. In some cases, the killers utilized young children to tamp down the dead and the dying in the pits in order to fit more victims into the gravesite. Karl Jäger, leader of Einsatzkommando 3, consisting of 8–10 men, was in Lithuania. Here is an excerpt from his report on one killing action:

> The execution of such Aktionen is first of all an organizational problem. The decision to clear each subdistrict systematically of Jews required a thorough preparation of each Aktion and the study of local conditions. The Jews had to be concentrated in one or more localities and in accordance with their numbers, a site had to be selected and pits dug. The marching distance from the concentration points to the pits averaged 4 to 5 kilometers. The Jews were brought to the place of execution in groups of 500, with about 2 kilometers distance between groups. The hardships and nerve-racking that we had to suffer in carrying out this work is illustrated in this example that I have chosen at random: In Rokishkis, there was a need to transfer 3,208 people and it was 4–5 kilometers to their place of execution. In order to carry out this operation within 24 hours, it was necessary to allocate 60 out of the 80 Lithuanian partisans at our disposal, for transportation, and especially guard duties. The remaining ... did the work [shooting] with my people.... Only the efficient use of our schedule made it possible to carry out five actions a week.[31]

Notice how Jäger's unit had standardized their killing process, how they utilized local captured Lithuanian men to assist them in the "action," and how it was "nerve-racking" and a "hardship"—not for the Jewish victims being marched several kilometers to their deaths, but for the killers. No real thought or concern for either the victims or the local population factored into building a world safe for the Volksgemeinschaft.

The local population, even if they were not forced to assist in the actual killing process, were able to witness the shootings on a regular basis. In Ternivka, Ukraine, one witness named Petrivna recalled how the Germans entered the village to kill Jews. They were led by a local Gestapo commander named Hummel. The gathering point was at the center of the village. Jewish children and the handicapped were taken away from their families and put into horse-drawn carts. The rest of the Jewish population was marched out to a large pit located on the edge of the village. The Jews were then forced to walk down the slope into the pit in groups of twenty. They were ordered to lie down on top of the dead and dying Jews already in the pit and were shot in the back of their heads. How did Petrivna know such details? She was a young Ukrainian girl, out in the field tending the family cow when the Germans came into the village. One German saw her and ordered her to go to her mother's house and return to them with a spade. She, along with two other young girls, returned with spades. Their job was to enter the pit of dead and dying people and walk on top of their bodies to pack them in more tightly. They were called "pressers." Petrivna said, "After every volley of shots. We were three Ukrainian girls who, in our bare feet, had to pack down the bodies of the Jews and throw a fine layer of sand on top of them so that other Jews could lay down."[32] Petrivna, several times in her testimony, recalled her Jewish classmate who had sat next to her in school. "She saw her in the pit, naked. She saw her arrive and then shot, before she had to trample on her corpse."[33] The shootings lasted from 10:00 a.m. to 4:00 p.m. There were 2,300 Jews killed in that one day. Little barefoot Ukrainian girls were witnesses and, by force, became assistants in the genocidal project to make Soviet territory "Jew-free."

Not all of the civilians "requisitioned" into service by the Germans were used as "pressers." In Father Patrick DesBois's accounts of interviewing now elderly Ukrainians, he notes that

There were those who mixed lime with the blood of the Jews; those who tied the Jews' clothes up in bundles and then loaded them onto carts; those who patched up the clothes; those who prepared food for the oppressors during the executions; those who drove carts full of hemp or sunflowers with which to burn the bodies; those who placed sunflower or hemp on the layers of bodies; those who tore out the Jews' gold teeth while they awaited their execution, collecting them in a canvas bag that they gave to the Germans in the evening; those who transported Jews in their carts from the villages to the pits; those who stored the spades in their house at night, between shootings; those who packed down the bodies of the Jews in the pits and covered them with sand between shootings; those who surrounded the groups of Jews who arrived at the pit until all the families were shot; those who guarded the Jews to prevent them from escaping; and those who brought ash to clean up the ground after the executions. Most of them were children.[34]

From this list, one can readily see just how involved the killing process actually was, drawing in not simply the Einsatzgruppen, the Gestapo, and Wehrmacht soldiers but locals as well. In order for the German killing machine to work properly, others had to be sucked into the guilt. One witness said that after a mass shooting his mother refused to let him take clothes that had once belonged to the now dead Jews. She said to him, "Don't take the Jews' clothes; they are covered in tears."[35] Not every local had that opinion. One witness said, "One day we woke up in the village and we were all wearing Jews' clothes."[36]

Local cooperation

For many local civilians in the Soviet Union, the Nazis were able to focus their propaganda message in such a way that Lithuanians, Ukrainians, and so on could collaborate with the German occupiers. The general message was that Jews had been calling the shots in the Soviet Union and Jews were purposefully blocking each nationality from achieving their own independence. We have already seen in earlier chapters the long history of pogroms and anti-Semitic attitudes present in Eastern Europe, so in many cases, the Nazis provided the excuse to enact violence against local Jews. In some of the regions, Jews were also accused of being proponents of the Soviet oppression, therefore linking the propaganda image of "Judeo-'with'-Bolshevism." Timothy Snyder, in *Bloodlands,* has argued that nationalistic right-wing groups perceived Soviet and Jewish actions in their territories as part of a plot to prevent various nationalities from breaking free of Soviet rule.[37] This made the efforts of the Nazis all the easier as they could frequently rely on local populations to carry out at least initial acts of violence against the Jewish population.

Here is one German man's account of events in late June 1941 in Kovno, Lithuania, which underscores the way local Lithuanian nationalism combined with anti-Semitism:

Close to my quarters I noticed a crowd of people in the forecourt of a petrol station which was surrounded by a wall on three sides. The way to the road was completely blocked by a wall of people. I was confronted by the following scene: in the left corner of the yard there was a group of men aged between thirty and fifty. There must have been forty to fifty of them. They were herded together and kept under guard by some civilians. The civilians were armed with rifles and wore armbands, as can be seen in the pictures I took. A young man—he must have been a Lithuanian—...

with rolled-up sleeves was armed with an iron crowbar. He dragged out one man at a time from group and struck him with the crowbar with one or more blows on the back of his head. Within three-quarters of an hour he had beaten to death the entire group of forty-five to fifty people in this way. I took a series of photographs of the victims.... After the entire group had been beaten to death, the young man put the crowbar to one side, fetched an accordion and went and stood on the mountain of corpses and played the Lithuanian national anthem.[38]

In yet another Lithuanian town, called Shavli, one Jewish physician, Aron Pik, kept a diary of the events. He was forced to move into the ghetto in Shavli with his wife and son. He worked in the ghetto hospital until his death in 1944. When he died, his son, Tedik David Pik, buried his father's writings, escaped from the ghetto, and joined a partisan unit. After the war, Tedik dug up his father's diaries and took them with him to Israel.[39] Aron Pik's diaries reveal the changing situation of Jews in Lithuania. He noted how in the summer of 1940 life improved for most Jews when the Soviet Red Army moved in and took over the region. Dr. Pik recalled how suddenly the anti-Semites of the town disappeared and Jews were granted full rights by the Soviet occupying forces. Speaking of many working-class Jews, Pik wrote, "they all felt the sun of a new, free life shone with the Bolshevist regime. How great, therefore, was our desperation and heartache when, after one year of rule, the Bolsheviks suddenly abandoned us at the beginning of the war and we were left defenseless in the teeth and claws of the wild, bloodthirsty German beasts!"[40] Once the Germans took over Shavli, Dr. Pik saw the re-emergence of the Lithuanian anti-Semites who blamed the Jews for their families' suffering under Bolshevism. His account continues:

They [Lithuanians] were furious about the deportations of their families to Soviet Russia, which they considered to be the work of the Jews, disregarding the fact that more than a few Jewish families were also deported, suspected of being "counter-revolutionaries." They blamed all the deeds of the Bolsheviks on the Jews, whom they held responsible for everything that has taken place and that is presently taking place, including the war, according to the formula of the modern Haman and the clique of his followers.[41]

Dr. Pik was correct in his observations. The local Lithuanians killed approximately 1,000 Jews out of 8,000 in the first week of the German occupation.[42] Karl Jäger, an Einsatzkommando 3 leader, whom we have met before, noted that when he arrived in Kaunas, local Lithuanian units were under the command of Obersturmführer Joachim Hamann. Hamann and his Lithuanian shooters carried out operations against the Jews. Jäger noted in a report, "The goal of clearing Lithuania of Jews could only be achieved through the establishment of a specially mobile unit, under the command of SS Obersturmführer Hamann who ... was able to ensure the cooperation of the Lithuanian partisans and the relevant civil authorities."[43] It is a tragic irony that Hamann, the leader of the killing party, has the same biblical name as Haman who wanted to eradicate the Jews, and only the Jewish woman, Esther, was able to convince the king to save her people and murder Haman instead. There was no Esther in the small communities of Lithuania unfortunately, and entire villages and medium-sized communities were annihilated. For larger cities in Lithuania, the Nazis began the ghetto formation process with all of its attendant restrictions. The first ghetto created by the Nazis was located in Kaunas, requiring all Jews move into the Slobodka district of the city by August 15, 1941.

As soon as the Kaunas ghetto was formed, the Jews had to form a Judenrat. One day before the ghetto was closed (August 14), the Jewish Council was ordered to gather educated people to do archival work. Those who responded to the Jewish Council's request were taken out of the ghetto to the Seventh Fort, where they were all executed. According to Jäger's account, "698 Jews, 402 Jewesses, 1 Pole, 711 Jewish people of intelligence from the ghetto [were murdered] in reaction to an act of sabotage."[44] This was a smaller scale version of the A-B Aktion and the Commissar Directive orders whereby Jews with an education were to be targeted for death so they could not inspire resistance among the less-educated Jews. The ghetto was then fenced in with barbed wire. Lithuanian police guarded the perimeter. Further actions were taken against the Jewish population of the ghetto in September and October.

At the end of October 1941, Jews were told by the German officer in charge of the ghetto, Helmut Rauke, that everyone had to appear on "Democracy Square" at 6:00 a.m. This was an area inside the ghetto. Anyone who disobeyed the order would be shot. The assembly of people was then organized according to where each person worked. Rauke had the inhabitants march in front of him. Some people were sent to Rauke's left, others to the right. For the ones on the left, selected as "fit to work," they and their families were kept in the larger portion of the ghetto. For the 9,200 others sent to the right, they were moved into what was called the "small ghetto." The following morning, October 28, all of the people who had been moved into the small ghetto were taken to the Ninth Fort where they were executed.[45] The actual killings were carried out by Kaunas Police Battalion no. 1, a Lithuanian force under the command of Colonel Andreas Butkumas.[46]

Minsk: A turning point

From the example above, we can see how shootings and ghettoization policies were being carried out simultaneously in areas under Nazi control. But further changes were about to occur. Back in August 15–16, 1941, just two months into the German invasion of the Soviet Union, Heinrich Himmler made a visit to Minsk to watch the extermination process. Minsk at this time was under Einsatzgruppen B leader Arthur Nebe's control. Nebe, before joining the mobile killing squad, had made a name for himself in the "Euthanasia Project, Aktion T-4" so he already knew how to kill defenseless human beings. Now, Himmler ordered Nebe to collect 100 Jews and demonstrate how the men of the Einsatzgruppe did their work. According to eyewitness accounts, Himmler grew increasingly upset during the shooting operation. Two Jewish women had been shot first, but they did not die immediately and were suffering in the pit. Ninety-eight Jewish men were executed as well. Himmler reportedly became more and more nervous and looked down at the ground during the shooting. After the killings were completed, a visibly shaken Himmler made an impromptu speech to the killers. In the speech, Himmler noted that he would not like it if German men did such things gladly for what they were doing was a repulsive task. However, he continued, their consciences should not be impaired for they were soldiers who had to carry out all orders. He took responsibility for their actions, saying that only he and the Führer understood the necessity of the task. He then elaborated on how nature is about struggle and brutality, with combat everywhere.

As Himmler was leaving the site, he mentioned to Nebe to begin thinking about other, more humane, ways of killing. He did not mean more humane for the victims; their suffering was inconsequential to Himmler. Instead, he meant that there should be a way to lessen the psychological strain and the sense of responsibility placed upon the killers. The search, to combine efficient ways of murdering large numbers of people while simultaneously removing the sense of personal responsibility for the murder of innocents, led to the creation of the gas van.[47]

Since Nebe had participated in the T-4 project back in Germany, he decided to try to kill some mental patients in an asylum in Minsk using carbon monoxide. He contacted the Criminal Police (Kripo) and asked for assistance in murdering mental patients via poisoned gas. The Kripo sent Dr. Albert Widmann, a chemist. Twenty or thirty mental patients were collected in Mogilev. They were put into a sealed room and carbon monoxide from car exhausts were pumped into the room. At first, the victims did not die because the car exhaust was not strong enough; Nebe and Widmann then decided to use a truck's exhaust and finally Widmann could report, "It then took only another few minutes before the people were unconscious."[48] What he really meant to say was that the people were dead.

The two men reported to Heydrich that their experiment had worked. Heydrich got the technical personnel of the Reich Security Main Office to begin working on developing gas trucks. They came up with two different models: one type of truck, resembling an ambulance, could hold 50–60 victims in the back, while the smaller model could take 25–30 people. Carbon dioxide was pumped out of each truck's exhaust pipe through another pipe which connected to the sealed compartment for the victims. The first trial run of the gas trucks occurred in the fall of 1941 at Sachsenhausen concentration camp. Soviet POWs were loaded into the trucks, the engines started, and after thirty minutes of driving around, all of the men had perished.[49] By December 1941, the first gas vans were sent to Riga, to Ukraine and eventually to the Chelmno concentration camp.[50]

Because there were technical issues, such as seals leaking, combined with the low number of vans operating inside Soviet territory, most of these early gas vans were used in small-scale actions, but the issue of using gas to kill was placed on the local administrators' agenda. On October 25, 1941, Dr. Ernst Wetzel, serving in the Ministry of the Eastern Occupied Territories, wrote to Lohse: "I must inform you that Oberdienstleiter Victor Brack, from the Führer's Chancellery, has agreed to cooperate in establishing the necessary buildings and instruments for using gas…. In the current situation, we must not doubt the advantages of using Brack's installations in exterminating Jews who are unsuited for work."[51] Nothing was done however, as Lohse seemed uninterested in building permanent gassing installations, so mass shootings continued to be the method most frequently used to kill Jews living in the Soviet Union.[52]

By the end of 1941, the Einsatzgruppen and their collaborators had murdered approximately 500,000 Jews in occupied Soviet territory. In Latvia, Lithuania, and Estonia, only 48,000 Jews were still alive in December 1941. Out of a population of almost 280,000 people, the order to cleanse the area of Jews had been deemed successful. Most of the killings in this area temporarily halted for a time, primarily because various Nazi offices and the military were at odds over what to do with the remaining Jews. To some officials, there was an extreme labor shortage and Jews with valued skills should be allowed to work for the war effort in ghettos and work camps. To others, however, all Jews, whether they could perform valuable labor or not, should be "liquidated." Karl Jäger, after hearing that an order had been given to keep the remaining "work Jews" alive, wrote:

> There are no more Jews in Lithuania, apart from working Jews and their families…. I wanted to liquidate these working Jews and their families as well, but the civil administration and the Wehrmacht attacked me most sharply and issued a prohibition against having these Jews and their families shot…. The remaining working Jews and Jewesses are urgently needed, and I presume that this manpower will continue to be urgently needed even after the winter is over … I am of the opinion that it is imperative to start at once with the sterilization of the male work-Jews to prevent propagation.[53]

Jäger did not get his wish to see Jewish male workers forcibly sterilized in Lithuania; however, the shootings and ghetto formation continued throughout occupied lands. The men of the killing squads competed with other units to see how many Jews they could murder in each "action." Christopher Browning's *Ordinary Men* shows the police reservists keeping score and participating in "Jew hunts," looking for any Jews who might have evaded the round-ups and shootings. Behind the idea of competition was the desire to "de-Jewify" the East, making the territories a scene of absolute horror.

Babi Yar

One such event occurred near Kiev, at Babi Yar. While very few individuals survived these types of mass shootings, we do have the words of one woman, Dina Wasserman, who described what happened to the Jews of Kiev. On September 28, 1941, notices were put up ordering the Jews of Kiev to report at 6:00 a.m. on September 29, 1941. The street listed as the collection point was in the vicinity of the cemetery and Jews were notified to bring warm clothes, their papers, and any valuables such as jewelry. Failure to comply would result in execution. In typical Nazi fashion, vague statements were made that Jews were going to be moved "elsewhere." On the appointed day, Dina Wasserman joined thousands of Jews walking to the ravine at Babi Yar. Her elderly mother was with her.

> As we approached Babi Yar, we heard gunfire and barbarous shouting…. As we passed through a gate, we were ordered to hand over our personal documents and valuables and to undress. A German came up to Mother and pulled a gold ring off her finger…. I went to a table at which sat a fat officer. I showed him may passport and said quietly, "I'm a Russian." Suddenly a [Ukrainian] policeman came running up and said, "Don't believe her. She's Jewish. We know her."[54]

Wasserman was instructed to stand aside by the officer and she was able to watch the events going on around her while her own fate hung in the balance. She continued:

> I watched as each group of men, women, old people, and children whose turn it was, undressed. They were all led to the open trench and shot…. I saw a young woman, completely naked, nursing a naked baby, and then a policeman ran up to her, snatched the baby away from the woman's breast, and hurled it still alive into the trench. The mother jumped in after him…. The German who had ordered me to wait led me to his commander, showed him my passport, and said, "The woman claims to be Russian, but the policeman knows her as a Jew." The commander looked at the passport and said, "Dina isn't a Russian name. You're a Jew. Take her away." The policeman ordered me to undress and pushed me toward the steep slope, where a group stood waiting for its fate. But, before the shots were fired, out of fear, I fell in, onto the corpses…. I pretended to

be dead. Beneath me and on top of me, lay dead and wounded—many of them still breathing, others were groaning. I pushed the bodies off me. I was afraid of being buried alive…. It started getting dark. Germans with submachine guns went past and shot at the wounded…. I showed no sign of life…. When it was completely dark and there was silence, I opened my eyes and saw that no one was around…. Suddenly I felt someone moving behind me…. I turned back and asked quietly, "Who are you?" I was answered by a soft, childish voice: "Auntie, don't be afraid, I'm Fima Schneidermann. I'm eleven"…We both started moving.[55]

Wasserman and Schneidermann are two of the few people to have survived such an event. They had to escape the scene and go into hiding.

The killings at Babi Yar, done over the course of two days, resulted in "de-Jewing" Kiev by murdering 33,771 Jews. Einsatzgruppen reports asserted that in actuality 36,000 Jews had been killed, as some were found hiding in the vicinity and were shot.[56]

In the passage by Wasserman, one can see the collaboration of Ukrainian policemen in the destruction of the Jews. Had the Ukrainian policeman not intervened when Dina Wasserman showed her Russian passport to the first German officer, he might have thought the paperwork was in order and excused her from the execution site. Unfortunately, neighbors and even relatives were often all too eager to rid themselves of the Jewish presence. Such was the case in the region of Novo-Zlatopol, near the Dnieper River. Novo-Zlatopol was occupied by the Germans in October 1941. Approximately 2,000 Jews were still residing in this area when they were ordered to "take their best clothing and food for the journey … They were taken to the back of the gendarmerie building, told to dig eight pits in the ground, and then [the Germans] began executing them…. Eight hundred people were murdered."[57]

In reality, the Germans were joined by local Ukrainians and Volksdeutsche in the killing operation. One German family in Novo-Zlatopol had two sons. One German son had married a Jewish woman and they had children together. The other German son (unmarried) had joined the local police force once the German occupation began. When the killings began, the married brother was already in the Red Army away from the town. The unmarried brother gathered his Jewish sister-in-law, his nieces. and nephews, and escorted them to the execution site. The children cried out, "Uncle, save us, we don't want to die!" They were all killed. Once again, local populations—even relatives of Jews—who had once been co-existing side by side with Jews were now complicit in these murders.[58]

The Wannsee Conference

As the winter of 1941–1942 approached, Heydrich wanted to move on the "Final Solution to the Jewish Question." He had mailed out invitations to various government officials for a "Final Solution Conference," but it had been postponed due to Japan's attack on the United States. Hitler responded to the attack on Pearl Harbor by declaring war on the U.S. on December 11, 1941, thus transforming the war into a truly worldwide conflict. For Heydrich, this delay led him to reschedule his conference for January 20, 1942. The meeting, which took place in a luxurious villa in a suburb outside of Berlin called Am Grossen Wannsee, became the site where Heydrich made it clear to all the various government agencies that he and Himmler had been put in charge of settling the "Jewish Question." No Nazi official higher than Heydrich was present at the meeting.

The conference began with Heydrich announcing that he would be the "plenipotentiary for the preparation of the 'Final Solution of the Jewish Question' in Europe."[59] Nazi mastery of euphemistic language is in full force in the minutes of the Wannsee Conference. Heydrich stated that forcing the Jews out of the life of the German people and forcing Jews out of the living space of the German people were the most important aspects of fighting the enemy. Much time was devoted to speaking about the emigration of the Jews, the various obstacles that had been encountered so far in trying to get Jews away from Germans. Now, Heydrich decreed, emigration was closed to Jews. Instead, it would be replaced with "evacuation" of the Jews "to the East as a further possible solution, in accordance with previous authorization by the Führer."[60] However, moving Jews to the East was only a provisional solution. The "Final Solution of the Jewish Question" involved 11 million Jews according to the charts Heydrich and Eichmann had produced for the meeting. What was to be done with that many Jews?

Heydrich stated that Jews would be assigned to labor units in the East, segregated by sex. He expected that "a large part will undoubtedly disappear through natural diminution."[61] What was to happen to those Jews who could survive forced labor? Heydrich argued that those who survived, "being undoubtedly the part most capable of resistance, will have to be appropriately dealt with, since it represents a natural selection and in the event of release is to be regarded as the germ cell of a new Jewish renewal."[62] This was a roundabout way of stating that Jews who were strong enough to survive deportations and harsh labor conditions would have to be killed.

The rest of the Wannsee Conference then went into the details that had been troubling Heydrich, so the discussion was what to do with Jews over the age of sixty-five, Mischlinge, Jews in mixed marriages, Jews working in the armaments industries, and so on. One of the officials, Dr. Stuckart, advocated for the forced sterilization of Jews and Mischlinge. He also argued for the dissolution of mixed marriages.[63] Secretary of State Dr. Bühler added that Jews in the General Government region should be done away with first as the Jews there were unfit to work and they would not need transportation to the East since they were already in the East. His only request was "that the Jewish question in this territory be solved as quickly as possible."[64] Bühler also recommended that no alarms should be raised among the Jewish population. With that, the men at the meeting all agreed to support Heydrich in his task to implement the "Final Solution to the Jewish Question" and the meeting adjourned.[65] With that, the fate of millions of European Jews was sealed.

After the meeting, Eichmann typed up the minutes and then thirty copies were circulated to different government agencies. Both Himmler and Goebbels gave separate speeches where they both articulated the same message: the "Final Solution" had to happen here and now because, they said, there was only one Adolf Hitler in history and the war had presented the German leadership with a unique way of solving the Jewish problem. "They warned that later generations would not have the strength nor the opportunity to 'finish off' the Jews."[66] For Germans on the home front, the propaganda continued to stream forth, stressing that Jews represented an existential threat to the Volksgemeinschaft and therefore, extreme measures against the Jews were absolutely necessary.

The Judeo-Bolshevik conspiracy and the home front

From the early days of the invasion of the Soviet Union, the Reich Security Main Office in Berlin wanted to gather information about the general populations' attitudes toward the Bolshevik threat. Leaders such as Heydrich must have been pleased to read reactions to newsreels from July 12–18, 1941:

> All reports received confirm that the images of the victims of Bolshevik terror in Lvov have been the object of the greatest discussion…. the by far most common conviction expressed is that precisely such pictures of the true nature of Bolshevism and Jewry, in all their realistic horror, must today be shown again and again, so that each and every Volksgenosse may be convinced, through this cool and objective factual material, of the danger which Jewish Bolshevism harbors, and be given a palpable visual impression of the ultimate meaning and import of the German struggle.[67]

Apparently, the weekly newsreels became so popular that additional showings were scheduled, with audiences packing the theaters and howling and cheering whenever Jews were depicted. In one report, the author notes that people have watched a reel called the "March of the Jews" which depicted various "types" of Jews, provoking "comments of disgust; a number of persons asked what would actually be done in future with these hordes."[68]

One suggestion that also began to appear in reports by August 1941 was the visible marking of Jews with badges of some sort. Jews in occupied Poland were already forced to wear armbands or badges that designated them as Jews, but as of August 1941, Jews in Germany were not yet marked as such. One office in Bielefeld, asking for a special badge, argued that "the Volksgenossen think it insufferable that in the streetcars, in buses, and elsewhere in public transport, they are forced to stand next to members of a people who bear the major guilt for the present war, and whose racial compatriots are trying in every way to destroy Germany."[69] The numerous demands to mark Jews were answered with the decree that, beginning on September 19, 1941, all Jews in Germany would have to wear a marking badge in public. The reports then note, "It is not exaggerated to assert that this police order has been received with genuine satisfaction in all strata of the population."[70] But not everyone was pleased, as some reports also trickled in stating that Aryans who were married to Jews should also be forced to wear the Star,[71] while still others were not pleased that Jews tried to hide the badge by holding a briefcase or purse in front to block the view.[72]

Still not content with restrictions placed upon the remaining Jews in Germany, some individuals demanded clarifications regarding the wearing of the Star of David. In the town of Warburg, an Aryan man and his Jewish wife became a source of controversy. Because theirs was a "privileged mixed marriage," the Jewish wife did not have to wear the Star. The townspeople were in an uproar because Jews were not allowed to use the sidewalks, but "If this Jewess walks on the sidewalks, she gravely annoys those Volksgenossen who know her. But if she does not use the sidewalk, she causes a disturbance, because she is not wearing the Star of David." The report concluded that this "loophole" needed to be closed immediately so that all Jews, whether married to Aryans or not, would have to display the Star even though most Jews "find it quite unpleasant to be marked and identified in this manner."[73] Connected to the increasing demands for Jews to be marked were the corresponding requests that areas of Germany become truly "judenfrei." In Lübeck, the NSDAP official submitted a report complaining about the severity of housing shortages for Aryans while Jews still occupied "quite good apartments." The recommendation was that "thought should be given to whether it is conceivable to deport these unpleasant fellows to the East, so that they might disappear completely from the townscapes of our Gau."[74] Deportations of Jews from the Altreich (Old Reich) would not be far behind public sentiment.

Deportations from the Old Reich

Beginning in October 1941, one month after Jews in Germany were compelled to wear the Star of David, the Nazi regime began its program of deportation of Jews from the Old Reich, including Germany, Austria, and the Protectorate region (Czech lands). Joseph Goebbels noted in his diary on September 24, 1941, "The Führer believes that the Jews must be gradually removed from Germany. The first cities to be made free of Jews will be Berlin, Vienna, and Prague."[75] However, the next question that needed to be addressed was the location of deportation: Where would the Jews of the Old Reich be sent? In an earlier chapter, we have already explored the deportation of Viennese Jews to the East and the appalling living conditions they encountered in the Lodz ghetto. Hitler himself had selected the cities which would receive the deported Jews. The first transports of Jews, taken in batches of 1,000 people at a time, were to Lodz, Minsk, Riga, or Kaunas. The deportations would be carried out in two separate phases. Between October and November, 19,593 Jews had been transported out of the Old Reich and into the Lodz ghetto. On November 8, the second phase of deportations began, lasting until mid-January 1942. In the second phase, Jews were sent even further east to Riga, Kaunas, and Minsk. However, the vast majority of the Jews sent to Riga, then rerouted to Kaunas, never made it to the ghetto. Instead, they were taken in groups to the Ninth Fort where they were all executed.[76] This was, according to the research of Yitzak Arad, "the Holocaust's first act of mass murder of Reich Jews."[77]

In addition, 10,000 Jews who had been living in the Kovno ghetto and 13,000 Jews in Minsk were shot before the transports, presumably to "make room" for the incoming Jews from the Old Reich territories.[78] Himmler began to receive letters of complaint that German war veterans and Mischlinge had been included in the massacred transports. He responded that "no liquidation" of the Jews deported from Berlin to Riga "should take place."[79] However, the order reached Riga too late, and Friedrich Jeckeln of the local Einsatzgruppe had already carried out the mass shootings as part of the usual extermination policy in occupied Soviet territories. Back in August 1941, Jeckeln had boasted at a gala that he had killed 44,125 people. He was also the man in charge of the mass killings at Babi Yar. By the time German Jews were being deported in October 1941, Jeckeln and his men had murdered at least 100,000 people.[80]

In early October 1941, Hitler delivered a speech in which he said:

There can be no compromises, an absolutely clear and unambiguous solution is essential, and that means especially here in the east the total annihilation of our enemies. These enemies are not even human beings by the standards of European culture, but they are raised up from childhood to be criminals and are trained as criminal animals. Such animals must be destroyed.[81]

He underscored this point by stating, "the law of existence demands endless killing, so that the better can live."[82] Having made it perfectly clear that in order for the Volksgemeinschaft to thrive, Jews had to die, the simultaneous processes of "clearing the ghettos" of Jewish inhabitants and the deportations of Jews from the Old Reich continued, as did plans to resettle ethnic Germans in the East.

Das Ungeziefer

Das Leben ist nicht lebenswert,
Wo man nicht dem Schmarotzer wehrt,
Als Nimmersatt herumzukriechen.
Wir müssen und wir werden siegen.

FIGURE 7.1 *Image titled "Vermin" with caption reading: "Life is not worth living, / when one does not resist the parasite, / Never satisfied as it creeps about. / We must and will win." From* Der Stürmer, *September 28, 1944, Issue #39. Courtesy Randall Bytwerk, German Propaganda Archive, Calvin College.*

By October 21, 1941 Hitler delivered yet another tirade against the Jews. In this instance he declared:

Jesus was not a Jew; the Jew Paul falsified Jesus' teaching in order to undermine the Roman Empire. The Jews' aim was to destroy the nations by undermining their racial core.... The Jews continued to torture people in the name of Bolshevism, just as Christianity, the offshoot of Judaism, had tortured its opponents in the Middle Ages. Saul became Saint Paul. Mordechai became Karl Marx.[83]

The ending then summarized his intent: "By exterminating this pest, we shall do humanity a service of which our soldiers can have no idea."[84]

This theme was revisited in yet another speech, on November 8, 1941, to Nazi "Old Fighters." After listing all of the terrible and dangerous things Jews supposedly did, Hitler told his loyal followers: "This struggle, my old party comrades, has really become not only a struggle for Germany, but for the whole of Europe, a struggle [that will decide] between existence and annihilation!"[85] Following the German declaration of war against the United States, Hitler spoke to a group of Gauleiter on December 12, 1941. Goebbels summed up Hitler's speech stating that Hitler reminded the audience that he had once prophesied that if world war came, it would lead to the annihilation of the Jews. "The world war is here, the extermination of the Jews must be its necessary consequence. ...We are not here to have compassion for the Jews, but to have compassion for our German people."[86]

Although Hitler's December 12 speech was to his hardcore fanatical "Old Fighters," the reports on the general mood of the German population seem to reflect the increasing acceptance that Jews needed to die in order for Germans to live. One report noted that based on newsreels showing "Jewish crimes" comments were made saying, "It would be better to just take these rascals and shoot them."[87] The Governor of Franconia reported that in the course of an "evacuation" of the 1,001 Jews and nine children from Nuremberg for Riga, three Jewish women committed suicide. In another part of his jurisdiction, he noted that a gallows had been built and the words "For the Jewess" was attached "in protest against the only Jewish person still resident in the district, the spouse of the watchmaker Reuter."[88] The Gendarme of Forchheim sent in their report regarding the "evacuation" of Jews from Forchheim to Bamberg then on to Nuremberg and finally to Riga. Back in Forchheim, it was noted that "While they [the Jews] were being readied for transport at the local Paradeplatz, a large number of local residents gathered, who watched them being sent off with great interest and satisfaction.... The apartments of the Jews evacuated were closed and sealed.... It is certain that Forchheim will be 'judenfrei' by Christmas 1941."[89]

There were those in Germany who voiced some disagreement about the necessity of deporting Jews to the East. In Minden, the Security Office reported that as the Jews of the locality were being prepared for evacuation, some Germans expressed concerns that "it is probably very questionable to ship the people specifically to the East now, during winter with all its dangers. It is quite likely that many Jews will not survive the transport.... People think that for many Jews, this decision is too harsh."[90] However, the SD report also added, "But Volksgenossen who are well informed about the Jewish Question are absolutely in favor and approve of this action."[91] Despite the reservations expressed by some Germans living in Minden, the first transport of Jews began on December 11, 1941. Jews from the area were brought to a central location where they were held for two days while their luggage was searched. The transport, destined for Riga, left on Saturday, December 13. The SD Main Office noted that the transport elicited a great deal of discussion among the general population, adding "people were grateful to the Führer for liberating us from the pestilence of Jewish blood." One worker said: "They should have done this with the Jews 50 years ago. Then we wouldn't have had to go through a world war or the present war we've got." The author of the report also noted how many people were "astonished" that "well-appointed buses" were used to transport the Jews to the train station.[92]

No difficulties arose as the Jews were forced out of Minden and its local area; however, a few days after the deportation, the Gestapo and the local Revenue Office were already engaged in an argument over which office had the right to use and dispose of Jewish assets left behind in the wake of their evacuation.[93] This type of response was fairly typical. In Göttingen, even before the Jewish population had been deported, there was a scramble among the local Germans to stake a claim for a Jewish apartment. The Party District Chief wrote, "The district head office is being swamped by requests for assignment of apartments."[94]

For those Jews about to be deported, fear and uncertainty dominated their mood. On November 15, 1941, Willy Cohn, his wife, and their two young daughters received notification that they were to be deported from Breslau on November 25. Cohn wrote in his diary, "But now all this must be dealt with, and one must try to bear up, on behalf of the children, and the words I've called out to other people—chazak ve'ematz [Hebrew: be strong and have courage]—now apply to me as well."[95] On November 29, Willy Cohn and his family were shot in Kovno. The German police officer in charge of the executions stated dryly: "693 male Jews, 1155 female Jews, 152 Jewish children. 2000 [total] (Resettled from Vienna and Breslau)."[96] According to the language of the policeman's report, Willy Cohn and family had been "resettled" in Kovno.

Still other Jews from the Old Reich were deported and kept at least temporarily alive in ghettos. Shlomo Frank, living in the Lodz ghetto, recorded the transports as more and more Jews from the Old Reich were dumped into the already overcrowded ghetto. On October 19, 1941, he noted that 1,000 Jews from Vienna arrived, on October 21, 1,050 Jews from Prague, on October 22, 1,200 Viennese Jews, on October 23, Jews from Frankfurt, and so on.[97] What life awaited the newly deported Jews in these ghettos? A life of deprivation and misery. Irene Hauser, a forty-year-old married woman with a five-year-old son Eric (Bubi), and her husband Leopold were deported from Vienna to the Lodz ghetto. Irene kept a notebook documenting what was happening to their family. Her entries reflect the onslaught of extreme hunger, dysentery, rashes, fevers, and overall weakness due to starvation.

On July 24, 1942, Irene wrote:

As of today we've been here for 9 months, also a Friday. Two executions for stealing half a loaf of bread and 60 RM. 18-year old young men are collapsing. My neighbors below me, woman of 40 and daughter of 17, 2 year-old child, starved to death, etc. We must be rescued soon or we'll all be dead, God help us.[98]

On September 11, Irene and her son were sent on to Chelmno where they were murdered.[99]

Many of the German Jews who now found themselves struggling to survive in the ghettos were mistakenly convinced that they were placed in the East to work for the German war effort and that the fate of the East European Jews was something that would not happen to them as Germans. For example, in Riga, two ghettos co-existed side-by-side: the "German ghetto," which was the larger of the two, and the smaller ghetto for the local Riga Jews. The "German ghetto" by February 1942 held approximately 14,300 people while the Riga Jews' smaller ghetto held close to 4,000. Upon arrival in the "German ghetto," the Jews from the Reich discovered that they were being housed in apartments that had belonged to Riga Jews. They found dishes, clothing, and even frozen corpses. The "Reich Jews" understood that the former "inhabitants had been murdered, but they still believed that their own fate would differ from that of the 'Ostjuden' [Eastern Jews]."[100] One woman in the deportations noted, "The Jews from Germany ... did not expect the same fate.... Thus, after recovering from the first shock at the sights of death and bloodshed, they believed that what had happened to the Latvian Jews could not happen to them."[101] This was, of course, misplaced hope for Nazis did not see any difference between a German Jew and a Latvian Jew.

"Reich Jews" underwent selections and those who were deemed unfit for labor were murdered in gas vans. Still others were removed from the ghetto and were taken to the forests for execution. Tensions existed between the small ghetto of local Jews and the "German ghetto" mainly because the Riga Jews believed (correctly) that their family members had been killed in order to make room in the larger ghetto for the incoming transports of Reich Jews. The divisions between the locals and the Reich Jews began to diminish somewhat in February and March 1942 when selections and executions were carried out against Reich Jews. From that point on, both ghetto inhabitants came to recognize that "no one was safe."[102] For a brief six-month time, no further deportation transports were brought into Riga; however, they resumed in August 1942 and continued on till the end of October 1942. Most of the Jews brought in to the ghetto in Riga were from Frankfurt and Theresienstadt. Further selections were made; many were simply shot.

The Riga ghetto was closed in November 1943. Approximately 2,000 Jews were sent to Auschwitz. For those left behind, they were sent to various labor camps while some were also sent to Stutthof concentration camp. By the end of the war, of the thousands of Reich Jews who had been deported to Riga, 600–800 of them remained alive. Arad concludes, "The Reich Jews who were deported to Minsk and Riga believed naively that they were being taken to settle and work in far-off regions of Eastern Europe. In the ghettos and camps of Minsk and Riga they faced the cruel realization that Nazi Germany's policies of extermination were directed not only against Ostjuden but also against them."[103] German Jews were not included in the Volksgemeinschaft. They were the enemy in Hitler's mind and they had to be exterminated or else the German people would die.

In January 1942, Hitler spoke at the Berlin Sportplast. He declared, "We are fully aware that this war can end either in the extermination of the Aryan peoples or in the disappearance of Jewry from Europe.... the result of this war will be the annihilation of Jewry. For the first time, the old, truly Jewish rule of 'an eye for an eye, a tooth for a tooth' will obtain."[104] In the next chapter, we will examine the further radicalization of Hitler's war of extermination.

For your consideration

Below you will find two accounts of mobile killing squads' actions. Read both accounts and then compare them: What seems different? Have the procedures of killing been modified? Who are the victims in each encounter? Where do the shootings take place in each incident? Are there eyewitnesses to these accounts? Do you see an evolution in the work of the Einsatzgruppen?

The first account is from Przemysil, Poland on September 20, 1939. The men of Einsatzgruppe I and Einsatzgruppe z.b.V., most likely assisted by Wehrmacht soldiers, committed the single largest murder action against a civilian population to date in the Polish campaign. Here is a private citizen's account of what he witnessed:

> Several days after the arrival of the Germans I was driving along Mickiewicz Street, one of the main thoroughfares in Przemysil, when I saw a ragged line of people running down the middle of the street, all with their hands clasped behind their necks. I pulled over to one side and stopped my truck. Around a hundred people ran past, and as they did, I saw that they were Jews. They were half-naked and crying out as they ran, "Juden sind Schweine" ("Jews are swine."). Along the line, revolvers in hand, German soldiers were running, young boys about eighteen years old, dressed in dark uniforms with swastikas on the sleeves, with light blond hair and rosy faces. When someone fell behind or broke pace, they beat the victim with the butts of their revolvers or with whips, or simply kicked him. Poles gathered on the sidewalks, incredulous, some crossing themselves at this monstrous sight. The face of the old Jews were contorted with pain, and the young boys were crying, but the Germans ran along the street almost joyfully drunk with power. As I later found out, the soldiers had fallen

on the Jewish section of town that morning and had driven all the men and boys out of their houses with blows and kicks. They made them do calisthenics for several hours in the street, and now they were driving them toward the railway station and on, until they crossed the city limits.

I returned home, shaken. Only in the afternoon, when I had calmed down somewhat, did I go out again to return my truck to the power station. Now a new horror met my eyes: distraught, weeping women were running toward the cemetery, for they had heard that all the Jews taken in the morning had been shot in Pikulice, the first village outside town. I put a load of these wailing women in my truck and headed for Pikulice. Right at the edge of the village, beside a small hill, a swarm of people had gathered. I drove up and stopped. What I saw surpassed all belief; it was a scene out of Dante's hell. All the men driven through the streets in the morning lay there dead. Some of the men from the nearby houses told me what had happened. The Jews had been driven up to the side of the hill and ordered to turn around. A truck was already standing there. A canvas had been lifted off a heavy machine gun, and several bursts of fire rang out, sweeping back and forth. Then a few more shots were fired into the few bodies that were still writhing. All was still. The soldiers climbed into the truck, and drove away.

I went quietly up to the little hill. The corpses were lying on their backs or sides in the most contorted positions, some on top of others, with their arms outstretched, their heads shattered by the bullets. Here were pools of blood; there the earth was rust colored with blood; the grass glistened with blood; blood was drying on the corpses. Women with bloodied hands were hunting through the pile of bodies for their fathers, husbands, sons. A sickish sweet smell pervaded the air.

I felt something inside me die, as though my heart had turned to stone. I was choking from the smell, from the sight, from the cries filling the air. I saw everything, but I could not grasp what I saw. Before my eyes I had an image of the laughing young Germans, the proud representatives of Hitler's New Order.

> *Document taken from Jürgen Matthäus, Jochen Böhler,*
> *and Klaus-Michael Mallmann, eds.,* Documenting Life and Destruction
> Holocaust Sources in Context: War, Pacification, and Mass Murder, 1939:
> The Einsatzgruppen in Poland, *93–95, quote from 94–95.*

Second account: This selection consists of two men's reporting regarding the murder of the Jews at Babi Yar in Soviet occupied territory. The shootings lasted for two days, September 29–30, 1941.

Statement of Kurt Werner, member of Sonderkommando 4a:

That day the entire Kommando with the exception of one guard set out at 6 o'clock in the morning for these shootings. I myself went there by lorry. It was all hands on deck. We drove for about twenty minutes in a northerly direction. We stopped on a cobbled road in the open country. The road stopped there. There were countless Jews gathered there and a place had been set up where the Jews had to hand in their clothes and their luggage. A kilometer further on I saw a large natural ravine. The terrain was sandy. The ravine was about 10 meters deep, some 400 meters long, about 80 meters wide across the top and about 10 meters wide at the bottom.

As soon as I arrived at the execution area I was sent down on the bottom of the ravine with some of the other men. It was not long before the first Jews were brought to us over the side of the ravine. The Jews had to lie face down on the earth by the ravine walls. There were three groups of marksmen down at the bottom of the ravine, each made up of about twelve men. Groups of Jews were sent down to each of the execution squads simultaneously. Each successive group of Jews had to lie down on top of the bodies of those that had already been shot. The marksmen stood behind the Jews and killed them with a shot in the neck. I still recall today the complete terror of the Jews when they first caught sight of the bodies as they reached the top edge of the ravine. Many Jews cried out in terror. It's almost impossible to imagine what nerves of steel it took to carry out that dirty work down there. It was horrible....

I had to spend the whole morning down in the ravine. For some of the time I had to shoot continuously. Then I was given the job of loading sub-machine gun magazines with ammunition. While I was doing that, other comrades were assigned to shooting duty. Towards midday we were called away from the ravine and in the afternoon I, with some of the others up at the top, had to lead the Jews to the ravine. While we were doing this there were other men shooting down in the ravine. The Jews were led by us up to the edge of the ravine and from there they walked down the slope on their own. The shooting that day must have lasted until ... 17.00 or 18.00 hours. Afterwards we were taken back to our quarters. That evening we were given alcohol (schnapps) again.

Anton Heidborn (Sonderkommando 4a) on the days that followed:

The third day after the execution we were taken back to the execution area. On our arrival we saw a woman sitting by a bush who had apparently survived the execution unscathed. This woman was shot by the SD man who was accompanying us. I do not know his name. We also saw someone waving their hand from among the pile of bodies. I don't know whether it was a man or a woman. I should think that this person was finished off by the SD man as well, though I did not actually see it.

The same day work began to cover up the piles of bodies. Civilians were used for this task. The ravine walls were also partly blown up.

After that day I never returned to the execution area. The next few days were spent smoothing our banknotes belonging to the Jews that had been shot. I estimate these must have totaled millions. I do not know what happened to the money. It was packed up in sacks and sent off somewhere.

Documents taken from Ernst Klee, Willi Dessen,
and Volker Riess, eds., "The Good Old Days:"
The Holocaust as Seen by Its Perpetrators and Bystanders, 66–68.

Suggestions for further reading

Yitzhak Arad, *The Holocaust in the Soviet Union* (Lincoln, NE, 2009).

Christopher Browning, *Ordinary Men: Reserve Police Battalion 101 and the Final Solution in Poland* (New York, 1996).

Patrick DesBois, *The Holocaust by Bullets* (New York, 2008).

Richard J. Evans, *The Third Reich at War* (New York, 2009).

Lauren Faulkner-Rossi, *Wehrmacht Priests: Catholicism and the Nazi War of Annihilation* (Cambridge, MA, 2015).

Robert Gerwarth, *Hitler's Hangman: The Life of Heydrich* (New Haven, CT, 2012).

Daniel Jonah Goldhagen, *Hitler's Willing Executioners: Ordinary Germans and the Holocaust* (New York, 1996).

Sonja M. Hedgepeth and Rochelle G. Saidel, eds., *Sexual Violence against Jewish Women during the Holocaust* (Lebanon, NH, 2010).

Radu Ioanid, *The Holocaust in Romania: The Destruction of Jews and Gypsies under the Antonescu Regime* (Ivan R. Dee, 2008).

Emil Kerenji, ed., *Documenting Life and Destruction Holocaust Sources in Context: Jewish Responses to Persecution*, Vol. 4, *1942–43* (Lanham, MD, 2015).

Ernst Klee, Willi Dressen, and Volker Riess, eds., *"The Good Old Days": The Holocaust as Seen by Its Perpetrators and Bystanders* (Old Saybrook, CT, 1991).

Wendy Lower, *Nazi Empire Building and the Holocaust in the Ukraine* (North Carolina, 2007).

Jürgen Matthäus, Jochen Böhler, and Klaus-Michael Mallmann, eds., *Documenting Life and Destruction Holocaust Sources in Context: War, Pacification, and Mass Murder, 1939: The Einsatzgruppen in Poland* (Lanham, MD, 2014).

Geoffrey Megargee, *War of Annihilation: Combat and Genocide on the Eastern Front* (New York, 2007).

Richard Rhodes, *Masters of Death: The SS Einsatzgruppen and the Invention of the Holocaust* (New York, 2003).

Mark Roseman, *The Villa, the Lake, the Meeting* (London, 2002).

Ben Shepherd, *War in the Wild East* (Cambridge, MA, 2004).

Anton Weiss-Wendt, *Murder without Hatred: Estonians and the Holocaust* (Syracuse, NY, 2009).

Michael Wildt, *An Uncompromising Generation: The Nazi Leadership of the Reich Security Main Office*, translated by Tom Lampbert (Madison, WI, 2009).

8

The Final Solution

If you talk with combat soldiers from the East, you'll see that the Jews
here in Germany are still being treated far too humanely. The correct
approach, people are saying, is to destroy the whole pack of them.
(FEBRUARY 1942)[1]

Introduction

In this final chapter, we will see how the traditions of hate-filled language and
rhetoric against the Jews culminated in the gas chambers of death factories.
In the Nazi universe, Jews had to perish so that the Volksgemeinschaft could
live. Even when it was apparent that Germany would not be able to win the
war, these destructive notions continued to drive German behavior. It was no
longer enough to humiliate, starve, or deport Jews—the "Jewish threat" had
to be completely removed for the sake of future German generations. German
fears regarding Jews coming back to seek revenge for all of the suffering and
degradation inflicted upon them also worked to bind the Volksgemeinschaft into
a killing community, leading to ever-increasing acts of brutality and destruction.

Reactions to the invasion of the Soviet Union

While the Einsatzgruppen continued to perform mass executions and
experiment with the use of gas vans, the military campaign inside the Soviet
Union seemed to founder. When the initial invasion began on June 22, 1941,
the Wehrmacht had 3 million men plus another 500,000–600,000 soldiers
from Allied Powers such as Hungary and Romania. Within three weeks of
the invasion, German forces had penetrated close to 400 miles inside Soviet
territory. Some of the German generals were optimistic that they had done
the unthinkable—invade and conquer the vast expanses of Russia. General
Halder wrote in his diary entry on July 3, 1941, that war with the Soviet
Union would be over in two more weeks.[2]

Goebbels wrote in his diary about what Hitler had told him on July 8: "We will still have some heavy battles to fight, but the Bolshevik armed forces will not be able to recover from the present series of defeats."[3] However, as August rolled around, the Soviet Red Army was still in the fight, the Wehrmacht's progress had been slowed down, and the Germans were taking large numbers of casualties. For the German home front, there were worries that perhaps this war was not going to end as quickly as had once been thought. Goebbels, after that meeting with Hitler on July 8, was told to intensify his propaganda: "We must continue to expose the cooperation between Bolshevism and plutocracy and now increasingly stress the Jewish aspect of this common front. In a few days, the anti-Semitic campaign will begin."[4]

True to his word, Goebbels began to intensify anti-Semitic propaganda. The German press were instructed to focus attention on the Jewish aspects of and influence over the Russian Bolshevik system. In Goebbels' more "intellectual" publication, *Das Reich*, he himself authored the article which depicted how Jews were mimics, able to camouflage themselves in order to trick unsuspecting innocents as they worked to manipulate situations to their benefit. He concluded with, "From every corner of the earth the cry would rise: 'The Jews are guilty! The Jews are guilty!'....As the fist of awakening Germany smashed this racial filth, so one day the fist of awakening Europe will smash it too."[5]

The Minister of Propaganda was helped in his efforts to "prove" how manipulative and threatening Jews were when he found a New Jersey Jew, Theodor N. Kaufman, had self-published a pamphlet called *Germany Must Perish*. In the pamphlet, Kaufman argued that German men should be sterilized and that Germany should be divided and distributed to other neighboring countries. Once Goebbels found this goldmine, he ran articles that portrayed Kaufman as a personal friend of President Franklin D. Roosevelt (he was not) and tried to prove that Kaufman's ideas were really Roosevelt's opinions. Millions of translated copies of Kaufman's pamphlet were released to the German public in September 1941, at precisely the same time German Jews were forced to wear the Star of David.[6]

SD reports representing the mood of the population of Bielefeld were able to report that despite some individual complaints about the duration of the war, "Virtually all Volksgenossen have realized that the Jew is the real instigator of this war. And that is largely due to the exceptional influence of the propaganda....An important recent factor for bringing such broad circles of the population to this realization has been the distribution of the manuscript by the American Jew Kaufmann."[7] Clearly, Goebbels' line of attack against the Jews was working to persuade the Volksgemeinschaft.

The Propaganda Ministry soon had other issues to address. Soldiers were coming home on leave from places such as Warsaw or Lodz and they were "talking in public about the way Jews are being eliminated in these cities; they may be exaggerating....The population is likewise disturbed by this, and it serves to bolster enemy propaganda."[8] Rumors continued to spread. One SD officer in Erfurt wrote, "The wildest rumors are in circulation.... Thus, people are saying that the Security Police has the task of exterminating the Jews in the occupied territories. They say Jews are being rounded up by the thousands and shot after having first been forced to dig their own graves."[9] Of course, these were not "wild rumors" at all. Germans on the home front continued to speculate what the deportations of Jews "to the East" really meant; however, there were no organized protests to the overall "resettlement" process.[10]

Reports continued to flow in that "evacuations" of Jews were moving along smoothly, although the reports usually contain references to Jews committing suicide rather than going on to an undetermined fate.[11] Occasionally, schoolchildren were present during the removal of local Jews. In the Bad Neustadt/Saale region, "The removal and transport of the Jews proceeded without incident. But level-headed among the population were offended by the fact that a large group of schoolchildren, hooting and jeering, accompanied the procession of Jews down to the train station, and continued their howling until the train departed."[12] Apparently yelling and taunting schoolchildren did not qualify as an "incident."

Deportations to the East

For many of the deported Reich Jews, if their transport was headed toward the Lodz ghetto, they would more than likely be completely unaware that Jews living in the ghetto were being killed to "make room" for them prior to their arrival. As we saw in Chapter 7, in the case of Riga's "German ghetto" and the smaller "Latvian" ghetto, thousands of Jews were taken out and executed before the German Jews' arrival. In the case of the Lodz ghetto, the Nazi administrators at first demanded that 20,000 Jews be "resettled" out of Lodz to make room for Reich Jews. Chaim Rumkowski, head of the Jewish Council in Lodz, negotiated the number down to 10,000 people instead. On the same day that the Reich Jews arrived, December 6, 1941, Rumkowski's local Jews were made ready for "labor deployment outside of the ghetto." The vast majority of the 10,000 Jews were deported from Lodz to Chelmno where the gas vans were operational. Between January 12 and 29, 10,103 Jews were gassed. The deportations out of Lodz to Chelmno continued. By April 1942, 34,073 ghetto inhabitants had been gassed.[13]

Most Jews of the Lodz ghetto were unaware of what was happening; however, news did begin to arrive in December 1941, warning them:

Dear cousin Mote Altszul, as you know from Kolo, Dabie, and other places Jews have been sent to Chelmno to a castle. Two weeks have already passed and it is not known how several thousands have perished. They are gone and you should know, there will be no addresses for them.

They were sent to the forest and they were buried.... Do not look upon this as a small matter, they have decided to wipe out, to kill, to destroy. Pass this letter on to learned people to read.[14]

The letter writer was quite accurate in depicting what has occurred in the "heartland of the Holocaust."[15] Throughout the summer of 1942 and continuing on through 1943, the Nazi regime continued to escalate its killing of Jews. Major deportations of Jews out of the East European ghettos, to death factories such as Treblinka and Chelmno, were occurring. The numbers of Jews murdered in this time period is staggering: 265,000 Jews from Warsaw ghetto sent to die in gas chambers in Treblinka; 40,000 Jews from Lwow ghetto taken to be killed in Belzec; 20,000 from Lodz ghetto; and the list goes on. From the Old Reich, mass deportations of Jews began in February 1943 with approximately 11,000 from Germany; 50,000 Jews from the Netherlands; 15,000 Jews from Belgium. With each transport sent away "to the East," the Nazi regime moved closer to Hitler's goal of annihilating the Jews of Europe.[16]

Goebbels noted in his diary as early as March 1942, "In this matter [the question of the Jews], the Führer is inexorable as ever: the Jews are to be thrown out of Europe, if necessary with use of the most brutal means."[17] However, by the end of March 1942, Goebbels had a much clearer vision of what the Führer envisioned, writing, "Jews are now being deported to the east from the territory ruled by the General-Government, starting with Lublin. Here will be used a fairly barbarous method that one can't come close to describing, not much will remain of the Jews themselves." His entry estimated that at least 60 percent of the Jews sent East would have to die as they were unfit for labor. He continued,

The former district leader of Vienna, who is in charge of the action, is showing a good deal of circumspection in following a method that does not attract a lot of attention. Justice is being meted out to the Jews; although it is barbarous, they deserve it... If we did not defend ourselves against the Jews, they would destroy us. It is a struggle of life and death between the Aryan race and the Jewish bacillus.... In this respect too the Führer is the constant champion and spokesman of a radical solution.[18]

Indeed, Hitler's personal manservant, Linge, reported that the Führer had several private meetings with Himmler throughout this time period. Speculation suggests that they were discussing the methods to be employed in the annihilation of the Jews. The procedure that they mapped out, from what we have already seen, followed the pattern of emptying the ghettos of their Jewish populations while killing the Jews of the Soviet Union in pits and gas vans, followed by the "resettlement" of Jews from Germany and Western Europe to the East where the same procedure of annihilation could continue. In Hitler's mind, Jews were not human beings, but rather "they were animals and beasts." He reportedly said, "If valuable men had to die each day at the front, then it was really of no consequence if such vermin like the Jews were killed. They were no different from 'tuberculosis bacilli'." Why should Germans lose their lives while Jews continued to live? This made absolutely no sense to Hitler.[19]

By September 30, 1942, Hitler could confidently make his "prophecy" once again that Jews would be annihilated if there was a world war. Speaking at the Berlin Sportpalast for a "Volk Rally," Führer laid out his plans: "First, since this war was forced on us, neither the power of arms nor time will defeat us. Second, should Jewry instigate an international world war in order to exterminate the Aryan people of Europe, then not the Aryan people will be exterminated, but the Jews."[20] He continued by referencing America's entry into the war, which widened the conflict even further, and then he made yet another prediction:

> Correspondingly, however, a wave of antisemitism swept over one nation after another. And it will continue to do so, taking hold of one state after another. Every state that enters this war will one day emerge from it as an anti-Semitic state. The Jews once laughed about my prophecies in Germany.... Today, too, I can assure you of one thing: they will soon not feel like laughing anymore anywhere. My prophecies will prove correct here, too.[21]

Hitler already knew, by the time he made his "prophecies" in September, that Jews who were living under German domination were facing extermination. By September 1942, the main death camps of Auschwitz, Belzec, Treblinka, Sobibor, Chelmno, and Majdanek/Lublin were operating in full force. Alongside of the killing machinery of these death camps, hundreds of thousands of Jews were being used as slave labor in work camps, factories, and in ghettos. Others were being killed in the "standard" way of shooting on the spot. For many Jews within these spheres of Nazi control, despair was mounting, as were rumors about what was actually taking place when Jews were "deported" or "resettled."

Jewish responses to deportation

For many Jews, living in closely monitored and shrinking ghettos, they had to consider whether mass deportations out of the ghetto with all of its attendant violence were isolated incidents or whether these "actions" were part of a larger, more coordinated German policy.[22] They also had to address the new realities of living in a greatly reduced ghetto community, readjusting their modes of survival to the changing circumstances under which they were now forced to live.[23] As the ghetto environments shrunk in size, some inhabitants came to believe that although they could work for the Germans for a time, it was only a temporary situation before the Germans decided to murder them all.[24] Jews also had different responses to these new situations. Some thought only of today, such as an eighteen-year-old named David Briner, who had lost all of his family in the deportations from the Warsaw ghetto.

Briner had become a looter, scavenging through the empty apartments, selling whatever items he could find on the black market, and using the money for food. Speaking to an interviewer from the Oyneg Shabes network, he said, "So I eat and drink. Should I save money? Money is worthless. Should I bring some to Treblinka? Yesterday my dinner cost 220 zl [zloty]... I don't think about it. I don't want to know what tomorrow will bring."[25] Briner's despair had led him to live only for the day, but others focused on preparing hideouts in the ghetto to escape the further deportations they fully anticipated would come. Emanuel Ringelblum noted,

> Hideouts are currently, in December 1942, a popular phenomenon. Everybody is now making hideouts. They are being built everywhere, in all the shops in the ghetto.... A new series of hideouts began after the selection.... People learned not to believe the Germans. People understand that as long as the current system is in place another action against the Jews will take place sooner or later, and that ultimately the Jewish ghetto will be liquidated.[26]

Rumors continued to flood into places such as the diminished Warsaw ghetto, with survivors from other work camps and smaller ghetto liquidations, making their way to Warsaw, giving chilling accounts of the organized murder of the Jews. However, as these testimonies came in piecemeal, some Jews in the remaining ghettos and work camps did not have a complete picture of all that was unfolding.

Some individuals, however, were not willing to wait and hope that a hideout might save them. There were calls to action:

> Be Vigilant. The uncertainty of the morrow poisons every minute of the bitter slave life of the Jewish community in Warsaw. Every day brings various "certain" news, rumors, terms concerning the fate of the Warsaw ghetto. They "give" us two weeks, three weeks, three months, four months to live. Frayed nerves twitch, the exhausted spirit feverishly vacillates between hope and resigned despair. Has terrible experience taught us nothing? Will we still allow ourselves to be lulled by the good word of this or that German murderer, by this or that canard spread by Jewish Gestapo men, traitors who have been bought, or credulous people? There is no doubt that Hitlerism has set for itself the goal of destroying all Jews. [emphasis in the original] It is just doing it gradually, in stages. Its main tactical principle: fooling, luring in the Jewish masses.[27]

This document, written as an editorial in the Warsaw ghetto in December 1942, attempted to shake Jews out of their belief that they might still survive the war. The author reminded them, "We remember all the lies, beginning with the 'evacuation to the east' [and] ending with the [identification] numbers, mass ID issuing, selections, and registrations. We all know the truth about the gigantic slaughterhouse at Treblinka, where hundreds of thousands of fathers and mothers, brothers and sisters, sons and daughters have been killed in such an inhumane and refined-bestial manner."[28] The rest of the editorial warns the remaining Jews of Warsaw not to be fooled. The writer points out the euphemistic language employed by the Germans to kill Jews, showing phrases such as "for work," "tailors needed," "transfer site," or "fed" have all led to the same ending: death. The final segment of the editorial calls for all Jews to reject the lies being fed to them by Judenrat leaders, by police officers, and by German officials. "Prepare to defend your lives....Let us defend our honor with bravery and dignity."[29] The authors' words did not fall on deaf ears, for ultimately, one of the largest armed ghetto uprisings would occur inside the Warsaw ghetto in April 1943.

Deportations continue

Outside of the General Government region, plans were under way to deport large numbers of Jews from regions outside of Poland "to the East." The first area to deport "their" Jews, following Germany, Austria, and the Protectorate, was Slovakia. The March 1942 transport had 999 young Jewish women. They were sent to Auschwitz. For the Slovakian political leaders, it was a straightforward economic calculation: the Jews of Slovakia had been robbed of their property and were now economic liabilities. It made good economic sense to deport the Jews away. In fact, the Slovak government paid the Germans 500 Reichsmarks per Jew to take the Jews away. In exchange, the Slovak government got to keep all confiscated Jewish property left behind. They also received the welcome news that "the deported Jews would not return."[30] In this way, at least 20,000 Slovakian Jews were deported.

The plans to deport Jews living in Holland, Belgium, and France (both occupied and unoccupied portions) fell into place following the assassination of Reinhard Heydrich in Prague in 1942. "Operation Reinhard" unleashed a venomous wave of increased violence—both in Eastern Europe and in the West. The man placed in charge of making "Operation Reinhard" work was Odilo Globocnik. Globocnik was an Austrian Nazi who had earned the trust of Heinrich Himmler. Nicknamed "Globus" by Himmler, the SS leader came to be in charge of the SS and Police forces located in the Lublin district. He was the highest authority in the region. At first Lublin district was envisioned as a future "Jewish reservation"; however, by 1941–1942, Jews were being deported from Germany, Austria, and Slovakia to the area in large numbers. Globocnik set up Majdanek camp to be a center of forced labor for the Jewish deportees. By the time Heydrich had convened the

FIGURE 8.1 *Image titled "When the Vermin Are Dead, the German Oak Will Flourish Once More." In this image, a Nazi is pumping poison gas into the base of a tree, with dead rats representing Jews around the tree. The rats are labeled "stock exchanges," "the press," and "trusts." The branches of the tree labeled "Germany" are "industry, agriculture, commerce, the arts, business, the sciences, social welfare, civil service, and workers." This is perhaps the earliest Nazi image that suggests poison gas as a way of killing the Jews. From* Der Stürmer, December 1927. *Courtesy Randall Bytwerk, German Propaganda Archive, Calvin College.*

Wannsee Conference in January 1942, Lublin had emerged as the preferred site for removing Jews "to the East." Yitzhak Arad argues that

> The choice of the Lublin district as the center for the extermination actions could, therefore, serve as a cover for the claim that the Jews were being sent to the East. Their disappearance after their extermination in the death camps could be explained by saying that they had been sent further east, for forced labor in the vast expanses of the Nazi-occupied areas of the Soviet Union.[31]

Under Globocnik's control, "Operation Reinhard" was to establish death camps while also coordinating the deportation and extermination of Jews. Their tasks also included seizing the valuables of the Jews and then handing them over to the proper authorities. None of Himmler's orders to loyal Globocnik were written down. On principle, Himmler was against committing anything regarding the extermination of the Jews to written documents. In October 1943, Himmler spoke to a group of SS and police officers in Posen, stating, "I refer to the evacuation of the Jews, the annihilation of the Jewish people.... In our history, this is an unwritten and never-to-be-written page of glory."[32]

To fulfill Himmler's commands, Globocnik recruited manpower. He incorporated the personnel who had worked in the euthanasia project because they had vast experience in constructing gas chambers and killing the mentally and physically challenged in Germany. As the men from the T-4 project were brought to Lublin, they all had to sign under oath a document swearing them to secrecy regarding the murder of the Jews. The number of SS men assigned to the death camps of Belzec, Treblinka, and Sobibor were supplemented by Ukrainians and Volksdeutsche. The Ukrainians were trained at Trawniki to become guards in the death centers. The Volksdeutsche, many of whom spoke both Ukrainian and German, were generally placed in charge of the Ukrainians. The SS men were placed as platoon and company commanders in each killing facility.[33]

"Operation Reinhard" camps open

Belzec, Sobibor, and Treblinka death camps were similar in that they were all meant to be located near the General Government region to make transporting condemned Jews easier. They were also required to be in fairly remote, isolated regions in order to keep "Operation Reinhard" as much of a secret from the locals as possible. Finally, they all had to be close enough to Soviet territories to maintain the illusion that deported Jews were only in temporary transit camps until they were then sent further eastwards.[34] By February 1942, Belzec camp was ready to receive the first transports of Jews. The victims were there primarily to be experimented upon to see whether the gas chambers would be efficient. Several transports of 100–250 Jews were brought in to "test" out the facility; afterwards all of the Jewish slave laborers who had been used to construct the camp were also gassed there.[35] SS Oberscharführer Christian Wirth, an experienced euthanasia operative, was placed in charge of Belzec.

Wirth began to establish many of the methods and actions that victims would face at other killing centers. Victims would receive the dual Nazi method of intimidation and lies; a welcoming speech would be given, assuring the victims that they were only there to be transported on to their final destination; they were there to get cleaned up in baths, their clothes would be cleaned, and then they would be moving on to the work camp, farm or factory to work for the German war effort. According to Wirth's instructions, the victims would have to be kept off balance so that they could not collect themselves, nor would they be able to get their bearings. Speed was of the essence. Wirth insisted that Jews should be made to run throughout the entire process, until it was too late for them to recognize that this would be their last stop.

Not all Jews brought into Belzec were gassed immediately upon arrival. Some dozen or more strong, relatively healthy young Jews were kept alive out of each transport to perform labor in the camps. They were designated as tailors, shoemakers, and skilled workers. They were called "Hofjuden" (Court Jews), referring to those few Jews in early modern Europe who were permitted to serve men of power and privilege. Part of these victims' jobs entailed removing the corpses of Jews from the gas chambers, some worked to bury the bodies, others were forced to sort through the clothing and other effects of the now dead Jews. Wirth believed that having the Jews involved in their own extermination process was a good idea.[36] After a time, those Jews involved in the killing process could themselves end up in a gas chamber, replaced by a new set of strong Jews.

The Ukrainian guards were positioned to guard the camp's perimeter, patrol the area, and work the watchtowers. They also guarded the undressing barracks when transports arrived and they stationed themselves along the walkway, called "the tube," which led victims to the gas chambers. The Volksdeutsche were primarily the commanders of each Ukrainian unit. The SS men in the camp served as administrators. Belzec was ready to receive transports by the middle of March 1942.[37] Sobibor death camp would be built in March 1942 and was fully operational by April. The Nazis were ready to provide victims for each camp, but one last camp, under "Operation Reinhard," was yet to be constructed; it was Treblinka.

The building of Treblinka began in late April 1942. The plan was similar to that of Belzec, but the Nazi administrators had learned from trial and error that certain "improvements" could be made. Like Belzec, the area was remote with dense pine forests all around to keep prying eyes out. It was conveniently located close to railway lines which led to Warsaw, Bialystok, Siedlce, and Lomza. The railroad lines all intersected at Treblinka, making it a central hub from different areas of occupation. The remote area allowed trains to come with Jews from the Warsaw and Bialystok ghettos, unload their victims, and return to the ghettos in less than one-and-a-half hours. Four hundred Jews from nearby villages and ghettos were brought in to begin the construction of Treblinka. Not one of them would survive.

The layout of the camp, like Belzec, was relatively small. There were two sections, referred to as Treblinka I and Treblinka II. Treblinka I was a prison work camp that was used to hold Jews temporarily as workers to sustain the needs of the Ukrainian, Volksdeutsche, and German guards. Treblinka II was the extermination center. When transports first arrived at Treblinka, there was the "sorting" process where young and "healthy-looking" Jews were designated for work in Treblinka I by the German officers. Those individuals would find themselves in the camp "for the living" where they performed carpentry, dress making, shoe making, and other jobs. At any given time, Treblinka I held approximately 1,200 Jews. Most of those pulled from the transports for work in the camp were Jewish men; however, Ukrainian guards were also allowed to select some Jewish women to use for sex.[38] All of the work done by the Jews within the camp were forced to wear patches on their clothing that showed what job they were assigned to perform. So, for example, those designated as "Blues" had the job of unloading the train transports, removing the bodies of those who had died in transit to pits, and carrying the clothing to a sorting station. "Reds" were workers selected to reinforce the lies told to the victims—pacify them, help them undress, and hand in their valuables, assuring them that this was only a transit camp. The "Goldjuden" were those in the prison elite who sorted confiscated money and melted down the gold fillings removed from their victims' teeth. The "Goldjuden" sat in a warm barracks and were better dressed than the rest of the prison inmate population. Still others collected pine branch twigs to weave into the barbed wire fencing; others were wood cutters, road builders, bricklayers, and so on. Under the watchful eye of first Dr. Irmfried Eberl, then by his replacement, Franz Stangl, fourteen Germans in total administered the camp at Treblinka.[39]

Treblinka II was known as the "Totenlager" (death camp). Only two roads lead to the camp. One road was for the guards to patrol, making sure that no one escaped and that no curious onlookers saw inside. The other road was surrounded by barbed wire interlaced with pine twigs. There was no return from this road as it led to three gas chambers. The gas chambers were attached to one room where a diesel engine could pump in the poisonous carbon monoxide gas through pipes into the chambers.[40] The path that led to the gas chambers, called "the tube," was also called the *Himmelstrasse* ("road to heaven") by the Germans. It was covered in white gravel and the Germans decided to plant flowers along the way, with signs that read "to the baths" as further reinforcement of the lies told to victims. The gas chambers themselves were also designed to simulate a shower room. The walls inside were covered by white tiles, and shower heads and piping were on the ceilings. The piping did not, of course, carry water; it carried the poisonous gas. There were two doors, locked from the outside, and once the doors were shut, there was no lighting inside.[41] There were only two groups of workers in this section of the camp. They were either gravediggers or "dentists." The dentists knocked out teeth with gold fillings and the gravediggers removed the corpses from the gas chambers and transported them to burial pits. The first major transports of Jews for gassing arrived on July 23, 1942, from the Warsaw ghetto.[42]

Treblinka operated from July 23, 1942 to August 19, 1943. Fourteen SS men and anywhere from 90 to 120 Ukrainian and Volksdeutsche guards were able to murder approximately 870,000 Jews in thirteen months. Although that figure addresses the number of Jews killed in gas chambers, the reality was that Jews were being destroyed even before they arrived at Treblinka. As Jews were packed into freight cars, with no proper ventilation, no sanitary facilities, and no water or food, the hellish trip to the death camps resulted in Jewish deaths long before they arrived at the killing site. One man, Abraham Kszepicki, explained his experiences in one of the deportations from Warsaw:

> Over 100 people were packed into our car…. It is impossible to describe the tragic situation in our airless, closed freight car. It was one big toilet. Everyone tried to push his way to a small air aperture. Everyone was lying on the floor…. The stink in the car was unbearable. People were defecating in all four corners of the car.[43]

Kszepicki's ordeal continued when the train stopped temporarily and Lithuanians working for the Nazis entered the car in order to rob Jews of whatever valuables they still had with them. The conditions worsened in the summertime heat. People in the freight car yelled out to railroad workers to bring them water.

> I paid 500 zlotys … for a cup of water—about half a liter. As I began to drink, a woman, whose child had fainted, attacked me. I drank; I couldn't take the cup from my lips. The woman bit deep into my hand—with all her strength she wanted me to leave her a little water. I paid no attention to the pain. But I did leave a few drops at the bottom of the cup, and I watched the child drink. The situation in the car was deteriorating.[44]

The journey continued on, arriving at Treblinka twenty hours later with many Jews already dead due to the extreme conditions. Although technically the transport of Jews from Warsaw to Treblinka on paper was said to take about one and a half hours, in reality, the inefficiency of the trains, due to logistical problems with the war in the East, meant that mortality rates for Jews soared in these unbearable conditions.[45]

Round-ups of Jews from the West

In a meeting called by Eichmann, on June 11, 1942 in Berlin, it was decided that 10,000 Jews were to be deported from Belgium, 15,000 from Holland, and 100,000 from France's two zones.[46] To the German occupiers, rounding up 100,000 Jews from France proved too difficult to accomplish in the summer months, so they upped the number of deportees to be taken from Holland to 40,000 instead.[47] The deportation of Jews from France began on March 27, 1942. Over 75,000 Jews from France were deported to death camps, most of them were foreign-born Jews who had an unprotected status under the Vichy regime.

In France, the German authorities believed that it would be easier to deport foreign-born Jews than French Jews. In many respects, their assessments were correct. France had been a refuge for fleeing Jews since Hitler's rise to power and now they were caught in the grip of the Nazis once again. The Nazis could rely on traditional anti-Semitism within France to assist them in their deportation plans. One official noted that it would be best to begin with the deportations of foreign-born Jews in order to achieve "the right psychological effect" among the population.[48] French author Lucien Rebatet wrote in the spring of 1942: "Jewish spirit is in the intellectual life of France a poisonous weed that must be pulled out right to its most miniscule roots.... Auto-da-fes will be ordered for the greatest number of Jewish or Judaic works of literature, paintings, or musical compositions that have worked toward the decadence of our people."[49] Rebatet is perhaps not totally indicative of French attitudes, yet his work *Les Decombres* received 200,000 orders. The book, however, could not be published due to paper rationing.[50] Author Robert Brasillach, also anti-Semitic, wrote of his complaints in a September 1942 publication, *Je Suis Partout*, that as Jews were being deported, children should be included with their families.[51] Brasillach had no need to worry; beginning in the summer of 1942 and continuing throughout the summer of 1943, the Nazi Holocaust would be at its peak of killing, children included.

Mass deportations of Jews from Holland began in July 1942; some transports ended in Auschwitz while others were sent to Sobibor, while a few were sent to Theresienstadt and Bergen-Belsen. From July 1942 through September 1944, some 105,000 Jews were rounded up by German authorities and the "Green Police," Dutch police officers who collaborated with the occupying authorities. According to sources collected by the Red Cross, of all the transports to Sobibor from Holland, only nineteen people survived.[52] Saartje Wijnberg, a 21-year-old woman from Holland, remembered her arrival at Sobibor:

We arrived at this camp at 2 o'clock this afternoon [April 9, 1943]. Much screaming by Ukrainians with mean faces and with sticks in hand. There is an old woman walking in front of me who gets beaten. All of a sudden we hear, "Packs to be thrown down!" So we threw down our backpacks, walking on we see 2 Krauts [Germans] who ask us, "Are you married?" We say no. "Then stand there." We stood there with about 20 girls picked from a transport of 3000 people. We were taken away from there. We arrive at a small barrack and are again asked for our names and told where we are to sleep.[53]

Saartje's account continues, providing details about being assigned to sort through the discarded backpacks. It did not yet occur to her what was happening at Sobibor.

Till the evening when I spoke with Mauritz Zukendelaar and also Mau Troostwijk from Zwolle who told me that all the people that I came along with and those that followed were gassed and murdered, burned. They then pointed to a large fire burning in Camp 3 where all 10,000 Jews had been burned. It is not to be believed.[54]

Himmler visited Sobibor and Treblinka in either late February or early March 1943. The purpose of Himmler's visit was to inspect the camps of "Operation Reinhard" in their final stages of operation. Belzec had already been closed down. Himmler had decided that with 1.7 million Jews murdered in Belzec, Sobibor, and Treblinka, the camps could now be closed. He also knew that Auschwitz-Birkenau was operating at full capacity with larger gas chambers and more crematoria to handle the Nazi project of exterminating all of the remaining Jews of Europe.

At Sobibor, the authorities wanted to demonstrate to Himmler how their camp worked even though no regular transport of Jews had arrived that day in the camp. Instead, they took a group of several hundred young Jewish girls from a labor camp in Lublin and gassed them for Himmler. One witness testified:

Himmler arrived. The commandants of the camp welcomed the important guests and toured the area with them. The youngsters were taken to Camp III for extermination. Himmler and his group attended the gassing and cremation of the youngsters. After this killing operation, all of them went to the canteen, where tables with food and flowers had been prepared for these murderers.[55]

At the end of his visit, Himmler told the staff of Sobibor that once they had gassed the incoming transports from Holland, the camp would be closed down. Promotions would be handed out to the SS and German police.

Treblinka was to be dismantled as well, but only after the thousands of corpses that had been buried there were exhumed and burned. In the end, Treblinka and Belzec were shut down; however, Himmler changed his mind regarding Sobibor and ordered it turned into a concentration camp.

Following the dismantling of the "Operation Reinhard" camps, Himmler ordered that all traces of the camps' work be destroyed. This led to SS Standartenführer Paul Blobel's appointment as the man to figure out how to destroy all of the remains of the victims' bodies. His team was called *Sonderaktion 1005* ("Special Action 1005"). There were to be no written orders and Blobel's team began their experiments on disposal of human remains in the forests of yet another death center, Chelmno.[56]

Chelmno

Chelmno death camp was unlike most other death camps created by the Nazi regime. It was not much of a camp, as victims were not going to be staying there for any great length of time. Chelmno was the first extermination camp and it served as the prototype for "single-purpose" (killing) camps. Chelmno, located in a small village in rural Poland, aimed to murder using industrialized, assembly-line processes. The killing center grew out of the T-4 euthanasia project. In the spring of 1941, the SS began Operation 14f13. The operation's mission was to remove concentration camp inmates who had been earmarked for death, transport the inmates to gassing facilities, and murder them. Between 1941 and 1943, at least 20,000 inmates were killed in this manner. The next step, as we have seen in earlier chapters, was to make the killers mobile.

Herbert Lange, born in 1909, was a fanatical Nazi who had participated in the murder of psychiatric patients in 1940; he had also assisted in shooting 30,000 Polish civilians as a member of Einsatzgruppe VI. His special unit, Sonderkommando Lange, consisted of fifteen men. They drove throughout Poland, killing mental patients. They decided to disguise a truck as a "Kaiser Kaffee" van (this was a well-known coffee company in Germany) and turn it into a mobile gas chamber. Polish prisoners were used to attach steel cylinders to the van, connect the cylinder to a valve, and then one of the men in the Sonderkommando was in charge of opening the valve. The victims, in the back of the sealed van, suffocated to death. The van then had to be emptied, the bodies had to be buried in pits in the forest, and the back of the van had to be cleaned so as to fool the next group of victims. Polish prisoners were generally the ones forced to do this dirty work. The turning point for Sonderkommando Lange occurred when Arthur Greiser, in charge of the Warthegau region, decided that he wanted to establish a "Model Gau," which meant getting rid of approximately 90 percent of the "sub-human material" already living in his region.[57]

Greiser had a plan in mind to "cleanse" his region. Much like the German administrators back in Berlin, he believed that ethnic Germans should be transferred in to become "settlers" while the "sub-human" Poles and Jews were deported further east. When deportations of Reich Jews to the Lodz ghetto began, Greiser had thousands of Jews in Lodz taken out of the ghetto and shot. These killings were carried out by Sonderkommando Lange. Lange decided, however, that taking victims out to forests to be shot in mass graves was inefficient and labor intensive for his men. He believed, based on his T-4 experience, that mobile killing vans would be more convenient. He later decided that a permanent killing location was needed. Lange had established a death camp. Greiser did not mind how the Jews were killed, he only cared that they were gone. Greiser later wrote a letter to Hitler asking for permission to "solve his Jewish problem." The letter is dated May 1, 1942. Hitler responded, granting Greiser permission to go forward with his plans. By that time, Chelmno was already operational.

Lange selected the village of Chelmno primarily because it had a mansion on an estate with a large basement area. The mansion was situated on the edge of the village so it was relatively removed from the center of the village, which had approximately 250 permanent residents. The mansion was confiscated, all Polish people living there in apartments were forced out, and the basement windows were boarded up; later they would be bricked in. An eight-foot tall wooden fence was built around the grounds of the mansion to keep prying eyes out, a large gate was constructed, and a second fence was built to enclose a courtyard leading into the mansion. The back of the mansion faced the River Ner. It was sealed off with a barbed wire fence. Once inside the mansion, a door led victims down to the basement. There was a long hallway with seven rooms on one side of the hall and four rooms on the opposite side. At the very end of the hallway there was another door leading to the outside. Lange's men built a wooden ramp which would be level with the back of the van.

Much like with the Einsatzgruppen, the killing method became standardized. Guards would be divided up into groups, some guarded the gate, the courtyard, or the undressing rooms in the basement. Others made sure the victims did not escape. Still others had to transport the victims from a holding pen on the estate, a former mill. The victims would be driven in trucks from the mill site to the courtyard of the mansion. Once the victims were unloaded from the trucks, they stood in the courtyard as Lange (or later, another leader, Hans Bothmann) greeted their "guests."

Using the combination of terror coupled with lies, the victims were told that they were on their way to a better camp in Austria, but first they needed to get cleaned up. They were told that they were going to undress, then take showers, and then move on to a more permanent camp. As they left the undressing rooms and rooms for valuables, they were ushered down the long hallway which had signs that read "To the baths." As the victims climbed the wooden ramp, it appeared that they were entering a shower room. Instead, they were actually walking into the back of the gas van. Once enough victims were inside the van, usually 35–40 people, the truck pulled away from the ramp, locking the victims inside.[58]

The victims locked inside the "Kaiser Kaffee" trucks were taken out to the nearby forest. They suffocated as the fumes from the truck exhaust were piped back into the van. Former Polish prisoners, now turned into employees, along with several shackled Jewish slave laborers waited under armed guard in the forest for the trucks to arrive. They were responsible for dragging the corpses out of the vans, digging the pits for the bodies, and cleaning out the vans for the next load of victims. The truly final step in the killing process involved the cataloging of the victims' valuables. Cash went into a wicker basket, larger items went into handcarts. Most of the goods were then packed up and sent by truck back to the Lodz ghetto administrators.

The first time this procedure was carried out was December 7, 1941. The victims were Jews from the Lodz ghetto. Approximately 700 people were killed in this manner on the first day, but the process was repeated for four days. They were able to murder 10,003 people in fourteen days. The killers took a break for the Christmas holidays, but their work resumed in January 1942.

The Chelmno killing process also created another issue—burying that many bodies in pits left too many traces as the corpses decomposed. The camp halted the killings for a time while they searched for an appropriate method to dispose of large numbers of corpses. The team of investigators, Sonderaktion 1005, tried various methods of destroying the evidence. At first they experimented with blowing the dead bodies up; however, that only left human remains scattered over a wider area, and it lit the forest on fire. They then opted to have Jewish laborers exhume the bodies and burn them out in the open. Once again, this was deemed inefficient mainly due to the need for copious amounts of wood. They then tried a furnace dug into a hole in the earth, but that left a terrible odor. Next they constructed a crematorium with tall chimneys; however, the locals could see the smoke and smell the burning human flesh. Finally, the Commandant of Auschwitz concentration camp, Rudolf Höss, visited the site in the summer of 1942, and it was determined that a crematoria built with bricks combined with a bone grinder to destroy the fragments left unburned would be the way to go. The ashes and ground bones were then scattered over the forest floor.[59] Heinz May, a forest inspector, was traveling through the forest with Kreisleiter Becht, the district chief. Becht pointed and said, "The trees will be growing better soon"; he then added, "Jews make good fertilizer."[60]

Chelmno was closed in March 1943 but there is no real explanation as to why. One theory is that Greiser had estimated that he had 100,000 "useless eaters" in his region and that number of victims had been reached in the killings. The German team was given four weeks' vacation but first all of the Jewish workers had to be killed and the mansion had to be scrubbed clean of all traces of the murderous work carried out there. Even the eight-foot high fence was removed. On April 7, 1943, the team blew up part of the mansion; the rest of it was removed by hand. A local farmer was invited in to farm the area. He did.

This was not the complete end of Chelmno though. In March 1944, the camp was reestablished. Hans Bothmann was reassigned to the camp and since the mansion was destroyed, they used the granary on the estate for their main structure. They did not bother to build a wooden fence the second time around. Barbed wire was all that was needed. Wooden barracks, tents, and storerooms were set up. The equipment was returned as well. The Sonderkommando Chelmno was back.[61]

To create the illusions they were looking for in 1944, in order to fool the victims, the men of the Sonderkommando reenacted the welcome speech which was laced with lies. The first barracks had signs posted "To the Doctor." Some of the men wore white lab coats and visually inspected the victims, telling each one that they were "fit to work" and handing them a bar of soap and a towel. Then, the victims were told to move on to the next "barracks" for a bath. "To the bath" signs were everywhere to reinforce the lies. Once inside, what had looked like a barracks was only the inside of a gas van. It pulled away and within six minutes the dead and dying would be at the crematoria. All valuables left behind would be sorted and made ready for shipment to Lodz. Despite the high numbers of Jews killed in the Chelmno camp, the higher administrators thought that its work was inadequate. By July 1944, the Red Army was fast approaching the site. In August 1944, the Sonderkommando attempted to dismantle and destroy all traces of the killing center, then fled. The Red Army found mostly smoldering ruins.[62]

The largest death camp facility: Auschwitz

Chelmno was just one in a vast network of camp systems run by the Nazi regime. It differed from most other "death camps," that is, camps whose sole purpose was murder, in that it was never a site where Jewish victims found temporary work. They were there to be killed. Unlike Chelmno, with its mobile gas vans, Auschwitz concentration camp perfected the use of stationary killing facilities and combined that work with a series of work camps as well. Also, unlike the "Operation Reinhard" camps and Chelmno, Auschwitz was not originally intended to be a camp that killed Jews.

The first transport of prisoners to Auschwitz arrived on June 14, 1940, and the camp evolved over time to reflect the policies of the Nazi regime. The man who supervised the camp's construction, from its very beginning, was Rudolf Höss. Höss had gathered experience first in Dachau concentration camp and then in Sachsenhausen and, at the age of thirty-nine, he was promoted to commandant for the new camp located in a desolate village in Poland called Oswiecim. Like Hitler, Höss had grown up in a Catholic household, had served in the First World War, and had felt desperately betrayed by the November 1918 armistice. He blamed a Jewish conspiracy for Germany's unexplainable loss in the war. Also like Hitler, Höss preferred the anti-Semitism of reason over that of emotional anti-Semitism. Even at his execution by hanging at the end of the war, Höss remained convinced that he was helping to "cleanse" the world of Jewish vermin.[63]

The first prisoners to arrive in 1940 at Auschwitz were German criminals. They were to be used as "kapos," men who were inmates in the camp but who kept other prisoners in line. The kapos acted as intermediaries between the SS and the rest of the camp population. The next prisoners brought into the camp were Poles, some 20,000 of them, who had been arrested for a variety of reasons. Some of them were university students and represented the intellectual class; others were there because they were accused of working with the Polish underground, and the list goes on. These men would be used to construct the camp.

The camp continued to expand, adding supplies such as sand and gravel to the German war effort through the use of slave labor. Other German companies expressed interest in working with the camp, particularly I.G. Farben. As the war expanded into the Soviet Union in 1941, the camp also had an influx of Soviet POWs, many of whom were simply shot in the gravel pits. As more prisoners were dumped into Auschwitz, a solution had to be found that promised an effective means of killing large numbers of inmates, but without the psychological drawbacks for the killers. One of Höss's deputies, a man named Fritzsch, in either late August or early September 1941, decided that a disinfectant called crystallized prussic acid (cyanide) that was being used to disinfect lice and other vermin at the camp could potentially be used to kill human beings. Experiments were conducted on inmates in Block 11 of the camp. Höss returned from a trip and was shown the process. The chemical compound, marketed as Zyklon B, became the preferred method of killing at Auschwitz. Höss was relieved that a new way to murder had been found. "No longer would the killers have to look into the eyes of their victims as they murdered them."[64]

As the war continued, plans for Auschwitz continued to evolve. By October 1941, when the first transports of German Jews from Hamburg were being sent "to the East," some of the deportees would end up in Auschwitz. Another portion of the camp was going to be built, called Birkenau on a swampy site. Birkenau, the future site of mass killings of the Jews, at this point in time was meant to be a POW camp.[65] Since the Birkenau site was intended to hold "subhuman" Soviet POWs, the plans drawn up included a barracks to hold 744 inmates with only a quarter of the space allotted to prisoners in camps such as Dachau. The plan to hold so many Soviet POWs was designed in such a way as to ensure that as many of the captured soldiers as possible would die. Soviet POWs were also the first inmates at Auschwitz to have numbers tattooed on their bodies. This was considered to be an "improvement" as it allowed camp personnel to identify the corpses by their registered number. At first prisoners were tattooed on their chests; later markings would be made on prisoners' arms.[66] The Soviet POWs were the people forced to construct the Birkenau camp.

Following the Wannsee Conference, Jews who had been deemed "unfit for work" from the surrounding area were sent to Auschwitz. The procedure with new arrivals was created to avoid "incidents." As new arrivals to the camp, the inmates would be told that they were there to be disinfected by showering. This made it easier to get their victims into the gas chamber, plus it had the bonus that all of the belongings of the victims were already removed and neatly folded with shoe laces tied together. However, Commandant Höss did not like that the improvised gas chamber was located near his office and he could hear the screaming of the victims once the Zyklon B pellets were released. The staff tried to mask the screams by having two motorcycles revving their engines to drown out the noise; however, this was unsuccessful.[67]

To solve this problem of too much noise as victims died in the gas chamber, Höss and his staff began to look for new ways to conduct the killings. Auschwitz began to emerge as the dual entity it would become at this time: one portion of the camp held prisoners who were used as slave labor while another portion of the camp existed only to kill new arrivals who might be at the camp for no more than a few hours before they were gassed.[68] By 1942, the stalemate with the Soviet Union brought still another evolution to the camp. Since there would be relatively few Soviet POWs entering Birkenau, Himmler switched policy and offered to use Birkenau for deported Jews. The Jews of Slovakia would be part of this change.

In February 1942, the Slovakian leader Vojtech Tuka had held meetings with SS Major Dieter Wisliceny, a representative of Adolf Eichmann. Tuka argued that it would be "un-Christian" to deport only the male head of Jewish households, leaving the Jewish women and children "defenseless." As we have seen earlier, there was also a financial concern that women and children left behind would become a financial burden on the government, so the bargain was struck that the Slovakian government would pay 500 Reichsmarks for every Jew deported.[69] Deportations began in March 1942. One woman, Silvia Vesela remembered walking from the holding camp in Slovakia to board the train that would transport her to Auschwitz:

> They spat at us and shouted, "Jewish whores, it serves you right! You'll finally work!" They also threw stones at us. They used every possibility to humiliate us. There were also some people who just stood still and just witnessed the humiliation. Some of those people cried. However, the majority, older and younger generation, humiliated us. I wouldn't wish this kind of experience on anyone. It is a horrible feeling.[70]

One of the Slovakian men who guarded and then loaded the Jews onto the trains, Michal Kabic, recalled,

> I was feeling sorry for them, but on the other hand I was not sorry for them considering they were stealing from the Slovaks. We were not very sorry. We thought it was good that they were taken away. That way they could not cheat us anymore. They were not going to get rich at the expense of the working class anymore.[71]

Much like his German counterparts, Kabic was combining his Slovakian nationalism with anti-Semitism. In order for the Slovakian people to be "free," they also had to be rid of the "Jewish threat."[72] The Slovakian transport arrived in March 1942 and the victims were admitted to the camp as inmates. A group of 1,000 men from the transport were sent running to Birkenau, sinking into the swampy soil. Off in the corner of Birkenau's camp was Höss's solution to the screaming of victims: a little red cottage that had been sealed up and converted into two gas chambers. It was secluded and could kill 800 people at one time.[73] It was first used to murder local Jews who had been classified as no longer being productive workers.

Höss continued to make "improvements" to his camp, and a new gas chamber was built at Birkenau; this one was a little white house, also called Bunker 2. The ventilation system was better in Bunker 2 which allowed the Zyklon B to dissipate faster after a gassing. It was also "better" because it could kill 1,200 people at one time.[74] Throughout the spring and summer of 1942, thousands of Slovakian Jews lost their lives in the little red cottage and in Bunker 2. To Höss, however, it was clear that these two killing areas were going to be insufficient if Auschwitz-Birkenau was going to be transformed into an industrialized killing center. One of the big transformations, by March 1943, was the opening of the first crematorium at Birkenau. In addition, rooms that had once been designated as mortuaries were transformed into undressing areas and a gas chamber. These areas were in the basement with the ground floor consisting of a crematorium. A small elevator carried the corpses from the basement to the ovens. By the summer of 1943, further gas chambers and crematoria had been built. By the time these "improvements" were completed, Auschwitz-Birkenau had the ability to kill 120,000 people per month.[75]

Now, Hitler's cold anti-Semitism of reason was realized in physical form at Auschwitz-Birkenau. The buildings were made of neat red brick, the killing process had been streamlined, and the sense of personal responsibility for the guards and administrators had been greatly reduced.[76] It also combined the ability to first utilize Jewish labor for the German war effort, then dispose of Jews too weak to produce for Germany. Since Auschwitz itself ended with some twenty-eight satellite camps, such as Monowitz, the number of inmates to be used as slave labor rose to approximately 80,000 in early 1944.[77] It is estimated that the slave laborers of Auschwitz contributed close to 30 million Reichsmarks of pure profit for the Nazi regime.[78]

For the transports destined for gassing upon arrival, there was a standardized procedure. The camp personnel would be put on alert that a train was due. Some of the inmates were selected to pull Jews off the trains. These individuals were supposed to lie to the victims, telling them that everything would be fine so long as they cooperated and followed instructions. Occasionally, these inmates would try to warn the victims. Camp physicians, the most notorious at Auschwitz being Josef Mengele, would make "selections" as to who should be set aside for slave labor and who should be gassed that day. For some victims, they had only a few hours left to live.

These selections were devastating for the Jews brought into the camp. For survivors, one of the most poignant memories they have is that last time that they saw their family members. The elderly, the obviously ill, the very young, children under the age of sixteen, mothers with young children—all were taken away immediately upon arrival. Some Jews were also initially pulled from the first selection if they were twins or had interesting abnormalities that the camp physicians wanted to experiment on. Those who survived this first experience remember the overpowering smells and sounds of the camp. Ruth Kluger, only twelve years old, remembered, "We were surrounded by the odious, bullying noise of the men who had hauled us out of the train with monosyllables, 'raus, raus' ('out, out') and who simply did not stop shouting as they were driving us along, like mad, barking dogs."[79] For those such as Kluger, they were led away, tattooed on their lower left arm, and were given their striped prisoner uniform with its corresponding patch. The patch designated what "crime" an inmate had committed. In the case of the Jews, two overlapping triangles made the Star of David.[80]

For those now selected for "special treatment," that is, the camp language for those about to be gassed, the standardized procedure of lying to the victims began. New arrivals were told that they were being taken to be "disinfected." SS men and Jewish Sonderkommandos circulated among the victims in the undressing hall, telling them to fold their clothes neatly. Amid soothing comments, victims were told to place their clothes on numbered hooks—this was done to reinforce the lie that victims would be getting their clothing back following the "disinfection." The victims were then led into the gas chamber, designed to look as if it was a large shower room. At least one of the Jewish Sonderkommandos would stay with the victims until they were all inside, again to reinforce their misunderstanding of what was about to occur. An SS man would often linger in the doorway as well. Once the victims were inside the chamber, the Sonderkommando man and the SS man would exit, closing the door and sealing the victims inside to their fate. The Zyklon B pellets were released through the ceiling vents.[81]

A physician was required to be present at all gassings. The doctor would watch through a peep hole in the door and he determined when all of the victims were dead. Dr. Johann Paul Kremer, from the University of Münster, kept a diary of his daily activities at Auschwitz.

> 2 September 1942. For the first time, at three this morning, present at a special operation (Sonderaktion)...5 September 1942.... In the evening around 8 o'clock again attended a Sonderaktion from Holland. The men [the Sonderkommando inmates] push themselves to participate in these operations, because special provisions are passed out, including a fifth of liquor, 5 cigarettes, 100 grams of baloney [bologna], and bread.... 6 September: Today, Sunday, excellent lunch: tomato soup, one-half chicken with potatoes and red cabbage (20 grams fat). Sweets and fantastic vanilla ice cream.... Evening at 8 o'clock outside again for a Sonderaktion.[82]

Kremer's account almost defies all limits of humanity, yet he had adjusted to the daily workings of the camp and softened its brutality by using the special language of the camps to lessen the severity of killing the process; victims did not exist as individual human beings, this was only a "special action," and he could dream about the next fantastic meal he would be enjoying. It should also be noted that Kremer conducted experiments on inmates on the effects of starvation on the human body.

Inside the Sonderkommando

Let us look at the "Sonderaktion" from the perspective now of a man who was in the Jewish Sonderkommando. The "Special commando/unit" had perhaps the worst assignment of any imaginable in the hell of Auschwitz. These Jewish men were selected to escort victims through the killing process. They were also the ones assigned to reenter the gas chamber after the killing, remove the corpses, pull out gold teeth, search body cavities of the deceased for hidden valuables, cut the long hair off of the dead women, and deliver the bodies to the crematoria to be burned. They often also were the ones assigned to dispose of the ashes. At Auschwitz, some of the ashes were used as fertilizer in the vegetable gardens, but there were so many ashes that most had to be dumped in nearby forests and rivers. All of the clothing and valuables left in the undressing rooms also had to be sorted and delivered to the barracks, called "Canada" by the inmates. (They called it Canada as they imagined this was a country of great riches.) This brutal work lasted usually for several months, at which point the SS would gas all of the Sonderkommando men and then select replacements. One must also remember that not all victims were unsuspecting of what was about to happen to them. In the winter of 1943, a transport of all children was brought into the camp. They were sent to the undressing barracks.

> A girl of eight years old undresses her little brother of a year old. A member of the [Sonder]kommando comes over to undress him. The girl calls out, ["]Go away, Jewish murderer! Don't lay your hand, drenched in Jewish blood, upon my beautiful little brother. I have become his good mother. He will die in my arms, together with me.["]A boy of 7–8 years old stands nearby. He calls out[, "]You are a Jew after all! How can you lead such dear children in to be gassed, only for you to live longer. Is your life among a band of murderers really dearer to you than the lives of so many Jewish victims?["][83]

One man, Shlomo Venezia, was a member of the Sonderkommando at Auschwitz for eight months and survived to share his experiences. Venezia was part of a Jewish-Italian community in Thessaloniki, Greece, who found themselves sent to Auschwitz on a transport on April 11, 1944. Venezia immediately lost his 44-year-old mother and two young sisters at the initial selections. After being held in the quarantine camp for three weeks, Venezia, one of his brothers, and some of his cousins were among those selected during a roll call to become the next Sonderkommando. Venezia, a young man in his early twenties, did not know what the job actually entailed, but the promise of extra food and the potential to stay alive sounded better than most jobs at Auschwitz. Of course, the reality was that Venezia had no choice in the matter. He was selected for this job. If he refused to carry it out, then he would be killed and another inmate would be forced to take his place. In his account, Venezia discusses his first experiences in the Sonderkommando. He, like so many of the men in the unit, deadened his feelings.

> Until that point I'd more or less forbidden myself to think about everything that was happening; we had to do what we were ordered to do, like robots, without thinking. But on seeing the body burning I thought the dead were perhaps luckier than the living; they were no longer forced to endure this hell on earth, to see the cruelty of men.[84]

By the summer of 1944, Auschwitz had emerged as the lead killing center out of all the various camps the Nazis had established. The vast number of Hungarian Jews, approximately 725,000 of them in 1944, had not yet been decimated as a community. The German army entered Hungary on March 19, 1944, and soon thereafter Eichmann, now SS Lieutenant Colonel, drove in to expropriate and plunder as much as possible from the Jews.[85] As the Nazi regime desperately needed laborers at this time in the war, Auschwitz was the ideal destination: some Jews could be worked there while unfit Jews would simply be gassed upon arrival. Eichmann was able to send close to 400,000 Hungarian Jews to Auschwitz. According to estimates, with each transport of Jews, 10–30 percent were selected for forced labor while the vast majority of deportees were gassed. Some 320,000 people were murdered in less than eight weeks.[86]

In a meeting with the Hungarian Prime Minister Sztojay, Hitler argued that he was helping Hungary by "de-Jewifying it." Hitler added:

> When, moreover, he had to remember that in Hamburg 46,000 German women and children had been burnt to death, nobody could demand of him to have the least pity for this world pest; he now went by the ancient Jewish proverb: "an eye for an eye, a tooth for a tooth." ... If the Jewish race were to win, at least 30 million Germans would be exterminated and many millions would starve to death.[87]

Hitler had inverted the perpetrators and the victims. Many of the Hungarian Jews would be deported to Auschwitz. The vast majority were earmarked for death upon arrival. The efficiency of Auschwitz continued on; the number of people murdered in Auschwitz totalled close to 1.1 million, 90 percent of them Jews.

A key element to the success of these killing centers was to murder in an efficient, standardized way. For the murderers, the success of the camps was contingent upon secrecy. In particular, language was used to hide the true meaning of the killing procedures. It gave the killers a layer of protection, so they held onto the official terms. We have already seen how the terms "deportation," "evacuation," "resettlement," and "to the East" were all meant to hide what was happening to Jews forced to board trains that would take the vast majority of them to their deaths. Phrases such as "Harvest Festival" might sound harmless enough; however, in the lexicon of the Nazi regime, "Harvest Festival" referred to the murder of 40,000 to 50,000 Jews in the Lublin district, taken from various work camps to be shot on the grounds of Majdanek concentration camp. These particular killings were completed in two days. In Nazi documents, Jews ready for deportation are often referred to as "Stücke," meaning "pieces," as in pieces of furniture. Even within the camps, we have seen the use of "special treatment," "special action," and "Stücke." Shlomo Venezia, working in the Sonderkommando of Auschwitz asked his kapo if it would be possible to have his brother transferred to Shlomo's unit. He found the kapo agreeable to the suggestion, stating, "To bring my brother over from Crematorium IV to Crematorium III, we had to exchange a Stück, in other words a 'piece' since we were considered to be nothing more than pieces.... For the Germans and the kapos, it was all the same, one 'piece' here or there."[88] An official working for a railway line could also try to convince himself that Jews were being relocated to "transit camps" or that they were destined for "special installations" without bothering to think about what these phrases actually meant. These were stock expressions used repeatedly which dulled their effect. In reality, these expressions meant that Jews were destined for major killing centers equipped with gas chambers. One of those involved in the killings was Kurt Möbius. Looking back after the war had ended he stated,

Although I am aware that it is the duty of the police to protect the innocent I was however at the time convinced that the Jewish people were not innocent but guilty. I believed all the propaganda that Jews were criminals and subhuman [Untermenschen] and that they were the cause of Germany's decline after the First World War. The thought that one should oppose or evade the order to take part in the extermination of the Jews never entered my head either.[89]

The German home front

Despite camp personnel swearing to an oath of secrecy, the rumors about what was really happening to Jews "in the East" continued on the German home front. By the end of 1942 into early 1943, however, the German home front not only speculated on the fate of the deported Jews, but also grew increasingly concerned that the Volksgemeinschaft would be punished for what was being done to the Jews. Time and again, SD reports on popular mood document this combination of rumors and fear. From Schwabach in December 1942, the SD officer noted,

> in the rural population are at the moment tales from Russia which speak about shooting and extermination of the Jews. This news leaves a sense of great anxiety, emotional distress, and worry among many in the circles of the population mentioned. As broad circles of the rural population see the situation, it is not yet certain that we will win the war, and if we do not, when the Jews return some day, they will take a horrible revenge.[90]

In Swabia, the District Governor wrote after the German surrender at Stalingrad, "In many circles, there are fears that the men taken prisoner there by the Russians could be killed as revenge for supposed mass executions of Jews by Germans in the East."[91] By June 1943, church leaders in Munich were telling parishioners not to complain about the Katyn massacres:

> The National Socialists have no right whatsoever to be indignant about the bestial slaughter. In combating the Jews in the East, the SS has, they stated, employed similar methods of slaughter. The awful and inhumane treatment meted out to the Jews by the SS clearly calls for the punishment of our people by the Lord.... The German people has taken upon itself such a burden of bloodshed that it cannot hope for mercy and forgiveness; there is bitter revenge for everything.[92]

The war was turning against Germany by 1943, and now the German people were concerned that if they did not win the war, the Jews would come back to seek revenge. Now, the Nazi regime had to convince the German people that they had to remain in the fight and win, or else the Volksgemeinschaft would be annihilated. If the war was lost, then all of the Volksgemeinschaft would have to pay. NSDAP reports continually stressed that thorough indoctrination of the people should follow the line that "the Jew, if he should succeed to break back into Europe and seize power, will not restrain his Old Testament hatred, especially toward the German people."[93]

What is also interesting in these reports is that the majority of them state that Germans were not blaming Hitler for the bombings and continuous air raids over Germany; rather they accepted the devastation as part of their communal fate, tied together by their crimes committed against the Jews. In one such report, the author wrote, "Often you could hear people say that this was retribution for what we did to the Jews in November 1938." Notice how it is "what we did" and not what the government leaders were doing. The situation inside of Germany continued to deteriorate and with each air raid, more Germans were beginning to lose faith that the war could be won. In a truly remarkable and cynical move, some were looking to improve relations with Jews because "People don't believe in final victory. Today they would really prefer to take precautionary measures and get on good terms with the Jews, if only that were possible."[94] Despite this, German people's knowledge about the extermination of the Jews did not soften anti-Semitic attitudes. In fact, it seemed to only increase their fears about what Jews might do to them.

As so many Germans came to understand that the war would be lost, they continued to fight on despite the odds being against them. They had seemingly accepted Hitler's proposition that this would be a war of either total victory or total destruction for the German people. Their fears of Jewish revenge coupled with their knowledge that they were complicit in the crimes committed against the Jews led some to proclaim, "The Volk say that as a consequence of a victory that is not ours, Jewry will pounce on the German Volk body and realize all its devilish and bestial plans, as described in our press. Which is why we have the slogan: Death and destruction to the Jews—the future and life are ours!"[95] Once again, one can see the dichotomy—Jews must die in order for Germans to live. It is "us" versus "them." As the circle tightened around Germany, Himmler gave the order sometime in January 1945 for all the camps in the East to be evacuated. Postwar testimonies vary; some say that Himmler made it clear that Hitler expected camp commandants to prevent any and all inmates from falling into enemy hands alive. Others testified that it was left up to camp commandants. In the face of ever-increasing chaos, the marches started westward, closer and closer to the Old Reich.

Closing of the camps and death marches

The transporting of inmates came to be called "death marches," an apt description given that the inmates were already in poor health, and were now going to be subjected to forced marching (some were also put on freight trains) under armed guard. There would be no concern shown for hunger or thirst, nor would the vast majority of inmates be given adequate clothing or shelter when the marching stopped. Although Himmler gave the evacuation order in January, the first forced death march had already taken place on July 28, 1944, from Majdanek concentration camp. The longest death march lasted for one month: 35,000 Hungarian Jews were marched from Budapest to Austria—some 260 miles—under Hungarian guard.[96] Auschwitz's evacuation began on January 17, 1945. Some 60,000 prisoners were led 60 miles away, then boarded trains to take them to various concentration camps. Other Auschwitz inmates were marched 170 miles away to Gross-Rosen. It is estimated that between March and April 1945, approximately 250,000 prisoners, one-third of them Jews, were sent out on these terrible marches.[97] Historian Daniel Blatman, examining the death marches, argues convincingly that these evacuations were but a continuation of the Holocaust. While the marches were not efficient ways of murdering Jews, they still achieved the same "final solution" in bringing about the slow and often excruciating death of the Jews.[98]

Those on the marches, such as Michael Kraus, witnessed the unending horror of suffering.

> In January…I participated in the so-called death march. Yes, indeed it was a death march because it claimed many victims, and only a few of us survived. We walked for three days. Ahead of us lay the victims of previous marches who had been shot, and behind us were guards who spent their time shooting prisoners who were not able to continue. They had a lot of work. It was a horrible sight … At night they herded us into some kind of farm…. With the inadequate clothing many froze to death or were shot because their legs had given out.[99]

The march was not over, for the guards marched the prisoners to Leslau where they were then pushed onto open freight cars: "There wasn't even room to sit down. And so we rode four days without food in open railroad cars to a new concentration camp."[100]

Shlomo Venezia, who had been transferred out of Auschwitz earlier on, was imprisoned in Ebensee camp. He noted that suddenly the kapos in his camp became less abusive, and one morning the camp commandant assembled the 5,000–6,000 inmates in the central square and announced that the Americans and the Russians were heading toward the camp. The commandant claimed he and his men would put up a fight. They did not. Instead, the commandant and other camp guards fled, but the prisoners were still not free. Now they found themselves under the control of Wehrmacht reservists who held them captive as the Americans advanced toward the camp. With the commandant gone, there was no food distribution to the inmates. They all awaited the Americans' arrival. Venezia and his group of friends were able to survive for four days on a sack of potatoes he "organized" from the camp's kitchen. He and his friends took turns sitting on the sack of food in order to prevent other inmates from stealing and eating it. When the American troops did enter the camp on May 6, 1945, Venezia and those still alive in the camp were given many different types of foodstuffs. Venezia, wisely, ate only potatoes and tins of pork to get his stomach accustomed to heavier food. He also described the thirst for revenge.[101]

Since the German oppressors had fled, the liberated inmates now focused their anger on the kapos. "The twenty-four hours that followed the Liberation gave rise to a veritable kapo-hunt."[102] He and some friends also went down to the local village to look for food: "We soon saw that the inhabitants were terrified. We only had to ask for what we wanted and they gave it to us without demur. They were as scared of us as if we were wild beasts. We just asked for some beans and salt."[103] For Venezia, liberation was followed by seven years of hospitalizations from tuberculosis.[104] He did not speak of his experiences after trying to explain to a Jewish man what he had gone through and finding that

> All of a sudden, I realized that, instead of looking at me, he was looking behind me at someone who was making signs to him. I turned around and was surprised to catch one of his friends gesturing that I was completely mad. I shut up and from that time on I didn't want to talk about it anymore. For me, it was painful to talk, so when I came across people who didn't believe me, I told myself there was no point.

Shlomo Venezia would take another forty-seven years before he spoke publicly about Auschwitz again.[105] His interviewer asked him, "What was destroyed in you by that extreme experience?" His answer was devastating:

> Life. Since then I've never had a normal life. I've never been able to pretend that everything was all right and go off dancing.... Everything takes me back to the camp. Whatever I do, whatever I see, my mind keeps harking back to the same place. It's as if the "work" I was forced to do there had never really left my head.... Nobody ever really gets out of the Crematorium.[106]

In the final weeks of the war, Germany lay in ruins. Down in his bunker in Berlin, Hitler and his long-time mistress Eva Braun were married. They then decided to commit suicide. Hitler took one of his secretaries, Traudl Junge, aside and dictated both his private will and his political testament. The political testament begins with Hitler's profession of love for the Volk: "In these three decades, all my thoughts, actions, and life have been guided for my love for and loyalty to the Volk.... I have used up my time, my working power, and my health in these three decades."[107] Of course, Hitler had to portray himself as self-sacrificing. He was, according to his testament, also innocent of all blame for the war: "It was desired and instigated exclusively by those international statesman who are either of Jewish origin or work for Jewish interests."[108] Eschewing any responsibility for the conflict, Hitler laid the blame squarely on the shoulders of Jewish capitalists: "should the nations of Europe again be regarded only as the portfolio of stocks of these international monetary and financial conspirators, then the race would be held responsible that actually is guilty in this murderous struggle: Jewry!"[109] Claiming that the war would go down in history "as the most glorious and brave avowal of a Volk's will to live," Hitler announced that he would commit suicide rather than fall into the enemy's hands, "who, for the amusement of its incited masses, needs a new spectacle directed by the Jews."[110] He asked the German people to continue to fight their enemies and promised them that, in their sacrifice, they would be bringing about the "shining rebirth of the National Socialist movement and the realization of a true Volksgemeinschaft."[111]

In the second portion of the political testament, Hitler expelled Göring and Himmler from the Nazi Party as traitors to him and to the country. He named Admiral Dönitz as the new President of Germany and appointed the loyal Goebbels to the position of Reich Chancellor. He then appointed others as officers in the new government and issued strict instructions that all Germans should remain obedient to the new leaders. As his final statement Hitler ended with, "Above all, I oblige the leadership of the nation and its followers to a meticulous observance of the racial laws and to a merciless resistance to those world-wide poisoners of all Völker, international Jewry."[112] The documents were witnessed and signed by Goebbels, Martin Bormann, Wilhelm Burgdorf, and Hans Krebs at 4 a.m. On April 30, 1945, Hitler and his bride committed suicide and, as per his instructions, their bodies were taken out of the bunker and lit on fire.

Hitler had bound the German people to him in the destructive project to build a Volksgemeinschaft by eliminating any and all who were deemed unworthy to be members of the community. Using familiar language that associated Jews with destruction, evil, the devil, conspiracies, and pollution, Hitler capitalized on preexisting stereotypes, myths, and legends about Jews in order to isolate and then persecute, and ultimately murder them. The Volksgemeinschaft accepted this bond. The end result was 5 to 6 million dead Jews.

For your consideration

Below is a portion of Szlama Winer's accounts of working as a slave laborer in the forests of Chelmno. Winer eventually escaped from his guards at Chelmno and made his way to Warsaw. His experiences at the death camp were recorded in the Warsaw ghetto and were found after the war. As you read his description, think of how Chelmno's killing apparatus differed from all other death camps. How was it different? How were victims killed? How were their bodies disposed of at the time of Winer's account? What was Winer's life like as a laborer in Chelmno? How does he describe his experiences?

On Wednesday, January 7, at seven in the morning, the guard on duty banged on the door screaming: "Get up." But none of us had slept anyway because of the cold. After an hour they brought unsweetened black coffee and bread from our packs. It comforted us a little; we whispered that there is still a God in heaven and that we will be going to work.

At half past eight (the reason it was so late was that the nights were long), they led us into the courtyard. Several people were left behind. They were taken to the neighboring cell in the basement. They carried out two Jews who had hung themselves (I don't know their names). They were prisoner/gravediggers from Klodawa. The corpses were thrown onto a truck. We met again with the other prisoners from Izbica. As soon as we came out of the basement, we were surrounded by 12 guards and Gestapo men with machine guns. There were 29 prisoners in the truck as well as the two corpses and six guards. A vehicle with ten guards and two civilians followed behind us.

We drove down the highway in the direction of Kolo. After going about seven kilometers the truck suddenly turned left into the forest. There was a half kilometer well-worn path. At the end of the path the SS men stopped the truck and ordered us to get out, undress and line up double file. (We remained in our shoes, underwear, pants, and shirts.) Although there was a severe frost, we had to leave our overcoats, hats, sweaters, and gloves on the ground. The two civilians brought shovels and pickaxes and gave each of us one of them. Only eight of us didn't get a tool. They were ordered to take the two corpses from the truck.

As we arrived in the forest we immediately saw the prisoners from Klodawa who had arrived before us. They were already at work in their shirtsleeves. The scene looked as follows: 21 people with pickaxes and shovels, behind them eight people and two corpses, and all around us Germans with machine guns. Those from Klodawa were also guarded by about 12 guards. Therefore we were surrounded by 30 guards.

As we approach the ditch, those from Klodawa greeted us in a whisper: "Where are you from?" "From Izbica," we answered.... We talked while working. We threw both bodies down into the ditch. Shovels were brought from the truck for those who still didn't have one. However, we didn't have to wait long before the next van arrived with fresh victims. The van was specially constructed and appeared normal; the size of a normal truck, gray, hermetically sealed with two rear doors. The inside was covered with sheet metal. There were no seats inside. The floor was covered with a wooden grating, as in public baths, and with a straw mat. Between the driver's cab and the rear compartment were two peepholes. Using a flashlight one could observe whether the victims were dead or not. Under the wooden gratings were two tubes of about 15 centimeters long that came out of the cab. The tubes had openings on the end from which gas came out. The gas apparatus was located in the cab, in which only the driver sat. It was always the same driver who wore a uniform with the SS skull and crossbones. He was about 40 years old. There were two of these vans.

The van stopped about eight meters from the grave. The leader of the guard detail, a high ranking SS man, was an absolute sadist. He ordered eight men to open the doors of the vehicle and the strong, sharp odor of gas hit us immediately. Dead Gypsies from Lodz were in the van.... The Jews ran to the van and threw out the corpses. As the work initially didn't go quickly enough for them, the supervising SS man pulled out his whip and screamed, "Hellblaue, ich komme sofort zu euch!" (I'm coming for you now), beating us about our heads, ears, eyes, in all directions, until everyone collapsed on the ground....

The corpses were thrown out of the vans like garbage onto a heap. They were dragged by their feet and the hair. Two people stood at the edge and threw the bodies into the grave. Two others were in the ditch and placed them in layers, face down, in such a way that the head of one was placed next to the feet of another. A special SS man directed this. If there was an empty place, the corpse of a child was stuffed in there.... A layer numbered from 180 to 200 corpses. After every three van loads about 20 of the gravediggers were used to cover up the corpses.

Excerpt taken from Patrick Montague, Chelmno and the Holocaust: The History of Hitler's First Death Camp, *98–99.*

This excerpt is from a trial transcript. In the transcript, one young woman, Magda Szabo, testifies about her experiences from a ghetto in Hungary to the camp at Auschwitz. She describes the experience of holding her sister-in-law's two-year-old toddler in her arms as they exit the cattle car. How does she describe the ride in the cattle car? What happens when they arrive at Auschwitz to Magda and to the rest of her family?

Presiding Judge:	Then you were first assembled in a ghetto—
Magda:	[interrupting] Yes.
Judge:	Near Tirgu Mutes, yes?
Magda:	In the brick factory, yes.
Judge:	And there you were together with your family?
Magda:	Yes, yes.
Judge:	Who belonged to your family?
Magda:	Father, mother, sister-in-law and her children and her sister, the sister-in-law of her sister, and her parents ...
Judge:	And did you have children? Did you already at this time—
Magda:	[interrupting] Myself, no, no, I was still unmarried.
Judge:	Now when were you sent to Auschwitz?
Magda:	At the end of May. I think it was May 29th, 30th. 1st of June or so. My sister-in-law had a little child, two years old: she had her birthday in the cattle car. It was—I don't know—the last day in the car or so.
Judge:	So you think the end of May?
Magda:	In any case at the end of May, early June, to the 1st of June. I can't remember exactly any more...
Judge:	Do you know approximately how many people were in your transport? Naturally you didn't count them, but....
Magda:	I didn't count, but we were eighty people in that car, and that was a very long...
Judge:	Very long train.
Magda:	Transport. Forty, fifty cars there were at least.

Judge:	Tell me, please, during the transport, did you receive any provisions?
Magda:	No. As we got into the car, we got a small piece of bread, every person, no water, nothing. We climbed in. We brought some food with us, but we ate it sparingly—we thought that we were going somewhere to work, [and] the children should have some of it.
Judge:	Did you at least receive anything to drink?
Magda:	No. Once it rained, I remember very well, and we caught the water in a glass.
Judge:	Some rainwater.
Magda:	A little water so we could give the children in the car at least a little water.
Judge:	When you arrived at Auschwitz, do you know who opened your cars and had you get out?
Magda:	There were prisoners there who helped us. And they said we should leave our baggage there. We should get out. And then immediately five to a row....
Judge:	They lined you up?
Magda:	Women separately, yes, lined us up. And I was with my sister-in-law; she had a small child, two years old. I took it in my arms because she was still younger and weaker [than I was]. And as we stood there in the row, a prisoner came to me and asked me if the child belonged to me. "No," I said. He said, "Give it to the mother." And I understood that I should give the child to my mother. Perhaps she would get lighter work. And so I gave it to her. Probably he meant that I should give it to an older...
Judge:	Woman.
Magda:	[An older woman], yes. And I also said to my mother, "Mother, say that you are old. Perhaps you can stay there, if you are older, so you could care for the children when my sister-in-law goes to work."
Judge:	Yes.
Magda:	And because this officer, the SS officer who was there, spoke so nicely to me and even spoke in Hungarian. I said, "Oh Mama, how good it would be if you could be with the children. Say that you are old."
Judge:	Yes.
Magda:	And I was taken out of the row, and I never saw her again....

Taken from Patricia Heberer, Documents of Life and Destruction Holocaust Sources in Context: Children during the Holocaust, *156–158.*

Suggestions for further reading

Yitzhak Arad, *Belzec, Sobibor, Treblinka: The Operation Reinhard Death Camps* (Bloomington, IN, 1999).

Hannah Arendt, *Eichmann in Jerusalem: A Report on the Banality of Evil* (New York, 2006).

Michael Berenbaum, *The Holocaust and History* (Bloomington, IN, 1998).

Daniel Blatman, *The Death Marches: The Final Phase of Nazi Genocide* (New York, 2011).

Witold Chrostowski, *Extermination Camp Treblinka* (Portland, OR, 2004).

Catherine Epstein, *Model Nazi: Arthur Greiser and the Occupation of Western Poland* (Oxford, 2012).

Sir Martin Gilbert, *The Righteous: Unsung Heroes of the Holocaust* (New York, 2004).

Wolf Gruner and Jörg Osterloh, eds., *The Greater German Reich and the Jews: Nazi Persecution Policies in the Annexed Territories* (New York, 2015).

Patricia Heberer, ed., *Documenting Life and Destruction Holocaust Sources in Context: Children during the Holocaust* (Lanham, MD, 2011).

Sarah Helm, *Ravensbrück: Life and Death in Hitler's Concentration Camp for Women* (New York, 2014).

Eric Katz, *Death by Design: Science, Technology, and Engineering in Nazi Germany* (New York, 2006).

Ian Kershaw, *The End: The Defiance and Destruction of Hitler's Germany* (New York, 2012).

Ruth Kluger, *Still Alive: A Holocaust Girlhood Remembered* (New York, 2003).

Primo Levi, *Survival in Auschwitz* (New York, 1995).

Patrick Montague, *Chelmno and the Holocaust: The History of Hitler's First Death Camp* (Chapel Hill, NC, 2012).

Laurence Rees, *How Mankind Committed the Ultimate Infamy at Auschwitz: A New History* (New York, 2005).

Jacques Semelin, *Purify and Destroy: The Political Uses of Massacre and Genocide* (New York, 2007).

Timothy Snyder, *Bloodlands: Europe between Hitler and Stalin* (New York, 2012).

Nechama Tec, *Resilience and Courage: Women, Men, and the Holocaust* (New Haven, CT, 2004).

Zoltan Vagi, Laszlo Csosz, and Gabor Kadar, eds., *Documenting Life and Destruction Holocaust Sources in Context: The Holocaust in Hungary: Evolution of a Genocide* (Lanham, MD, 2013).

Shlomo Venezia, *Inside the Gas Chambers: Eight Months in the Sonderkommando of Auschwitz* (Malden, MA, 2010).

Elie Wiesel, *Night* (New York, 2006).

Leah Wolfson, ed., *Documenting Life and Destruction Holocaust Sources in Context: Jewish Responses to Persecution*, Vol. 5, 1944–1946 (Lanham, MD, 2015).

GLOSSARY OF TERMS

A-B Aktion: Codename for the order to murder Polish intelligentsia, skilled workers, Catholic priests, political leaders, and former aristocrats upon the invasion of Poland in September 1939. The killing actions would be largely carried out by the Einsatzgruppen.

Ahlwardt, Hermann: (1846–1914) Originally, Ahlwardt was an elementary school teacher; however, upon being fired from his position, he became a prolific anti-Semitic author. He also helped to establish the Anti-Semitic People's Party in Germany.

Aktion T-4: Codename for the Nazi "Euthanasia" program. T-4 refers to the address of the project's headquarters, Tiergartenstrasse 4.

Anschluss: (Joining) This is the term employed by the Nazi Regime when it annexed Austria to Germany in March 1938. Austria was then incorporated into what was called "the Greater German Reich." It was greeted with public acclaim by many people in Austria; however, it meant the beginning of terror for Austrian Jews.

Article 48: A clause of the Weimar Constitution which allowed the President of Germany to declare an emergency situation in the country and thereby circumvent parliamentary democracy. Beginning in 1930, President Paul von Hindenburg enacted Article 48 to appoint presidential cabinets, undermining the power of the parliament.

Article 231: The "War Guilt Clause" of the Treaty of Versailles which stipulated that Germany bore sole responsibility for starting the First World War. Most Germans, no matter what their political beliefs, rejected this clause as a lie.

"Aryan": Originally a linguistic category used in nineteenth-century ethnology that was later incorporated into eugenics and racial discourse. Although the term is not clearly defined, its concept was used to distinguish among a hierarchy of races, with "Aryans" being the supposedly superior race. Nazi ideology used this concept to define who could be included in the Volksgemeinschaft. It excluded Jews as "non-Aryans" and it also excluded people of mixed blood (Mischlinge) as well.

Aryanization: This was a euphemistic term used by the Nazis to describe the confiscation of Jewish property, businesses, and other assets to "de-Judaize" the Aryan economy. This policy aimed to impoverish Jews, thus harming them both economically and socially.

Augustine: (345–430) One of the most influential of early Church Fathers, Augustine served as Bishop of Hippo in North Africa. He developed a doctrine that taught Christians that they should not seek to convert Jews, nor should they murder them. He did, however, teach that Jews could be humiliated and debased to remind them of their refusal to acknowledge Jesus as the Messiah.

Babi Yar: Ravine near Kiev where approximately 33,700 Jews were brutally murdered on September 29–30, 1941, by some of the men of Einsatzgruppe C.

Barbarossa: Code name for the Nazi military plan to invade the Soviet Union on June 22, 1941.

blood libel: Also known as "Ritual Murder," blood libel charges were brought against Jews for supposedly killing Christian children and then using the dead child's blood for ritualistic purposes. The first known formal accusation of blood libel appeared in Norwich, England in 1144. The last official charge was in 1946 in Kielce, Poland.

Centralverein deutscher Staastsbürger jüdischen Glaubens: Abbreviated as CV; translated as Central Association of German Citizens of Jewish Faith. Founded in 1893, the CV fought to defend against growing anti-Semitic acts while simultaneously encouraging Jews to cultivate strong German identities. With the rise of Hitler to power, the CV began to refocus its mission on assisting Jews with emigration issues and with charitable assistance to those Jews still living in Germany. The organization was forced to change its name in 1935 to the Centralverein der Juden in Deutschland (Central Association for Jews in Germany), and it would eventually be abolished after Kristallnacht.

Chamberlain, Houston Stewart: (1855–1927) Chamberlain, trained as a botanist, became a leading "expert" in racial theory. His work, *Foundations of the Nineteenth Century*, proclaimed Germans as the superior race and the inheritors of Aryanism.

Commissar Directive: Hitler's order to the invading German Wehrmacht and the Einsatzgruppen to eliminate Soviet commissars engaged in a "Judeo-Bolshevik" conspiracy. This action was modeled on the A-B Aktion carried out in Poland.

Constantine: Emperor who converted to Christianity in 313, ushering in a rise of conversions to Christianity within the Roman Empire.

conversos: Spanish term for Jews who converted to Roman Catholicism in 1492. Some of the population converted out of genuine faith while others may have converted due to threats of expulsion from Spain. A derogatory term developed for the converts, "marranos," which means "swine."

Czerniakow, Adam: (1880–1942) Czerniakow was a Polish Jew who was an engineer and an activist in Warsaw before the Second World War. In September 1939, the mayor of Warsaw pointed him out to Nazi forces and Czerniakow was named the Chairman of the Jewish Council for Warsaw. He held that position, trying to protect and save as many Jews as he could in the ghetto, but he committed suicide in July 1942.

Degrelle, Leon: (1906–?) A Belgian political leader who created the "Rexist movement" in 1930. Degrelle became a leading collaborator with the Nazis during the war. He established the "Walloon Legion" in the SS. His unit fought for Germany in the Soviet Union and Degrelle became the most highly decorated foreigner in the German military. He fled to Spain at the end of the war where he evaded Belgium extradition attempts.

deicide: "[T]he murder of a king/god." An accusation against the Jews by Christians that Jews were guilty for the death of Jesus of Nazareth and were therefore "Christ-killers."

Donin, Nicholas: Jewish convert to Christianity. Donin engaged in a public debate in 1239 in Paris that was designed to use his knowledge of Judaism in order to ridicule it. The point of the disputation was to prove that Jews were "blind" to the teachings of Jesus of Nazareth.

Drexler, Anton: (1884–1942) Original founder of the German Workers' Party (DAP), which was opposed to both capitalism and communism. Drexler's small right-wing political party became the foundation for Adolf Hitler's National Socialist German Workers' Party in 1920. Drexler was ousted from political leadership by 1921, as he was quickly eclipsed by Hitler's charismatic leadership.

Dreyfus Affair: Captain Alfred Dreyfus was accused of selling French military secrets to the Germans in 1894. He was the only Jewish man to be an officer in France and his court martial took on the character of a public spectacle. Dreyfus was publicly humiliated, his reputation was destroyed, and he was sentenced to life imprisonment on Devil's Island. Dreyfus was completely innocent of all charges.

Eichmann, Adolf: (1906–1962) Eichmann was born and raised in Austria where as a young man he joined the Austrian Nazi Party. Once he moved to Germany, he joined Reinhard Heydrich's staff at the SD. He played a major role in the "de-Jewing" of Austria after the Anschluss and thereafter was utilized as a "Jewish expert" deployed to various occupied countries to begin the Aryanization and deportation processes that resulted in the deaths of millions of Jews. He escaped at the end of the war, was finally captured by Israeli secret service, and was placed on trial in Israel.

He expressed no remorse for his actions. He was sentenced to death by hanging in 1962.

Einsatzgruppen: (special attack unit/group) Mechanized units of the SS who remained independent of military control as they operated under the command of the chief of the Security Police as well as the Security Service. They were used repeatedly in various campaigns, but their most well known activities occurred during the campaign against the Soviet Union. Inside of Russian territory, Einsatzgruppen A, B, C, and D followed on the heels of the advancing German army. Their mission was to enforce the Commissar Directive. In particular, their work focused on annihilating the Jewish population as Hitler had argued that Jews spread Bolshevism. At first the Einsatzgruppen executed only Jewish men; however, after August 1941, they targeted all Jewish people—men, women, and children—for execution.

Einsatzkommandos: Special commandos/Sonderkommandos, smaller sub-groups of the larger Einsatzgruppen.

euthanasia: "Mercy killing." The Nazi regime took the concept of "mercy killing" and twisted it to mean the eradication of "life unworthy of living," targeting the mentally and physically disabled, the elderly, and others the regime had deemed "unproductive." The first program to eliminate "useless eaters" began in 1939 against children. Then a second "adult euthanasia" program began as well. The adults targeted for death in the T-4 operation were primarily killed in gas chambers between 1939 and 1941. Approximately 70,000 adults were killed in the program and 5,000 children were murdered.

Fichte, Johann Gottlieb: (1762–1814) Fichte earned the dual titles of "Father of Modern German Nationalism" and "Father of Modern German Antisemitism" by his public lectures dedicated to fighting against Napoleon Bonaparte and the spread of French revolutionary ideas. Fichte's argument fused German nationalism with German anti-Semitism, arguing that Jews living in German lands were a "divisive presence" who could never be included in a German nation-state.

First Crusade: Preached in 1095 by Pope Urban II calling on Christian knights to go on an armed pilgrimage to wrest control of the Holy Land away from Islam. As Crusaders embarked, they attacked Jews all along the Rhine River as "unbelievers," resulting in the decimation of Jewish communities in Western Europe.

forced sterilization: Program initiated by the Nazis beginning in July 1933 when the "Law for the Prevention of Hereditary Ill Offspring" was announced. This led to the establishment of Hereditary Health Courts where individuals who had been denounced as "hereditarily diseased" or "feeble-minded" were forced to appear and receive a sentence of forced sterilization. Couched in the eugenics language of the day, the Nazi regime insisted that this program would protect the healthy Aryan people from degeneration. Approximately 320,000 Germans were forcibly sterilized under this program.

Franco, Francisco: (1892–1975) Leader of the coalition of Spanish nationalists and Falangists against the Popular Front liberal Republican government of Spain. Franco took leadership of the right-wing extremists in the summer of 1936, and with the help of Hitler and Mussolini, his coalition of forces won the Spanish Civil War in 1939.

Frank, Hans: (1900–1946) Frank was an early supporter of the NSDAP, using his legal training to defend Nazi party members when they were arrested. He was trusted enough by the Führer to research into Hitler's family tree. During the war, Frank was sent to be Governor-General in Polish territory. He set himself up in the castle in Krakow where he entertained lavishly while enacting brutal policies toward the Polish population. He was captured at the end of the war and was executed in 1946 after the Nuremberg Trials.

gas vans: Used by the Einsatzgruppen as a mobile killing facility to murder Jews and other "enemies." These vehicles were primarily used on the eastern front beginning in 1941.

Gau: An old term for a particular region, revitalized by the Nazi regime as the word implies "tribes" and racial cohesiveness.

Geiger, Abraham: (1810–1874) Geiger established "Reform Judaism" in the nineteenth century. He also argued against the supersessionist myth, stating that Christianity should recognize its debt to Judaism. In addition, he argued that Jesus of Nazareth was a liberal Pharisee.

Generalgouvernment: After the conquest of Poland, the Nazi regime designated an area of Polish land as a collateral or separate region not directly incorporated into Greater Germany. Hans Frank became the chief administrator of this region. The Generalgouvernment region served as a dumping ground for unwanted Jews and other ethnic "enemies" of the Reich. It was also the area from which vast numbers of ethnic Poles were taken to be used as forced laborers as well as the region slated for the ghettoization of the Jews.

Generalplan Ost: Plan developed to "fortify the German nation," it was signed by Heinrich Himmler in June 1942. This plan served as the official Nazi regime's occupational policy for the East. The plan involved the forced displacement of millions of Eastern Europeans which would allow the Volksgemeinschaft to extend its boundaries in the quest for Lebensraum. It involved the murder of millions of "Slavic inferiors and Jews" and the enslavement of hundreds of thousands more. It was never completely enacted due to the deterioration of the German forces in the war.

genocide: A term coined by Polish Jewish jurist Raphael Lemkin: "genos" meaning "a people" and "cide" meaning "to kill." Lemkin fought tirelessly in the post-Second World War environment to push the United Nations delegates to adopt his concept of genocide. Although the U.N. did not embrace Lemkin's entire definition of what constitutes a genocide, it did ratify genocide as a crime in December 1948, under the Agreement for the Prevention and Punishment of Genocide.

Germanization: The concept that was applied to certain areas of Eastern Europe implying the need to "re-Germanize" the lands with ethnic Germans at the expense of the indigenous populations. This idea was part of the concept to build a Volksgemeinschaft, or a racially united community of Aryans.

German Völkisch Movement: A term used to encompass numerous organizations arising in the early twentieth century to promote nationalism, racism, and anti-Semitism.

Gestapo: Acronym for "Geheime Staastspolizei" meaning "Secret State Police."

ghetto: The first Jewish ghetto was established in Venice, Italy, in the sixteenth century. This was established following a decree of Pope Paul IV who required that Jews move from outlying areas into an urban environment where certain streets would be designated as appropriate for Jews. Most early ghettos also forced Jews to be inside before nightfall, where they would be locked in for the night. The Nazis revived Jewish ghettos, of many sizes, throughout areas of occupied Europe. The largest Jewish ghetto created during the Second World War was in Warsaw.

Globocnik, Odilo: (1904–1945) Globocnik was born in Austria and was an active Nazi party member there even before the Anschluss with Austria. As part of the SS, Globocnik participated in Einsatzgruppen killing activities in Poland. In 1942, Himmler placed Globocnik in charge of carrying out Operation Reinhard. Globocnik committed suicide as the Allies closed in on him in 1945.

Gobineau, Arthur de: (1816–1882) Gobineau was a French diplomat and author. He became well known for his writings encouraging nineteenth-century thinkers to acknowledge "lower" and "higher" races. He influenced men such as Houston Stewart Chamberlain and Richard Wagner.

Goebbels, Joseph: (1897–1945) An aspiring (and failed) author, Goebbels joined the völkisch movement in the 1920s, joining the early Nazi Party and rising to become one of the most powerful leaders surrounding Hitler. Ultimately, Goebbels became the Minister of Propaganda and

Enlightenment in 1933, and he used his rhetorical skills to crush would-be opponents of the Nazi regime. Born with a crippled foot, slight in stature, he dutifully served Hitler, preferring to commit suicide in Hitler's final bunker as the Soviet Red Army entered Berlin.

Göring, Hermann: (1893–1946) Göring, who had grown up in affluent circles, became one of the most successful fighter pilots for Germany in the First World War. He met Hitler in 1922 and participated in the Beer Hall Putsch of 1923. He became addicted to morphine as a result of injuries he suffered during the Beer Hall Putsch, finally beating his addiction in the late 1920s. Once Hitler became Chancellor of Germany, Göring entered the new cabinet as Minister Without Portfolio. Göring was ruthless in his ambition and limitless in his greed, acquiring more and more power for himself throughout the twelve years of the Third Reich. He was captured by Allied forces and was put on trial at Nuremberg. He received the sentence of death by hanging; however, he was able to commit suicide in his jail cell before his sentence could be carried out.

Graetz, Heinrich: (1817–1891) Graetz was a Jewish historian who wrote the monumental 11-volume work *The History of the Jews*. Graetz argued throughout this work that a true test of a society's moral health resided in how Jews were treated by that society.

Grynszpan, Herschel: (1921– ?) Grynszpan was a young student in Paris when the rest of his family was forcibly deported from Germany into Poland. In his rage, he planned to assassinate the German Ambassador in Paris; however, he shot and killed Ernst vom Rath, an undersecretary at the embassy instead. The assassination of vom Rath sparked off the government-sponsored pogrom against German Jews called Kristallnacht on November 9–10, 1938. Grynszpan was arrested by the French for vom Rath's murder; however, when France fell to Germany in 1940, he was taken into German custody. He was a prisoner at Sachsenhausen concentration camp but his date of death is unknown.

Henrici, Ernst: Henrici founded the Reich Social Party in the late 1870s which preached anti-Semitism. He authored the "Antisemites' Petition" which was presented to Kaiser Wilhelm I in 1880.

Hereditary Health Courts: Established by the Nazi regime in 1933 to combat hereditary illnesses within the German nation. The courts functioned in the forced sterilization program to prevent individuals with potentially hereditary diseases from reproducing.

Herzl, Theodore: (1860–1904) Herzl, a Viennese lawyer and journalist, became the lead organizer of the First Zionist Congress in Basle, Switzerland, in 1897. Herzl had covered the anti-Semitic trial of Captain Alfred Dreyfuss and had concluded that anti-Semitism was inescapable and incurable. He resolved to bring Jews together on the world stage to pursue the creation of a Jewish nation-state. His death at an early stage prevented him from seeing the establishment of a Jewish homeland.

Heydrich, Reinhard: (1904–1942) Heydrich, nicknamed the "Blonde Beast" due to his Aryan racial characteristics, came from a middle-class family. He held a position as an officer in the navy, briefly, before he was dismissed due to a broken promise to marry a young woman. He interviewed for a position with Heinrich Himmler in the SS. Himmler appointed Heydrich to form an intelligence-gathering unit called the SS Security Service (SD) in 1932. By 1936, the ambitious Heydrich had accumulated more control over police and intelligence units to become the Chief of the Security Police and the SD. These offices were joined together in 1939 to become the Reich Security Main Office. Heydrich is the person to whom Göring wrote in July 1941 authorizing the "Final Solution of the Jewish Question." Heydrich summoned various representatives of German government agencies to a villa in Wannsee to discuss the implementation process of the Final Solution. Heydrich was assassinated by Czech resistance fighters in May 1942. In retaliation for the murder of Heydrich, Himmler ordered the "Operation Reinhard" action to be taken against Jews. The inhabitants of the Czech village of Lidice were murdered and the village was razed to the ground. The accusation was that the village had harbored Heydrich's assassins.

Himmler, Heinrich: (1900–1945) Born into a middle-class Roman Catholic household, Himmler went on to join the German army in the First World War; however, he never made it to the front. After the war ended, Himmler tried his hand at various occupations, none of which were very successful. He also came into contact with Hitler in 1924 and joined the early Nazi Party. Himmler was particularly interested in ideas regarding race, blood and soil, and farming. He established the elite SS (Schutzstaffeln/Protection Squad) to protect Hitler, then evolved the SS

into a powerful organization that ultimately ran the vast majority of the ghettos and concentration camps. He was also, by 1936, the Chief of the German Police, providing Himmler with still further reach into German lives. By 1939, he was also placed in charge of the "Fortification of the German-Volk Nation" which allowed him to exercise his plans for the Germanization of the East. By the end of the war, Himmler had been disavowed by Hitler for seeking to negotiate a separate armistice with the Allied Powers. He went in disguise through British lines and ultimately committed suicide in a displaced persons' camp.

Hindenburg, Paul von: (1846–1934) Hindenburg, a Prussian aristocrat, fought in the German Wars of Unification and retired from military service in 1911. With the outbreak of the First World War, Hindenburg returned to the army and became a war hero in the Battle of Tannenberg and the Masurian Lakes in 1914. By 1916, Hindenburg was the Supreme Commander and exercised a near-military dictatorship throughout the rest of the war. After the war ended, Hindenburg, no lover of the Weimar Republic, did support the new government in the name of law and order. By 1925, he was elected as President of the Weimar Republic. He was re-elected as president in 1932. Using Article 48, the emergency clause of the Weimar Constitution, Hindenburg appointed Hitler as Chancellor of Germany on January 30, 1933.

Hirsch, Simon Raphael: (1810–1888) Hirsch developed "Neo Orthodoxy," which meant that German Jews should practice Judaism as it always had been. He also pushed for German Jews to engage with German secular society.

Höss, Rudolf: (1900–1947) Höss was a First World War volunteer who later joined (in 1922) the Nazi Party. He served time in prison during the 1920s for murdering a teacher, but he was pardoned in 1928. By 1934, he was in the SS, training first at Dachau Concentration camp and then at Sachsenhausen. By 1940, Himmler promoted Höss to commandant of Auschwitz concentration camp. Höss turned the camp into the largest killing facility of the Nazi era. He was captured by the British in 1946, put on trial at Nuremberg, and sentenced to death. He was brought back to Auschwitz and was hanged outside of his former commandant's house at the camp.

Jahn, Friedrich Ludwig: (1778–1852) Jahn was the founder of the German gymnastics movement which emphasized the need for German youth to be physically fit to fight off French invasion. Jahn's concepts of the pure Volk influenced other racial thinkers, including Nazi theorists.

Kahr, Gustav von: (1862–1934) A middle-class jurist and politician, Kahr became the civilian leader in Bavaria following the 1920 Kapp Putsch. He was a conservative nationalist who wished to see an end to the Weimar Republic. Along with Otto von Lossow, he conspired with Hitler to begin the Beer Hall Putsch in November 1923. Kahr disavowed the putsch and continued on in his legal career until the summer of 1934 when Hitler enacted revenge against him, ordering Kahr's brutal murder.

Klemperer, Victor: (1881–1960) Klemperer was raised in a Jewish household but he converted to Protestantism. Classified under Nazi law as a Jew, Klemperer, a literary scholar and diarist, survived the war years because he was married to a non-Jewish woman. Their union was classified by the Nazis as a "privileged mixed marriage." Klemperer's astute observations regarding the Nazi's manipulation of language was published after the war, titled LTI—Linga Tertii Imperii.

Kristallnacht: Night of Broken Glass. A government-sponsored, nationwide pogrom enacted against Jewish people, property, and houses of worship. The nights of violence erupted upon the news that Ernst vom Rath had died of his wounds in Paris on November 9, 1938. Hitler and Goebbels worked to encourage acts of destruction and violence be perpetrated against the Jewish community in Germany. Thousands of businesses, synagogues, and private homes were destroyed in the two nights of violence. Approximately 30,000 Jews were arrested and sent to German concentration camps and at least ninety-one Jews were reported as dead.

Kulturbund deutscher Juden: Abbreviated: Kulturbund/Culture League of German Jews. This organization was formed in June 1933 to provide Jews with a creative outlet in the increasingly restrictive Nazi environment. The Kulturbund gave opportunities for Jews to participate in the performing arts and it provided entertainment for Jews. It was strictly monitored and controlled through Joseph Goebbels's Ministry of Propaganda and Enlightenment.

KZ: Most common abbreviation for Konzentrationslager/Concentration Camp. The official abbreviation in German was KL.

Lagarde, Paul de: (1827–1891) Lagarde, a professor of the "Orient," decried the Jews as aliens within

Germany. His völkisch views along with his critique of civilization were picked up by Nazi party members including Alfred Rosenberg.

Lebensraum: Living space. A concept first popularized during the founding of Germany in 1871, associated with expansionism and colonialism. However, a professor of geopolitics, Karl Haushofer and many of his followers began to apply this concept to the idea of European conquest. Hitler, in particular, looked to the East as a place of expansion for the German people. The quest to acquire more Lebensraum was used frequently to justify Hitler's foreign policy. It was also used to justify the "Final Solution of the Jewish Question" since Hitler argued that Bolshevism had come from the mind of a Jew (Karl Marx) and Bolshevism had rendered the vast territories of the Soviet Union an ideal place for conquest and resettlement by Aryans.

Ludendorff, Erich: (1856–1937) Ludendorff rose to become Quartermaster General of the German army during the First World War, partly due to his success in the Battles of Tannenberg and the Masurian Lakes (with Paul von Hindenburg). By 1916, Ludendorff, alongside Hindenburg, was running a virtual military dictatorship in Germany. Ludendorff left the military in October 1918, and he denounced the defeat of the German army and the November armistice, popularizing the "Stab in the back Legend." He participated in the failed Beer Hall Putsch of 1923 with Hitler, and was tried for treason, but was acquitted. He largely turned against Hitler by 1928, and practiced a type of neo-paganism, but was left alone by the Nazis.

Lüger, Karl: (1844–1910) Lüger, a Viennese lawyer and politician, is credited with making the language of political anti-Semitism acceptable and respectable in Austrian circles. Elected Mayor of Vienna many times over, Lüger's example inspired Hitler with his ability to manipulate the masses and achieve community improvements for the local Viennese.

Luther, Martin: Luther shattered medieval Christendom with his revolutionary doctrine of "justification by faith alone," sparking the Protestant Reformation. Luther, at various times of his life, weighed in on Jews, producing by 1543 a writing, "Concerning the Jews and Their Lies," which suggested a Final Solution to the Jewish Question in German territories.

Machtergreifung: Seizure of power. Refers to Hitler's appointment as chancellor by President Paul von Hindenburg on January 30, 1933.

Madagascar Plan: First discussed by men such as Paul de Lagarde and other racial theorists, the plan called for the removal of Jews from Europe to the island of Madagascar in order to "solve" the "Jewish Problem." The Nazi leadership adopted this forced emigration plan in 1938, and held some Jews in transit camps in France during the war, but by 1940–1941 this plan was no longer feasible since the Nazi regime had not been able to defeat the British domination of the high seas.

Marr, Wilhelm: Marr became one of the very first political anti-Semites with publications denouncing "Jewish influence" in German life. Marr's writings were so popular that his new terminology for "Jew hatred," called "anti-Semitism," became a household word.

Mendelssohn, Moses: (1729–1786) Mendelssohn was a leading Jewish intellectual during the Enlightenment. In one of his most famous works, *Jerusalem*, Mendelssohn attempted to show how the principles of Judaism and the Enlightenment could be compatible.

"Mischling" (pl. "Mischlinge"): Defined as "mixed breed," this terminology had been in use since the nineteenth century; however, it became codified under the Nazi regime beginning with the 1935 Law for Protection of German Blood and German Honor. Under the Nazi definition, a person who had both "Aryan" and "non-Aryan" blood was a mixed breed. Nazi leaders debated what to do with Mischlinge since some of their blood was "Aryan"; however, during the war most Mischlinge in occupied Eastern Europe were persecuted and targeted for death just as full-blooded Jews were.

Night of the Long Knives: June 30–July 2, 1934. A bloody purge within the Nazi Party aiming to remove Ernst Röhm and other leaders of the SA (Sturmabteilung/Storm Division) from power. Hitler used these nights of violence to also rid himself of political opponents such as former Chancellor Kurt von Schleicher.

Nisko Plan: Part of Adolf Eichmann's plan to deport Jews to the Generalgouvernement region in Poland beginning in October 1939. This plan was part of the Nazi scheme to deport Jews from the Reich to the Lublin district which would serve as a giant reservation for Jews. Himmler ordered the transports stopped in November 1939 as he was focused on bringing ethnic Germans to Poland to Germanize it. The program was officially shut down in April 1940.

November Criminals: Epithet used by right-wing extremists to denounce supporters of the Weimar Republic. In particular, the phrase reminded audiences of the devastating November 11, 1918, unconditional surrender of Germany in the First World War.

Old Reich: A term used to designate Germany before the Anschluss with Austria.

Operation Reinhard: (also called Aktion Reinhard) After the assassination of Reinhard Heydrich, Himmler ordered Odilo Globocnik to begin planning for the Final Solution, which included planning for deportations, building killing centers, coordinating transports to the campsites, and the killing of Jews.

Pale of Settlement: Area of land belonging to the Russian Empire where Jews were required to live. First established for Jews by Catherine the Great following the 1791 Partition of Poland.

Papen, Franz von: (1879–1969) Catholic conservative aristocrat and a leading member of the Catholic Zentrum (Center) Party. Papen was Chancellor of the Weimar Republic briefly in 1932 and was instrumental in convincing President Paul von Hindenburg to appoint Hitler as Chancellor in 1933. Von Papen served in Hitler's first cabinet as Vice-Chancellor.

pogrom: A Russian word implying devastation, it has come to be identified with attacks against Jews. Kristallnacht would be an example of a German pogrom.

Preuss, Hugo: Preuss was a constitutional law scholar who was elected to the National Assembly in 1919. His primary task in the Assembly was to draft a constitution for the German people. His work was ratified in the summer of 1919 when the constitution of the new Weimar Republic was proclaimed. Preuss also happened to be Jewish.

protective custody: (Schutzhaft) Euphemistic terminology employed by the Nazi regime for an arrest of an individual. This was originally a law in Prussia that police officers could take a person into custody in order to protect them from mob violence, but the person was to be released by the next day. Under the Third Reich, the idea of protective custody was abused, allowing police greater flexibility in terms of how long they detained a person.

Protocols of the Elders of Zion: Forged document, thought to have been created by the Russian secret police. The Protocols purport to be secret speeches given by Jews that call for world Jewry to spread chaos and anarchy throughout the world. Jews were then supposed to rise up amid the chaos and take over the world. This forgery is used repeatedly to "prove" that an international Jewish conspiracy exists.

Race and Settlement Main Office: Abbreviated as RuSHA, this was an office created in 1931 by the SS leadership of the Nazi Party. Much of this office's work centered on Waffen-SS marriage applications, searching for racial purity but during the war years it also was in charge of funeral and cemetery arrangements for Waffen-SS.

Rassenschande: (Race Defilement) According to the Law for the Protection of German Blood and German Honor of 1935, extramarital intercourse between Aryans and non-Aryans was prohibited. If an individual was accused of having an intimate relationship, it could result in charges of race defilement.

Rath, Ernst vom: (1909–1938) Rath, working as a legation secretary in the German Embassy in Paris in 1938, was assassinated by Herschel Grynszpan. Rath's death on November 9, 1938, sparked a massive pogrom against Jews in Germany called Kristallnacht.

Reich Germans: A term used to designate Germans who had grown up in Germany proper, to distinguish them from ethnic Germans who were living outside of Germany's boundaries. The ethnic Germans were designated as *Volksdeutsche*.

Reich Security Main Office: Abbreviated RSHA this was an organization created by joining the Security Police with the Security Service. Himmler was in charge but he appointed Heydrich to be its head until Heydrich's assassination in 1942. Ernst Kaltenbrunner became the next leader of the RSHA in 1943. The RSHA was a massive organization that was dedicated to gathering intelligence, inflicting terror and violence against opponents. It was ultimately the RSHA which was placed in charge of managing the Einsatzgruppen and handling the "Final Solution."

resettlement: A term used euphemistically by the Nazi regime to often mask forced deportations of groups of people deemed to be a threat to the Volksgemeinschaft.

Ribbentrop-Molotov Pact: Also known as the Nazi-Soviet Non-Aggression Pact. This agreement shocked the world as it promised neutrality if either Germany or the Soviet Union went to war with a third party. Secret protocols were added to the treaty in which the Soviet Union promised to support the German war effort with supplies. It also divided much of Eastern Europe into spheres of influence between the two powers. Once Hitler had this agreement signed, he was able to wage war against Poland without the fear of Germany fighting a two-front war as it had in 1914.

Ringelblum, Emanuel: (1900–1944) Ringelblum, a trained historian with a strong social conscience, had been active in left-wing Jewish circles for many years. Once the Nazis had created the Warsaw ghetto, Ringelblum helped to organize Jewish aid societies and soup kitchens. He was the driving force behind a project, Oyneg Shabes (Joy of the Sabbath), whereby he and other scholars interviewed men and women living in the ghetto in order to document what was happening to Jews in Warsaw. Ringelblum participated in the Warsaw ghetto Uprising, and escaped to the Aryan section of Warsaw, but was captured by the Germans. He, his wife, and his son were all executed by the Nazis in 1944.

Röhm, Ernst: (1887–1934) Röhm hated the Weimar Republic and joined the Nazi Party in the early 1920s. He organized the Sturmabteilung (SA) as the street fighters of the NSDAP. Röhm was interested in making his SA Brownshirts the new German army; however, his ambitions were squelched during the Night of the Long Knives when he was arrested on Hitler's orders and was executed.

Rosenberg, Alfred: (1893–1946) Rosenberg was an ethnic German who had been raised in Estonia. After the First World War he came to Germany, and joined many volkish organizations as well as the German Workers' Party (DAP). He became known as an anti-Semitic writer and his *The Myth of the Twentieth Century* revealed his anti-Christian attitudes as well.

He held various political offices under the Third Reich and despite some of his arguments over Nazi exterminationist policies, he was sentenced to death by hanging at the Nuremberg Trials.

Ruhs, Christian Friedrich: (1781–1820): Ruhs was a professor of history at the University of Berlin. He contributed to the development of language that designated Jews as divisive, disloyal, and aliens who should be forced to wear special markings on their clothing to distinguish Jews from Christians.

Schleicher, Kurt von: (1882–1934) Schleicher was a German general and politician. He was supportive of ending the Weimar Republic and replacing it with some type of authoritarian regime. He served as chancellor in 1932 but was replaced as chancellor with the appointment of Hitler in January 1933. Schleicher had plotted to divide the Nazi Party and for that, Hitler added the general's name to the list of opponents who would be assassinated during the Night of the Long Knives in 1934.

Schönerer, Georg Ritter von: (1842–1921) Austrian politician who adopted the language of political anti-Semitism and *völkisch* nationalism to gain votes. He authored the Linz Program which advocated for the removal of Jews from public sectors of Austrian life. He stressed the need for ethnic Germans in Austria to be united into one large Germanic Empire. Hitler admired Schönerer and mentioned him by name in his autobiography, *Mein Kampf.*

SD: Acronym for the Sicherheitsdienst des Reichsführer-SS—the Security Service, an intelligence-gathering and surveillance organization established in 1931 under Heinrich Himmler.

Himmler then appointed Reinhard Heydrich to be in charge of the organization. By 1937, the SD had been granted the authority to watch potential enemies of the German State. By 1939, the SD was merged with the Security Police to create the Reich Security Main Office.

Spanish Civil War: Conflict that took place between 1936 and 1939 between the legally established Liberal, republican government of Spain and the extreme conservative-nationalist, Falangist-fascist forces. The war began in July 1936 in Spanish Morocco and quickly was taken over by General Francisco Franco. Franco sent representatives within days of the conflict's beginning to meet with Hitler who then pledged his support in the fight against the Communists, Socialists and Republican forces. Franco declared the war over in April 1939; half a million people died in the three years of warfare.

Special Commandos: (Sonderkommandos: SK) Part of the Einsatzgruppen. These units were typically the smallest in number carrying out executions and other tasks.

special handling: Euphemistic terminology used by the Nazi regime to describe the murder of Jews and other enemies. More than likely the phrase was first used by Reinhard Heydrich in his directive of September 29, 1939, regarding the murder of Jews and other Poles. Over the course of time, the phrasing used by bureaucrats and SS changed to words such as "resettlement," "transfer," and "deportation" as it was well known that "special handling" meant death for Jews.

SS: Full name: Schutzstaffeln/Protection Squad. The SS began in 1923 when it was determined that Hitler should have a guard service. Over time the squads spread all over Germany, and linked together by their oath to serve Hitler with unconditional loyalty. Once Heinrich Himmler took over the SS in 1929, he worked to recruit the elites and sons of elites of German society into the SS. He raised the membership to 52,000 men by 1932. By 1933, the SS had grown to approximately 200,000 members. Himmler envisioned the SS as the racial, biological elite of the New Germany under Hitler. They were also to be the "racial enforcers" who aimed to restore the Volk to its rightful place in history. It was under Himmler's direction that the SS came to play an important role in occupation policies, using Einsatzgruppen to terrorize local populations, carry out murder, create ghettos, and eventually to run concentration camps as death factories.

Stab-in-the-back Legend: Idea put forward by nationalists at the end of the First World War arguing that the German military had not lost the war on the field of battle, but rather, weak civilians on the home front, combined with internal enemies, sought to end the war to destroy German greatness. This legend was loudly proclaimed by General Erich Ludendorff in the immediate postwar years. It was picked up by Hitler and used repeatedly throughout Hitler's rise to power.

Stoecker, Adolf: (1835–1909) German Evangelical Lutheran pastor who decided to establish his own political party to combat the spread of secularization in German society. He also attacked socialism and Jews as being responsible for moving the German people away from religious values.

Streicher, Julius: (1885–1946)
Originally an elementary school
teacher, Streicher fought in the First
World War and afterwards, in 1921,
he joined the Nazi Party. In 1923, he
founded the anti-Semitic newspaper,
Der Stürmer, the only newspaper
that Hitler supposedly read in
its entirety each week. Streicher
was Gauleiter of Franconia and
amassed great wealth through the
Aryanization process; however, he
fell out of favor and was banished to
a country estate. Hitler allowed him
to continue to publish *Der Stürmer*.
At the end of the war, Streicher was
trying to escape in disguise, but was
discovered and arrested. He was
placed on trial at Nuremberg as
Germany's "no. 1 Jew-baiter" and
was sentenced to death by hanging.

Sturmabteilung: (Storm Division/
Storm Troopers) Abbreviated as SA,
also known as the "Brown shirts"
for the color of their clothing.
The SA, led by Ernst Röhm, was
a mass organization known as
the street fighters of the Nazi
party. Membership in the SA grew
exponentially in the early 1930s,
having approximately 700,000
members by 1933. Once Hitler was
appointed Chancellor, the SA ran
wild in the streets, settling political
scores against their enemies and
often dragging opponents off to
"wild" concentration camps. After
the Night of the Long Knives in
June 1934, the SA declined in
membership and in power; however,
the SA men participated actively in
violent attacks against Jews in events
such as Kristallnacht. Once the war
began, SA men were not exempted
from military service. Those who
did not enlist were used as auxiliary
support for the regular German
army, the air defense, border patrol,
and so on.

supersessionism: An idea that
developed within the early Christian
Church that Jews who refused to
convert to Christianity had forfeited
their special relationship as God's
chosen people. The Christians
were now portrayed by the Church
Fathers as God's new chosen ones,
with the church triumphing over the
synagogue.

T-4: See entry on Euthanasia.

Talmud: Rabbinic texts interpreting
and advising how to follow Biblical
texts.

Theodosius the Great: Emperor of
Rome who ordered that all of his
subjects within the empire convert to
Christianity, outlawing the worship
of pagan Gods. Christianity became
the dominant religion of the Roman
Empire following this decree in 380.

Thomas Aquinas: (1225–1274) One
of the most influential medieval
theologians, Aquinas further
developed St. Augustine's doctrines
on Jewish-Christian relations. Like
St. Augustine, Thomas Aquinas
allowed for public humiliation of
Jews to remind them of the error of
their beliefs.

Vernichtungslager: Extermination
camp.

Versailles, Treaty of: (1919) The
treaty which ended the First World
War for Germany. It was extremely
unpopular among the German
population due to its restrictive and
humiliating clauses. In particular,
"Article 231" of the treaty became
the most hotly debated clause as
it stated that Germany bore sole
responsibility for starting the war.
This clause led to the idea that
Germany must pay reparations for
all of the wars' damage.

Volksdeutsche: Ethnic Germans
who were residents of countries
other than Germany. Nazi
propaganda made every effort to

encourage ethnic Germans to push for annexation of their lands to Germany.

Volksgemeinschaft: "People's community" was a concept utilized by Hitler through Nazi propaganda to emphasize the building of a dynamic, racially homogeneous community of healthy Aryans. Those who were included in the Volksgemeinschaft were considered to be racially valuable members who would contribute to the Third Reich. For members of the community, Hitler promoted the idea that all Aryans must be ready to stand and fall together as they attempted to build their ideal society. Those individuals not classified as healthy Aryans were to be excluded from the community as they were deemed racially inferior and a threat to the health of the German nation. Jews, as "non-Aryans," were excluded from participating in the Volksgemeinschaft.

Volkgenosse (m.), Volkgenossin (f.): A common form of address used during the Third Reich, it implied that one was a racially fit member of the Aryan community. It was part of the Nazi propaganda effort to portray the Third Reich as a place of equality among Aryans. It was also used to contrast with those people deemed unworthy to be members of the Aryan community. In the NSDAP party platform, point 4 stipulated that only a Volk Comrade can be a citizen.

Volunteer Helpers (Hilfswillige; "Hiwis"): A term used for foreigners who were used as auxiliaries to the German military, the police, and the SS. They were most notoriously used in concentration camps and Einsatzgruppe shooting sites. These men had generally been captured

and were POWs; however, they were offered the chance to help the Nazis as volunteers.

Wagner, Richard: (1813–1883) German composer and virulent anti-Semite. Wagner wished to revive Teutonic mythology for the German Volk in his operatic works. He also railed against Jewish "influence" in music as well as in other areas of German life. His son-in-law, Houston Stewart Chamberlain, continued Wagner's legacy of anti-Semitism and glorification of all things German. Of all the Germanic composers, Wagner was Hitler's favorite. The performances of Wagnerian operas were celebrated in Germany with great fanfare.

wandering Jew: The image of the eternally wandering Jew comes from an ancient story of a shoemaker, Ahasuerus, who would not allow a stranger knocking at his door into his home at night. The story eventually took on the religious connotation that the "stranger" had been Jesus and therefore Ahasuerus symbolized Jewish rejection of the Messiah. The story reasoned that the shoemaker was condemned to wander the earth seeking a place of safety to rest for his rejection of Jesus.

Wannsee Conference: Reinhard Heydrich summoned representatives of various government ministries and agencies to coordinate the "Final Solution of the Jewish Question" in January 1942. Heydrich made it clear that his office, the RSHA, would coordinate and organize the murder of millions of European Jews. The meeting to decide the fate of millions took less than two hours.

Wehrmacht: (Defense Power) A term used after 1935 to designate the German military. Prior to this time, the military was referred to as the Reichswehr (Reich Defense Force). According to the law of March 1935, Hitler was named as the supreme commander of the Wehrmacht.

Weimar Republic: (1919–1933) The first democratic republic of Germany. Established after Germany's loss in the First World War, the Weimar Republic was plagued with problems ranging from its association with the hated Treaty of Versailles to inflation, unemployment, and inefficient government. It enjoyed a brief respite from 1924 to 1929, but with the stock market crash in America, the Weimar government spiraled into further debt and instability. Parliamentary democracy truly came to an end in 1930 once President Paul von Hindenburg began to invoke Article 48, the "emergency clause" of the constitution. This clause enabled him to bypass election results and appoint a cabinet of ministers at his own discretion. On January 30, 1933, he appointed Hitler as Chancellor, thus effectively ending the democratic republican form of government for Germany.

Zionism: A movement that aimed to establish a Jewish state in Palestine as a national homeland for the Jews. The founder of the modern Zionist movement was Theodore Herzl, who wished to combat anti-Semitism he encountered in France during the Dreyfus Affair. Zionism arose out of a mixture of motivations, including religious, nationalistic, and political ones.

Zyklon B: Hydrogen cyanide. Originally Zyklon B was used as a disinfectant to destroy vermin and other pests. Eventually Rudolf Hoess, commandant of Auschwitz concentration camp, decided to use the chemical in the gas chambers. It was produced by the German companies DEGESCH Firm, which was a subsidiary of Degussa/I.G. Farben, and Tesch and Stabenow. The company produced Zyklon B in a crystalline form so that it could be thrown into the gas chambers. When the product is exposed to the air, it forms a cloud of noxious gas which results in death by suffocation.

NOTES

Chapter 1

1 A member of the Sonderkommando at Auschwitz-Birkenau. His eyewitness account was found in 1962, buried in the yard of Auschwitz crematorium. Venezia, *Inside the Gas Chambers: Eight Months in the Sonderkommando of Auschwitz*, VIII.

2 Kühne, *Belonging and Genocide: Hitler's Community, 1918–45*, 2.

3 Friedländer, *Nazi Germany and the Jews: Years of Extermination*, xviii–xix.

4 Friedländer, *Years of Extermination*, xx.

5 Ruderman, "Jewish Intellectual History," *The Great Courses*, 93.

6 Hilberg, Staron, and Kermisz, eds., *The Warsaw Diary of Adam Czerniakow*, diary entry June 14, 1942, on starving children in the Warsaw ghetto.

Chapter 2

1 Gager, *The Origins of Antisemitism: Attitudes toward Judaism in Pagan and Christian Antiquity*, 67–115.

2 This is not to imply that all Jews believed in a Messiah, but for those Jewish communities who did await a Messiah, they were also generally expecting to experience the ushering in of a messianic age which often included the idea of the resurrection of the dead.

3 Much of what the historical Jesus of Nazareth was preaching was in fact not new, nor even particularly revolutionary for some in the Jewish community. See Amy Jill Levine, *The Misunderstood Jew: The Church and the Scandal of the Jewish Jesus, passim*. Levine argues that much of Judaism has been distorted and filtered through centuries of Christian stereotypes and that in order to understand Jesus's teachings, one must have a deep understanding of first-century Judaism.

4 Levine, *The Misunderstood Jew*, 19. See Hans Hermann Henrix, "The Son of God Became Human as a Jew: Implications of the Jewishness of Jesus for Christology," in Philip A. Cunningham et al., *Christ Jesus and the Jewish People Today: New Explorations of Theological Interrelationships*, 115–138.

5 Levine, *The Misunderstood Jew*; see especially Levine's explorations of how Christian seminaries and divinity schools continue to stereotype Judaism as a system of beliefs which rejected everything Jesus had preached (121–125).

6   For a brief explanation of Matthew's agenda when writing this portion of the Gospel, see Amy Jill Levine, *The Misunderstood Jew*, 99–102. In particular, Levine argues that Matthew had aligned Jerusalem and the people living in Jerusalem with the rejection of Jesus's message.

7   For a discussion of how the Roman Catholic Church has sought to separate its teachings from the idea that all Jews throughout time are "Christ-killers," see Mary C. Boys, "Facing History: The Church and Its Teaching on the Death of Jesus," in Philip A. Cunningham et al., *Christ Jesus and the Jewish People Today*, 35–41.

8   Bauer, *A History of the Holocaust*, 7.

9   This is not to imply that the early Church leaders were in agreement. In fact, Peter was preaching his interpretation of Jesus's message to primarily Jewish communities while Paul went out to preach and convert non-Jews, i.e., the gentiles. Ultimately, after much in-fighting, it was Paul's leadership that came to dominate the early church's formation.

10   See the work of Daniel J. Harrington, S.J., "The Gradual Emergence of the Church and the Parting of the Ways," in Philip A. Cunningham et al., *Christ Jesus and the Jewish People Today*. In particular, Harrington illuminates the latest scholarship on interpreting Paul's mission by stating, "it appears more likely that Paul, far from disavowing Judaism, regarded Jesus as the fulfillment of God's promises to Israel, the Christian movement as a group within Judaism, and himself as part of the loyal remnant of Israel" (p. 94).

11   Harrington, "The Gradual Emergence of the Church and the Parting of the Ways," 103–104.

12   For an explanation of the supersessionsim debate among scholars, see Jesper Svartvik, "Reading the Epistle to the Hebrews without Presupposing Supersessionism," in Philip A. Cunningham et al., *Christ Jesus and the Jewish People Today*, 77–91.

13   Gager, *Origins of Antisemitism*, 117–133.

14   Fredericksen, *St. Augustine and the Jews, passim.*

15   Gager, *Origins of Antisemitism*, 162–167.

16   Gager, *Origins of Antisemitism*, 90.

17   Ruderman, "Between Cross and Crescent," 44.

18   Eidelberg, *The Jews and the Crusaders*, 23.

19   Chazan, *Reassessing Jewish Life in Medieval Europe*, 146.

20   Chazan, *Reassessing Jewish Life in Medieval Europe*, 146–147.

21   Hilberg, *The Destruction of European Jewry*, 9–13.

22   Trachtenberg, *The Devil and the Jews, passim.*

23   Friedman, Connell Hoff, and Chazan, *The Trial of the Talmud, Paris, 1240, passim.*

24   Ruderman, "Between Cross and Crescent," 72–75.

25   Ruderman, "Between Cross and Crescent," 80–83.

26   Ruderman, "Between Cross and Crescent," 80–83.

27   Ruderman, "Between Cross and Crescent," 84–87.

28 Hochstadt, *Sources of the Holocaust*, 13–15.

29 Ruderman, "Between Cross and Crescent," 97–100.

30 Ruderman, "Between Cross and Crescent," 99–100.

31 Ruderman, "Jewish Intellectual History," 27–31.

32 Pulzer, *Jews and the German State*, 71–73.

33 Pulzer, *Jews and the German State*, 16.

34 Pulzer, *Jews and the German State*, 15.

35 Pulzer, *Jews and the German State*, 16.

36 Pulzer, *The Rise of Political Antisemitism in Germany and Austria,* "The Rejection of Liberalism," 29–74.

37 Bauer, *A History of the Holocaust*, 27–36.

38 Bauer, *A History of the Holocaust*, 27–36.

Chapter 3

1   Pulzer, *The Rise of Political Antisemitism in Germany and Austria*, 49–52.

2   Bauer, *A History of the Holocaust*, 43.

3   See J. Trachtenberg's work, *The Devil and the Jews, passim.*

4   Pulzer, *The Rise of Political Antisemitism in Germany and Austria*, 62–63.

5   Pulzer, *Jews and the German State*, 96–99.

6   Pulzer, *The Rise of Political Antisemitism in Germany and Austria*, 95–101.

7   Pulzer, *The Rise of Political Antisemitism in Germany and Austria*, 249.

8   Ruderman, "Jewish Intellectual History," *Great Courses*, 36–39.

9   Ruderman, "Jewish Intellectual History," *Great Courses*, 40–41.

10 Ruderman, "Jewish Intellectual History," *Great Courses*, 44–45.

11 Pulzer, *The Rise of Political Antisemitism in Germany and Austria*, 153.

12 Pulzer, *The Rise of Political Antisemitism in Germany and Austria*, 162–187.

13 Pulzer, *The Rise of Political Antisemitism in Germany and Austria*, 266–267.

14 Ruderman, "Jewish Intellectual History," *Great Courses*, 67.

15 Bein, *Herzl: A Biography, passim.*

16 Wildt, *Hitler's Volksgemeinschaft*, 15.

17 Wildt, *Hitler's Volksgemeinschaft*, 18.

18 Wildt, *Hitler's Volksgemeinschaft*, 18.

19 Wildt, *Hitler's Volksgemeinschaft*, 16.

20 Kühne, *Belonging and Genocide*, 9–31.

21 Remarque, *All Quiet on the Western Front, passim.*

22 Adas, *Men as the Measures of Machines, passim.*

23 Hitler, *Mein Kampf*, 204.

24 Bauer, *A History of the Holocaust*, 75.

25 Pulzer, *The Rise of Political Antisemitism in Germany and Austria*, 314.

26 Steinweis, *Studying the Jew*, 36.

27 Wildt, *Hitler's Volksgemeinschaft*, 36–37.

28 Wildt, *Hitler's Volksgemeinschaft*, 53–54.

29 Wildt, *Hitler's Volksgemeinschaft*, 55.

30 Wildt, *Hitler's Volksgemeinschaft*, 57.

31 Friedrich, *Before the Deluge*, 96.

32 Haffner, *Defying Hitler*, 20–28.

33 Burleigh, *Death and Deliverance*, 15–21.

34 Steinweis, *Studying the Jew*, 25.

35 Steinweis, *Studying the Jew*, 29.

36 Steinweis, *Studying the Jew*, 34.

37 Steinweis, *Studying the Jew*, 38.

38 Steinweis, *Studying the Jew*, 39.

39 Steinweis, *Studying the Jew*, 39.

Chapter 4

1   See works by Gay, *Weimar Culture*; Deak, *Weimar Germany's Left-Wing Intellectuals*; Lane, *Architecture and Politics in Germany, 1918–1945*.

2   Kershaw, *Hitler: Hubris*, 127.

3   Kershaw, *Hitler: Hubris*, 125.

4   Steinweis, *Studying the Jew*, 7.

5   Steinweis, *Studying the Jew*, 7–8.

6   Wildt, *Hitler's Volksgemeinschaft*, 37.

7   Wildt, *Hitler's Volksgemeinschaft*, 36.

8   Wildt, *Hitler's Volksgemeinschaft*, 36.

9   Wildt, *Hitler's Volksgemeinschaft*, 48.

10 Noakes and Pridham, *Nazi Reader*, 35.

11 Domarus, ed. by Patrick Romane, *The Essential Hitler*, 31.

12 Kühne, *Belonging and Genocide*, 6.

13 Kühne, *Belonging and Genocide*, 91.

14 Wildt, *Hitler's Volksgemeinschaft*, 38.

15 Wildt, *Hitler's Volksgemeinschaft*, 60–65.

16 Wildt, *Hitler's Volksgemeinschaft*, 66.

17 Wildt, *Hitler's Volksgemeinschaft*, 61.

18 Kershaw, *Hitler: Hubris*, 377.

19 Wildt, *Hitler's Volksgemeinschaft*, 77–78.

20 Haffner, *Defying Hitler*, 107.

21 The Jewish population in Germany in 1933 stood at approximately 525,000 in a nation of approximately 65 million.

22 Wildt, *Hitler's Volksgemeinschaft*, 78.

23 Matthäus and Roseman, *Jewish Responses to Persecution*, Vol. 1, 8.

24 Matthäus and Roseman, *Jewish Responses*, Vol. 1, 10.

25 Matthäus and Roseman, *Jewish Responses*, Vol. 1, 10–11.

26 There is some indications that this law was drafted even before the Reichstag fire. See Benjamin Carter Hett, *Crossing Hitler: The Man Who Put the Nazis on the Witness Stand*.

27 Wildt, *Hitler's Volksgemeinschaft*, 78.

28 Wildt, *Hitler's Volksgemeinschaft*, 79.

29 Wildt, *Hitler's Volksgemeinschaft*, 79.

30 Kaplan, *Between Dignity and Despair*, 18.

31 Wildt, *Hitler's Volksgemeinschaft*,

32 Kulka and Jäckel, *The Jews in the Nazi Secret Reports on Popular Opinion in Germany* (*Secret Reports* hereafter), 3.

33 Kulka and Jäckel, *Secret Reports*, 4.

34 Kulka and Jäckel, *Secret Reports*, 6.

35 Kulka and Jäckel, *Secret Reports*, 7.

36 Kaplan, *Between Dignity and Despair*, 20.

37 Matthäus and Roseman, *Jewish Responses*, Vol. 1, 11–12.

38 Domarus, *Essential Hitler*, 374–380.

39 Kaplan, *Between Dignity and Despair*, 22–23.

40 Matthäus and Roseman, *Jewish Responses*, Vol. 1, 22.

41 Dawidowicz, *A Holocaust Reader*, 39.

42 Dawidowicz, *A Holocaust Reader*, 40.

43 Originally this April 7, 1933, law contained a loophole that allowed Jewish men to be exempted if they could demonstrate that they had served on the front-lines in the First World War for Germany. This was done as a concession to President Hindenburg. Once Hindenburg died in 1934, the exemption was removed.

44 Dawidowicz, *A Holocaust Reader*, 41.

45 Matthäus and Roseman, *Jewish Responses*, Vol. 1, 29.

46 Matthäus and Roseman, *Jewish Responses*, Vol. 1, 30.

47 Matthäus and Roseman, *Jewish Responses*, Vol. 1, 30.

48 Kaplan, *Between Dignity and Despair*, 37.

49 Kaplan, *Between Dignity and Despair*, 37.

50 Wildt, *Hitler's Volksgemeinschaft*, 91.

51 Kaplan, *Between Dignity and Despair*, 41.

52 Kaplan, *Between Dignity and Despair*, 41.

53 Kulka and Jäckel, *Secret Reports*, 16.

54 Kaplan, *Between Dignity and Despair*, 67.
55 Hitler's speech is available online: www.jewishvirtuallibrary.org/jsource/ Holocaust/knives.html
56 Kulka and Jäckel, *Secret Reports*, 55.
57 Kulka and Jäckel, *Secret Reports*, 62.
58 Kulka and Jäckel, *Secret Reports*, 69.
59 Matthäus and Roseman, *Jewish Responses*, Vol. 1, 92–93.
60 Matthäus and Roseman, *Jewish Responses*, Vol. 1, 108.
61 Kulka and Jäckel, *Secret Reports*, 73.
62 Kulka and Jäckel, *Secret Reports*, 83.
63 Kulka and Jäckel, *Secret Reports*, 95.
64 Kulka and Jäckel, *Secret Reports*, 99.
65 Kulka and Jäckel, *Secret Reports*, 99.
66 Kulka and Jäckel, *Secret Reports*, 104.
67 Matthäus and Roseman, *Jewish Responses*, Vol. 1, 135.
68 Matthäus and Roseman, *Jewish Responses*, Vol. 1, 151.
69 Kulka and Jäckel, *Secret Reports*, 108.
70 Dawidowicz, *A Holocaust Reader*, 45.
71 Dawidowicz, *A Holocaust Reader*, 48.
72 Matthäus and Roseman, *Jewish Responses*, Vol. 1, 186.
73 Matthäus and Roseman, *Jewish Responses*, Vol. 1, 188.
74 Matthäus and Roseman, *Jewish Responses*, Vol. 1, 188.
75 Kulka and Jäckel, *Secret Reports*, 153.
76 Kulka and Jäckel, *Secret Reports*, 175.
77 Kulka and Jäckel, *Secret Reports*, 176.
78 Kulka and Jäckel, *Secret Reports*, 167.
79 See works of Kershaw, "The Persecution of the Jews and German Popular Opinion in the Third Reich," 261–269; Sarah Gordon, "Hitler, Germans, and the 'Jewish Question'," 171–174; Bankier, *The Germans and the Final Solution*, 76–80; Kulka, "Die Nürnberger Rassegesetze und die deutsche Bevölkerung im Lichte geheimer NS Lage- und Stimmungsberichte," 582–624. All cited by M. Wildt in *Hitler's Volksgemeinschaft*, 164.
80 Wildt, *Hitler's Volksgemeinschaft*, 173.
81 Wildt, *Hitler's Volksgemeinschaft*, 174.
82 Gellately, *Die Gestapo und die deutsche Gesellschaft: die Durchsetzung der Rassenpolitik, 1933–1945*, 185.
83 Frevert, "Ehre-männlich/weiblich," 21–68. See also Wildt, *Hitler's Volksgemeinschaft*, 187.
84 Wildt, *Hitler's Volksgemeinschaft*, 187.
85 Matthäus and Roseman, *Jewish Responses*, Vol. 1, 194.
86 Matthäus and Roseman, *Jewish Responses*, Vol. 1, 194.

87 Matthäus and Roseman, *Jewish Responses*, Vol. 1, 195.

88 Adam, *Judenpolitik im Dritten Reich*, 153. See also Wildt, *Hitler's Volksgemeinschaft*, 216.

89 Wildt, *Hitler's Volksgemeinschaft*, 215.

90 Wildt, *Hitler's Volksgemeinschaft*, 216.

91 Wildt, *Hitler's Volksgemeinschaft*, 216.

92 Griech-Polelle, "The Catholic Episcopacy and the National Socialist State," 229.

93 Domarus, *Essential Hitler*, 386.

94 Kulka and Jäckel, *Secret Reports*, 212.

95 Kulka and Jäckel, *Secret Reports*, 214–215.

96 Griech-Polelle, "The Catholic Episcopacy and the National Socialist State," 223–236.

97 Griech-Polelle, "The Catholic Episcopacy and the National Socialist State," 229.

98 Griech-Polelle, "The Catholic Episcopacy and the National Socialist State," 230.

99 Kulka and Jäckel, *Secret Reports*, 227.

100 Matthäus and Roseman, *Jewish Responses*, Vol. 1, 263.

Chapter 5

1   Matthäus and Roseman, *Jewish Responses*, Vol. 1, 291.

2   Kulka and Jäckel, *Secret Reports*, 247–248.

3   See Pine, *Nazi Family Policy*, 88–116.

4   See works by Michael Phayer, *Protestant and Catholic Women in Nazi Germany*; Henry Friedlander, *The Origins of Nazi Genocide: From Euthanasia to the Final Solution*; Claudia Koonz, "Single Issue Dissent" in Michael Geyer and John Boyer, *Resistance*.

5   Pine, *Nazi Family Policy*, 153.

6   Pine, *Nazi Family Policy*, 154.

7   See works such as Aly, *Hitler's Beneficiaries*; Dean, *Robbing the Jews*.

8   Pine, *Nazi Family Policy*, 155.

9   Dean, *Robbing the Jews, passim*. See also Kwiet, "To Leave or Not to Leave," 142.

10 Pine, *Nazi Family Policy*, 159.

11 Kaplan, *Between Dignity and Despair*, 44.

12 Kulka and Jäckel, *Secret Reports*, 292.

13 Wildt, *Hitler's Volksgemeinschaft*, 228.

14 Matthäus and Roseman, *Jewish Responses*, Vol. 1, 278.

15 Matthäus and Roseman, *Jewish Responses*, Vol. 1, 285.

16 Matthäus and Roseman, *Jewish Responses*, Vol. 1, 288.

17 Matthäus and Roseman, *Jewish Responses*, Vol. 1, 289.

18 Matthäus and Roseman, *Jewish Responses*, Vol. 1, 291–292.

19 Matthäus and Roseman, *Jewish Responses*, Vol. 1, 292.

20 Kulka and Jäckel, *Secret Reports*, 306.

21 Kulka and Jäckel, *Secret Reports*, 307.

22 Kulka and Jäckel, *Secret Reports*, 322.

23 Kulka and Jäckel, *Secret Reports*, 322.

24 See Kaplan, *Dominican Haven, passim.*

25 Matthäus and Roseman, *Jewish Responses*, Vol. 1, 322.

26 Dawidowicz, *Holocaust Reader*, 52.

27 Matthäus and Roseman, *Jewish Responses*, Vol. 1, 325.

28 Matthäus and Roseman, *Jewish Responses*, Vol. 1, 325.

29 Kulka and Jäckel, *Secret Reports*, 332.

30 Kulka and Jäckel, *Secret Reports*, 332.

31 Stein, ed., *Great Lives Observed: Hitler*, 477–478.

32 Stein, ed., *Great Lives Observed: Hitler*, 480.

33 Kulka and Jäckel, *Secret Reports*, 333.

34 Wildt, *Hitler's Volksgemeinschaft*, 237.

35 Wildt, *Hitler's Volksgemeinschaft*, 237.

36 Kulka and Jäckel, *Secret Reports*, 342.

37 Matthäus and Roseman, *Jewish Responses*, Vol. 1, 341.

38 Gilbert, *Kristallnacht*, 67–68.

39 Gilbert, *Kristallnacht*, 24.

40 Gilbert, *Kristallnacht*, 24–26.

41 Gilbert, *Kristallnacht*, 26.

42 Gilbert, *Kristallnacht*, 27.

43 Friedlander, *Nazi Germany and the Jews: The Years of Persecution*, 272.

44 See Michael Wildt's *Hitler's Volksgemeinschaft* for this argument.

45 Pine, *Nazi Family Policy*, 163.

46 Pine, *Nazi Family Policy*, 162.

47 Kaplan, *Between Dignity and Despair*, 69.

48 Kaplan, *Between Dignity and Despair*, 69.

49 Kaplan, *Between Dignity and Despair*, 69.

50 Kaplan, *Between Dignity and Despair*, 71.

51 Kaplan, *Between Dignity and Despair*, 71.

52 Kaplan, *Between Dignity and Despair*, 72.

53 Kaplan, *Between Dignity and Despair*, 72.

54 Dawidowicz, *Holocaust Reader*, 53.

55 Gilbert, *Kristallnacht*, 95.

56 Matthäus and Roseman, *Jewish Responses,* Vol. 1, 356.

57 Matthäus and Roseman, *Jewish Responses,* Vol. 1, 372–373.

58 Kulka and Jäckel, *Secret Reports*, 370.

59 Kulka and Jäckel, *Secret Reports*, 370.

60 Kulka and Jäckel, *Secret Reports*, 370, 371, 379.

61 Kulka and Jäckel, *Secret Reports*, 385.

62 Kulka and Jäckel, *Secret Reports*, 372.

63 Kulka and Jäckel, *Secret Reports*, 396.

64 Domarus, *Essential Hitler*, 393–399, quote from 399.

65 Domarus, *Essential Hitler*, 400.

66 Garbarini, ed., *Jewish Responses to Persecution*, Vol. 2, 1938–1940, 104–105.

67 Garbarini, ed., *Jewish Responses to Persecution*, Vol. 2, 105.

68 Gruner, "Protectorate of Bohemia and Moravia," 104.

69 Gruner, "Protectorate of Bohemia and Moravia," 104–105.

70 Gruner, "Protectorate of Bohemia and Moravia," 106.

71 Gruner, "Protectorate of Bohemia and Moravia," 106–107.

72 Gruner, "Protectorate of Bohemia and Moravia," 108.

73 Gruner, "Protectorate of Bohemia and Moravia," 110–111.

74 Gruner, "Protectorate of Bohemia and Moravia," 112–122.

75 Kulka and Jäckel, *Secret Reports*, 435.

76 Garbarini, ed., *Jewish Responses to Persecution*, Vol. 2, 81–84.

77 Grabarini, ed., *Jewish Responses to Persecution*, Vol. 2, 76–77.

78 Garbarini, ed., *Jewish Responses to Persecution*, Vol. 2, 93.

79 Garbarini, ed., *Jewish Responses to Persecution*, Vol. 2, 115.

80 Pine, *Nazi Family Policy*, 167.

81 Kulka and Jäckel, *Secret Reports*, 471.

82 Kulka and Jäckel, *Secret Reports*, 473.

83 Kulka and Jäckel, *Secret Reports*, 476.

84 Kulka and Jäckel, *Secret Reports*, 477.

85 See Burleigh's *Death and Deliverance, passim.*

86 Griech-Polelle, *Bishop von Galen, passim.*

Chapter 6

1 Kulka and Jäckel, *Secret Reports*, 462.

2 Loose, "Wartheland," 191.

3   Friedlander, *Nazi Germany and the Jews: The Years of Extermination*, 11.
4   Garbarini, *Jewish Responses*, Vol. 2, 124.
5   Garbarini, *Jewish Responses*, Vol. 2, 125.
6   The Polish government escaped and eventually relocated to England.
7   Friedlander, *Years of Extermination*, 11.
8   Friedlander, *Years of Extermination*, 11.
9   Friedlander, *Years of Extermination*, 12.
10 Friedlander, *Years of Extermination*, 12.
11 Dawidowicz, *Holocaust Reader*, 59–60.
12 Dawidowicz, *Holocaust Reader*, 60–64.
13 Loose, "Warthegau," 193.
14 Garbarini, *Jewish Responses*, Vol. 2, footnote 39, 137.
15 Garbarini, *Jewish Responses*, Vol. 2, 138.
16 Garbarini, *Jewish Responses*, Vol. 2, 138.
17 Garbarini, *Jewish Responses*, Vol. 2, 135.
18 Garbarini, *Jewish Responses*, Vol. 2, 141.
19 Garbarini, *Jewish Responses*, Vol. 2, 141–142.
20 Gilbert, *The Holocaust*, 116.
21 Dawidowicz, *Holocaust Reader*, 65.
22 Dawidowicz, *Holocaust Reader*, 66.
23 Loose, "Warthegau," 193–194.
24 Loose, "Warthegau," 194.
25 Loose, "Warthegau," 194.
26 Friedlander, *Years of Extermination*, 22.
27 Friedlander, *Years of Extermination*, 24.
28 Kulka and Jäckel, *Secret Reports*, 478.
29 Kulka and Jäckel, *Secret Reports*, 485.
30 Kulka and Jäckel, *Secret Reports*, 483.
31 Kulka and Jäckel, *Secret Reports*, 488.
32 Kulka and Jäckel, *Secret Reports*, 487.
33 Dawidowicz, *Holocaust Reader*, 66–67.
34 Hilberg, ed., *The Warsaw Ghetto Diary of Adam Czerniakow*, introduction.
35 Garbarini, *Jewish Responses*, Vol. 2, 176–177.
36 Garbarini, *Jewish Responses*, Vol. 2, 351.
37 Friedlander, *Years of Extermination*, 35–36.
38 Loose, "Warthegau," 192.
39 Levin, *The Holocaust: The Destruction of European Jewry*, 207–208.
40 Levin, *The Holocaust*, 208.
41 Levin, *The Holocaust*, 208.

42 Browning, *Remembering Survival*.

43 Garbarini, *Jewish Responses*, Vol. 2, 381–382.

44 Hilberg, ed., *The Warsaw Ghetto Diary of Adam Czerniakow*, 239.

45 Hilberg, ed., *The Warsaw Ghetto Diary of Adam Czerniakow*, 366.

46 Garbarini, *Jewish Responses*, Vol. 2, 372.

47 Levin, *The Holocaust*, 230.

48 Garbarini, *Jewish Responses*, Vol. 2, 404.

49 Garbarini, *Jewish Responses*, Vol. 2, 410–411.

50 Churchill and Cannadine, *Blood, Toil, Tears and Sweat: The Great Speeches*, 149.

51 Kulka and Jäckel, *Secret Reports*, 495–496.

52 Kulka and Jäckel, *Secret Reports*, 499.

53 Kulka and Jäckel, *Secret Reports*, 501.

54 Kulka and Jäckel, *Secret Reports*, 504.

55 Kulka and Jäckel, *Secret Reports*, 507.

56 Kulka and Jäckel, *Secret Reports*, 507.

57 Kulka and Jäckel, *Secret Reports*, 517.

58 Kulka and Jäckel, *Secret Reports*, 516.

59 See Alan E. Steinweis, *Studying the Jew*; Robert Ericksen, *Complicity in the Holocaust: Churches and Universities in Nazi Germany*; Claudia Koonz, *The Nazi Conscience*; and Elizabeth Harvey, *Women and the Nazi East*.

60 Schoentgen, "Luxembourg," 291.

61 Schoentgen, "Luxembourg," 291.

62 Schoentgen, "Luxembourg," 294.

63 Schoentgen, "Luxembourg," 294–295.

64 Schoentgen, "Luxembourg," 295.

65 Schoentgen, "Luxembourg," 295.

66 Schoentgen, "Luxembourg," 295–298.

67 Schoentgen, "Luxembourg," 299.

68 Schoentgen, "Luxembourg," 301.

69 Schoentgen, "Luxembourg," 311.

70 Garbarini, *Jewish Responses*, Vol. 2, 316.

71 Garbarini, *Jewish Responses*, Vol. 2, 316.

72 Matthäus, with Emil Kerenji, Jan Lambertz, and Leah Wolfson, eds., *Documenting Life and Destruction Holocaust Sources in Context: Jewish Responses to Persecution*, Vol. 3, 1941–1942, 10–12.

73 Garbarini, *Jewish Responses*, Vol. 2, 336.

74 Garbarini, *Jewish Responses*, Vol. 2, 338.

75 Garbarini, *Jewish Responses*, Vol. 2, 338.

76 Pine, *Nazi Family Policy*, 168–169.

77 Pine, *Nazi Family Policy*, 169.

78 Kulka and Jäckel, *Secret Reports*, 521.

79 Kulka and Jäckel, *Secret Reports*, 520.

80 Kulka and Jäckel, *Secret Reports*, 521.

81 Kulka and Jäckel, *Secret Reports*, 523.

Chapter 7

1   Kulka and Jäckel, *Secret Reports*, 525.

2   Kitchen, *The Third Reich*, 310.

3   Kitchen, *The Third Reich*, 311.

4   Friedlander, *Years of Extermination*, 160.

5   Friedlander, *Years of Extermination*, 162–163, quote from 163.

6   Friedlander, *Years of Extermination*, 191.

7   Kitchen, *The Third Reich*, 312.

8   Kitchen, *The Third Reich*, 312.

9   Arad, *The Holocaust in the Soviet Union*, 212–213.

10 Kitchen, *The Third Reich*, 312–313.

11 See works such as R. Hilberg, *The Destruction of European Jewry*; Browning, *Ordinary Men: Reserve Police Battalion*, 101; Rhodes, *Masters of Death*; for a controversial challenge to Browning, see also Goldhagen, *Hitler's Willing Executioners*.

12 Rhodes, *Masters of Death*, 113.

13 Rhodes, *Masters of Death*, 113.

14 Rhodes, *Masters of Death*, 113.

15 Rhodes, *Masters of Death*, 113.

16 Kitchen, *The Third Reich*, 313.

17 Kitchen, *The Third Reich*, 312.

18 Kay, *Resettlement and Exploitation*, 100.

19 Kitchen, *The Third Reich*, 312.

20 Kay, *Resettlement and Exploitation*, 101.

21 Kay, *Resettlement and Exploitation*, 101.

22 Kay, *Resettlement and Exploitation*, 101.

23 Rhodes, *Masters of Death*, 112–113.

24 Hilberg, *The Destruction of European Jewry*, 263.

25 The ranks of the Einsatzgruppen would be quickly supplemented with thousands of men under direct SS control as well as by some 20,000 Orpo men.

26 Hilberg, *The Destruction of European Jewry*, 104–120.

27 Arad, *Holocaust in the Soviet Union*, 133.

28 Bartov, *Hitler's Army, passim.*

29 Arad, *Holocaust in the Soviet Union,* 134.

30 Arad, *Holocaust in the Soviet Union,* 134.

31 Arad, *Holocaust in the Soviet Union,* 135.

32 DesBois, *Holocaust by Bullets,* 83–84.

33 DesBois, *Holocaust by Bullets,* 85.

34 DesBois, *Holocaust by Bullets,* 97.

35 DesBois, *Holocaust by Bullets,* 97.

36 DesBois, *Holocaust by Bullets,* 97.

37 Snyder, *Bloodlands,* 126, 141–143.

38 Klee et al., *"The Good Old Days,"* 31.

39 Matthäus, *Jewish Responses,* Vol. 3, footnote 131.

40 Matthäus, *Jewish Responses,* Vol. 3, 133.

41 Matthäus, *Jewish Responses,* Vol. 3, 134.

42 Matthäus, *Jewish Responses,* Vol. 3, 134.

43 Arad, *Holocaust in the Soviet Union,* 142.

44 Arad, *Holocaust in the Soviet Union,* 142.

45 Arad, *Holocaust in the Soviet Union,* 144.

46 Arad, *Holocaust in the Soviet Union,* 144.

47 Hilberg, *Destruction of the European Jews,* 136–138.

48 Arad, *Holocaust in the Soviet Union,* 138.

49 Arad, *Holocaust in the Soviet Union,* 138.

50 Arad, *Holocaust in the Soviet Union,* 138.

51 Arad, *Holocaust in the Soviet Union,* 139.

52 Arad, *Holocaust in the Soviet Union,* 139.

53 Arad, *Holocaust in the Soviet Union,* 161.

54 Arad, *Holocaust in the Soviet Union,* 174–175.

55 Arad, *Holocaust in the Soviet Union,* 175.

56 Arad, *Holocaust in the Soviet Union,* 176.

57 Arad, *Holocaust in the Soviet Union,* 183.

58 Arad, *Holocaust in the Soviet Union,* 183–184.

59 Dawidowicz, *Holocaust Reader,* 74.

60 Dawidowicz, *Holocaust Reader,* 76.

61 Dawidowicz, *Holocaust Reader,* 78.

62 Dawidowicz, *Holocaust Reader,* 78.

63 Dawidowicz, *Holocaust Reader,* 81.

64 Dawidowicz, *Holocaust Reader,* 82.

65 Dawidowicz, *Holocaust Reader,* 82.

66 Hilberg, *Destruction of the European Jews,* 231.

67 Kulka and Jäckel, *Secret Reports*, 527–528.

68 Kulka and Jäckel, *Secret Reports*, 532.

69 Kulka and Jäckel, *Secret Reports*, 533–534.

70 Kulka and Jäckel, *Secret Reports*, 537.

71 Kulka and Jäckel, *Secret Reports*, 539.

72 Kulka and Jäckel, *Secret Reports*, 538.

73 Kulka and Jäckel, *Secret Reports*, 541.

74 Kulka and Jäckel, *Secret Reports*, 552.

75 Matthäus, *Jewish Responses*, Vol. 3, 147.

76 Friedlander, *Years of Extermination*, 266–267.

77 Arad, *Holocaust in the Soviet Union*, 389.

78 Friedlander, *Years of Extermination*, 267.

79 Friedlander, *Years of Extermination*, 267.

80 Kitchen, *The Third Reich*, 315.

81 Kitchen, *The Third Reich*, 316.

82 Kitchen, *The Third Reich*, 317.

83 Friedlander, *Years of Extermination*, 273.

84 Friedlander, *Years of Extermination*, 273.

85 Friedlander, *Years of Extermination*, 275.

86 Friedlander, *Years of Extermination*, 280.

87 Kulka and Jäckel, *Secret Reports*, 555.

88 Kulka and Jäckel, *Secret Reports*, 560.

89 Kulka and Jäckel, *Secret Reports*, 560–561.

90 Kulka and Jäckel, *Secret Reports*, 563.

91 Kulka and Jäckel, *Secret Reports*, 564.

92 Kulka and Jäckel, *Secret Reports*, 565.

93 Kulka and Jäckel, *Secret Reports*, 567.

94 Kulka and Jäckel, *Secret Reports*, 570.

95 Matthäus, *Jewish Responses*, Vol. 3, 154.

96 Matthäus, *Jewish Responses*, Vol. 3, 154.

97 Matthäus, *Jewish Responses*, Vol. 3, 159–160.

98 Matthäus, *Jewish Responses*, Vol. 3, 178–179, quote from 179.

99 Matthäus, *Jewish Responses*, Vol. 3, 179.

100 Arad, *Holocaust in the Soviet Union*, 393–394.

101 Arad, *Holocaust in the Soviet Union*, 394.

102 Arad, *Holocaust in the Soviet Union*, 395.

103 Arad, *Holocaust in the Soviet Union*, 396.

104 Domarus, *Essential Hitler*, 400–401.

Chapter 8

1 Kulka and Jäckel, *Secret Reports*, 576.

2 Kitchen, *Charisma*, 343.

3 Friedlander, *Years of Extermination*, 199.

4 Friedlander, *Years of Extermination*, 204.

5 Friedlander, *Years of Extermination*, 204–205.

6 Friedlander, *Years of Extermination*, 205–206.

7 Kulka and Jäckel, *Secret Reports*, 579.

8 Kulka and Jäckel, *Secret Reports*, 580.

9 Kulka and Jäckel, *Secret Reports*, 582.

10 The only recorded time a mass open protest against deportations of Jews from Germany was in Berlin in February 1943. See Nathan Stoltzfus, *Resistance of the Heart* for an examination of the "Rosenstrasse" protest of Aryan wives demanding the release of their Jewish husbands.

11 Kulka and Jäckel, *Secret Reports*, 584.

12 Kulka and Jäckel, *Secret Reports*, 585.

13 Friedlander, *Years of Extermination*, 314–315.

14 Friedlander, *Years of Extermination*, 317.

15 Kerenji, *Jewish Responses to Persecution*, Vol. 4, xxvi.

16 Kerenji, *Jewish Responses*, Vol. 4, xxvi.

17 Domarus, *Essential Hitler*, 403.

18 Domarus, *Essential Hitler*, 403–404.

19 Domarus, *Essential Hitler*, 404.

20 Domarus, *Essential Hitler*, 405.

21 Domarus, *Essential Hitler*, 405–406.

22 Kerenji, *Jewish Responses*, Vol. 4, 6.

23 Kerenji, *Jewish Responses*, Vol. 4, 6.

24 Kerenji, *Jewish Responses*, Vol. 4, 8.

25 Kerenji, *Jewish Responses*, Vol. 4, 8–9, quote from 10.

26 Kerenji, *Jewish Responses*, Vol. 4, 10–11.

27 Kerenji, *Jewish Responses*, Vol. 4, 26.

28 Kerenji, *Jewish Responses*, Vol. 4, 27.

29 Kerenji, *Jewish Responses*, Vol. 4, 28.

30 Friedlander, *Years of Extermination*, 372–373.

31 Arad, *Belzec, Sobibor, Treblinka: The Operation Reinhard Death Camps*, 15–16.

32 Arad, *Belzec, Sobibor, Treblinka: The Operation Reinhard Death Camps*, 16.

33 Arad, *Belzec, Sobibor, Treblinka: The Operation Reinhard Death Camps*, 20–22.

34 Arad, *Belzec, Sobibor, Treblinka: The Operation Reinhard Death Camps*, 23.

35 Arad, *Belzec, Sobibor, Treblinka: The Operation Reinhard Death Camps*, 26.

36 Arad, *Belzec, Sobibor, Treblinka: The Operation Reinhard Death Camps*, 26.

37 Arad, *Belzec, Sobibor, Treblinka: The Operation Reinhard Death Camps*, 29.

38 See works such as Sonja M. Hedgepeth and Rochelle G. Saidel, eds., *Sexual Violence against Jewish Women during the Holocaust.*

39 Chrostowski, *Treblinka, passim.*

40 Arad, *Belzec, Sobibor, Treblinka: The Operation Reinhard Death Camps*, 42.

41 Arad, *Belzec, Sobibor, Treblinka: The Operation Reinhard Death Camps*, 42.

42 Chrostowski, *Treblinka, passim.*

43 Arad, *Belzec, Sobibor, Treblinka: The Operation Reinhard Death Camps*, 63–64.

44 Arad, *Belzec, Sobibor, Treblinka: The Operation Reinhard Death Camps*, 64.

45 Arad, *Belzec, Sobibor, Treblinka: The Operation Reinhard Death Camps*, 67.

46 Friedlander, *Years of Extermination*, 374.

47 Friedlander, *Years of Extermination*, 375.

48 Friedlander, *Years of Extermination*, 380.

49 Friedlander, *Years of Extermination*, 380.

50 Friedlander, *Years of Extermination*, 381.

51 Friedlander, *Years of Extermination*, 381.

52 Arad, *Belzec, Sobibor, Treblinka: The Operation Reinhard Death Camps*, 148–149.

53 Kerenji, *Jewish Responses*, Vol. 4, 56.

54 Kerenji, *Jewish Responses*, Vol. 4, 56.

55 Arad, *Belzec, Sobibor, Treblinka: The Operation Reinhard Death Camps*, 166.

56 Arad, *Belzec, Sobibor, Treblinka: The Operation Reinhard Death Camps*, 170–171.

57 See Patrick Montague's *Chelmno and the Holocaust: The History of Hitler's First Death Camp, passim.*

58 Montague, *Chelmno, and the Holocaust: The History of Hitler's First Death Camp, passim.*

59 Montague, *Chelmno, and the Holocaust: The History of Hitler's First Death Camp, passim.*

60 Friedlander, *Years of Extermination*, 136.

61 Montague, *Chelmno, and the Holocaust: The History of Hitler's First Death Camp, passim.*

62 Montague, *Chelmno, and the Holocaust: The History of Hitler's First Death Camp, passim.*

63 Rees, *Auschwitz*, 1–10.

64 Rees, *Auschwitz*, 54–55.

65 Rees, *Auschwitz*, 62.

66   Rees, *Auschwitz*, 65.
67   Rees, *Auschwitz*, 82–83.
68   Rees, *Auschwitz*, 84.
69   Rees, *Auschwitz*, 93–94.
70   Rees, *Auschwitz*, 95.
71   Rees, *Auschwitz*, 95.
72   Rees, *Auschwitz*, 96.
73   Rees, *Auschwitz*, 96–97.
74   Rees, *Auschwitz*, 101.
75   Rees, *Auschwitz*, 168–169.
76   Rees, *Auschwitz*, 170.
77   Friedlander, *Years of Extermination*, 501.
78   Rees, *Auschwitz*, 171.
79   Klüger, *Still Alive*, 94.
80   Friedlander, *Years of Extermination*, 506.
81   Friedlander, *Years of Extermination*, 506.
82   Friedlander, *Years of Extermination*, 506–507.
83   Kerenji, *Jewish Responses,* Vol. 4, 62.
84   Venezia, *Inside the Gas Chambers*, 61–62.
85   Rees, *Auschwitz*, 220.
86   Rees, *Auschwitz*, 227–228.
87   Friedlander, *Years of Extermination*, 618.
88   Venezia, *Inside the Gas Chambers*, 63.
89   Klee et al., *"The Good Old Days,"* 220–221.
90   Kulka and Jäckel, *Secret Reports*, 608.
91   Kulka and Jäckel, *Secret Reports*, 623.
92   Kulka and Jäckel, *Secret Reports*, 627.
93   Kulka and Jäckel, *Secret Reports*, 633.
94   Kulka and Jäckel, *Secret Reports*, 636.
95   Kulka and Jäckel, *Secret Reports*, 652.
96   Wolfson, *Jewish Responses,* Vol. 5, 1944–1946, 46.
97   Wolfson, *Jewish Responses,* Vol. 5, 46
98   Blatman, *The Death Marches, passim.*
99   Wolfson, *Jewish Responses,* Vol. 5, 50.
100   Wolfson, *Jewish Responses,* Vol. 5, 50.
101   Venezia, *Inside the Gas Chambers*, 141–144.
102   Venezia, *Inside the Gas Chambers*, 144.
103   Venezia, *Inside the Gas Chambers*, 146.
104   Venezia, *Inside the Gas Chambers*, 151.

105   Venezia, *Inside the Gas Chambers*, 153.
106   Venezia, *Inside the Gas Chambers*, 155.
107   Domarus, *Essential Hitler*, 804.
108   Domarus, *Essential Hitler*, 804.
109   Domarus, *Essential Hitler*, 805.
110   Domarus, *Essential Hitler*, 805.
111   Domarus, *Essential Hitler*, 806.
112   Domarus, *Essential Hitler*, 808.

SELECT BIBLIOGRAPHY

Published primary sources

Dawidowicz, Lucy, ed., *A Holocaust Reader*. West Orange, NJ, 1976.

Domarus, Max and ed. Patrick Romane, *The Essential Hitler: Speeches and Commentary*. Wauconda, IL, 2007.

Eckhart, Dietrich, *Bolshevism from Moses to Lenin*. Translated by William Pierce. Nuremberg, 1925.

Friedman, John, Jean Connell Hoff, and Robert Chazan, eds., *The Trial of the Talmud, Paris, 1240*. Toronto, 2012.

Garbarini, Alexandra, with Emil Kerenji, Jan Lambertz, and Avinoam Patt, eds., *Jewish Responses to Persecution*, Vol. 2, *1938–40*. Lanham, MD, 2011.

Goebbels, Joseph, *Communism with the Mask Off and Bolshevism in Theory and Practice*. Nuremberg, 1935 and 1936.

Heberer, Patricia, ed., *Documenting Life and Destruction Holocaust Sources in Context: Children during the Holocaust*. Lanham, MD, 2011.

Hilberg, Raul, ed., *Documents of Destruction. Germany and Jewry, 1933–1945*. Chicago, IL, 1971.

Hilberg, Raul, ed., *The Warsaw Ghetto Diary of Adam Czerniakow*. Warsaw, 1999.

Hitler, Adolf, *Mein Kampf*. Translated by Ralph Manheim. New York, 1999.

Hochstadt, Steve, ed., *Sources of the Holocaust*. New York, 2006.

Kaufman, Theodore and Wolfgang Diewerge, *Germany Must Perish! and the War Goal of World Plutocracy*. New Jersey, NJ, 1941.

Kerenji, Emil, ed., *Documenting Life and Destruction Holocaust Sources in Context: Jewish Responses to Persecution*, Vol. 4, *1942–43*. Lanham, MD, 2015.

Klee, Ernst, Willi Dressen, and Volker Riess, eds., *"The Good Old Days:" The Holocaust as Seen by Its Perpetrators and Bystanders*. Old Saybrook, CT, 1991.

Kulka, Otto dov and Eberhard Jäckel, eds., *The Jews in the Nazi Secret Reports on Popular Opinion in Germany, 1933–1945*. Translated by William Templer. New Haven, CT, 2010.

Matthäus, Jürgen and Frank Bajohr, eds., *Documenting Life and Destruction Holocaust Sources in Context: The Political Diary of Alfred Rosenberg and the Onset of the Holocaust*. Lanham, MD, 2015.

Matthäus, Jürgen and Mark Roseman, eds., *Documenting Life and Destruction Holocaust Sources in Context: Jewish Responses to Persecution*, Vol. 1, *1933–38*. Lanham, MD, 2010.

Matthäus, Jürgen, Jochen Böhler, and Klaus-Michael Mallmann, eds., *Documenting Life and Destruction Holocaust Sources in Context: War, Pacification, and Mass Murder, 1939: The Einsatzgruppen in Poland*. Lanham, MD, 2014.

Morgan, Michael L., *A Holocaust Reader: Responses to the Nazi Extermination.*
New York, 2001.
Noakes, J. and G. Pridham, eds., *Nazism, 1919–1945*, Vol. 3: *Foreign Policy, War
and Racial Extermination. A Documentary Reader.* Evanston, IL, 1997.
Ringelblum, Emmanuel, *Notes from the Warsaw Ghetto.* New York, 2006.
Stackelberg, Roderick and Sally A. Winkle, eds., *The Nazi Germany Sourcebook.
An Anthology of Texts.* New York, 2002.
Stein, George, ed., *Hitler: Great Lives Observed.* Englewood Cliffs, NJ, 1968.
Vagi, Zoltan, Laszlo Csosz, and Gabor Kadar, eds., *Documenting Life and
Destruction Holocaust Sources in Context: The Holocaust in Hungary:
Evolution of a Genocide.* Lanham, MD, 2013.
Venezia, Shlomo, *Inside the Gas Chambers: Eight Months in the Sonderkommando
of Auschwitz.* Malden, MA, 2010.
Wolfson, Leah, ed., *Documenting Life and Destruction Holocaust Sources in Context:
Jewish Responses to Persecution*, Vol. 5, *1944–1946.* Lanham, MD, 2015.

Secondary sources

Adam, Uwe D., *Judenpolitik im Dritten Reich.* Droste, 2003.
Adas, Michael, *Machines as the Measure of Men: Science, Technology and
Ideologies of Western Dominance, Ithaca, NY, 1990. Erich Maria Remarque, All
Quiet on the Western Front*, translated by A.W. Wheen. New York, 1987.
Altmann, Alexander, *Moses Mendelssohn: A Biographical Study.* University, AL,
1973.
Aly, Götz, *Final Solution: Nazi Population Policy and the Murder of European
Jews.* Translated by Belinda Cooper and Allison Brown. Baltimore, MD, 1994.
Aly, Gotz, *Hitler's Beneficiaries: Plunder, Racial War, and the Nazi Welfare State.*
Picador Press, 2008.
Aly, Götz, Christian Pross, and Peter Chroust, eds., *Cleansing the Fatherland: Nazi
Medicine and Racial Hygiene.* Baltimore, MD, 1994.
Arad, Yitzhak, *Belzec, Sobibor, Treblinka: The Operation Reinhard Death Camps.*
Bloomington, IN, 1999.
Arad, Yitzhak, *The Holocaust in the Soviet Union.* Lincoln, NE, 2009.
Arendt, Hannah, *Eichmann in Jerusalem: A Report on the Banality of Evil.* New
York, 2006.
Bankier, David, *The Germans and the Final Solution: Public Opinion under
Nazism.* New York, 1996.
Bartov, Omer, "Defining Enemies, Making Victims: Germans, Jews and the
Holocaust," *American Historical Review* 103 (June 3, 1998): 771–816.
Bartov, Omer, *Hitler's Army: Soldiers, Nazis, and the War in the Third Reich.* New
York, 1991.
Bauer, Yehuda, *A History of the Holocaust.* New York, 1982.
Ben-Itto, Hadassa, *The Lie That Wouldn't Die: The Protocols of the Elders of
Zion.* New York, 2005.
Berenbaum, Michael, *The Holocaust and History.* Bloomington, IN, 1998.
Bergen, Doris, "Catholics, Protestants, and Christian Antisemitism in Nazi
Germany," *Central European History* 3 (1994): 329–348.

Bernauer, James and Robert A. Maryks, eds., *"The Tragic Couple:" Encounters between Jews and Jesuits*. Boston, MA, 2014.

Biale, David, ed., *Cultures of the Jews*, vols. 1–3. New York, 2002.

Blatman, Daniel, *The Death Marches: The Final Phase of Nazi Genocide*. New York, 2011.

Bonfil, Robert, *Jewish Life in Renaissance Italy*. Los Angeles, CA, 1994.

Bredin, Jean-Denis, *The Affair: The Case of Alfred Dreyfus*. New York, 1986.

Breitman, Richard, *Architect of Genocide: Himmler and the Final Solution*. New York, 1991.

Browning, Christopher, *Ordinary Men: Reserve Police Battalion 101 and the Final Solution in Poland*. New York, 1996.

Browning, Christopher, *Remembering Survival: Inside a Nazi Slave-Labor Camp*. New York, 2011.

Burleigh, Michael, *Death and Deliverance: "Euthanasia" in Germany, 1900–45*. New York, 1995.

Chazan, Robert, *Church, State, and Jew in the Middle Ages*. West Orange, NJ, 1980.

Chazan, Robert, *In the Year 1096: The First Crusade and the Jews*. Philadelphia, PA, 1996.

Chazan, Robert, *Medieval Jewry in Northern France*. Baltimore, MD, 1973.

Chazan, Robert, *Reassessing Jewish Life in Medieval Europe*. New York, 2010.

Chodakiewicz, Marek, *Between Nazis and Soviets: Occupation Politics in Poland*. New York, 2004.

Chrostowski, Witold, *Extermination Camp Treblinka*. Portland, OR, 2004.

Churchill, Winston and David Cannadine. *Blood, Toil, Tears and Sweat: The Great Speeches*. New York, 2007.

Cohen, Jeremy, *Living Letters of the Law: Ideas of the Jew in Medieval Christianity*. Los Angeles, CA, 1999.

Cohen, Mark R, *Under Crescent and Cross: The Jews in the Middle Ages*. Princeton, NJ, 1995.

Dawidowicz, Lucy S., *The War against the Jews, 1933–45*. New York, 1975.

Deak, Istvan, *Weimar Germany's Left-Wing Intellectuals: A Political History of the Weltbuhne and Its*. Berkeley, CA,, 1968.

Dean, Martin, *Robbing the Jews: The Confiscation of Jewish Property in the Holocaust*. Cambridge, MA, 2010.

Dembowski, Peter, *Christians in the Warsaw Ghetto*. Indiana, 2005.

Desbois, Patrick, *The Holocaust by Bullets*. New York, 2008.

Elon, Amos, *The Pity of It All*. New York, 2003.

Eidelberg, Shlomo, ed., *The Jews and the Crusaders: The Hebrew Chronicles of the First and Second Crusades*. Jersey City, NJ, 1996.

Epstein, Catherine, *Model Nazi: Arthur Greiser and the Occupation of Western Poland*. Oxford, 2012.

Ericksen, Robert P., *Complicity in the Holocaust: Churches and Universities in Nazi Germany*. Cambridge, MA, 2012.

Evans, Richard J., *The Coming of the Third Reich*, Vol. 1. New York, 2004.

Evans, Richard J., *The Third Reich in Power*, Vol. 2. New York, 2005.

Evans, Richard J., *The Third Reich at War*, Vol. 3. New York, 2009.

Faulkner-Rossi, Lauren, *Wehrmacht Priests: Catholicism and the Nazi War of Annihilation*. Cambridge, MA, 2015.

Flannery, Edward, *The Anguish of the Jews*. New York, 2004.

Frevert, Ute. "Ehre-männlich/weiblich: Zu einem Identitätsbegriff des 19," *Jahrhunderts, Tel Aviv Jahrbuch für deutsche Geschichte* (1992): 21–68.

Fredericksen, Paula, *St. Augustine and the Jews: A Christian Defense of Jews & Judaism* New Haven, CT, 2010.

Friedlander, Henry, *The Origins of Nazi Genocide: From Euthanasia to the Final Solution*. Chapel Hill, NC, 1995.

Friedländer, Saul, *Nazi Germany and the Jews, 1933–39*. New York, 1998.

Friedlander, Saul, *Nazi Germany and the Jews: Years of Extermination*. New York, 1998.

Friedlander, Saul, *Nazi Germany and the Jews: Years of Persecution*. New York, 1998.

Friedrich, Otto, *Before the Deluge: A Portrait of Berlin in the 1920s*. New York, 1972.

Gager, John, *The Origins of Antisemitism*. New York, 1983.

Gay, Peter, *Weimar Culture: The Outsider as Insider*. New York, 2001.

Gellately, Robert, *Die Gestapo und die deutsche Gesellschaft: Die Durchsetzung der Rassenpolitik, Schoeningh*. Germany, 1994.

Gellately, Robert, *The Gestapo and German Society: Enforcing Racial Policy*. Oxford, 1990.

Gellately, Robert, *Backing Hitler: Consent and Coercion in Nazi Germany*. New York, 2002.

Gerwarth, Robert, *Hitler's Hangman: The Life of Heydrich*. New Haven, CT, 2012.

Geyer, Michael and John W. Boyer, eds., *Resistance against the Third Reich, 1933–1990*. Chicago, IL, 1994.

Gilbert, Sir Martin, *Kristallnacht: Prelude to Destruction*. New York, 2006.

Gilbert, Sir Martin, *The Righteous: Unsung Heroes of the Holocaust*. New York, 2004.

Goldhagen, Daniel Jonah, *Hitler's Willing Executioners: Ordinary Germans and the Holocaust*. New York, 1996.

Griech-Polelle, Beth A., *Bishop von Galen: German Catholicism and National Socialism*. New Haven, CT, 2002.

Griech-Polelle, Beth A., "The Catholic Episcopacy and the National Socialist State," in Jan Nelis, Anne Morelli, and Danny Praet, eds., *Catholicism and Fascism in Europe, 1918–45*. Hildesheim, Germany, 2015, 229.

Grunberger, Richard, *The 12-Year Reich*. New York, 1971.

Grüner, Wolf, *Jewish Forced Labor under the Nazis: Economic Needs and Racial Aims*. Cambridge, 2008.

Grüner, Wolf and Jörg Osterloh, eds., *The Greater German Reich and the Jews: Nazi Persecution Politics in the Annexed Territories*. Translated by Bernard Heise. New York, 2015.

Haffner, Sebastian, *Defying Hitler: A Memoir*, translated by Oliver Pretzel. New York, 2000.

Harvey, Elizabeth, *Women and the Nazi East*. New Haven, CT, 2003.

Hastings, Derek, *Catholicism and the Roots of Nazism: Religious Identity and National Socialism*. New York, 2010.

Hedgepeth, Sonja and Rochelle G. Saidel, eds., *Sexual Violence against Jewish Women during the Holocaust*. Lebanon, NH, 2010.

Helm, Sarah, *Ravensbrück: Life and Death in Hitler's Concentration Camp for Women*. New York, 2014.

Hilberg, R., *The Destruction of the European Jews*. New York, 1985.

Hilberg, Raul, Stanislaw Staron, and Josef Kermisz, eds., *The Warsaw Diary of Adam Czerniakow*. New York, 1982.

Ioanid, Radu, *The Holocaust in Romania: The Destruction of Jews and Gypsies under the Antonescu Regime*. Chicago, 2008.

Jones, Larry Eugene, *Between Reform, Reaction, and Resistance: Studies in the History of German Conservatism from 1789 to 1945*. Providence, RI, 1993.

Kaplan, Marion, *Between Dignity and Despair: Jewish Life in Nazi Germany*. New York, 1998.

Kaplan, Marion, *Dominican Haven: The Jewish Refugee Settlement in Sousa*. New York, 2008.

Katz, Eric, *Death by Design: Science, Technology, and Engineering in Nazi Germany*. New York, 2006.

Katz, Jacob, *Out of the Ghetto: Social Background of Jewish Emancipation, 1770–1870*. New York, 1998.

Kay, Alex J., *Exploitation, Resettlement, Mass Murder: Political and Economic Planning for German Occupation Policy in the Soviet Union*. New York, 2011.

Kershaw, Ian, *The End: The Defiance and Destruction of Hitler's Germany*. New York, 2012.

Kershaw, Ian, *Hitler: Hubris. Nemesis. 2 volumes*. New York, 2000.

Kershaw, Ian, *The Hitler Myth: Image and Reality in the Third Reich*. New York, 2001.

Kershaw, Ian, "The Persecution of the Jews and German Popular Opinion in the Third Reich," *Leo Baeck Institute Yearbook* 26 (1981): 261–269.

Kershaw, Ian, *Popular Opinion and Political Dissent in the Third Reich. Bavaria, 1933–45*. New York, 1985.

Kitchen, Martin, *The Third Reich: Charisma and Community*. New York, 2008.

Klüger, Ruth, *Still Alive: A Holocaust Girlhood Remembered*. New York, 2003.

Koonz, Claudia, *The Nazi Conscience*. New York, 2005.

Kühne, Thomas, *Belonging and Genocide: Hitler's Community, 1918–45*. New Haven, CT, 2010.

Kulka, Otto dov, "Die Nürnberger Rassegesetze und die deutsche Bevölkerung im Lichte geheimer NS Lage- und Stimmungsberichte," *Vierteljahrshefte für Zeitgeschichte* 32 (1984): 582–624.

Kwiet, Konrad, "To Leave or Not to Leave. The German Jews at the Crossroads," in Walter Pehl, ed., *November 1938: From 'Kristallnacht' to Genocide*. Oxford, 1990.

Lane, Barbara Miller, *Architecture and Politics in Germany, 1918–1945*. Boston, MA, 1968.

Langmuir, Gavin, *Toward a Definition of Antisemitism*. Los Angeles, CA, 1990.

Levi, Primo, *Survival in Auschwitz*. New York, 1995.

Levin, Nora, *The Holocaust: The Destruction of European Jewry*. New York, 1973.

Lower, Wendy, *Nazi Empire Building and the Holocaust in the Ukraine*. North Carolina, 2007.

Lukacs, Richard, *The Forgotten Holocaust: The Poles under German Occupation*. New York, 2012.

Massing, Paul, *Rehearsal for Destruction: A Study of Political Antisemitism in Imperial Germany*. New York, 1949.

Megargee, Geoffrey, *War of Annihilation: Combat and Genocide on the Eastern Front*. New York, 2007.

Mendelssohn, Moses, *Jerusalem*. Translated by Allan Arkush. London, 1983.

Montague, Patrick, *Chelmno and the Holocaust: The History of Hitler's First Death Camp*. Chapel Hill, NC, 2012.

Mouton, Michelle, *From Nurturing the Nation to Purifying the Volk*. Cambridge, 2007.

Nelis, Jan, Anne Morelli, and Danny Praet, eds., *Catholicism and Fascism in Europe, 1918–45*. Hildesheim, Germany, 2015.

Perechodnik, Calel, *Am I a Criminal? Testament of a Jewish Ghetto Policeman*. New York, 1996.

Petrovsky-Shtern, Yohanan, *The Golden Age Shtetl: A New History of Jewish Life in Eastern Europe*. Princeton, NJ, 2014.

Phayer, Michael, *Protestant and Catholic Women in Nazi Germany*. Detroit, MI, 1990.

Pine, Lisa, *Education in Nazi Germany*. Oxford, 2010.

Pine, Lisa, *Hitler's "National Community": Society and Culture in Nazi Germany*. London, 2007.

Pine, Lisa, *Nazi Family Policy*. London, 1999.

Poliakov, Leon, *A History of Antisemitism*. Translated by Richard Howard, vols. 1–3. New York, 1965–75.

Poliakov, Leon, *A History of Antisemitism: Suicidal Europe, 1870–1933*, Vol. 4. Pennsylvania, PA, 2003.

Pulzer, Peter, *Jews and the German State: The Political History of a Minority, 1848–1933*. Detroit, MI, 2003.

Pulzer, Peter, *The Rise of Political Antisemitism in Germany and Austria*. New York, 1964.

Rees, Laurence, *How Mankind Committed the Ultimate Infamy at Auschwitz: A New History*. New York, 2005.

Rhodes, Richard, *Masters of Death: The SS Einsatzgruppen and the Invention of the Holocaust*. New York, 2003.

Roseman, Mark, *The Villa, the Lake, the Meeting*. London, 2002.

Ruderman, David B., "Between Cross and Crescent: Jewish Civilization from Mohammed to Spinoza," *Great Courses*. Chantilly, VA, 2005.

Ruderman, David B., *Early Modern Jewry: A New Cultural History*. Princeton, NJ, 2011.

Ruderman, David B., "Jewish Intellectual History: 16th to 20th Century," *Great Courses*. Chantilly, VA, 2002.

Rutherford, Phillip, *Prelude to the Final Solution: The Nazi Program for Deporting Ethnic Poles*. Kansas, 2007.

Schleunes, Karl, *The Twisted Road to Auschwitz: Nazi Policy towards German Jews*. Illinois, 1990.

Schoentgen, Marc, "Luxembourg," in Gruner and Iseloh, eds., *Greater German Reich*.

Seltzer, Robert, *Jewish People, Jewish Thought*. New York, 1980.

Semelin, Jacques, *Purify and Destroy: The Political Uses of Massacre and Genocide*. New York, 2007.

Shatzmiller, Joseph, *Cultural Exchange: Jews, Christians, and Art in the Medieval Marketplace*. Princeton, NJ, 2013.

Shepherd, Ben, *War in the Wild East*. Cambridge, MA, 2004.

Snyder, Timothy, *Bloodlands: Europe between Hitler and Stalin*. New York, 2012.

Spicer, Kevin P., *Hitler's Priests: Catholic Clergy and National Socialism*. Northern, IL, 2008.

Spicer, Kevin P., *Resisting the Third Reich: The Catholic Clergy in Hitler's Berlin*. Northern, IL, 2004.

Stein, George, ed., *Great Lives Observed: Hitler*. Englewood Cliffs, NJ, 1968.

Steinweis, Alan, *Studying the Jew: Scholarly Antisemitism in Nazi Germany*. Cambridge, MA, 2008.

Stern, Fritz, *Gold and Iron: Bismarck and Bleichröder and the Building of the German Empire*. New York, 1979.

Tec, Nechama. *Defiance: The Bielski Partisans*. Oxford, 2008.

Tec, Nechama, *Resilience and Courage: Women, Men, and the Holocaust*. New Haven, CT, 2004.

Tent, James, *In the Shadow of the Holocaust: Nazi Persecution of Jewish-Christian Germans*. Kansas, 2003.

Trachtenberg, Joshua, *The Devil and the Jews*. New Haven, CT, 1943.

Wachsmann, Nicholas, *Hitler's Prisons: Legal Terror in Nazi Germany*. New Haven, CT, 2004.

Weinberg, Gerhard, *Hitler's Foreign Policy: The Road to World War II*. New York, 2010.

Weiss-Wendt, Anton, *Murder without Hatred: Estonians and the Holocaust*. Syracuse, NY, 2009.

Wiesel, Elie, *Night*. New York, 2006.

Wildt, Michael, *Hitler's Volksgemeinschaft and the Dynamics of Racial Exclusion: Violence against Jews in Provincial Germany, 1919–39*. New York, 2012.

Wildt, Michael, *An Uncompromising Generation: The Nazi Leadership of the Reich Security Main Office*. Translated by Tom Lampbert. Madison, WI, 2009.

INDEX